Handbook
of
Health Care
Material Management

Handbook
of
Health Care
Material Management

Edited by
William L. Scheyer
Bethesda Hospital, Inc.
Cincinnati, Ohio

AN ASPEN PUBLICATION®
Aspen Systems Corporation

1985

Rockville, Maryland
Royal Tunbridge Wells

Library of Congress Cataloging in Publication Data
Main entry under title:

Handbook of health care material management.

"An Aspen publication."
Includes bibliographies and index.
1. Hospitals—Materials management. I. Scheyer, William L.
[DNLM: 1. Materials Management, Hospital—handbooks. WX 39 H2356]
RA971.33.H36   1985   362.1′1′0687   85-4016
ISBN: 0-87189-102-6

Editorial Services: Jane Coyle

Library of Congress Catalog Card Number: 85-4016
ISBN: 0-87189-102-6

Printed in the United States of America

1 2 3 4 5

To my wife, Trisha,
whose constant support
makes all my effort worthwhile.

CONTENTS

FOREWORD

In the late 1960s, I began, on behalf of the American Sterilizer Company, Inc. (AMSCO), to do research in the area of hospital material management systems. My familiarity with industrial material management suggested to me that the concept could be adapted to hospitals and, if this were true, it would make a significant contribution to their productivity and efficiency. I soon realized that I was too early. There was little evidence that it existed, much less was practiced, in the mode that I visualized. The zealot who did preach the concept of material management (but who never called it by that name) was Gordon Friessen. However, few understood his complex concepts and even fewer knew how to apply them.

In the early 1970s, my AMSCO colleagues and I went a step further, visiting many hospitals to discuss the concept of material management. To my personal dismay, we found that we were explaining the problem to administrators, rather than discussing possible solutions. However, time often has swift wings. By 1976, a group of us formed the Health Care Material Management Society. That name was to come later because, at the outset, we were a section under the International Material Management Society.

When books discussing hospital material management finally began to appear, the emphasis was primarily upon purchasing and inventory control. This was understandable. Most of those who advocated or practiced material management in hospitals came out of the purchasing department. In truth, many hospitals, even today, call the purchasing manager the director of material management, while concentrating only on the art and science of purchasing.

All of this has been a roundabout way of zeroing in on Bill Scheyer's *Handbook of Health Care Material Management*. He is correct in calling it a handbook, for it is a reference book that will suggest to professional material managers interesting ways to operate all of the activities related to this subject. It also will be of interest to hospital administrators—not, in this instance, to practice material management but to understand in its complexity what a great contribution it can make to good management. After all, the supplies, services, and labor that are related to material management can make up 40 percent of the hospital's total operating budget.

This is an important handbook in another sense, as well. For the first time, it brings together in one volume a comprehensive treatment of the three subsystems of material management (inventory management, processing, and distribution) as they relate to hospitals. It also discusses important related subjects in a fresh perspective that can help translate individual components into an integrated system. Challenging, sometimes provocative, topics, such as space management, internal auditing's role in material management, ethylene oxide safety, marketing new services, and many others are treated here.

Bill might have chosen to research and write the book himself. Instead, he opted for a wiser approach: He invited experienced managers from around the country to contribute chapters on their particular areas of expertise. Thus, readers not only can have access to a single reference source covering a multitude of topics but also can share the years of experience of a diverse and respected group of managers.

The publication of this handbook is more than sufficient evidence that health care material management has truly arrived and that this concept, which has proved so indispensable in other industries, will prove equally so in hospitals. Health care material management, in all of its facets, is being tested in the renaissance that is taking place in the industry.

It appears, too, that the burgeoning diversification of the industry, as evidenced by the proliferation of home care services, free-standing ambulatory and surgical care centers, and shared service arrangements, both local and regional, can be well served by the application of material management as a tie to bind the system together.

All of us who were asked to contribute to this project consider ourselves fortunate to be part of this well-balanced handbook, and our thanks go to Bill Scheyer, who has done an excellent job in organizing it all.

Donald G. Soth, Director
Consultant in Health Care
Material and Space Management
Erie, Pennsylvania

PREFACE

This book is intended as a standard reference for material managers, both experienced and newly assigned, as well as for administrators with interest in or responsibility for material management functions. It does not contain fully detailed information about every topic. It does include descriptions of how to accomplish a wide variety of material management objectives and provides assessment tools, such as checklists and specific action plans, for improving operational performance.

The basic purpose is to bring together in one volume the best thoughts of experienced managers around the country concerning the various aspects of hospital material management. This provides working managers with quick access to information regarding daily issues without having to do extensive research.

I have attempted to strike an appropriate balance between traditional topics, such as purchasing management and inventory control models, and issues not usually treated in standard material management texts, such as management of linen, pharmacy, printing, and central processing services. I also have tried to strike an optimal balance between the overview approach and the treatment of specific details. Only the reactions of you, the readers, will provide an actual measure of the success of this effort.

Another aspect is the treatment of topics that "everyone understands" but that usually do not receive formal analysis. These include chapters on how to gain support for a program, how to select appropriate products, and how to conduct effective meetings.

The management of this handbook project has been a challenging logistical task. It also has been extremely rewarding. It has allowed me to synthesize my grasp of individual aspects of the field into an integrated whole. It also has given me the opportunity of working with colleagues around the country, and of learning from their experience. In fact, it has done for me what I hope it will do for every person who reads the book.

As the project concludes, I have only one regret: That is that additional topics come to mind every day in a field that is developing so rapidly and that to capture every subject in one volume is really an impossibility. My hope is that in future volumes these areas can be addressed.

I hope that everyone who uses this book will be able to benefit, either by reading it in its entirety or by using individual sections as they become of concern in daily operations. In addition, I would like to have your suggestions on additional topics for future editions. Please, feel free to share your reactions with me. Above all, enjoy the opportunity of sharing ideas with your colleagues in the field and use the ideas to meet the emerging needs of our patients and of our blossoming industry.

I wish to express my sincere appreciation to the members of the Editorial Advisory Board. Their efforts in identifying potential topics and authors and in reviewing manuscripts went above and beyond the call of duty.

William L. Scheyer
Director of Supply, Processing, and
Distribution
Bethesda Hospital, Inc.
Cincinnati, Ohio
July 1985

PART I
ESTABLISHING A FIRM FOUNDATION

Whether you are preparing to establish the first material management program in your health care facility or to take an existing program into the future, you must have laid a proper foundation. Just as an elaborate home that has been built upon a weak foundation will not withstand the test of time, neither will a material management program that lacks a firm foundation be able to survive and flourish in today's rapidly changing health care environment.

Nearly everyone spends time writing goals and objectives and discussing them with others throughout the organization. In many cases, however, managers fail to invest sufficient time and energy in the process of learning the details of the organization; establishing a detailed plan of operation; determining how to measure, document, and report results; and establishing a strong network of supportive relationships.

This part, Chapters 1 through 8, provides specific guidelines for completing these vital processes successfully.

1. Justifying the Centralized Concept

EDWIN E. CARTY, JR.

In the past, there has been a significant amount of discussion on centralization of the material management function—unfortunately, much discussion and not a whole lot of action. Material management operations are discussed as if they were totally centralized. But if you ask about pharmacy, you find an exception; ask about food, you find an exception; maintenance, lab, x-ray, often exception after exception. Being centralized means that the material manager accepts both the responsibility and authority for the activities of purchasing, receiving, and distribution, or the total supply function for the entire facility from acquisition through disposition. The alternative is decentralization, with certain of these functions delegated to department heads who may or may not be skilled in key material management responsibilities.

In the new prospective payment environment, decentralization should generate concern. This is because in the past, although centralization was accepted in theory, it rarely was proved through practice. With diagnosis related groups (DRGs), the author's feeling is that it will prevail. Most managers like to think that their facilities are centralized and consequently under their control. The fact is that it is like being pregnant—there is no halfway, one either is or is not. The reality is that few facilities are centralized in the truest management sense and most are not even close. This lack of commitment could seriously jeopardize a hospital's financial viability under DRGs.

This fact should be considered much more seriously than it is. The prospective payment system is generating changes that will make material management centralization virtually essential for hospitals to be truly cost efficient.

This concept is nothing new. Centralization has long been thought of as a necessary road to success in material management. The author's contention is that without it, managers are only partially fulfilling this concept of a total supply system—the very reason for their existence.

Why has there been so long a delay in implementing centralization? There are a variety of reasons, such as lack of administrative support, other priorities within administration, and the fact that department heads suffer as many do from resistance to change along with the view that they may lose control. It can be argued that in the past the whole reimbursement structure was a negative factor in that higher cost meant higher payback. Heavy revenue producers such as laboratory, x-ray, and pharmacy were given a laissez-faire approach. Those days are over. Survival depends on the managers' ability to gain rightful control of the material functions in areas such as surgery, lab, pharmacy, and dietary.

Essentially, material managers have taken a nonaggressive approach toward centralization. Many such managers feel unable and bogged down, or simply are too lackadaisical, in obtaining or developing proof of the advantages of centralization. Many get caught up in their own daily routines, unable to develop a necessary master plan. It can be said that they have been their own worst enemies—in short, they have no one to blame but themselves. Much of the problem in advancing toward the goals of centralization may lie in the managers' perception of themselves as professionals. Most have capabilities far beyond what they are using.

Managers have been trained well and can assume much more responsibility. Their basic role to assure adequate, dependable sources of supply should be a springboard toward greater

3

control within their institutions. The time has come when they need to step out of the position of simply being "order processors" and mesh themselves into the control of this very expensive side of hospital operations. Most managers have developed skills to uncouple this buyer/user function and can provide this service both efficiently and effectively.

Why not exercise this ability? The author has found that material management basically can be doing a good job in the central storeroom—that is, buying right or turning inventory at an acceptable rate of 12 to 15 times annually—but have no control over other areas such as surgery, which may have a supply need that as a percentage of total inventory is considerably greater than the central storeroom itself yet often turning at a rate of less than three times per year. Material managers' capability to sell themselves and their programs to nursing, surgery, pharmacy, and laboratory is a key element of success. The days of isolation in the basement are gone forever.

THE ADVANTAGES OF CENTRALIZATION

To be successful, one must enumerate the advantages that can be obtained via centralization. Most managers are aware of the advantages of reduced inventory as it applies to freshness of supply, cash flow, and control; the advantages of mutual enhancement of standardization and centralization; the greater ease in evaluating products from a total house perspective; the reduction in distribution responsibilities; and the elimination of duplication in effort, thus saving valuable time of trained department heads as well as reducing recordkeeping and enhancing the ability of administration to focus control on a single department.

Managers know these facts, but do their administrators? Numerous articles state that in order to succeed in the new DRG environment, health care facilities must reduce cost, increase productivity, and improve data processing capability. For example, facilities must concen-

trate on enhancing their infection control program, thus reducing patients' length of stay. These are the very goals that managers would lay out to improve their own material control program. Each one represents goals and opportunity especially tailored for material management.

As staffing, the biggest cost in this labor-intensive industry, comes under microscopic scrutiny, department heads throughout the institution will come under the conflicting strains of improving, yet not expending dollars to do so. This situation opens the door for material management to enter, providing effective support programs such as automated or manual traveling requisition systems, automated or manual physician preference documents, and proper case cart management—all welcome advantages to department heads. Based on experience, the author never has seen a department head be displeased with the results of such types of systems where the directors had adequate input—if the concept was presold and implemented properly.

A plan of action needs to be developed for administration. Issues regarding DRGs are omnipresent facts, and continued government regulation as well as private sector control will provide constant pressure. The changes in material management in the next few years will be greater than the total changes in the last decade. The plan of action should push for the concept of inventory management that encompasses the whole hospital, not just the central storeroom.

This is not to say that all acquisition and control begin immediately via the material manager's desk but that individual must become the conceptualizer and strategist to put forth innovative approaches, working in that direction and planning for such changes. The Latin phrase festine lente, or hasten slowly, should apply. Since material management is a glove-fit-the-hand situation, no firm action plan can be dictated across the board. The new environment brings with it scrutiny of all past practices; for example, exchange carts vs. par level stock. The use of fully automated systems to track usage and replenishment will make the full exchange cart concept obsolete. Automation also will make obsolete the terminology of "official" and "unofficial" inventory. Managers cannot rest on the laurels of their past practices; all positions require close examination.

It is obvious that a set system or total cookbook approach is not realistic. A 50-bed hospital is different from a 300-bed hospital, which is considerably different from a 600-bed tertiary care facility. Individuals' expertise and ability to manage people and to presell ideas to department heads all are crucial to success.

It has been said that the single most important trait top management values in purchasing or negotiating personnel is the planning skill. In personal life as well as in business, planning is the key to success. A second major attribute is people management. Material managers spend more time managing people than they do managing material. This is especially important because of the overlap into departments where they do not necessarily have the authority but should have the responsibility for supplies.

This people management aspect goes far beyond managers' own personnel and gets to the very core of their ability to sell their ideas to their peer department heads as well as to administration. The author has seen many technically qualified material managers fail miserably in this area. Their "bull-in-the-china-closet" approach has proved disastrous and, although their concepts were solid, their inability to get these points across resulted in abysmal failure. Development of skills in this people management area is more important than technical ability alone and, consequently, must be part of managers' strategy.

PHILOSOPHY

Republic Health Corporation, a multihospital health care corporation, continuously addresses the goals of centralization and standardization, the support aspect of which is filtered up through material managers, regional material managers, and directly to top management. Creating the perception of being part of the architecture, having everyone in the loop so to speak, goes a long

way in support. The common denominator for all facilities, regardless of size, is that strong internal support is a must. For example, if a manager reports to an assistant administrator, the latter's superior also must be 100 percent sold on the program. This is because the material manager's span of control will encompass much territory well outside the immediate superior's field, creating the likelihood of conflict. As this conflict arises, it is necessary to know that the philosophies at higher levels are in synchronization.

The operating philosophy of Republic Health is to provide quality health services in the most efficient and cost-effective manner possible to provide competitive pricing as a means for increasing market share. This is accomplished via innovative marketing programs and effective business management practice. Republic has proved this concept by turning poor-performance hospitals into winners despite significant operational and geographic/market difficulties. Material management, particularly centralization, is an important vehicle toward attainment of these goals.

In some ways, the industry faces problems similar to those of the airline industry. The health care industry must cut cost and bring in volume. Airlines fill seats, health facilities fill beds. It is that simple, yet that complex. Obviously, material management's role does not fill all of this bill; marketing and physician relations, for example, play major parts. A point to consider is where to cut costs after completion of staffing analysis and adjustments.

Enter material management, which introduces a major factor for control: centralization. Centralization focuses directly on the goals of reduced staffing, reduced product costs, and increased productivity through systemization. It is, therefore, a vital element in coping with the problems of the DRG era.

Centralization makes it easier to pursue another of Republic Health's important goals, that of product standardization for increased leverage in its group purchasing program. This is particularly valuable and is heavily supported by top management. Negotiating deals based on committed volume is the key to cost containment. Groups that can standardize their product needs always can achieve more favorable pricing. Health care facilities have entered the age of commitment, and groups that maximize this aspect may just be ensuring their own survival.

Republic Health's structure in material management demonstrates its commitment in this field. Each region has a material manager who is responsible for the institutions in that area and reports to an assistant vice president of the region. There also is dotted-line responsibility from the regional to the corporate material manager. Policy is agreed upon through routine meetings and is set by the operations department at the corporate office. For example, an automated inventory system is recommended for use by Republic's facilities; an exception recommended by one of the facilities would require approval by corporate material management. Another example is the method and frequency of taking physical inventories, as well as targets for inventory turns or days supply on hand.

Regional and corporate material managers communicate frequently, meet individually during routine hospital visits, and formally as a group each quarter to discuss strategy, set goals, and measure performance. An important means of obtaining input from institutions is through blue-ribbon committees composed of select material managers from the regions. This philosophy also involves laboratory, dietary, and pharmacy, which provide the direct linkage necessary from the people performing the jobs. After all, who else could sell concepts to a lab person better than another lab person or a pharmacist to another pharmacist?

In individual facilities, a cost-containment committee could provide similar results. This concept is not new. In industrial settings, committees have been used successfully to incorporate centralization because they provide results based on broad input and sufficient flexibility. This committee would be chaired by the material manager and include heads of such departments as laboratory, pharmacy, housekeeping, and the director of nursing or nursing supervisors.

Managers' ability to sell themselves as the materials' watchguard is important. Gaining rapport and credibility with the department heads is crucial to success, but begins with the ability to muster administrative backing. Developing ways to cut or contain costs via standardization or systemization will provide success. Managers' planning in this endeavor is important and they must look for ways to increase their span of control since they are the experts in material management. Therefore, it is up to them to relieve other department heads of these responsibilities.

(The specifics of expanded services such as messenger service, patient transportation, linen management, print shop, and security are covered in detail in other areas of this book. Suffice it to say here that these all are areas with significant cost-containment potential.)

Involvement in a variety of committees is essential because this puts managers in the power position of setting direction and policy. Involvement should include, but not be limited to, pharmacy and therapeutic, budget, capital acquisition, infection control, and product standardization/evaluation committees.

Product standardization/evaluation committees, especially, will gain in influence in the future. To date, they have not been fully effective; for example, they have spent an inordinate amount of time addressing nursing care items, which represent only 25 percent of supply costs. What about the other 75 percent? Real opportunity lies in other departments such as blood bank products, microbiology-prepared media, coagulation reagents, etc. All departments are targets for centralization and standardization, so the involvement of material managers with other department heads in this committee should be mandatory.

Physician involvement no longer may be optional; it is becoming a requirement. Physicians must be educated in regard to fiscal responsibility, product costs, and product compliance. Increased control obviously can generate physician resistance, so problems can occur. It is important to note that the administrator is, among other things, the marketing and public relations person who may be best equipped to deal with physicians. Extensive consultation with and preselling to this segment of individuals is important. It is probable, however, that in the not too distant future, individuals who are unsympathetic toward fiscal responsibility and whose costs are excessive from a DRG standpoint could be invited to leave the staff.

CHANGE AND RESISTANCE

Change, as always, is inevitable and everyone can remember the time not too long ago when material managers would not even think of discussing something as sensitive as surgeons' gloves. Many items will become commodity products and fewer therefore will be sacrosanct. The marketplace is changing. It is time to look at the bare-bones products and demand reasons for the various whistles and bells. For example, if a less expensive product will work from an infection control point and provide proper patient care, then it should be used. The product does not have to be the best or have the largest market share, it simply needs to work. Undeniably, cost is increasingly important.

The main resistance to total centralization seems to be in the dietary and pharmacy areas, while the laboratory, radiology, and maintenance departments have become less sensitive. There is no reason why pharmacy and dietary cannot be handled in the same way as other departments. However, it is essential that material managers do their homework in these areas before moving to assume control. A first step may be the total centralization of receiving. They should sell this point as a way of gaining efficiency, not as loss of control by a department. Receiving departments are best equipped for this activity and provide the most efficient utilization of staff time. Objectors will cite physical plant problems or security difficulties and will marshal an unending list of excuses for nonparticipation, but managers can be creative in building control yet offering them some flexibility.

It is true that dietary and pharmacy may be more subjective and sensitive issues because of problems associated with dating, spoilage, frozen handling, and so on, but the solution lies in training materials personnel and requiring expertise from other departments to help ensure compliance with specifications. Many products such as canned food and vacutainers are no different from the type of product on any general store's shelves. Distribution can be handled via replenishment against a typical par stock type system similar to that on nursing units. The advent of notebook computers will go a long way in helping install controls in these areas since the data collected on site can be downloaded onto the computer in material management. Food purchasing often was loosely controlled but now requires a formalized system.

Drugs and Pharmacy

The acquisition of drugs through the wholesale or depot method can provide efficiencies that allow pharmacy to provide its own input via the telecommunication system. The accessibility of certain information such as inventory reports and stock analysis from wholesalers, plus rapid delivery that enhances inventory reduction, has allowed pharmacy to continue control in this area. Involvement with purchasing groups, as well as new approaches with generic and therapeutic drug substitution, have reduced the importance of price as an issue at individual health care facilities.

From the author's perspective, it basically comes down to inventory control. For example, the pharmacy director, as well as other department heads, should know that inventory is the responsibility of material management. If a problem exists in this area—that is, if statistics indicate lags in inventory turns or controls— material management will step in and assist the pharmacy in pursuit of these goals. All departments should be viewed the same. Managers' ability to carry out sourcing strategies and be the professional in control of the materials at issue must be underscored. Most department heads tend to claim that their particular situation is different and requires their own hands-on effort. Material managers must work with these individuals, and administrative support will help prove their point.

Value Analysis, Forms, Linen

Value analysis is an important factor in product evaluation. It removes much of the subjectivity and sales ballyhoo from the decision process. Value analysis has been a standard tool in industry for years, and the health care field can adapt it with substantial benefit.

Forms management also looms in importance. Many facilities claim to have forms management programs, but the proof of such systems is difficult to quantify. In most cases, forms represent a significant portion of the general stores inventory. Such a costly category obviously merits close attention. Centralization by its nature requires crossing the borders of all departments, and forms management is a perfect example of this opportunity. It can produce a positive effect as a direct link with other departments' procedures, involving benefits of work simplification and cost savings across the whole spectrum.

A final area for dramatic cost reductions is in linen management. Savings can be significant, not just on the production or raw cost side but specifically on the consumption or use side. Unfortunately, there are few health care facilities that cannot stand improvement in consumption control. It is rare to find one that cannot be improved to the tune of 30 to 50 cents per patient day. The laundry function should report to material management. (Again, details on this are covered later in this book.)

PLANNING

Anyone in the health care industry who is satisfied with the status quo will not survive. Today's dramatic changes will not allow it. A key element in material managers' success is selling themselves and their programs, through administration, to nursing, pharmacy, laboratory, and other departments. This therefore requires a plan. This means building up responsibility in a methodical manner so as not to assume too much too soon, which could result in disaster.

Regardless of official reporting relationships, material management should control the functions of purchasing, receiving, distribution, and inventory management throughout the organization. This proactive position must be taken to ensure full control of items from acquisition to disposition. This highlights the importance of having effective interpersonal communication skills so managers can orchestrate control and work with those who do not necessarily have line reporting relationships. Communication is a key ingredient. Material managers must develop a network of people within the facility to help provide ideas to solve problems. The advantage of Republic Health Corporation's regional material managers is the ability to provide routine total operational reviews. A similar approach may be used by facilities not connected with a chain but it requires intense resolve by the material manager to do so. Self-audit or self-analysis is not easy.

Operational Analysis and Centralization

Republic requires a total operational analysis at least annually, segments of which are examined routinely. In this way, problems are corrected and new approaches are created and monitored as they are installed. The primary objective of a material management operational review is to audit the operation of the department, including inventory, all systems, departmental relations, and staffing, as well as performance in product standardization and purchasing program compliance. Facilities' turning inventories four times a year no longer is acceptable. With that type of performance, no one would survive long in a manufacturing environment. It is interesting to note that centralization of purchasing took place in some large companies such as General Motors and General Foods in the early 1970s and others, such as IBM and Raytheon, have had it for years.

Material managers will find that doing their homework in pursuit of consolidation pays off. They must investigate the time spent by department heads on duties that belong under material management, such as requisitioning, inventorying, and interviewing sales representatives, as well as determining ways to control amounts of stock maintained in departments and identifying obsolete and excessive merchandise. Identifying this duplication and demonstrating how it can be corrected require much investigation, including meeting with department heads, blending persistence and diplomacy to prove the point. The author never has seen a decentralized facility that has performed its inventory turns adequately. This point may be the crux of material managers' beginning to prove their worth. Some departments will be operating efficiently in turning inventory appropriately. That's fine, leave them for last. By and large this is not the case and in a decentralized setting it never happens in all departments. Interestingly, department satisfaction levels are lower with decentralization, a fact they often do not realize until the advantages of centralization are addressed.

A delicate point in any situation is justification of personnel. Staffing is based on workload and without proper analysis of their own operations, material managers will find that they are either (1) overstaffed, or construed as such, and thereby risk losing personnel or (2) understaffed and unable to assume the responsibilities required to carry out centralization adequately. Unfortunately, material management often seems to be an area invariably considered early if staff cuts are required, a point that makes mandatory a complete analysis of the department and its interrelationship with other departments in moving material control functions to where they belong.

Physical Inventory

As routine as it may sound, a good place to start is taking a total physical inventory. Especially in a multifacility setting, the need for a uniform method of counting is required. This takes considerable effort and a policy can become quite detailed. For example, there is much subjectivity in areas such as laboratory reagents, open cases, and drug floor stock. For example, are sutures counted by the dozen, individually, or by the box?

Republic recommends taking a physical inventory twice a year, with facilities that do not reach preset goals required to do so more frequently. The stress is on such things as cycle counting, which works well in conjunction with Republic Health's automated system. The hospitals are required to supply physical inventory summary sheets for each category. The summary sheet breaks down the various departments so that a dollar figure for each department (A) is listed down the column; next to this is indicated the average daily supply expense (B) for that department; the division of B into A equals the days expense of inventory. The final column allows a space to figure a goal for that department.

For example, if an operating room had $200,000 worth of inventory and expenses of $3,740 per day, the days expense in inventory would be 53.4. If the goal was 45 days, that would call for a reduction of $30,000 in the OR inventory. This method permits concentration on individual departmental inventories, with the net effect of addressing the total. These segments of inventories also are reviewed as a percentage of the whole. If it is found that physical plant normally runs 3 percent to 5 percent of the total inventory and a particular hospital is higher, the count sheets can be examined to determine whether a real problem exists. One such finding showed $5,000 worth of light bulbs, much of which can be returned for credit.

In Republic's setting, obsolete inventory is closely scrutinized and slow-moving items can be shared with sister hospitals. This can be used as a joint effort by facilities in a city or community where limited sourcing requires large initial orders. Obsolete inventory is a bigger problem than most hospitals care to admit and much has to do with inattention, lack of control, or both.

From the corporate side, Republic Health's group purchasing program uses such tactics as elimination of a 25 percent restocking fee or specifying low minimum orders or open case shipments for its smaller hospitals, as well as minimum dollar requirements for orders. This permits frequency of delivery. Republic also strives for maximum cash discount terms, which the material manager must ensure are taken. Given the sophistication of automation, especially automated entry, the sales representative's function is changing. This change is capitalized on at the corporate level by demanding the reps' assistance in the field to avoid the pitfalls of inventory mismanagement. Much of the burden of presell and product change is placed on these persons as it is practical to assume that, with their vested interest, they will do a good job.

Evaluation Flow Chart

An evaluation flow chart of a facility's distribution process also will point out ways to eliminate duplication. Central sterile can be a primary target for change. Unfortunately, it sometimes has significant physical design limitations in its ability to serve the hospital. This results in limited service and little interaction between CS and OR. With the recent onslaught of prepackaged sterile items and the modularization of product concept, the central sterile's role has changed. An example is the modularization (prepacked kit) concept. Although it appears to be a quick fix for cost identification, and the theory may make sense, the question is whether it reduces cost. Reduce items and cost, is the author's theory, and managers should be sure they are headed in the right direction before making major changes.

Central sterile has gone from reprocessing to distribution in many locations. Instead of expanding the facilities to accommodate better sterilization techniques, hospitals allowed this function to decentralize and, indeed, grow within the OR and OB departments. This is unfortunate as facilities now find themselves in a position where centralization of sterilization is important but the logistics and equipment costs make it difficult. It should be obvious that central

sterile's role is becoming more vital in these days of greater emphasis on infection control and its direct relationship to length of stay. In many cases, facilities may be in a situation where they would like to look at certain reusable goods but do not have the space, staffing ability or equipment to cope with them. Since the expenditures in this area are most often cost-prohibitive, no great shift toward reusables can be foreseen; like it or not, limited budgets and continued staff reduction are foregone conclusions.

Republic Health uses a basic philosophy of limited location for supplies. Proliferation of storage sites leads to increased inventory and subsequent loss of control. CS and general stores provide the perfect example of this duplication. When CS is involved in distribution, it often creates a less even flow and adds to inventory value. Additional storage sites impose demands on the total system for more stock, more paper work, and less control, resulting in more stock outages. This increase in stock occurs very simply. Usage stock is fixed on a number of units—that is, general stores, central sterile, and departments. All stock locations by nature must include safety units so each situation proliferates stock, and adds personnel time to support additional control of records. Obviously, the advantages in this area include greater efficiency in and reduction of paper work.

With the exception of case carts, central sterile should not be in the business of distribution of disposable items. Instead, it should be concerned mainly with the manufacturing process, that is, decontamination, sterilization, and packaging of reusable trays and equipment. Limited distribution might be appropriate, but if this is the case, it should handle only the product, such as IV cassettes for infusion devices. The advantages of consolidation of distribution are numerous. It avoids the double layers of inventory in these departments. Computerized physician preference lists, case cart sheets, and traveling requisitions should be used exclusively for both inpatient and outpatient surgery areas.

Surgery will be the driving force in supply usage, and inventory management actually will begin with the OR surgery schedule. Therefore, there must be a closer tie between central sterile and surgery. The OR inventory, in a sense, will be absorbed into the computer in material management. Even where automation is not present, material managers should be in total control of inventory for the operating room. Republic Health is convinced, as its philosophy has dictated in the past, that nurses should not be assigned to nonnursing functions, and scrub nurses and technicians should not be charge ticket collectors or inventory counters. Material managers must get into the operating room both mentally and physically.

Health care facilities should use the same concept, Pareto's Law or the 80-20 theory (which states that 80 percent of your results come from 20 percent of your effort) that is used to control general stores inventory, on the balance of the material management program. Tighter control will bring with it the use of fewer items at less cost per unit. Identification of where dollars in inventory exist is the beginning. This same 80-20 theory can be applied toward examination of DRG activity, i.e., most surgery will fall into a small number of DRGs. It will become a requirement that managers be familiar with cost accounting methods in the DRG environment.

Material managers should provide monthly reports in as detailed fashion as possible. This book details much of what will be needed in such reports so it is not emphasized here. Republic Health stresses that monthly reviews pay attention to statistics on the contribution margin of the department or the cost of goods as they relate to revenue. Calculations of revenue per patient day (cost per patient day in the future) are monitored in relation to other facilities. Inventory, of course, is an important item in attaining goals. Managers should point out programs they have implemented that reduced or avoided costs to the institution.

RESPONSIBILITY VS. AUTHORITY

The whole health industry, not just acute care hospitals, is changing:

- Major distributors have cut back significantly on their sales force.
- Several large national distributors have gone the way of the dinosaur.
- Certain large manufacturers have eliminated major distributors to better position themselves for future markets.
- Major manufacturers have created new lines and turned away from those for which they were famous.
- Distributors have merged.
- Consortia have been developed to provide regional geographic coverage in response to corporate requirements.
- Equipment manufacturers are engaged in intense competition and now are stressing the more important advantages of their products in terms of future productivity and cost effectiveness as opposed to revenue potential and the simple addition of whistles and bells.

And the list goes on and on.

DRGs bring with them the requirement that managers stay abreast of these and other changes and gauge their ramifications. Managers' expertise and the continued development of these skills to provide the best possible linkage for the supplies and equipment of all department heads is rapidly becoming part of their future.

In summary, the centralization effort requires administratively guided teamwork, and today's environment, with its cost restrictions, makes this process mandatory for survival. In its system, Republic Health is fortunate to have the resources of such important personnel as regional material managers; these, with a proper blend of blue ribbon panels from dietary, laboratory, and pharmacy, constitute a solid formula for success.

The climate is changing away from an era when few supported centralization efforts; the burden of proof has always been on material managers as professionals to gather the evidence and push for control. The time is at hand so managers should not let it pass them by. They should not be the ones who get into trouble for not properly identifying their responsibilities. They should not be perceived as having authority and responsibility for a centralized system where none exists. It is not uncommon to find a hospital where material managers' responsibility essentially is limited to general stores. They could be doing an excellent job in general stores and general distribution to nursing units, and even though the span of control stops there, many are held accountable for what goes on in areas such as the operating and emergency rooms. Are they, for example, responsible for inventory held in pharmacy, or the orthopedic hardgoods in the surgery suite? For their own good, managers must identify both their authority and their responsibility.

A typical example would be the case of a material manager in a decentralized setting with a total house inventory of $500,000. Under the purview of general stores is $125,000 worth of inventory, in the operating room $200,000, in the pharmacy $75,000, and in the laboratory $60,000, with the rest spread throughout other departments. Unfortunately, this is not an uncommon inventory scenario in many hospitals. The statistics show that only 25 percent of the inventory is indeed under the control of the material manager; even if that individual were to decrease the general stores inventory by an astounding 50 percent ($62,000) it would affect only 12 percent of the total house inventory. Indeed, many managers control only 20 percent to 25 percent of the dollars.

It is the author's belief that the timing is right for managers to lay out a plan to obtain from administration both the authority and the responsibility for housewide management of materials. They cannot be held accountable for what they cannot control. Once centralization and control are harnessed, advantages toward true cost containment abound. To use the famous words of Rocky Balboa, "Go for it!"

2. Gaining Support for the Program

WILLIAM L. SCHEYER

Material management is a tool. Some people fall into the trap of thinking of it as an end in itself. They then feel that everyone in the organization should manage in a way that meets the needs of the material management division, never the other way around. This approach can lead to resistance and is ineffective. Material management, like all management concepts, is a tool to be used to serve the overall goals and needs of the organization. With this in mind, it becomes clear that support for the material management program comes first by making sure that its goals are in concert with those of the parent organization. If the goals are not congruent, then support will not be achieved, or last.

Once this is established, however, support comes from two sources. First, managers must tie into the goals of key people and groups within the organization. If program goals complement those of colleagues, it is likely that managers will be able to count on peer support. Second, they must establish positive personal relationships with key people. This does not mean that everyone must like everyone else. It means that managers should strive to maintain respect and a workable business relationship with those people who have influence in the organization.

Once this situation is in hand, three things are important in maintaining support for the program.

Managers must:

1. stay abreast of changes and trends both in the field and the health care facility—be the captain who keeps the ship in the mainstream
2. invest the time and energy necessary to nurture the supportive relationships thus established

3. avoid outright conflict. This does not mean that managers should not state their position, even disagreement, on important issues. However, most successful managers are skilled at managing conflict and keeping communication productive.

This chapter lays out a blueprint for accomplishing these goals and for building support for the program.

LEARN THE ORGANIZATION

Read and Read Between the Lines

In order to ensure that the goals of the program are in line with those of the organization, managers must know what the institution's goals are. The best way to learn this is to take the time to read what it has to say about itself and what others have had to say. The following list of sources is not meant to be comprehensive but will serve as a start:

- long-range plans
- history of the organization
- newspaper clippings
- annual reports
- Securities and Exchange Commission reports
- Joint Commission on Accreditation of Hospitals reviews
- committee minutes
- policy and procedure manuals.

In collecting this information, it is important to note how the reports change from year to year.

For example, as managers identify which elements of the long-range plan drop out and which stay in place year after year, they get a sense of where the organization is really going. One fascinating source of information that usually is overlooked is the file room of a local newspaper. Managers could well spend an afternoon reading clippings that go back a number of years; when finished, they will know more about the organization than 90 percent of their fellow managers.

It is essential to read between the lines, as well. Every organization says certain things about itself as part of its public posture. The key to building a power base is to figure out which things really matter to the daily operation of the business. By linking their program goals to these elements, managers can be assured of a certain amount of built-in support.

Figure Out Who Has the Power

From an egalitarian standpoint, everyone and every piece of business is of some importance. Realistically, however, managers have only a certain amount of time in the day and it is imperative that they use it wisely. The best way to ensure this is to make sure to spend time on items that will lead to accomplishment of primary objectives. Thus, it is reasonable to spend the most time with those who can have significant impact on the managers' objectives. It is important that they correctly identify people whose support is critical to the long-term success of the program. Some who belong on the list are obvious by virtue of the official power attached to their positions. These include:

- chief executive officer (CEO)
- the boss, if not the CEO
- chief financial officer (CFO)
- president of the medical staff
- heads of important medical staff departments, such as surgery and orthopedics
- director of nursing
- director of medical records

- director of internal auditing
- the manager's own department heads.

Other influential persons may not be so obvious. As has been said, everyone is important to one degree or another. How can managers identify those who warrant special attention? There are at least three good ways to answer:

1. Ask their own key people. This certainly will include their boss. It also should include their department heads, particularly if they have worked for the organization for a while. They probably have a good idea of whose opinion really counts.
2. Identify those whose opinions the managers have come to respect. These individuals probably are going to be part of the list anyway, just because managers feel good about working with them. They can be asked to list several persons who are particularly influential.
3. Use the reading material listed earlier and look for individuals whose names and statements stand out frequently.

A note of caution: The fact that a number of people point out a certain person as being influential does not necessarily mean that they are right. Managers will have to form their own conclusions and develop their own list of key people. This is part of the process of learning to wield organizational influence.

Meet with the Staff

Before officially beginning to build a support network, managers must be sure they have a clear sense of their own program and what it has to offer the organization. A good way to start is to meet with their department heads and their staff people. This will involve a series of one-on-one and group meetings. It should be made clear that the purpose of these meetings is not to form positions or to solve problems but to develop a picture of the current situation. Questions such as the following will get things started for managers:

- What are their main job-related concerns?
- What do they think the most important problems have been in the past?
- What would they identify as the underlying causes of these problems?
- What do they see as the greatest strengths of the present material management program?
- What people in the organization would they identify as being most supportive of material management? The least?
- What do they think material management can be in this organization?

Meet with Key People

Having developed a preliminary picture of the organization and where the current program fits in, it is time to start building a network of supportive relationships. The objective, at this point, is not to sell the program but to further clarify what it ought to be in terms of the true goals and objectives of the parent organization. This is a vital distinction and must be kept in mind. Managers are almost certain to fail if they approach people with the idea that they are here to convince these others of the appropriateness of their program and of why the others should get in step. Instead, the objective should be to look for points of agreement and commonality of interest.

This is not to say that managers can downplay areas of disagreement to the point of misstating their position. If it becomes obvious that there are areas of serious disagreement, note them for additional follow-up and move on to other areas where common interest can be established. Problems can always be worked on in future meetings but it is the commonality of interest that will serve as the cornerstone of a mutually supportive relationship and that must begin to be developed in the initial meeting.

Again, questions or points of discussion such as the following can get managers started:

- What do they see as the key issues and objectives of the organization?
- How do they feel material management fits in?
- How can it help in achieving the organization's objectives?
- What issues are most important to them and their department?
- How can their department make life easier for others and their departments?
- What suggestions do they have about how to set up or change the material management program?
- Do they feel they will be able to support this program?
- What other key people do they feel should be contacted for their opinions about material management in the organization?

During these meetings, they should be on the lookout for individuals with whom they feel particularly comfortable. As mentioned, they do not have to like everyone, just work effectively with them. This is one of the bases of official support. However, the role of unofficial support should not be minimized. There are times when managers need to be able to count on a crucial vote in committee or to know that someone will lend support during a heated debate. These are the times when they want to know that they have supporters they can rely on.

PLAN THE PROGRAM

Identify Priorities

At this point, there should be a clear picture of the organization that includes:

- history and projected future
- strengths and weaknesses of current material management practices and personnel
- sources of potential support
- sources of potential conflict.

It now is time for managers to assemble their plan for the operation of their program. This should reflect the information gathered during investigation and should, to the extent possible, represent the interests and desires of the staff and others identified as being important to the success of the program. However, it ultimately must be the managers' program, one in which they fully believe.

An effective way to envision the complete program is to brainstorm. Managers should write down everything they feel would be part of a perfect program, list all the elements missing in the current situation, then prioritize these. With this comprehensive and prioritized list of items that need to be accomplished, they can develop an action plan or strategy for achieving them. The following three priority ratings are appropriate:

1. Critical deficiencies must be corrected immediately.
2. Items that are directly related to major goals of the organization receive second priority.
3. Items that are directly related to goals of significant supporters receive third priority.

If an item does not fall into one of these categories, it probably should receive little or no attention.

State an Operating Philosophy

A mark of successful organizations is their adherence to clear and consistent value systems. One of the best ways to develop a reputation as managers who can be counted upon is to let everyone know their operating philosophy, then consistently operate within it.

Develop a Specific Plan

Once managers know where they want their program to go, they must determine how to accomplish it. First, they should develop a detailed operating plan that will include:

- priorities
- timetables
- accountabilities (exactly who is to do what by when)
- methods of monitoring progress.

Before proceeding, it is important to review the plan with immediate superiors to make sure of total support if needed. Some points may be controversial. In that case, manager and superior should seek a meeting with the chief executive to solicit support. This step must not be taken lightly. Many times people sidestep possible conflict by indicating their tacit support, even though they know they are not prepared to stand by it in a tough situation. This is not dishonest—it is simply natural conflict avoidance behavior. Managers must be aware that their superior may be placed in this situation by certain elements of the plan. The seeking of a clear statement of support from the CEO is a prudent, proactive management action. If at all possible, this should be in the form of a written policy statement.

Publicize the Plan

To some extent, managers will want everyone in the organization to know that a strong material management program is in operation and how they can benefit from it. This can be done through hospital newsletters, interoffice communication, and word of mouth. However, some persons must know the detailed plan. Managers' own department heads not only must know it in detail but also must share it with their department personnel. This is to be their primary operating document. In addition, all of those identified as significant supporters should be kept up to date with the main points. In their case, it serves as a working document to guide the continuing relationship between departments.

MAINTAINING SUPPORT

The ability to sustain continuing support of the program depends on information and people. It has been said that information is power. Managers will dramatically increase the amount of influence they wield in the organization by increasing the amount of information they receive and by disseminating information about the positive accomplishments of the program. Two effective ways managers can achieve these objectives are (1) to arrange to receive current information about financial performance, key committee decisions, and so on, and (2) to see that they or their representative sit on committees that are really effective.

Managers should never downplay the importance of people. They should make sure they nurture the supportive relationships that they took time to develop and stay current with those people, keeping them up to date with what is happening in the area, and making sure the managers know what is happening in these others' departments. It is important to be an information source for them, passing along interesting or important pieces of information. However, this must not degenerate into gossiping. Being seen as a reliable source of important and accurate information is valuable; being seen as a gossip must be avoided.

Managers should look for ways of supporting their supporters. Being sensitive to their concerns, as well as speaking well of them in public, is a good way of ensuring their continued support. Again, this can become negative if taken too far. It is important that effective managers not support one another in inappropriate positions. Instead, they must work together to find the proper positions in terms of achieving the organization's goals.

Finally, it is important to maintain strong ties with other material managers within the community. An excellent way to do this is through active participation in professional organizations.

MANAGING FOR EXCELLENCE

It is material managers' own concept of what their role is within the organization that will shape the daily performance of such functions in the hospital. Managers represent these interests to the administrators above them, sell the concept and gain support for it from colleagues, and represent the organization's interests outside the hospital. They also are the driving force behind the daily performance of subordinates. The program must have a reputation for high standards of quality.

To achieve this, it is essential to select competent employees for every section of the department, then inspire them to strive continually for high-quality performance. There are specific steps that will lead to this type of effort. Managers should:

1. Make sure that high quality is rewarded and that mediocre performance receives no reward.
2. Keep staff members informed of everything that can affect their jobs.
3. Stand behind staff members when they need support.
4. Demonstrate confidence in them by giving them the freedom to act on their own, make mistakes, learn from their mistakes, and grow.
5. Make sure that high-quality performance is recognized publicly.
6. Encourage this style of management throughout all levels of the department, down to the newest member of the team.
7. Encourage department heads to develop networks of supportive relationships, just as managers themselves do.
8. Strive to meet the needs of the "whole person" while making sure that the individual's daily efforts are tied to the primary goals of the organization.

The program will enjoy long-term success only if it continues to meet the changing needs of the parent organization and if it maintains a reputation for high-quality performance. Managers are responsible for seeing that their program stays in tune with the goals and objectives of the organization. They also are responsible for having a vision of excellence and for inspiring everyone around them to harness their energies to this vision. These are imposing respon-sibilities. However, the success of the program, as well as personal success as material managers, will be direct reflections of how well they are able to meet them.

3. Space Management

DONALD G. SOTH

Everyone uses enclosed space in homes, in certain leisure activities, and at work, whether it be in factories, offices, or hospitals. Furthermore, people take for granted space as a means of shelter, to control climate, or as protection.

Enclosed space has the connotation of psychological, sociological, and physical meaning. A complicating factor is the effect of time on this space, which invokes change upon people.

The study of man's relationship to space, and how he perceives it, is called "proxemics." It is a legitimate and fascinating study that can help people better understand how they perceive space and why they want a certain configuration and relation of components. It can help them understand why they want to make changes periodically for no good reasons—yet for very good reasons.

The hospital has some of the most expensive space cost and space complexity. Even more than industrial offices, it is subject to change not only "intra" but "inter" in terms of relationships with other areas and departments.

Even in hospital environments that can be considered as similar, individuals' physical, mental, emotional, social, and work culture traits are such that space requirements will greatly vary and must be taken into consideration in its planning and management.

Material management, because it is an important hospital function, occupies a significant share of available space in the facility. Much of the space is centralized but some of it is decentralized, such as storage areas in nursing units and consumer departments. The complexities of hospital space are examined here from various viewpoints and the principles then applied to material management.

DEFINITION OF SPACE MANAGEMENT

Hospital administration and department supervisors should be deeply concerned with their space and how it can best be used. Hospital space is subject to empirical laws, encroachment, change, growth, unattractiveness, and inefficiency, and it is very expensive. However, careful planning of space can create a pleasant configuration and environment and improve productivity. The space configuration and how it is used can be controlled by careful planning. It is imperative that hospitals be aware of the space environment, for how well the operations within the hospital function depends very much upon it. This means functional enclosed space that is used in hospital activities, not just one category such as office applications.

Space management can be said to be the planned use of enclosed space at a given time so that it can be utilized efficiently to accomplish specific functions. The phrase "at a given time" is stressed because it is so vital to this concept and so often overlooked. Planners often develop a space utilization plan that is inflexible and difficult to modify in response to changes in the organization. Thus, change can nullify an enclosure of space and its components. So, space must be evaluated and recommendations made with a given time frame in mind. In terms of usability, the question is: "What time is this space?"

PROXEMICS

The scientific name for this field is proxemics—man's social and personal relationship

19

to space and how he perceives it. To state it in another sense, proxemics is the interrelated observations and theories of man's use of space. Proxemics is advocated here in two ways—in the health care environment and in its changing nature.

Man is an organism with a wonderful and extraordinary past. He is distinguished from the other animals by virtue of the fact that he has developed elaborate extensions of his organism. He has made the computer an extension of the brain, as the telephone extends the voice, and the wheel extends the legs and feet. Language extends experience in time and space, while writing extends language. The relationship between man and his cultural dimension is one in which both man and his environment participate in molding each other. His use of space goes beyond mere shelter, and he makes real use of space for sensible reasons—to counteract the laws of physics (gravity), for sociological implications (privacy, prestige, etc.), and to work.

The monolithic appearance of a hospital is an illusion. It has been said that today's hospital is outdated the day it opens because of technological change that can take place between the end of the planning process and when the doors are opened to receive patients. The juxtaposition of hospital departmental spaces to each other could be tolerated more easily if change and growth did not take place or, if they did, at least would be predictable. However, particularly in hospitals, this has not been possible. Moreover, even if space change and growth were predictable, they develop at different rates. Change and growth can have so drastic an impact that a perfectly good building can become inefficient and have to be abandoned, or have a major overhaul, to keep it within functional reason. This suggests that equipment and walls, wherever possible, should be easily movable and/or adjustable to meet new requirements, concepts, and technology.

HOSPITAL DESIGN CHANGE

Until after World War II, hospital buildings often were monuments to the benefactors who furnished construction funds. Before the war, the basic design, such as the pavilion, was created. Hospitals had to be horizontal because of the lack of elevators and to allow the greatest exposure to fresh air to counteract miasma, a vapor that in those days was thought to emerge out of the ground and infect the air.

With the advent of the elevator and steel-clad construction, hospitals could be vertical. This eased distribution problems. Still later, a compromise was developed: a large horizontal base for support services and a vertical building to house patients. The complexity of hospital services has since given rise to connected buildings to cope with growth and change. This is a recognition of the fact that people are dynamic, so the space they work and live in needs to be dynamic.

SPACE/COST FACTOR

A modern short-term acute care general hospital can require 1,000 gross square feet (GSF) per bed and a teaching hospital 1,400 GSF per bed. GSF is the total space composed of net square feet (NSF), the usable functional space, plus the nonfunctional areas such as partition columns. The standard conversion factor for changing hospital square footage to GSF is 1.5, thus:

$$
\begin{array}{ll}
650 & \text{NSF} \\
\times\ 1.5 & \text{Converting Factor} \\
\hline
975 & \text{GSF/bed}
\end{array}
$$
(nonfunctional space)

Construction costs of approximately $120/GSF are common. Based on this, $120 × 1,000 GSF = $120,000 per bed. For a 400-bed hospital, construction could cost $48 million for 400,000 GSF.

Building life-cycle costs constitute an important factor that often is overlooked. Emphasis usually is placed on construction, but maintenance costs continue for the life of the building and increase as the facility becomes older. There also is adaptive cost—changing space to meet new functions or supporting new equipment as technology changes.

Finally, there are operating costs that begin the day the hospital opens, and of course, continue. These must be taken into consideration when the hospital is planned and constructed. Operating costs usually can equal the original construction cost in less than two years; in ten years, the cost of operation, maintenance, and adaptation (change and growth) might be four times the initial capital construction cost.

When viewed in this light, it would appear to be more practical to invest more heavily in initial construction if it can reduce the operation, maintenance, and adaptation costs over the 40-plus years of the building's existence.

The enclosing of space for whatever use is expensive, but few spaces are as costly as those in hospitals because they are so complicated technologically. Yet hospitals somehow must adapt to technological obsolescence. Hospital space is complicated for another reason: the intrarelationships and interrelationships with other functionally important spaces. The functions are somewhat like neighborhoods in a city, except that in hospitals many of these "neighborhoods" often are in competition with one another. The city analogy can be seen in another light: the budget of a 500-bed hospital may be as much as that of a small city.

Still another space factor is that a hospital usually is designed to be static yet is required to change and grow—by encroachment of one department upon another, if necessary.

This, then, is what is explored here: this rather new and exciting concept, the management of space by planning, evaluating, and reconstituting an activity to cope with its inherent problems.

There is a well-known adage that "form follows function." In health care facilities, this must be disputed for the planning phase of space management must make sure that the form can accommodate function not only now but in the future, since today's waiting room could be part of tomorrow's laboratory. Yet a comparison of the original hospital plans with the structure five to ten years later will show that the changes that have taken place are numerous and expensive and not necessarily satisfying to the occupants.

The changes actually began as soon as the first patient was admitted, if not before. In truth, in hospitals, form must adapt to function.

Space management in hospitals involves planning for the unpredictable. That seems to be a contradiction in terms, implying that space, function, dimensions, and occupancy are predictable. However, future requirements are truly unpredictable and such unpredictability must be managed from the planning stage onward.

ANATOMY OF A HOSPITAL

Support services constitute about 80 percent of the total hospital space, while the patients' environment (the rooms they occupy) takes the remaining 20 percent. It is no wonder, based on this ratio alone, why hospital costs are so high. In a hotel, the ratio of guest rooms to service areas would be the reverse.

This analysis of the anatomy of a hospital starts with the broadest space area, the facilities. These can be defined as a broad segment that contains one or more departments that have a central function. There are six basic facilities: (1) patient care, (2) administration, (3) diagnostic treatment, (4) material management, (5) engineering, and (6) environmental maintenance.

Within these facilities are departments that have specific functions related to the central responsibility. In diagnostic treatment, for example, are radiology, surgery, laboratory, and many others. Each department in turn breaks down into rooms or areas, which can be further classified. The technical or "hard" areas are those in which tasks generally related to patient care are accomplished. Administrative or "soft" areas support and document the activities of the department. "Soft" areas also include waiting rooms and those for ancillary uses (personal hygiene, lockers, and so on). Each of these rooms has a defined function or purpose in which tasks can be accomplished.

There always is a functional hierarchy from facilities to department to room. Each room or area will have equipment of some type, even if it is only furniture. Equipment can be classified as technical or nontechnical. If it is technical, it could be medical/surgical such as operating tables or nonmedical/nonsurgical such as a computer. Nontechnical can include items such as casework or furniture. The equipment can be considered fixed or major movable. Fixed means that it is attached to surfaces or to utility lines and is difficult to move, even should it be desirable to do so. "Major movable" is equipment that has an expected life of at least five years and costs more than $250. While it may be plugged into an electrical circuit, it is considered capable of being moved without construction considerations. All other items are supplies and are carried as an operating expense. This group ranges from surgical instruments to paper forms.

Because every department can be broken down into technical, administrative, waiting, and ancillary areas, each function can be defined precisely. In doing this, the equipment required becomes defined.

The author, in a review of a 550-bed hospital, found more than 225 departments and subdepartments. There were more than 400 room types, but many were represented over and over again throughout the departments, so that in a hospital of that size there were about 2,000 rooms, all susceptible to change and growth at different times and degrees.

Space planning is concerned not only with defining the facilities, departments, and rooms/ areas but also with the interrelationship among facilities and the intrarelationship within departments. It also is concerned with defining the function that has to be accomplished and the square footage and configuration required to house the people necessary to accomplish the function. Planners also must take into account the equipment that will be used in this function, and its placement. Those who occupy a space use their "space intelligence," or sense of the reasonable use of space, because they become aware of the environment and its impact. They also need this ability to change the environment when required to provide pleasant qualitivity (quality and productivity).

Space planning should not be thought of as intruding on the architect's province of the art and science of building. The architect is concerned with the details that give substance to the structure and thus needs to be told by the user what attributes will contribute to functional efficiency.

ZONING IN THE HOSPITAL

The functional relationships can be seen more clearly by zoning the hospitals (Figures 3–1 and 3–2). There are four facility zones: Zone 1, Inpatient and Administration; Zone 2, Outpatient and Ambulatory; Zone 3, Diagnostic and Treatment; Zone 4, Material, Environmental, and Engineering Maintenance. Each zone has a high degree of intrarelationship as well as a working relationship with each of the other zones in one way or another (Figure 3–3).

Zone 1

Zone 1 is shown as a multistoried vertical building. Administration and related functions such as fiscal management, admitting, and lobby occupy the first floor, with patients on the other floors. These floors generally are stacked; that is, each has the same basic arrangement and all of them have commerce with the ground floor by means of vertical movement devices. The ground level becomes patient- and visitor-oriented and contains the main entrance. Inpatients require relatively close proximity to Zone 3 for diagnostic and treatment facilities. Staff and personnel require interchange with Zones 2 and 3, and there is heavy supply commerce to and from Zone 4.

Zone 2

Zone 2 is an outpatient facility oriented to receiving patients and ambulances and providing immediate treatment. Since some of these patients will become inpatients, a good interrelationship with Zone 1 is a requirement. The outpatients also will use the treatment and diag-

Figure 3–1 The Zoned Hospital Gross Space Relationship

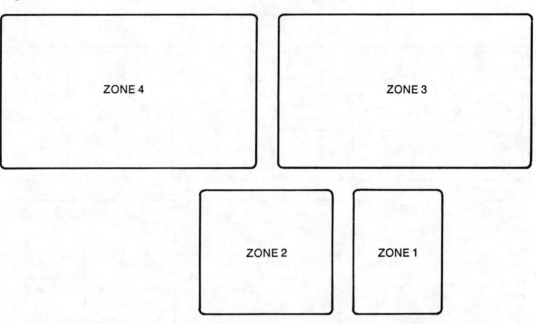

nostic departments in Zone 3. With the exception of outpatient pharmacy, there is no commerce with Zone 4.

Zone 3

Zone 3 houses all the diagnostic and treatment departments. Patients move from one department to another, as do hospital personnel and equipment. An exception is when outpatient sur-

Figure 3–2 3 Dimensions of the Zoned Hospital

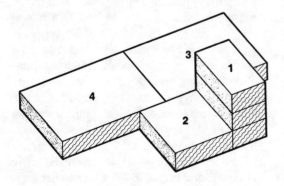

gery might be a separate free-standing building. Visitors usually are not encouraged.

Zone 4

Zone 4 contains material, environmental, and equipment management. The material management area involves inventory management, processing, and distribution. A characteristic of this zone is that it does not involve the presence of patients, with the exception of an outpatient pharmacy if it is located here. However, because of this potential affinity, the pharmacy is placed close to Zone 2 for the convenience of outpatients. This means that the more expensive space in the three other zones can be used primarily for patient-oriented activities. Zone 4 also is a good location for environmental management, which covers the cleaning of the structure and houses its supplies, beds, drapes, and so on.

EQUIPMENT MANAGEMENT

Equipment management involves the maintenance of the equipment and the building and may

Figure 3–3 The Zoned Hospital Functional Space Relationship

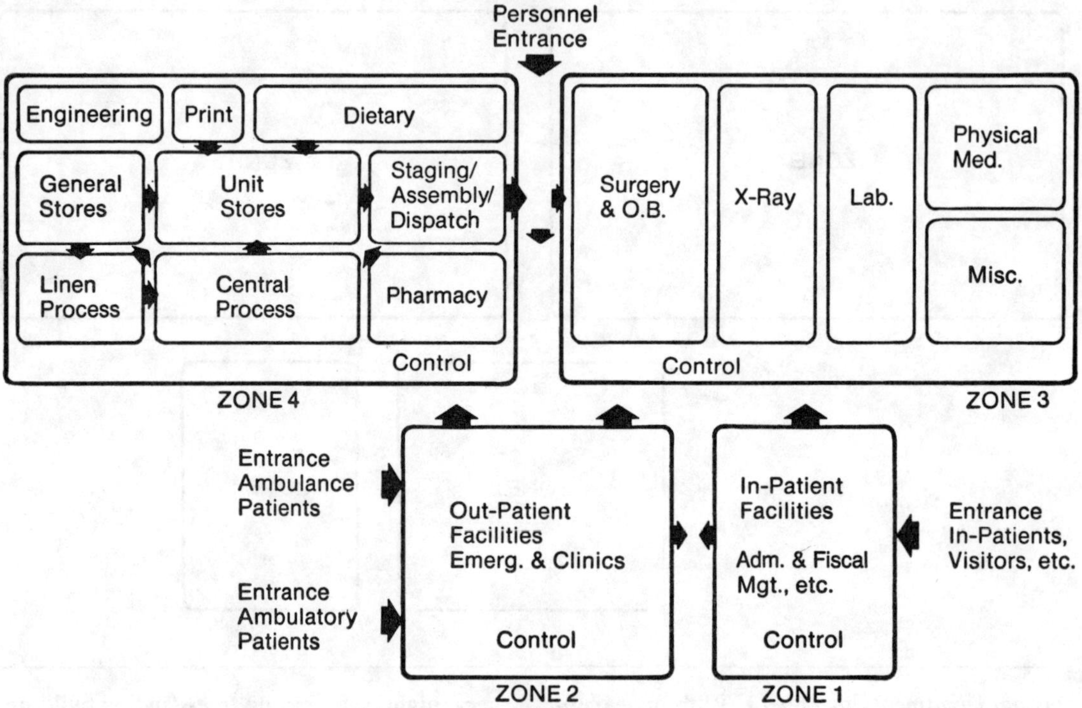

Source: Reprinted from Hospital Materiel Management Quarterly, vol. 5, no. 2, published by Aspen Systems Corporation, © 1983.

include the capital equipment location and related recordkeeping. There are reasons for making this activity part of the material management function.

Zone 4's basic construction usually is less expensive than the three other zones in terms of finishes and aesthetics and does not have to meet severe building codes because of the absence of patients. In some cases, this might be a separate building. Material management has a great deal of commerce with all other zones seven days a week, 24 hours a day. This includes a highly organized distribution system that is disciplined to a delivery schedule for meeting the consumer departments' needs in the other zones.

PLANNING FOR CHANGE

In the context of space management, the planning really is for the unpredictable. Why is this so? And if it is so, is there not a contradiction between planning, whose end result is often mistakenly thought to be permanency, and the unpredictable? The unpredictable relates to the functional space, which must be so designed that it can be changed to meet new conditions, which are not predictable at the time the space is constructed. Planning, therefore, should not lead to permanency but to form accommodating change.

All the data regarding space footage and cost are generally predicated on the idea that once it is constructed, what actually is built is a monument. At one time that was true, for hospitals were built to honor a benefactor and required a static form so that they could achieve permanence. In truth, though, a hospital should be likened to a living, growing organism that can achieve permanence only by adapting to change.

Herbert McLaughlin, a West Coast architect, made the astute remark that "the inherent nature of a hospital's physical structure is to be incomplete and irregular." Stated another way, change and growth constitute a continuing activity that takes place at different rates of intensity and time, even if from the outside this activity is not apparent.

CHANGE/GROWTH FACTORS

Too often when a hospital is opened, it is found that this "new" facility cannot adjust or adapt to change or growth. One reason is that in the planning, the initial outlay sometimes is curtailed, which may save space but leads to higher operating costs and frustrations. This inefficiency of the total space results in costly operation, and changes to rectify the situation often are physically impossible.

Hard space and soft space have been mentioned. Hard space next to hard space amounts to inflexibility when it comes to growth and change. A juxtaposition of hard and soft space is required for flexibility. Recognizing the certainty of change and growth, there are strategies that do help in planning for the unpredictable. Departments such as radiology and laboratory are dynamic in growth and consequent change because of technological impact. They also increase when patient loads expand or there is a growth in surgery.

Fixed equipment causes soft space to become hard space. Highly technical areas, such as radiology diagnostic rooms, operating rooms, laboratories, and microbiology areas, are called hard areas. All of these have a great deal of technical equipment so it is difficult to move them. Public hygiene areas because of their plumbing usually are hard areas. Soft spaces are places such as waiting rooms and reception areas that are necessary for the operation of a hospital but can easily be moved. It makes sense, then, to plan to have hard spaces next to soft spaces because expansion is simpler.

Departments or rooms that are expected to have the greatest growth should be so located that they can expand in two or three directions, with at least one direction as a minimum. Because change and growth in a hospital are inevitable, there are four ways this can take place: (1) a takeover of adjacent space, which means something has to be sacrificed; (2) the domino system, in which Space A takes over Space B and Space B takes over Space C; (3) open-ended expansion, so that a department can expand by moving external walls in one or two directions; (4) establishment of a large volume of enclosed space, in which mobile modular space units are placed for easy change.

Following are some of the change growth factors that can affect the size, configuration, and encapsulation of space:

- control of climate
- geometry of space, cube to cube, cube on cube
- privacy, which also can have the connotation of prestige or security
- establishment of territory
- security
- prestige
- effect of time (one walks through it and it becomes the fourth dimension); time contributes to the changes of the function of space, the fifth dimension
- technological obsolescence
- personal reasons, for example, a person assigned to a space where the former occupant was left-handed, or change of work methods, with a need to adjust components to suit new needs.

THE PLANNING PROCESS

It was said earlier that form does not follow function but that form must accommodate the function at any given time, so it is necessary to develop a workable plan for space management. "The plan is nothing," said Dwight Eisenhower, "planning is everything."

Planning involves a sequence of activities for developing an enclosed space that is functional, not static, and capable of adjustment. Planning for change and growth requires functional and space programming. These add up to continuing space management programs so that the space efficiently supports the functions that will be placed within it.

The main difference between adaptable and conventional planning is that restraint is used in filling large areas of space. The emphasis is on function and the efficiency of space, and flexibility to respond to future requirements. The enclosure of space and the components used are predicated on modules.

Adaptable Space Planning

This utilizes large planning areas that are developed so that self-contained partitions can be used to design space configurations that meet the operational requirements of how an area is to be used at a given point in time. These modules are used primarily in soft areas and are capable of being changed without the trauma of construction. To meet new functional requirements, utilities are fed by umbilical cord from utility lines in the ceiling or floor. Hard spaces, where fixed equipment will be placed, are more difficult to use with free-standing module enclosures, but even these problems can be managed if there is interstitial space—the space between floors that will contain utilities and some equipment. It is important that this be high enough for persons to service the equipment.

The important point is: do not let the functional space determine how a future function will be performed simply because the configuration is not adaptable. For example, a four-year-old hospital found: (1) general stores already undersized, (2) insufficient storage space for exchange carts, (3) insufficient alcove storage for carts on nursing units, and (4) no available space to solve these problems.

Creative Planning

It is easy to define creativity: to invest with a new form something produced through imaginative skill. Imagination is the ability to confront and deal with a problem. It is more difficult to tell someone how to be creative. Some people are more so than others. More people could be

except that some prefer to focus on the details that result from the creativity.

The imaginative-creative activity is an abstract process that is responsible for solving a problem. The solution often comes from two apparently unrelated factors that, when combined, can provide the answer. These factors are based on prior knowledge and often are related to a physical activity or law. The solution may require hardware if it is to be translated into a practical reality. The more flexible people can be in the environment, the more they can be creative.

THE WORKING ENVIRONMENT

There are four basic reasons for working in a particular environment that exist throughout a department in varying degrees:

1. Habit: For some people, routine work gives meaning and order to lives that otherwise would be chaotic. They like the formulas. The arrangement of work and storage surfaces for these people should be coherent.
2. Pleasure: More people than might be thought enjoy working, and in a pleasant atmosphere. Some may want isolation to work best, others can be extroverts who prefer contact with fellow workers.
3. Money: This is a powerful motivator. Money-seekers tend to be dynamic and may want changes of environment more often.
4. Power: These people desire prestigious quarters, such as a corner room.

Three basic space generators help define space planning requirements:

1. Workload: What processes are going to take place in the space?
2. Equipment: What type and quantity of equipment—including work and storage components—will assist in the workload?

3. Personnel: How many people, and of what types, will occupy the space to operate the equipment or accomplish the workload?

It is obvious that there has to be compromise, so space must be arranged to meet the objectives of a department. It must be kept in mind that the planning discussed here is the creative, as differentiated from the physical. It also involves factors such as the following:

- psychological and sociological reasons for change
- the effect of time on the plan
- technological obsolescence (or impact), which occurs before the physical obsolescence of the structure
- accommodation of future workloads
- accommodation of equipment
- accommodation of person (or personnel)
- rapidity of change
- clean environmental change (noise, dirt, etc.)
- accommodation to human design factors.

One example of inadequate planning is the use of static components in a newly designed laboratory that had been in operation for two months. Investigation found the following problems and led to the indicated design modifications:

1. There was not enough knee space for sit-down operation. Undercounter storage was torn out to make knee space.
2. Some personnel were handicapped, so work spaces had to be lowered. Standard 36-inch-high work surfaces were altered but unfortunately the end result was a make-do effort—and looked it.

Design Principles

Horizontal work surfaces should be capable of being changed in 1-inch increments to meet the requirements of normal and handicapped persons. This may be more desirable than changing seat heights. The adjustment can suit bench work, drafting table, and communication position.

Desks, tables, counters, and workbenches are task areas and should be at elbow height, whether the person is sitting or standing. Abnormal table heights can reduce efficiency and lead to fatigue. Insufficient leg and foot room creates poor posture and discomfort. The important dimensions of work surfaces are working height, working width and depth, knee room height and depth, and kick room.

Storage and Components

Shelves are more functional when their contents can be seen and reached. Therefore, the top shelf should be no higher than 72 inches. The depth is determined by the unit size of the item. Components should be arranged properly, with manual equipment based on visual, auditory, and tactile links between the person and the units. The major components, such as work surfaces, are linked by the function involved. Equipment determines the value of this linkage: frequency of use, importance to productivity, and time of usage.

Human Factors

Most comparative tables of body measurements are based on averages. At best, these are guidelines for planning work areas. These measurements are used to develop work areas for such occupations as secretary, executive, and technician. Work surfaces then are designed with emphasis on working height, working width and depth, and knee room height and depth.

There is no quarrel with seating design, it is important; but emphasis must be put on the ability of people to adjust their work space, size, and height positions for best accommodation of the function to be done.

Acoustical Considerations

Acoustics consultants look at the following in order of importance:

Voice Levels: People learn to talk at a level so they do not get feedback, i.e., other opinions of their voice levels. Ironically, feedback is difficult when individuals are in separate enclosed rooms. Voice levels tend to be louder, so the feedback will be louder.

Visual Awareness: Certain groups such as those in waiting and reception areas should have visual awareness of each other. This tempers voices to acceptable levels. The smaller the number of people who have to work together, the more they should be able to see each other and the more carefully they should be located in the space. This leads to a more comfortable situation and encourages lower voice communication within each space. On the other hand, when people are in a cluster of voices, even those in unrelated activity tend to feel more comfortable because of the blanket of sound.

Ceilings: These are one of the two prominent horizontal surfaces (the other is the floor) that are major acoustic influences. The ceiling offers the better acoustic performance because of soft conditions it can offer, such as absorptive properties. This significantly reduces reverberation and long-distance voice transmission. The ceiling should duplicate, as much as possible, outdoor space. This occurs when the ceiling is 90 to 95 percent absorptive. Ceilings also have an effect on space management decisions. The proper ceiling can be installed relatively inexpensively during initial construction but it is difficult to do this once the space is occupied. Numerous ceiling-mounted lighting fixtures are not always the best choice; they reflect sound, and there is less intimacy with lights so far removed.

Walls: Absorbent wall coverings greatly reduce sound. This has high aesthetic value.

Floors: Carpeting, along with ceilings and absorbent panels, contributes to sound control. The sound of movement is muffled. In some areas, carpeting breaks falls and may require less maintenance. In other areas, noise reduction must be traded for ease of cleaning. Select floor surfaces that serve the needs of the function to be performed.

Configurations: A variation of shape and size of dynamic space assists in grouping like activities and helps control sound. Modular panels covered with cloth help absorb sounds. Spoke layouts of space cubicles isolate personnel, as do mazes of small, indiscriminately placed cubicles, and are generally not effective arrangements. Configurations that are irregular or ''L'' shaped still allow interaction and encourage privacy.

PLANNING WITH CONSULTANTS

The consultant is hired by the board to develop a program that will be translated by the architect into a functional and efficient structure. The consultant may be given several tasks, such as determining the need for a renovation, an addition, a replacement for an existing hospital, or a new hospital where one did not exist. The basic need is determined by developing the patient service area, i.e., the geographical area from which the hospital is attracting patients as well as the location of the doctors. This essentially is a demographic study but it will help determine the size and scope of the services that will be offered.

In developing the functional program, the consultant ascertains each department's needs by function and space in terms of rooms (or areas), including, in many cases, the number of persons required in each department or room. The room area space requirements are totaled to determine the department size. Adding for circulation, as well as converting the net square footage (NSF) into gross square footage (GSF) by some ratio such as 1.3 or 1.5 × the NSF, provides the total space requirement.

Having the consultant hired by the board (not by the administrator, but who is in agreement with the choice) on the scene before the architect has a tremendous influence on the final building configuration, size, and internal relationships. Above all, it affects the treatment of space, for it is during this planning stage that the hospital determines whether the consultant will allow for the concept of planning for the unpredictable, and where the institution's influence will be felt.

The philosophy of space management needs to be explained carefully to the consultant. A related element is the factor of clean change— that is, that future changes in walls and components will be done with a minimum of disruption to hospital commerce. This includes the actual changeover itself, the rapidity of change, and doing it without noise or dust, as would not be the case with the conventional method of skeletal structure erection, wallboard, plaster, painting, hammering, etc., ad nauseam. In the long run, over the life of the building, the "clean change philosophy" is the least expensive route.

How convincing the hospital administrator is in explaining this philosophy will determine how much confidence the consultant will have in this new approach to growth and change, and the ultimate recommendation. Best of all, the end user will be satisfied.

PLANNING WITH ARCHITECTS

Architects are geared to fill space with enclosures. In many cases, for example, they will take a given area such as a storage space and have the drafts person simply copy a layout from another hospital of similar size. This is an instinctive economy action and in keeping with the architect's training.

However, as space management is visualized here, it is recognized that change of space will predominate. As a matter of fact, the time element will increase in the future and spatial changes will probably take place more rapidly in the future as the demands placed on hospitals continue to change. The hospital's problem is to convince the architect to leave large spaces that can be changed to meet future requirements. This is simply planning for the unpredictable. No one is a soothsayer so it pays to allow those who will use the space to decide how they want it to be developed, both in configuration and the components that will compose work surfaces and areas.

This new attitude expected from the architects is contrary to their normal design behavior and thus it may confront hospitals with the most difficult aspect of the dynamic planning program. This is not to dismiss static architecture, for it has a definite place in certain areas of the hospital, but not where intensive change is expected. The ability to take care of the patient in unforeseen conditions is the main requirement.

PLANNING MATERIAL MANAGEMENT

Zone 4 (Figure 3–3, above) houses all the material management departments and may include the related departments of environmental management and equipment management. The material management department generally includes central and unit stores, central process, linen process, dietary (but generally not the cafeteria), pharmacy, printing, and staging assembly of vehicles. None of these require the presence of the patients except possibly outpatient pharmacy.

All the material management functions have a real physical and functional interface with all departments (Figure 3–4). All departments furnish supplies to unit stores. The unit store, which operates similarly to a supermarket, holds the supplies that will be picked for the vehicles in the staging/assembly area, then dispatched to the consumer departments.

Zone 4 of course can be physically removed from the three other zones as long as there is adequate horizontal communication with them. Workflow in every department should move from soiled to clean, airflow in the opposite direction, from clean to soiled. Both movements should assist in reducing cross-contamination (Figure 3–5). If the worst soiled air is visualized as the highest number, it is possible to plot airflow properly. More than one air movement flow may be needed to accomplish this. The general workflow in material management is shown in Figure 3–6. Workflow in the central processing department in material management is shown in Figure 3–7.

Figure 3–4 Interface with Hospital Departments

From
Consumer Dept.

Soiled
Supplies
⇩

Laundry

Clean
Linen
⇩

Central Stores

Supplies (Disposables
& Reprocessables)
⇩

| DECONTAMINATION | ⇨ | Clean Supplies

TERMINAL PROCESSING

Sterile Supplies | ⇦ | Makeup Supplies

UNIT STORES | ⇨ | CART HOLDING

STAGING AND
ASSEMBLY

Clean Supplies

Sterile Supplies |

⇩
Dispatch Carts
to
Consumer Depts.

Source: Reprinted from *Hospital Materiel Management Quarterly,* vol. 5, no. 2, published by Aspen Systems Corporation, © 1983.

While all departments have some type of holding space, the focus here is the major centralized storage areas—those found in the nursing units. From the point of inventory, storage in consumer departments really is an extension of material management storage, even though it is for the use of the consumer department.

The nursing unit, the major receiver of these supplies, has various areas or rooms for storage. (In some designs the supplies actually are dispensed to each patient room via a nurserver.) The following information is from a new acute care general hospital with more than 500 beds.

The decentralized storage on the nursing units can be broken down into:

- Linen storage: for storage of linen supplies
- Clean miscellaneous storage: miscellaneous clean stores
- Clean holding: place to hold portable carts or wall-hung modules filled with clean supplies
- Clean utility: preparation of supplies before using them on patients
- Soiled utility: place to take soiled supplies
- Soiled holding: place to hold portable carts or wall-hung modules filled with soiled supplies
- Medicine rooms: storage/preparation of medicines
- Dietary: storage of dietary carts and meal nourishment preparation
- Treatment rooms: despite this designation, treatments often are given in patient rooms and these are converted into additional storage areas.

Figure 3–5 Workflow and Airflow Paths

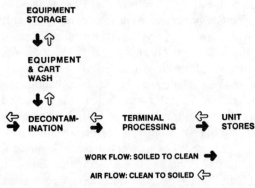

EQUIPMENT
STORAGE

⬇⬆

EQUIPMENT
& CART
WASH

⬇⬆

⇦ DECONTAM- ⇦ TERMINAL ⇦ UNIT
➡ INATION   ➡ PROCESSING ➡ STORES

WORK FLOW: SOILED TO CLEAN ➡

AIR FLOW: CLEAN TO SOILED ⇦

Source: Reprinted from *Hospital Materiel Management Quarterly,* vol. 5, no. 2, published by Aspen Systems Corporation, © 1983.

Figure 3–6 Material Management Workflow

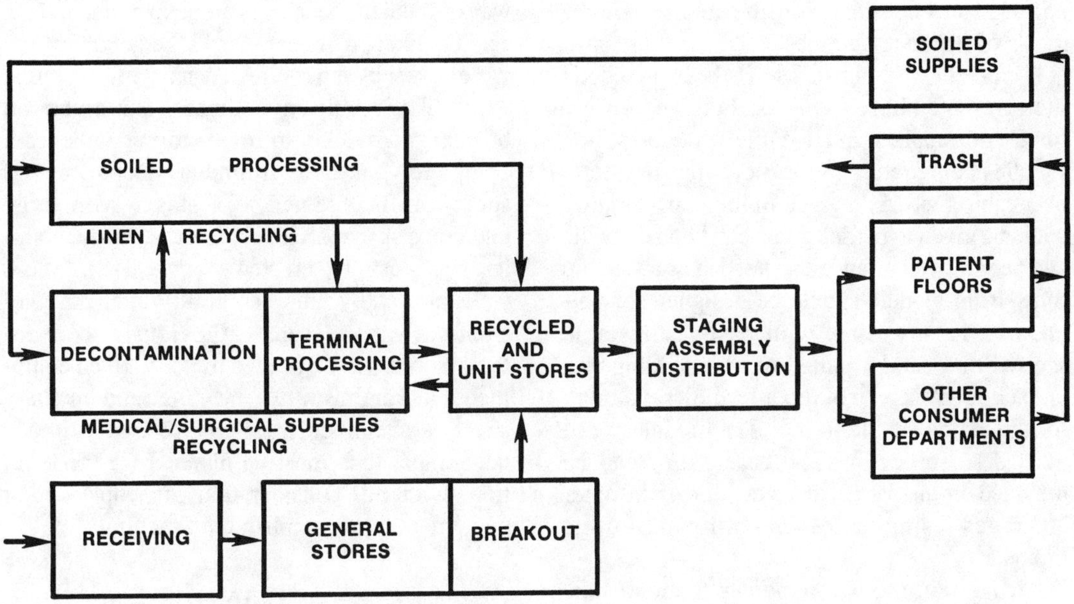

SOILED SUPPLIES
TRASH
PATIENT FLOORS
OTHER CONSUMER DEPARTMENTS
SOILED PROCESSING
LINEN RECYCLING
DECONTAMINATION
TERMINAL PROCESSING
RECYCLED AND UNIT STORES
STAGING ASSEMBLY DISTRIBUTION
MEDICAL/SURGICAL SUPPLIES RECYCLING
RECEIVING
GENERAL STORES
BREAKOUT

From the original building plans, the following storage changes took place:

- linen room became satellite pharmacy
- treatment room(s) became medical/surgical storage
- medical/surgical storage became paper supplies storage
- clean utility became medical/surgical/linen supply
- treatment room became cast room
- bath became orthopedic storage area
- shower became IV storage
- dietary room(s) became miscellaneous storage

Figure 3–7 Workflow Diagram, Central Processing

DISPATCH
STAGING, ASSEMBLY
UNIT STORES
CLEAN CARTS
PREPARATION AND PACKAGING
WASH
DECONTAMINATION
EQUIPMENT STORAGE

An analysis of the decentralized storage areas by function and net square footage (NSF) showed total storage space of 12,795, which was close to 9 percent of the total NSF of all nursing units. The total storage space on the nursing units almost equaled that in general bulk and unit stores. In spite of the amount of space, the hospital complained of inadequate storage. In truth, it had more storage space than it really required but it was in the wrong place and wrong configuration. It was not designed to adapt to new and present needs.

How did this happen? In the planning of the hospital, major space involved the architects and consultants, minor space, such as storage on the nursing units, was done by the draftspersons, who modelled the space size and the storage units on projects previously designed. The arrangement of static cabinets, drawers, shelves, and types of doors (sliding, hinged, solid glass),

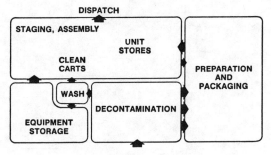

were at the discretion of the draftsperson and did not take into consideration the future requirements of different supplies.

If true, how could this have been avoided? Storage should have been based on 2 cubic feet for clean supplies and 1 cubic foot for soiled supplies being returned for recycling for a total of 3 cubic feet. As storage units, consideration could be given to modules that can hang on walls and be removed or added as needed at a specific time. Each module should be designed for volumetric density, i.e., with easily adjustable shelves that can be pulled out for loading and unloading. This type of module allows planning for the unpredictable future. The modules need much less space. In some cases, they can be mounted in alcoves in the corridor or in other "garages" similar to conventional storage rooms.

Alcove space to accommodate the total storage requirements would reduce the need to about 2,000 NSF. Based on a construction cost of $120/GSF, the space cost would be $240,000. The conventional example of 12,795 NSF is reduced to 7,864 to allow for ice units, dietary, and utility requirements, so 7,864 × $120 is $943,680. The module saving then is $703,680. It should be noted that future changes of the modules avoid the construction, noise, dirt, and time to accomplish.

PLANNING FOR THE UNPREDICTABLE

Due consideration must be given to physical obsolescence, which sometimes becomes so bad that it dictates how a hospital or unit is to function. Functional obsolescence is a change in technique or procedures. It can be an increase or decrease of supplies by type or quantity that may make inefficient the existing function to the degree that the patient (the end product) could be endangered. Technological obsolescence is created when new technology affects productivity, quality, and efficiency.

These three factors are victims of the passage of time. They all can cause change and growth,

so allowance must be made in the allotment for ways in which the space can be expanded. This can be likened to creating a stage on which various scenes can be created at a particular time to reveal a specific environment. This scene can be changed quickly to reveal to the audience a completely new environment. Departmental space can be likened to a stage, with large undefined space left in which free, sturdy modular walls can be erected (Figure 3–8). These walls are fed by umbilical utility lines for electricity or other services. Obviously, conventional room will be needed to house fixed equipment but administrative, waiting, and ancillary space can be modular, similar to scenery. Each department thus must be planned for the function, with full consideration of people and/or equipment to accomplish the function.

CONTINUING PLANNING

The planning process, as noted, consists of two major programming activities: functional and space (see Figure 3–9). This is a continuing program, however, for after the department goes into operation, space management is a neverending activity because change and growth can always be expected.

Too many hospitals do not have a director or manager of space management who is given the

Figure 3–8 Mobile Modular Spaces

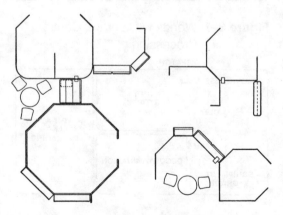

Figure 3–9 Space Management Program Sequence

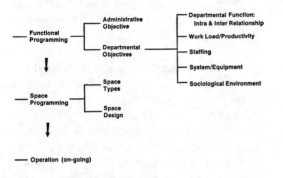

— Operation (on-going)

responsibility to anticipate space change and growth. Where there is one, that person identifies these emerging elements, then works with one or more departments to develop a need into a reality. In some hospitals a continuing planning committee is formed to do this, to review problems, and to resolve them. In either method, the data must be collected from several fronts, functions, and staffing, to ensure that the politics of design are not asserted over the logic of design.

Administrative Involvement

The administration obviously has as part of its strategy the planning aspects for the hospital and each of its facilities and departments. The hospital board actually employs the consultant and/or architect. If the building project is new or a major renovation, it may be advisable to have a consultant to handle both the first phase—the demographic studies of patient service areas and physician availability—and the second—the functional programming. If the planning involves only one department, the architect might be used.

The consultant or the architect will require a great deal of input from the department manager regarding workflow, activities, space, personnel, system, and equipment in the functional programming and space programming phases.

Departmental Involvement

Objectives need to be developed carefully because they determine subsequent planning activities. The objectives in turn are based on the following factors and should be on two levels:

Level 1—Short Term

- intradepartmental and interdepartmental relationships
- other departments necessary for interface
- supply input
- personnel input
- equipment
- airflows

The logistics of supplying all departments will determine staffing, workloads, and systems to use.

Level 2—Long Term

The long-term level is concerned with the effects of time. What are the workload, staffing, space requirement, and growth apt to be in the future? When change and growth is required, can the department respond? It is well to remember that objectives are not cast in concrete but are subject to change and should change when it is necessary.

Design elements should reflect the accurate interpretation of functional parameters:

- the correct size and configuration of functional space
- proper intrarelationship and interrelationship of facilities, departments, rooms
- workload, including flow and productivity
- types and numbers of staff
- the system defined and the equipment required to operate the system.

PREDICTABLE PLANNING

Planning for the predictable is accomplished by predictive planning; that is, by observing trends and drawing on the reservoir of information on the existing departments in the material management division. There should be quality-of-care studies. Demographic influences are helpful. A data base is particularly important for use with prospective payment programs when the hospital develops an efficient, cost-effective product.

To recapitulate briefly, the material management department is a major support element. It grows by two methods:

1. An increase in responsibility and supporting activities based on the consumer departments it supports.
2. Substantial changes in space and functions because the consumer departments it serves drastically increase their activities.

It should be kept in mind that these consumer departments do not change simultaneously, which makes change and growth within the material management department more difficult.

Material management should be housed in a separate building so it can grow in four horizontal directions. It should be connected with a pathway to the base hospital.

It will be difficult to find a part of the hospital that interfaces with more entities than the material management department. That is why it is so important and why it must be planned so carefully.

4. The Management Engineer

Larry E. Shear

The fundamental principle that enables a hospital to provide top-quality care is its ability to integrate the many disciplines and types of expertise necessary to form a cohesive team. The material manager is a major contributor to this team. Another team member, and one who may prove to be an invaluable resource, is the management engineer.

The management engineer is a person who applies knowledge of industrial engineering techniques to the hospital environment. Known also as a systems engineer, systems analyst, or consultant, the management engineer is concerned with the development, improvement, and installation of integrated systems of labor, supplies, and equipment.

This person is perhaps most visible today in relation to productivity enhancement and cost-containment efforts. Services may be provided by an in-house management engineer, through shared-service programs, or by an external consulting firm.

Often labelled as an "efficiency expert," the management engineer utilizes a cadre of specialized tools and techniques that assist in analyzing methods and systems quantitatively. The quantitative methods produce numerical results and findings that then may be used to evaluate, plan, and recommend more effective operational environments. Such tools and techniques include human factors analysis, work measurement techniques, work sampling, labor standards development, work distribution methods, and cost-benefit analysis. The management engineer usually is trained in computer technology, facilities layout, economic analysis, organizational development, and work simplification.

In addition to these quantitative and scientific techniques, the management engineer should be experienced in the system of human values that extends beyond numerical calculations. The efficiency component thus is balanced with the effectiveness component that recognizes the "people" element in designing better systems. In this regard, the management engineer may be trained in individual and group behavior, issues of morale and cohesion, motivation/incentives, and personnel development.

While not purporting to be an expert in all areas of endeavor, the management engineer is truly a generalist in the health care setting. With relatively few exceptions, the management engineer is perhaps the most versed in the multidisciplinary language of hospital systems. It is the management engineer who is apt to be cognizant of nursing, respiratory therapy, lab, and radiological systems, of administrative, financial, and personnel systems, and of all these systems as they interplay and interact with one another toward the delivery of better patient care. Perhaps most pertinent, it is the management engineer who is most apt to know how all these systems are interactive and mutually supportive to the material management system.

SUPPORT FOR THE MATERIAL MANAGER

An inherent component in the training of a management engineer (usually a B.S. in industrial engineering or an advanced degree) is exposure to material handling, distribution, inventory management, and value analysis. Significant emphasis is placed, academically, on logistical systems and the development of handling methods—the basis for an effective hospital material management program. In this regard, the management engineer is a trained material system analyst.

The management engineer is able to: (1) provide a hospital and its material manager with a broad organizational perspective, (2) act as a facilitator for new systems and as an educator in behalf of those systems, and (3) assist the material manager with the detailed systems analysis and design of supply networks.

The management engineer can provide specific support to the material manager in:

- formulating and recommending hospital inventory, purchasing, and control policies and procedures (exchange cart par levels, LIFO/FIFO, ABC inventory analysis)
- developing a fully integrated material management organization (laundry, maintenance, dietary, pharmacy, reproduction, mail/messenger, and so forth)
- developing a strategic plan for storage, distribution, space allocation requirements and facilities design (remote storage areas, warehouse design, delivery runs, supply and demand analysis)
- analyzing the economic prudence of capital equipment requests (medical equipment, office equipment, computers, photocopy machines, word processing equipment)
- developing labor and material control programs (exchange cart systems, unit dose, elevator systems, equipment/storage needs)
- assisting in making/buying, buying/leasing, providing/contracting decision analysis (IV solutions, disposables/nondisposables, equipment finance)
- developing preventive and remedial maintenance programs, equipment replacement protocols, and three-to-five-year capital budget projections (biomedical engineering maintenance programs, equipment upkeep, utilization, and life cycles)
- establishing and chairing cost-containment committees to review purchase requests and major expense categories (budget analysis, arbitration, cost-effective alternatives)

- developing detailed procedures, forms, and procedural steps for various systems and training employees in their use (playscript step-by-step procedures, workshops, formalized classroom sessions, one-on-one assistance)
- identifying actual costs of goods, developing cost profiles for diagnosis related group (DRG) input, and developing charging practices to reflect actual costs (value analysis, cost accounting, cost of handling, cost of inventory)
- designing and implementing management information systems that facilitate decisions (simulation techniques, format design, screen/output design, needs identification and quantification, liaison with data processing personnel)
- developing automated systems for inventory control, charging order backlogs, account aging, accounts payable, order entry, internal controls, labor performance, and budgeting
- evaluating and testing equipment, reviewing contracts, quality control programs, and user satisfaction surveys.

TOOLS AND TECHNIQUES

The management engineer employs a number of analytical tools that may be used to provide a considerable amount of analytical information. Many of these tools may be learned and applied with a minimal amount of research and/or training.

A number of these tools were developed in the more traditional industries but certainly have applicability in the health care industry. This is particularly so in the field of hospital material management. The tools are:

- work sampling
- work measurement
- control procedures
- workflow analysis
- labor/time standards

- methods/motion study
- operations research
- work simplification.

While some of these techniques require added training, some—such as work sampling, work simplification, and workflow analysis—may be learned quite readily.

Basic Concepts

Productivity, a key focus of a management engineer, is a term that has a number of different meanings, although it traditionally has been associated with labor efficiency in industry. In its simplest form, productivity is a ratio: a mathematical relationship between two variables, output to input. Input may be one, some, or all of the resources used to produce the output:

$$\text{Productivity} = \frac{\text{Output}}{\text{Input}}$$

Outputs are goods or services produced and may be either intermediate or final products, e.g., goods delivered, purchase orders processed, invoices processed, equipment installed, and supplies received. The inputs are resources that include labor, material, facilities, and capital. The resources are converted into outputs by an organizational unit, which can be anything from a hospital stores receiving area to a multi-hospital chain.

Productivity management involves manipulating this ratio. Its goal is the effective and efficient use of all resources. It requires the provision of a proper mix of inputs to ensure the maximum production of output, given quality considerations. Obviously, the quality of the output must meet the required standards, or one theoretically could continue to drastically limit the resources used to produce a given output.

Motion and Time Study Techniques

A body of knowledge has evolved over the years that is designed to increase the productivity of an organization and of the individuals who make it up. Motion and time study is the systematic study of work systems with the purposes of:

- developing the preferred system and method—usually the one with the lowest cost
- standardizing this system and method
- determining the time required by a qualified and properly trained person working at a normal pace to do a specific task or operation
- training the worker in the preferred method.

The two main parts of the motion and time study concept are:

1. motion study or work methods design—for finding the preferred method of doing work, and
2. time study or work measurement—for determining the standard time to perform a specific task.

The design of the method of performing an operation or the improvement of a current method is an important part of the industrial/management engineering approach. Because methods design is a form of creative problem solving, the general problem-solving process is an important tool. It entails the following seven steps in the logical and systematic approach to solving almost any problem:

1. problem definition
2. analysis of problem
3. search for possible solutions
4. evaluation of alternatives
5. recommendation for action
6. implementation
7. follow-up, feedback, and review.

Work Simplification

Work simplification is a process that utilizes the general problem-solving approach in the search for better and easier ways of doing work. It consists of an organized approach of challenging the "who, what, where, when, and how" of a particular work method or process. The approach closely parallels the general problem-solving process and directs the manager to take the following seven steps:

1. Select the job activity or situation.
2. Get the facts—make a breakdown of the work.
3. Analyze the facts—discover problems/opportunities.
4. Develop possible solutions/alternatives.
5. Evaluate solutions—testing and decision making to arrive at preferred solution.
6. Implement the improvement—plan of action.
7. Follow up—feedback and review.

The principles of eliminating all unnecessary work, combining operations where possible, changing sequences of operations and simplifying the necessary operations are applicable in searching for a better method.

Management Engineer's Support

Today's material managers are exposed to any number of consultants, systems design staff, and specialized experts in a variety of capacities. It is as important in dealing with these individuals as with a management engineer that objectives be defined clearly. In that sense the use of a management engineer could best be utilized when:

- Time is of importance. The material manager has an urgent problem but either cannot deal with it soon enough or does not have sufficient time. Management engineers have and can take the time that line managers may lack.
- Technical problems arise that are beyond the capability of the management staff. This could include a feasibility or cost study or a functional-facility design problem.
- Objectivity is needed because the organizational and political climates and inherent biases do not allow the material manager to

deal with the real issues. This could include a study to determine a reorganization issue, or whether the in-house laundry should be maintained or discontinued.

- Planning medium- to long-term goals is required and this requires a facilitator or educator who can structure the problem-solving process.
- Confirmation may be needed after the material manager has identified several alternatives but has difficulty in selecting the best one. Examples might include designing an automated material handling system for inventory control.
- Results are required immediately. Examples may include a surgical case cart system that has broken down, inventory controls that are out of hand, staffing that is excessive or lean, or lost charges that are beyond levels of acceptability.
- Specialized tools and techniques may be required beyond the ability of the material manager's scope. This might include sophisticated scheduling or simulation programs for the development of staffing plans.
- Interdepartmental communications require an individual to relate to the total operational process, thereby resolving departmental differences and/or developing systems that are best for the total hospital.

Maximizing Use of a Management Engineer

Once a management engineer is brought into a particular project, the material manager should make every effort to:

- Work very closely with the management engineer in determining who will coordinate the effort, in which form or format the results will be developed, and to whom they will be presented.
- Be sure to let staff know who the management engineer is, what the individual will be doing and why, and what roles may be

fulfilled to assist in project support. A group meeting would be helpful in many cases.

- Involve self and staff as required in the gathering of information, data, and documents. Not only is this a time saver, it also ensures that the correct sources are being identified and that participation is being solicited. It also optimizes the management engineer's time.
- Establish a plan of action with the management engineer to which there is mutual commitment. It should include timetables, key milestones, expectations, and outcomes.
- Work with the management engineer in understanding the individual's tools, techniques, processes, and data analysis methods. Understanding the result is also understanding the way the result was derived.
- Follow the course as defined. It is easy to become sidetracked in any study. Stick to the objectives and the plan of action. Keep the management engineer on track.

- Review the preliminary findings with the management engineer before finalization. Ensure accuracy, appropriateness, and completeness. Make sure it is what was asked for.
- Utilize the management engineer in the presentation phase, the "selling of recommendations" phase, and the implementation phase to optimize success.
- Identify the end of the project.

The complexities of today's hospital environment suggest that it is impossible for anyone to have all the answers or to be fully trained in every technique. Everyone seeks the help of the experts from time to time. One source that can be of true benefit to the material manager is the management engineer. Understanding the analytical and quantitative methods of the management engineer and utilizing the talents that each individual can lend will lead to a better material management function and make today's material managers better equipped for the future.

5. The Internal Auditor

Thomas J. Gruber

It is the managers' responsibility to define, design, modify, conduct, and provide continuing evaluation of the functions within their departments. For an experienced manager this is a challenging task; for a newly assigned manager it can be downright frightening. This chapter discusses a resource who also works for the same organization and is interested in its ultimate success: the internal auditor.

Many hospitals and health care institutions have established internal auditing departments and more are doing so. However, many, particularly smaller and more rural ones, cannot afford this service. If the hospital has internal auditing, managers should determine whether it also performs operations audits. This too is becoming more prevalent. If the institution does not have internal auditing, this chapter can be used as a primer to develop such audits.

Next, a definition of internal auditing:

> Internal auditing is an independent appraisal activity established as a service to management for the review of the operational processes of the organization.[1]

There are three key elements to this definition. Internal auditing is: (1) independent, (2) a service to management, (3) a reviewer of operational processes. These also are the three important elements in the relationship between the internal auditor and the material manager.

INDEPENDENCE

Independence implies objectivity. Objectivity is critical because no matter how hard the manager tries, complete objectivity cannot be achieved. Objectivity means that both strengths and weaknesses of the operation are identified, analyzed, and evaluated in a constructive fashion.

Independence also suggests ability to respond. The auditors, by virtue of their reporting relationship in the organization and their defined responsibility, should be able to work with managers in a timely fashion. More and more internal auditing departments report to chief executive officers or boards of trustees to assure organizational independence. Internal auditing charters (statements of responsibilities) and annual schedules normally provide time and resources to respond to specific management needs. These may include requests for assistance from the material manager.

SERVICE TO MANAGEMENT

Internal auditing truly is a service to management. The general objectives of an audit closely parallel the classical management objectives of planning, organizing, staffing, directing, and controlling. The difference is one of level and perspective. The manager has primary responsibility for department operations. The internal auditor has secondary responsibility for operations reviewed, with the primary responsibility focused on operating strengths and weaknesses. The auditor also can look at the operation from a different perspective and supply observations and recommendations based on that perspective.

"Can't see the forest for the trees" is a trite but often accurate phrase. Managers can get involved so intricately in the daily running of their departments that they lose sight of the bigger picture. The auditor is the resource or service the manager can turn to to provide independent, objective analyses. The manager can and should help define specific objectives for the audit. The final audit report provides a blueprint for action.

REVIEWER OF OPERATIONAL PROCESSES

This is a skill in itself. As a trained professional, the auditor does this for a living. The experience, training, and education developed by the auditor are assets of value for the material manager.

Internal auditing is a profession. The Institute of Internal Auditors (IIA) is an international organization composed of thousands of audit professionals. The Institute has published standards for the practice of internal auditing and conducts a rigorous certification program. Certified internal auditor (CIA) is the internal auditing equivalent of certified public accountant (CPA).

The Healthcare Internal Audit Group (HIAG) was established in 1982. This group numbers more than 500 professionals who work in the health care industry to advance the cause of internal auditing and is another resource to enhance the quality of operational reviews. HIAG does not restrict its membership to auditors. Material managers may wish to consider joining HIAG if their hospital does not have an audit function. HIAG members can access a large library of programs and other resources that can assist nonauditors attempting to develop audit routines.

Information pertaining to HIAG membership can be obtained by contacting the author of this chapter.

OPERATIONAL AUDITING

Unfortunately, the internal auditing profession has done a poor job of distinguishing terms such as internal auditing, compliance auditing, management auditing, financial auditing, electronic data processing (EDP) auditing, and operational auditing. For this discussion, internal auditing and operational auditing are considered synonymous. Operational auditing also is considered to be the composite package not only of operational but also of financial, management, compliance, and EDP auditing.

Thus, internal auditing provides a comprehensive, integrated review of all aspects of the material management function: financial, management, data processing, operating procedures, and legal and statutory compliance.

THE INTERNAL AUDITOR'S VIEW

It has been established that the auditor is a trained professional performing reviews of operations. The "auditor's view" seems to suggest approaching material management one way and other departments such as laboratory, personnel, or accounting in different ways. Actually, this is both true and false.

Internal auditing is a skill that combines science and art. As noted, the IIA has established standards for the practice of internal auditing. In this sense internal auditing is a science. Standards exist to ensure consistency, comprehensiveness, and completeness. Standards also recognize that all operations are composed of common elements, even though their purposes may be vastly different. Thus, standards provide guidelines.

Auditing also requires extensive use of judgment. This is the art. The evaluations and analyses of the audit require judgment where standards cannot be applied blindly. To do so would risk turning the audit service into a disservice.

For example, all businesses offer different products or services yet they all have common elements such as the need to manage people and assets, market to their customers, comply with contracts and laws, and, ultimately, earn a profit. Similarly, the material management role is different from other hospital functions. Yet all hospital functions can be effective only if they operate in congruence with the overall philosophy of the organization; effectively utilize assets and personnel; develop reliable and useful information systems; and comply with laws, regulations, and contracts.

The point is that the overall approach to auditing is constant, but the auditor uses professional judgment to tailor procedures that account for the uniqueness of the material management function.

THE AUDITOR'S OBJECTIVES

Having established the fact that the auditor's objectives are consistent, those objectives can be stated. The auditor has five integrated objectives and makes available a sixth for the manager. These are to determine:[2]

1. The operational objective: What is the purpose of this operation? How effectively is the purpose being accomplished?
2. The management objective: Is the purpose of the operation in congruence with the overall philosophy and purpose of the organization of which it is a part?
3. The financial objective: How effectively and efficiently are the assets and resources (including personnel) utilized, accounted for, and safeguarded?
4. The EDP objective: How reliable and useful is the information system supporting the operation? How well controlled is it?
5. The compliance objective: What is the extent of compliance with outside contractual obligations, industry standards, and governmental laws and regulations?
6. The manager's objective: What is the material manager seeking to achieve—specific, advisory, general?

The Operational Objective

What is the purpose of this operation? How effectively is the purpose being accomplished?

If, indeed, there is an unwritten, generally accepted approach for operational auditing, this approximates it. The idea is for the auditor to become familiar with the actual operation and its peculiarities. Flow charts, floor plans, statements of objectives, job descriptions, staffing schedules, inventory and equipment listings, operating budgets, and price and product lists should be gathered (if available) or prepared (if possible), then evaluated.

The primary end product is a determination of whether the operation is designed and functions to achieve its stated objectives. Control deficiencies, procedural breakdowns, and operating inefficiencies are additional important disclosures to be pinpointed.

The Management Objective

Is the purpose of the operation in congruence with the overall philosophy and purpose of the organization of which it is part?

The five primary responsibilities of management are (1) planning, (2) organizing, (3) staffing, (4) leading, and (5) controlling. The complexity of most organizations results in several layers of management, each of which addresses these responsibilities as applicable to its particular domain.

The typical operational audit may evaluate management performance at the operational level. Often overlooked is the link with middle management, executive management, or both. This is the first example of the integrated approach. The operational manager may have developed an outstanding operation but if it is not in accord with overall organizational direction, the effect can be detrimental.

The Financial Objective

How effectively and efficiently are the assets and resources (including personnel) utilized, accounted for, and safeguarded?

Material managers who may be CPAs probably feel a bit reassured at this point. After all, is this not what auditing is really about? The answer is yes—in part. Certainly, financial considerations are important, but they can be evaluated most effectively when considered in the overall perspective of the operation.

The financial objective also is integrated with the operational objective. Some of the information obtained to accomplish the operational objective is useful here. In fact, the auditing procedures to accomplish these objectives probably will be performed simultaneously. (These procedures are discussed later in this chapter.)

One final note about the financial objective. If they examine the financial statements, external auditors, to varying degrees of emphasis, will address these same issues. This is a good reason to use judgment and avoid excessive emphasis on this aspect of the audit.

The EDP Objective

How reliable and useful is the information system supporting the operation? How well controlled is it?

This is more accurately titled the information system objective. EDP normally is the primary and most complicated element of an operational information system. Manual communication in written and oral form also is important and should be evaluated.

The concept of integration probably is most critical here. How can an information system be evaluated for reliability, usefulness, and, to a lesser degree, control if the auditor does not understand the operation the system is designed to support? No operation in an organization exists in a vacuum. A hospital laboratory might do excellent clinical work but if the supporting information system does not report test results to physicians in a timely manner, the laboratory's overall effectiveness is diminished. The same analogy is applicable for material management.

The Compliance Objective

What is the extent of compliance with outside contractual obligations, industry standards, and governmental laws and regulations?

Legal, professional, and statutory obligations should be monitored routinely as part of an operational audit. Omission of these compliance evaluations precludes a total evaluation of the status of the operation under review.

It should be apparent at this point that these objectives have general applicability for material management as well as for almost any function that could be audited.

The Manager's Objective

The final objective is perhaps most important to the material manager because it is defined by that individual. An effective auditor permits the manager to provide input. This maximizes the effectiveness of the audit and makes it a tool truly tailored to serve the manager's needs. The objectives should be a collaborative byproduct of a trained professional analyst and a trained professional manager in the field being analyzed.

The audit objectives suggested by the manager are limited only by the imagination. Objectives can be:

- global, such as comparing standard costs to process a pound of laundry for the hospital to the same standards for the health care industry
- specific, such as categorizing inventory items into an ABC classification system
- advisory, such as preparing guideline instructions for conducting a physical inventory count
- general, such as identifying key indicator elements common to all aspects of material management, i.e., purchasing, pharmacy, laundry, central distribution, processing, and printing services, which the manager can employ to monitor the overall effectiveness of these departmental operations.

This illustrates that the potential objectives of an audit are vast and can be tailored to accommodate the manager's specific needs. At the same time, the manager receives the benefit of a solid overall operational assessment that is based on professional expertise and time-tested standards of practice.

THE AUDIT PROCESS

The audit process consists of nine steps:

1. establishment of objectives
2. research
3. investigation
4. assessment
5. testing
6. conclusions
7. recommendations
8. implementation
9. follow-up.

Process Step 1: Establishment of Objectives

A comprehensive operational audit encompasses, at a minimum, the five general objectives. These constitute the primary goals if the audit is initiated as part of the routine schedule of internal auditing.

The manager should be able to incorporate specific additional objectives as desired. These should be clearly defined, succinct, written statements aimed at ensuring mutual understanding between the internal auditor and manager. A good internal auditor will require written objectives from each party.

In the event no routine audit is planned, the manager should call the internal auditing department and request a review that will satisfy the objectives. This can be a full-scale operational audit of one or more material management departments or it may be limited to a special study of a specific problem.

It must be remembered that internal auditing is a service to management. The internal auditing director should be prepared to accommodate the manager's needs within a reasonable time.

The remaining steps in the audit process are important only to material managers planning to perform self-audits. As noted earlier, this most frequently is the case in smaller institutions without internal auditing departments. However, all institutional resources are limited, and internal auditing is no exception. Therefore, understanding the steps in the process can be useful to all material managers. The knowledge gained is an important tool for every managerial arsenal.

A word about the audit program: It is a set of instructions or guidelines. It can even be compared to a chef's recipe. A recipe lists ingredients and the steps required to prepare them to make the desired dish. An internal audit program documents the objectives and procedure to be performed to produce an opinion (the conclusion step) about those objectives.

The proof of the success of the recipe is the taste. The proof of the success of the audit program is to provide conclusions about the objectives in an informed fashion that does not require assumptions or statements of appearance but only statements of fact.

Most aspects of an audit generally are constant and have general applicability in every case. The unique steps in each audit are establishing objectives and testing; as noted, only some objectives will be unique while the primary objectives are general.

The typical audit program is composed of three portions (see Table 5–1). Their relationship becomes clearer as the remaining steps in the process are discussed. At this point, the objectives should be considered as the foundation upon which the rest of the program is constructed. The objectives must be delineated before any additional program steps can be developed.

Process Steps 2–4: Research, Investigation, Assessment

Appendix 5–A at the end of this chapter outlines a sample audit program. Program item 1 under "Audit Procedures" deals with setting objectives and has been discussed. Program

Table 5–1 Sections of an Audit Program

Program element	Steps in audit process
1. Listing of objectives	1
2. Standard audit procedures	2–4, 6–9
3. Specific audit test(s)	5

items 2 and 3 provide for the research, investigation, and assessment aspects of the audit.

Research: The Global Review

Research is important to provide a macro as well as a historical basis for comparison and to obtain the viewpoints of contemporary thinking on the subject.

Program items 2 and 3 are for the research process. The public library is the best place to begin this segment but there are others. Most managers and many hospitals maintain reference libraries. Of particular significance today are computerized data bases. Many of these exist and more are coming into the marketplace each year. They can be accessed through most microcomputers by using a telephone communication device known as a modem. Data bases, like magazines, normally are subscription services. If a hospital has a library, it probably subscribes to most of the relevant data bases. The hospital librarian can supply information and guidance.

Through this research process, the auditor becomes aware of current events in the field and the thinking of industry leaders. Information also may be obtained about regional and national productivity standards or specific experiences of similar or like hospitals. This information is of significant value in its own right but becomes more important when compared with the data collected from the internal review process.

One note of caution: Internal auditors and material managers should not jump to rash conclusions if the data comparisons show significant favorable or unfavorable deviations against the external data. There may be very valid reasons why the particular operations being reviewed should show this deviation, whether it be in number of inventory turns or pounds of laundry processed per patient day. This is where the science of auditing yields to the art, and that is the purpose of the next steps in the process—investigation and assessment.

Investigation: Formulating Fact from Appearance

Program items 4 through 14 are for investigation. This investigation includes interviewing, observation, and review of organizational and departmental goals, objectives, policies, and procedures.

As the heading states, investigation is designed to formulate facts from appearances. Just as importantly, investigation separates fact from fiction. Facts is the key word. An audit is of little or no value, and actually may be counterproductive, if not based primarily on facts.

Armed with the historical and macro research data, the auditor can begin the investigative process that places the internal operation into proper perspective.

Effective investigation starts with a comprehensive interview with the department director or manager. This is critical and must not be ignored, even if the manager is performing a self-audit. In such a case, the manager also must perform a self-interview.

Item 4 in the sample program in Appendix 5–A lists a series of generally applicable questions. These provide a starting point and by no means should be considered all-inclusive. As many questions as possible should require more than a yes-or-no answer. These are the "what," "where," "why," and "how" questions. This is not to suggest that the "is," "does," and "are" questions (the yes/no questions) are not important, because they are. Actually the yes/no questions generally establish the facts. The what/why questions then provide the insight that will be used in the assessment process. These questions are the ones that describe the unique aspects of the operation—and every operation is unique.

The interviewing process continues with key employees. These are a cross-section of the workers who perform the tasks that constitute the operation. Key employees should be asked the same questions in their areas of responsibility that the manager was asked. The purpose is not to cause dissension but to determine that the workers and manager have a similar understanding of the processes. If not, there are certain to be operational problems.

The auditor also should observe the employees performing their duties as they described them. This is the next part of the verification process (discussed in the Testing section later). Observation also is important to assess work conditions, adequacy of equipment, reasonableness of floor layout, and other factors.

Investigation concludes with a review and understanding of corporate and departmental goals, objectives, policies, procedures, job descriptions, and long-range plans, as well as compliance, regulatory, and statutory requirements. The key element here is continuity; i.e., if departmental objectives are not consistent with corporate objectives, or not in compliance with Joint Commission on Accreditation of Hospitals regulations, or the law, an operational problem exists.

Assessment: Determining the Impact

The legwork is now completed and it is time to start formulating opinions about the strengths and weaknesses of the operation. Program items 15 through 24 accomplish this.

The first of these items is a review of opinion poll data. The second item develops flow charts for the operation as discerned through research and investigation. The remaining steps entail a study of hard data such as financial, statistical, and engineering reports. The ordering of program items 17 through 24 is not important. Opinion polls (if available) and flow chart operations should be reviewed early in the assessment process.

Opinion polls are important for two reasons: (1) They measure the feelings of patients or other end users of the services produced by the operation under audit. In the final analysis, this opinion is the one that matters. (2) They should provide the auditors with corroborative evidence of their opinion. If the auditors' investigation has led to preliminary opinions and conclusions that differ significantly from those polled, they should look for reasons why. Perhaps the audit work was not properly focused or totally objective. Auditors should be sure, however, to consider the poll questions as well. Many opinion polls, if not prepared professionally, may be biased in their phrasing and many draw respondents to conclusions that may be tilted.

Flow charting is the most important step. It permits the auditor to construct a picture of what has been learned. This integrates the information so as to more effectively assess the impact of tasks and functions on each other. Writing a memorandum can be substituted for flow charting but it is not recommended. Memos usually take longer to prepare, require more pieces of paper, and tend to ramble. It also is easier to omit a task when writing a memo than when preparing a flow chart.

Flow charts should be simple. Purchase a simple template at an office supply store. A template will have eight or ten basic symbols with labels that are easy to understand. These symbols can be used in your flow charts.

Flow charts are like blueprints. They normally consist of one or two pages of pictures. The manager or employees being audited can review them and acknowledge whether or not they are complete. They make outstanding reference and training material. Finally, the auditor can use them as work sheets to record comments at steps in the process that are incomplete or are particularly well controlled. This becomes base material for subsequent substantive testing, conclusions, and recommendations.

Assessment is completed with a study of the hard data. Program items 17 through 24 present a basic list of points reviewed but should not be considered all-inclusive. Data items reviewed in these steps encompass elements common to most organizations. Auditors can select other appropriate hard data for study by using their knowledge of their organizations.

Financial and statistical reports, user manuals, computer program requests, productivity standards, and blueprints all are barometers used to measure the operation against itself. Data from these sources is the final assessment tool and a primary basis for determining if and what substantive testing is required.

Process Step 5: Testing

The sample audit program has one simple instruction for testing (Item 25): "Determine what, if any, additional audit testing is required.

Develop supplementary audit programs for these tests. Note audit findings.''

Testing is the unique portion of every audit whether it be a hospital material management function or a General Motors assembly line operation. Testing is judgmental. Is a test required? If yes, what type test? At this point in the audit, answers to these questions will be apparent if the previous four process steps were completed adequately and effectively.

Upon completing assessment, the auditor has identified procedures that are strong, i.e., safeguarding assets or controlling operational effectiveness and guaranteeing compliance; and also has identified weaknesses, i.e., areas where a procedure may be missing or where one individual exercises too much or too little control over a process.

An example of a missing procedure is failure of the receiving dock to count and verify incoming receipt quantities. Without this information, accounts payable must pay the invoice without assurance that quantities billed are correct.

An example of placing excessive control in one individual is a pharmacist who orders, receives, issues, and inventories stock. This failure to segregate duties places an employee in a position to defraud the company. It also increases the chance that an error will go undetected because no other individual has an opportunity to review the transaction.

Another reason to test is, as noted, to verify that procedures are being performed as represented by management and employees in the interview process and as observed by the auditor. Sometimes employees know what is supposed to be done but for any one of several reasons choose to not follow procedures. Testing can help determine this better than observation because most people will do what they are supposed to do if they know they are being watched. Observation is most effective in determining instances where employees do not understand a procedure and hence cannot follow it.

Once the necessary tests are determined, separate audit test programs should be written. Like the standard audit program, they begin with an objective. Test programs should be limited to one objective. The objective will be related to the reason the test is considered necessary in the first place.

For instance, if inventory storage and issuance controls are poor, the auditor may wish to observe the physical inventory. The purpose or objective is to determine that the inventory adjustment to the accounting records, generated as a result of the inventory, is reasonable. The auditor accomplishes the objective by performing program test steps designed to determine that all inventory items are counted once and only once, the counts are accurate, and the items are properly costed and accurately extended for compilation purposes.

Space limits prevent exhaustive discussion of testing so it should be remembered that most test procedures are based on common sense once the need has been primarily established and the objective is clearly stated.

Process Steps 6 and 7: Conclusions and Recommendations

The last two items in the standard audit program are devoted to conclusions and recommendations. These are like the old song about love and marriage, "You can't have one without the other."

Conclusions are made about the initial audit objectives, both of the standard audit program and of the special test programs. Once it has been established to what extent these have been satisfied, the report can be written and recommendations made.

It is important to note that the report should dwell on the strengths as well as the weaknesses of the operation. If something works well, the auditor should say so and recommend its continuance. Recommendations for improvement should offer specific suggestions. Of course, this is understood where the manager also has been the auditor.

Finally, the auditor (if not the manager) should be available in an advisory capacity to assist in implementing the recommendations.

Process Steps 8 and 9: Implementation and Follow-Up

Implementation and follow-up occur after the audit. The material manager can implement recommendations, the auditor cannot. The auditor should work with the manager in the advisory capacity.

Follow-up may be the most important element in the process. It should occur in stages, perhaps in the first several weeks, again in three to four months, and a final time in about a year. Follow-up is also judgmental with regard to frequency, extensiveness, and time frame. These comments are simply intended to provide guidance.

An effective follow-up program probably will resemble a miniaudit of the aspect of the operation that was revised. By its nature, it probably will be less formal than the original audit, but it should be based on the principles of the operational audit.

THE CHALLENGE TO MANAGERS

This chapter is intended to give the material manager an understanding of the purpose and work of an internal auditing department. While the thrust is as a guideline for performing an operational audit, the chapter has a broader purpose.

The principles, procedures, and methods used by the internal auditor are simply logical extensions of the fundamentals of effective management. Material managers should incorporate some of these concepts and ideas into their own everyday management practices. In this sense, material management will benefit from an internal audit whether or not the institution provides a formal internal auditing department as a resource.

NOTES

1. Thomas J. Gruber, "The Operational Audit—An Integrated Approach," *The Internal Auditor* (August 1983): 39.

2. Ibid., 39–42.

Standard Program for Operational Audits

OVERVIEW

An operational audit is an independent appraisal of the adequacy, effectiveness, and efficiency of an operational process. It entails determining the following general objectives:

1. What is the purpose of this operation? How effectively is the purpose being accomplished?
2. Is the purpose of the operation in congruence with the overall philosophy and purpose of the organization of which it is a part?
3. How effectively and how efficiently are the assets and resources (including personnel) utilized, accounted for, and safeguarded?
4. How reliable and useful is the information system supporting the operation? How well controlled is it?
5. What is the extent of compliance with outside contractual obligations, industry standards, and governmental laws and regulations?

The accompanying procedures provide general guidance for performing an effective operational audit.

AUDIT PROCEDURES

1. Consider the general objectives denoted in the introduction above, then record any other specific audit objectives. Work toward that end but be aware that other issues may surface during the course of an audit.
2. Perform a literature search at the library using the card catalog and/or have the staff perform a computerized literature search. Determine from the literature what the relevant issues are. If the literature suggests any evaluative criteria, employ these in the analysis.
3. Review the findings of past inspections, reviews, and studies. Note all shortcomings and recommendations. Review for compliance and/or progress. Examples:

   - past audit reports, or audit flow charts
   - Joint Commission on Accreditation of Hospitals reports
   - fire inspections
   - management engineering studies
   - insurance reviews
   - any other pertinent reviews, inspections, or studies.

4. Interview the department director. Obtain the following items from the department director:

   - department policy and procedure manual
   - quality assurance plan
   - self-audits
   - departmental goals and objectives
   - departmental data bases, e.g., logs, schedules, production records
   - user manuals for data systems, equipment, inservice documentation, maintenance schedules.

   Ask these sorts of questions:

   - What specific relationships exist with physicians, other departments, and external agencies, organizations, vendors, etc.?

- What credentials are necessary for the staff? How are they documented?
- What resource contraints exist in terms of staffing, equipment, space, supplies, and storage?
- What possibilities exist for marketing?
- Are departmental policies and procedures current?
- Is staff turnover a problem?
- Is recruitment difficult?
- Are any major projects planned or being implemented?
- Is the organizational chart in the department job description current and accurate?
- Does pricing adequately cover costs?
- What are the major problems the department faces?
- What sorts of routine analysis are performed?

Before concluding the interview, ask for a tour of the department and permission to interview the staff. Be observant of work conditions, employee attitudes, and diligence to the job during these periods.

5. Review the organization's long-range plan for applicable goals. Determine the current status of goal implementation.
6. Review applicable corporate policies and procedures and check for compliance.
7. Review departmental goals and objectives. Are they consistent with the long-range plan? Are they measured?
8. Review the departmental policy and procedure manual. Verify that required policies are in place and followed. Comment on discrepancies between policy and practice.
9. Review the quality assurance plan. (JCAH requires this.) Check for compliance. Review any written quality assurance reports prepared.

10. Review pertinent compliance and regulatory requirements, e.g., JCAH, Food and Drug Administration, local fire codes. Acquire evidence that each requirement is complied with. Comment on any deviation.
11. Review the department description. Verify its accuracy through interviews and personal observation.
12. Determine consistency of goals, objectives, and policies and procedures at the corporate and departmental levels.
13. Review the job descriptions for all department personnel. Determine their accuracy through interviews with department management and staff and personal observations. Note any discrepancies.
14. Review the staff personnel files for:

- proof of licensure
- discipline not in accordance with organizational policy
- excessive staff turnover.

15. Review patient or other opinion poll responses and incident reports. Note any repetition of complaints, or incidents that indicate areas of potential liability.
16. Prepare flow chart of operations where applicable, based on the understanding of department operations gained through the above work. Submit the preliminary flow chart draft to the department director for review. Incorporate any revisions into the final copy. Analyze the flow chart for control strengths and weaknesses and consistency with external, corporate, and departmental dicta.
17. Review computer programming or systems requests and their current status. Evaluate the logic for acceptance or rejection of these.
18. Review the financial and utilization reports prepared by the accounting department. Analysis of these should give the auditor an understanding of department utilization of financial and

personnel resources. Growth rates, seasonal variations in expenses and revenue, control of overtime, and so on should become evident.

19. Determine whether the department uses microcomputers; if so, record descriptions and quantities of hardware and software. Review the data base developed. Ask what controls exist to preclude the establishment of duplicate data (i.e., as compared with hospital data base). Evaluate whether the data are being used appropriately and effectively. Are controls over the data, and accessibility to them, sufficient and effective?

20. Review any formulas that compute departmental productivity standards. Determine whether or not these formulas and standards are reasonable as a basis for standards.

21. Review past capital budget requests. Determine the reasonableness of the rationale for acceptance or rejection of these requests. Identify capital requests that may require construction work for installation. Is the construction costed and included in the cost of the capital request? If not, why?

22. Obtain a blueprint of the department floor plan. Evaluate how well the floor plan design accommodates the department's needs.

23. Review user manuals. Are they informative? Adequate? Understandable? Understood? Complied with? Consistent with corporate policies and procedures?

24. Review the property ledger maintained in accounting for capital assets assigned to the department. Identify items requiring a high degree of control and safeguarding (consider acquisition cost, size, desirability, etc.). Verify that assets listed are in physical existence. Identify equipment in physical existence fitting the above description. Verify that this equipment is listed. Note any discrepancies.

25. Determine what, if any, additional audit testing is required. Develop supplementary audit programs for these tests. Note audit findings.

26. Conclude to audit objectives. Refer to the audit objectives at the beginning of the audit program. Evaluate to what extent the questions raised in the objective statements can be satisfactorily answered; e.g. (from objective 3), how much inefficiency was detected in the utilization of assets. Be specific.

27. Draft report. Include all noteworthy comments and recommendations.

28. Plan future review and follow-up.

6. Performance Indicators

Thomas J. Gruber

Performance indicators can be defined as systems of reporting data to management about meaningful operational activities. Managers then transform these data to information that aids their decision-making process.

Performance indicators dovetail nicely with auditing. Attention to these indicators may signal to the manager that an audit is necessary. On the other hand, they can serve as ideal trending and monitoring tools for the follow-up phase, the last step in the audit process.

Performance indicators are important but should be kept in perspective. Managers can use them in a distant or analytical fashion; however, they also should practice the concept of "management by walking around" (MBWA). MBWA encompasses managers' direct participation, not distant order giving.

The manager who participates directly with workers becomes knowledgeable about the purest and most direct indicators of the operation and the workers' thoughts, concerns, and attitudes. This knowledge then can be applied more effectively in the analytical indicator process as well.

Performance indicators can be quite varied. Table 6–1 provides a matrix listing of performance indicators for different operations in each material management division. This is only a sampling; a complete list probably would be longer than this book.

TYPES OF INDICATORS

For purposes here, three primary indicator types are considered:

1. historical
2. budget
3. external.

Historical indicators are comparisons against the operation itself in previous years, or other reasonable periods of measurement. Budget indicators are comparisons of the actual result of the operation against a projected result. External indicators are comparisons against similar operations, either individual or collective, in the hospital or in general industry.

Of course, there are the formal indicators such as cost to prepare a purchase order, average time to fill a prescription, or pounds of laundry processed per patient day. It is essential not to overlook the importance of management by walking around, or informal indicators such as worker attitudes and cleanliness of the workplace.

The rest of this chapter covers the identification, development, and use of the formal indicators, called performance indicators. The informal MBWA indicators normally should corroborate the trends identified from the analysis of these formal performance indicators. Thus, effective use of MBWA can help managers more effectively utilize time available for performance indicator analysis by disclosing specific conditions in individual departments.

ESTABLISHING THE SYSTEM

Establishing a performance indicator system for the first time requires a three-step process: (1) identifying sources of information, (2) selecting relevant indicators from those identified, and (3) establishing a data base of meaningful information.

Sources of performance indicator data are vast. Some of the more common types are discussed next.

Table 6–1 Performance Indicator Matrix

Internal statistical data	Purchasing	Receiving/ transp.	Inventory control	Supply distrib.	Central process.	Laundry	Print shop	Pharmacy
Consumption per patient day			X	X	X	X		X
Cost per patient day	X	X	X	X	X	X	X	X
Full-time equivalent (FTE) employees per patient day	X	X	X	X	X	X	X	X
Sick hours as percent of total labor hours	X	X	X	X	X	X	X	X
Rate of employee turnover (percent)	X	X	X	X	X	X	X	X
Inventory turnover			X	X			X	X
Cost to produce a purchase order	X							
Percentage of total hospital purchases processed through purchase orders	X							
Percentage of stock outages per stock issue requests			X	X			X	X
Percentage of job-related injuries per FTE	X	X	X	X	X	X	X	X
Worker compensation cost per employee	X	X	X	X	X	X	X	X
Percentage of spoiled, outdated, or damaged stock			X	X		X	X	X
Items issued per employee or department	X	X	X	X	X	X	X	X
Employee labor hours per patient day	X	X	X	X	X	X	X	X
Cost per unit processed	X	X	X	X	X	X	X	X
Overtime hours as percentage of total hours worked	X	X	X	X	X	X	X	X
Internal financial data								
Annual budget	X	X	X	X	X	X	X	X
Departmental financial statements	X	X	X	X	X	X	X	X
Physical inventory results			X	X			X	X
Inventory shortages and overages			X	X			X	X
Internal reference data								
Patient opinion poll summaries			X	X	X	X		X
Patient, visitor, and employee letters	X	X	X	X	X	X	X	X
Equipment down time records		X	X		X	X	X	X
Equipment idle time records		X	X		X	X	X	X
Equipment maintenance records		X	X		X	X	X	X
Schedule II narcotics inventory audit reports								X
Frequency of employee promotions	X	X	X	X	X	X	X	X
Standard costs	X	X	X	X	X	X	X	X
Standard of production per labor hour	X	X	X	X	X	X	X	X
External reference and statistical sources								
Monitrend (American Hospital Assn.)	X	X	X	X	X	X	X	X
Price indexes	X		X	X		X	X	X
State, federal, and local government bureaus	X	X	X	X	X	X	X	X
American Hospital Association	X	X	X	X	X	X	X	X
State hospital associations	X	X	X	X	X	X	X	X
Public library	X	X	X	X	X	X	X	X
Computerized data bases	X	X	X	X	X	X	X	X

Table 6-1 continued

Consultant Reports	Purchasing	Receiving/ transp.	Inventory control	Supply distrib.	Central process.	Laundry	Print shop	Pharmacy
Joint Commission on Accreditation of Hospitals	X	X	X	X	X	X	X	X
Internal auditors	X	X	X	X	X	X	X	X
Management engineers	X	X	X	X	X	X	X	X
Attorneys	X	X	X	X	X	X	X	X
Fire and other safety inspectors	X	X	X	X	X	X	X	X
Outside paid consultants	X	X	X	X	X	X	X	X

Company Statistics

This information generally includes financial and personnel reports on a departmental basis. Some more sophisticated hospitals may provide cost accounting reports that compare results of actual activities with predetermined standards.

If the hospital offers such information, the rest of this chapter will have limited meaning to readers. Their primary concern in such a case should be the continuing reasonableness of the standard and the relevance of activities measured with standards.

In-House Consultants

This group includes internal auditors, management engineers, and accounting and marketing personnel, among others. In-house consultants typically are used for special, one-time indicator studies.

External Consultants

The sources here are almost infinite. Primary ones include the hospital's external auditors, professional hospital industry groups such as the American Hospital Association, which issues a report called Monitrend; the Healthcare Financial Management Association, and hospital vendors.

Federal, state, and local government agencies can provide data on many relevant topics. This is particularly true for personnel data such as average sick time or employee turnover. The local office of the U.S. Department of Labor should be contacted.

Books, magazines, professional journals, audiocassettes, videocassettes, computer data bases—the list is extensive. The public library is the best resource for identifying and obtaining this information.

There are other sources of data as well but these five categories encompass the vast majority of indicator sources that the manager will require.

SELECTING DATA SOURCES

The manager is faced next with the task of selecting relevant data. This is accomplished initially by defining the purpose for the data and understanding the uniqueness of the operation itself.

For example, assume the manager monitors storeroom inventory turns. It is important to compare inventory turns to all three indicator types: historical, budget, and external. Still, knowledge of the operation is the critical factor in assessing the most relevant indicator(s).

Assume, for instance, that a hospital considers bulk storeroom items as inventory but expenses them when they are broken down to piece goods, even though the items initially remain in the storeroom after breakdown. In this case, inventory as recorded on the books is artificially low because piece goods, practically speaking, remain a part of inventory if physically present in the storeroom. It is reasonable to assume that most hospitals would account for these piece goods as inventory and not expense. This is consistent with generally accepted accounting principles.

Turnover is computed as follows:

$$\frac{\text{Value of inventory issued}}{\text{Average value of inventory on hand}} = \text{Inventory turns}$$

The hospital in this example records an artificially low inventory on-hand figure, one not calculated on a consistent basis by most facilities. The result is an inventory turn factor that is too high because of the mathematics of the equation. When a denominator (inventory on hand in this case) is lowered, the result is higher. The material manager of this hospital must be aware of this factor to avoid the risk of decision making based on inaccurate information.

Assume further that this same hospital expanded its total bed complement by 20 percent during the year. Typically, on-hand inventory quantity requirements rise at a lower percentage rate than the percentage of bed increase. The normal result is an increase in inventory turns. This requires the manager to reconsider the value of the historical data collected on inventory turns.

Finally, assume that the budgeted inventory turnover figure was based on an 85 percent bed occupancy factor. The major employer in town shuts down in midyear and occupancy drops to 70 percent. The original budget data no longer are relevant because new external determinants have had an impact on the equation.

These examples of differing conditions affecting the same activity illustrate the point that relevant indicators are effective tools but irrelevant indicators can be counterproductive.

ESTABLISHING THE DATA BASE

Now that the manager has identified relevant indicators and sources of data, the data base can be established.

Included in Table 6–1 are many typical indicators for the various activities constituting the material management division. This matrix can be used as a final source for relevant indicators that might have been overlooked.

Setting up the system to collect data required for performance indicators analysis entails four steps:

1. making necessary arrangements with the data supplier
2. determining the frequency the data are required
3. creating a logical filing system to facilitate analysis
4. assigning responsibility for maintaining the file.

Data source arrangements may not be necessary if, for example, the source is a routinely prepared company statistical report. On the other hand, the manager may need to confer with an in-house consultant, contract with an external consultant, or subscribe to a publication or other data source.

It is particularly important to know the frequency the data are required. This is especially true when working with the internal and external consultants to avoid ineffective use of each party's time. Most published subscription services cannot offer flexibility but computerized data bases and services such as Dun & Bradstreet reports are attractive because they are essentially pay-as-you-use services.

After completing arrangements to acquire the data, managers must create a logical filing system to facilitate their analysis. Logical means reasonable. Reasonable does not demand much explanation. It is sufficient to state that the data should be easily accessible and assembled in one place, especially if they are delivered in series. Consideration may be given to continuing graphs or charts if the data are supplied in singular numeric bits. There is truth in the colloquialism that a picture is worth a thousand words: graphs and charts can make effective pictures.

The final and most important step in setting up the data collection system is assigning responsibility for maintaining the data file. Whether it be the manager, that individual's secretary, or another subordinate, the responsibility must be delineated clearly and carried out or the entire process is defeated.

TRANSFORMING DATA TO INFORMATION

Data are the raw materials used to produce information. Data are transformed into information by the application of analysis and evaluation. Information is used by managers to make decisions.

Chapter 5 on internal auditing explained that data gathering, analysis, evaluation, and decision making are the products of the nine-step audit process. This relationship is shown in Exhibit 6–1.

This section addresses the second step in the performance indicator process—transforming data to information. The techniques used in data gathering are similar to the first three steps in the audit process. The techniques for transforming data to information are similar to the hard data analysis discussed in Chapter 5. Testing is then available for use at the manager's discretion. (Chapter 5 should be reviewed again before proceeding.)

The merits of charting, graphing, and other forms of trending data have been discussed. It was noted that the three comparative bases of data are budget, historical, and external, and the informal corroborative base is management by walking around. The risks of using irrelevant data in the analytical process were illustrated and the analytical techniques employed by the internal auditor were considered.

With these tools, the manager can do an effective job of transforming data to useful information to effectively manage by. Correct?

The answer is maybe. An important distinction is the difference between efficient and effective. Too often these terms are considered synonymous or considered in the wrong order. Sometimes efficiency is emphasized at the expense of effectiveness. If nothing else is remembered about this chapter, this point should be: Forget efficiency until you accomplish effectiveness!

Efficiency = output/input
Effectiveness = % of goal obtained

Productivity is efficiency not effectiveness.

Efficiency is to effectiveness what quantity is to quality, a secondary benefit. Just as quality must be achieved before quantity is beneficial, so must effectiveness be achieved before efficiency is beneficial.

For example, a hospital's pharmacy department might fill more prescriptions per pharmacist hour than any other hospital anywhere. That is a tremendous accomplishment of efficiency. But how would the manager evaluate that department's performance if it also had the highest incident of prescription filling error of any hospital? Obviously the pharmacists are not effective. Their efficiency serves no purpose, and probably detracts from their effectiveness.

This does not mean that efficiency and effectiveness or quantity and quality are mutually exclusive terms. There is a great deal of correlation between efficiency and effectiveness, or quantity and quality, up to a point. That point is the optimal point, or point of diminishing returns. The test for the manager is to develop an operation that produces at an optimal level of both efficiency and effectiveness. An example is the simple model shown in Figure 6–1.

Exhibit 6–1 Comparison of Audit and Performance Indicator Processes

Performance indicators process	*Audit process*
1. data gathering	1. establishment of objectives
	2. research
2. transforming data to information	3. investigation
	4. analysis
	5. testing
3. decision making	6. conclusions
	7. recommendations
4. repeating above steps.	8. implementation
	9. follow-up.

Figure 6–1 Relationship of Quantity and Quality

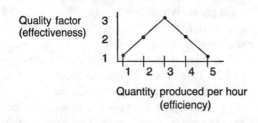

Quantity produced per hour (efficiency)

Assume that the market value per unit is:

$$\$1 \times \text{quality factor (Q.F.)}$$

The value produced per hour is shown in Table 6–2.

In this model the optimal level of efficiency and effectiveness is achieved at the No. 3 level of production. Beyond that point revenue generated declines because product quality has diminished. Up to that point, quality is poorer in addition to the lesser quantity.

THE VALIDITY FACTOR

There can be no arguing the mathematics of this model. The question is: Why are these relationships valid?

The human brain is much more powerful than any machine ever produced by man. The brain differs from man-made machines in another respect as well: Its comprehensive powers are vast but not subject to upward or downward adjustment. Translated, this means the brain will drift

sporadically into other areas of concentration if a person is performing a task at half speed or half-heartedly. The result of lack of concentration is poorer quality of work and reduced effectiveness.

On the other hand the brain is subject to finite limitations. This precludes the ability of man to continually increase task output and still maintain constant quality. If full concentration is devoted to a task, a balance must be found and maintained between quality and quantity or efficiency and effectiveness. That is the optimal point. Beyond that point, quality suffers if quantity is increased because of the brain's finite capacities. Short of that point, full concentration cannot be maintained effectively on the task at hand.

The other critical distinction in analyzing performance indicators is the difference between short-term and long-term considerations. As with effectiveness and efficiency, the manager must strike a balance between short-term and long-term operational factors. For purposes here, the short term is defined as less than one year.

Too much emphasis on the short term can cause the operation to be unprepared for changing conditions in the future. In contrast, too much emphasis on long-term planning results in lack of attention to current conditions. Employees often feel this lack of concern and their output declines.

The manager must be concerned with short-term and long-term operations and must analyze and evaluate performance indicators with both in mind.

Performance indicators are a byproduct of objective setting. Clearly defined and thoughtfully considered objectives will be responsive to the need to balance short-term and long-term operational priorities. Performance indicator analysis is simply applied in logical amounts to satisfy the need to measure the extent to which objectives are accomplished. The manager now has the blueprint to make the necessary decisions that keep the operation on a progressive, profitable, and effective track.

Table 6–2 Calculation of Value Produced

Units produced	Price/unit $1 × Q.F.	Total revenue
1	$1	$1
2	2	4
3	3	9
4	2	8
5	1	5

7. Developing a Regulatory Compliance Plan

DARLENE HARDWICK

The material manager has concerns other than the fundamentals of handling supplies. The effective individual must formulate practical policies and procedures that comply with regulatory agencies' regulations and meet basic requirements. The typical material manager in the health care setting may be responsible for departments such as laundry, receiving, purchasing, central storeroom, sterile processing, decontamination, and pharmacy. Each of these areas is subject to federal, state, and local regulations and standards.

Regulations are nothing new to the health care industry. In 1917, the first minimum standards for hospitals were published by the American College of Surgeons. Since then, the quality of care in hospitals has improved greatly, and continues to do so.

JCAH STANDARDS

The *Accreditation Manual for Hospitals*, published by the Joint Commission on Accreditation of Hospitals (JCAH), has been the recognized standard for measuring day-to-day health care services. The 21 members of the Joint Commission have the responsibility to review, update, suggest, and propose new standards in an extensive and elaborate process. Each hospital voluntarily invites the Joint Commission to the facility to evaluate its progress. If the facility meets or exceeds the established standards, it may advertise "JCAH Accredited." If certain standards or conditions are not met, the JCAH reviewers offer a guideline to assist the institution to do so. The guideline is presented at a summary conference at the end of the reviewers' visit. A time limit is given to meet the standards. To obtain a copy of the *Accreditation Manual*, write to:

Joint Commission on Accreditation of Hospitals
875 North Michigan Avenue
Chicago, Illinois 60611

Although material management is not mentioned specifically in the *Manual*, areas in that field are covered. Under infection control are central service, linen and laundry, and pharmacy. After receiving a copy of the *Manual*, the material manager should meet with the heads of each area, go over current policies and define which ones need to be rewritten or new ones developed.

These managers should be encouraged to join professional organizations related to their area and to share knowledge for educational reasons. The more informed managers are, the more skilled they become in the decision-making process. Sending personnel to seminars and in-service programs enhances their value to the facility and produces more knowledgeable employees.

Besides JCAH, several other agencies are interested in governing actions in material management. These are listed under the topics involving them.

ETHYLENE OXIDE

In the case of the safe use of ethylene oxide, several agencies have requirements the health care industry must follow. Among them is the Occupational Safety and Health Administration (OSHA), which has set a new standard for exposure at 0.05 parts per million (ppm) averaged over an eight-hour workday. Environmental monitoring is required annually, biannually, or quarterly, depending on the initial readings obtained from studies after June 15, 1983. All methods of compliance were set in February 1985 and any engineering requirements must be set by August 1985. Information on ethylene oxide may be obtained from:

> NIOSH Publications Dissemination
> Division of Technical Services
> 4676 Columbia Parkway
> Cincinnati, Ohio 45226
> "Use of Ethylene Oxide as a Sterilant in Medical Facilities"

> Health Industries Manufacturers Association
> 1030 15th Street, N.W.
> Washington, D.C. 20005
> "Monitoring Airborne Ethylene Oxide" (Report #81–1) and
> "The Safe Use of Ethylene Oxide" (Report #80–4)

> American Hospital Association
> 840 North Lake Shore Drive
> Chicago, Illinois 60611
> "Ethylene Oxide Use in Hospitals: A Manual for Health Care Personnel" (Catalog #031180)

> Environmental Protection Agency
> National Technical Information Service
> 5885 Port Royal Road
> Springfield, Virginia 22161

Data from these and related reports will help implement a plan to use ethylene oxide safely as a sterilant for complex and intricate surgical instruments.

REUSE OF DISPOSABLES

As to the issue of reusing disposable items, the Joint Commission and the Association for Practitioners in Infection Control (APIC) have taken similar stands. Legal considerations are important. For example, if an item intended by the manufacturer for one-time use is resterilized by the hospital and fails to perform properly when used for patient care, and the patient sues, the hospital, material manager, and central service supervisor may all be found liable for damages. Material managers should contact their risk manager or hospital attorney for advice. Cost-control measures currently in force, such as diagnostic related groupings (DRGs), are no reason to fall prey to negligence. If a hospital does not have policies that regulate the reuse of items, one should be developed and implemented before the next site visit.

The possibilities of reusing and resterilizing certain high-cost health care items, such as indwelling pacemaker wires, have many ramifications. The manufacturer must supply a written guide for decontamination and sterilizing and the number of times an item can be reused safely. Patients and their rights must be addressed. With health care costs soaring, the final determination as to whether a patient receives a resterilized single-use item must be given serious consideration. The patient's safety must always be the predominant concern.

COMPRESSED MEDICAL GASES

Since the receiving area of material management may handle several types of gases for patient use, the potential dangers and hazards should be explored. Since September 1960, the federal government has regulated the cylinders in which medical gases are contained and transported. Enforcement comes under the Department of Transportation (DOT). Among the specific criteria is the type of steel out of which the cylinders can be made. DOT cylinder regulations and specifications can be obtained by requesting Title 49, Code of Federal Regulations, Parts 170–179, from:

> Superintendent of Documents
> U.S. Government Printing Office
> Washington, D.C. 20402

> Association of American Railroads
> Bureau of Explosives
> 1920 L Street, N.W.
> Washington, D.C. 20036

Appropriate identifying labels, color coding, and information concerning safe practices in transporting cylinder medical gases are published in a pamphlet, "Safe Handling of Compressed Gases," available from:

Compressed Gas Association, Inc.
500 Fifth Avenue
New York, New York 10036

FIRE HAZARDS AND REGULATIONS

According to Richard Bland, chairman of the National Commission on Fire Prevention, in the film *America Burning*, fires each year cause 12,000 deaths, $11 billion in wasted resources, and more than 300,000 serious injuries. The statistics become a reality when in each adult's lifetime, the person will experience at least three fires; each day 33 people die as a direct result of fires. By alerting staff members to the peril and cautioning them in their work practices, the statistics can be lowered.

Material managers need to establish, post, circulate, and enforce policies for employee and fire safety. Combustibles such as paint and oil may be stocked in the storeroom. It is up to the manager to identify the problem and take corrective action. Good housekeeping practices do not need regulations, just common sense. Participation in fire drills and evacuation plans not only can save employees' (and patients') lives, but also can arouse interest in prevention of unsafe practices. A master plan for fire education and prevention should be developed. A planning process can be obtained by writing:

National Fire Prevention and Control
    Administration
P.O. Box 19518
Washington, D.C. 20036

DISPOSAL OF TOXIC AND INFECTIOUS WASTE

Regulations regarding the removal from the hospital of any and all potentially toxic or infectious waste are essential because thousands of pounds of solid wastes are produced in our hospitals each year. The waste includes disposable surgical linens, dressings, food, medicine, tubing sets for intravenous infusions, laboratory waste, and so on. Since hospital solid waste can contain pathogenic microorganisms, the responsibility to make working conditions as safe as possible to prevent cross-contamination and injury to workers and other patients becomes a hospitalwide endeavor.

By seeking the thoughts of authorities on the handling of toxic waste and prevention of industrial injuries, hospitals can develop policies and procedures to protect workers and also comply with legislation and regulations on the subject. The latest acceptable methods for making infectious waste safe for transport, both in the hospital and for ultimate disposal, can be obtained by writing:

Center for Infectious Disease
Centers for Disease Control
Atlanta, Georgia 30333
"Isolation Techniques for Use in
    Hospitals"

DEVELOPING AN ACTION PLAN

To be well informed, material managers should obtain copies of all regulations and standards that pertain to departmental and personnel actions and combine them in a notebook divided into areas of responsibilities such as storeroom, sterile processing, linen, and so on. Any applicable federal, state, or local regulation would then be accessible.

The next step is to develop policies and procedures that comply with current standards and regulations. The input of workers, managers, risk managers, and infection control practitioners should be sought. No policy or procedure is worth the paper it is printed on if no one follows it, or if it is about to become obsolete. Workers should become involved and have a say in developing the procedures; for example, those who have spent ten years wrapping linen packs should be able to describe what linen is acceptable for the operating room or nursery.

After the policies are written, the real task begins: educating personnel through inservice programs. The old adage, "you can lead a horse to water . . .'' applies to everyone. Each employee should have a looseleaf notebook to keep new and revised policies. Providing time to review changes is a necessary part of good management. Managers can obtain better cooperation by handing out to employees copies of the changes, then going over them during an inservice program.

By taking the approach that the institution must meet the new regulations and its workers are expected to comply to the best of their ability, managers can develop educated and trusting employees. After explaining a new regulation at an inservice class, it may be helpful to reward correct behavior, e.g., wearing goggles when handling toxic disinfectants. By making a chart with the listed behavior and the names of the employees and checking or starring the ones who abide by the new regulation, peer pressure can be made to work for the manager.

The compliance plan should be evaluated at least annually, with appropriate additions, dele-

tions, and revisions of standards. Material managers should meet often with department heads to discuss changes in the regulations. They should let the risk manager know they are interested in receiving all new information. It can be worthwhile to conduct a mock JCAH or OSHA inspection of the material department, writing down the areas in which it does not meet standards, and using these to begin an action plan to correct problem areas. A report should be made to the hospital administrator on the findings of the mock inspection and the actions to be taken.

During an official inspection by a regulatory agency, the main fact to remember is to cooperate. Material managers may have done their best to comply with regulations and standards, and any further advice from the experts will be welcomed and shared with counterparts all over the country. No one expects a perfect score every day. Therefore, material managers should learn how they can add or delete steps to make their department one of the best.

8. Developing Quality Assessment Programs

WILLIAM L. SCHEYER

Nearly all managers profess a belief in the value of providing high quality services. Yet why do they sometimes fail to provide consistently satisfactory levels of service? The answer lies in a lack of formal planning and documentation. There usually is so much activity each day that quality tends to be taken for granted until a complaint arises. At that point, time and energy are expended in investigating the complaint, identifying whether it is legitimate, and, if it is, taking corrective action.

There are two deficiencies in this system: (1) The reputation for quality service already has been damaged because the customer had to complain in order to have the problem corrected. (2) It usually takes a good deal of time and energy to follow up the problem. If managers accept the idea that time is money, they can see that this can be an expensive system. It also is frustrating for everyone involved because they usually are dealing in negative, as opposed to positive, terms.

The author proposes that it is more effective to invest the time and energy in developing a formal system of routinely monitoring and documenting quality of performance. This enables managers to identify and correct internal performance problems before they become apparent to customers. It allows them to establish and maintain a reputation for consistently high quality performance. It also is less costly to do this type of work in a planned way. Finally, because complaints hardly ever come at a convenient time, it reduces the managerial frustration level.

TERMINOLOGY

The classic manufacturing industry name for this type of program is quality control. The current health care industry name is quality assurance. Both are misnomers. Managers can neither control nor assure quality. All they can do is assess whether they are providing satisfactory quality, and take corrective action if they find that they are not maintaining standards. For this reason, the author prefers to call these quality assessment programs.

ORGANIZATION

The Ideal System

The most effective way to carry out these functions is to employ a quality assessment (QA) coordinator, who reports directly to the material manager. This person should be responsible for the following three activities:

1. assessment
   a. routine inspections
   b. problem and complaint follow-up
   c. surveys of employee and customer satisfaction.
2. training
   a. programs required to comply with policies and procedures
   b. programs identified as being needed as a result of QA findings.
3. documentation
   a. inspection results
   b. results of scheduled follow-up actions
   c. problem and complaint follow-up
   d. survey results
   e. training programs
   f. development, review, and revision of policies and procedures.

A case could be made for saying that these all are primary functions of management and that the manager should be responsible for carrying them out. However, management involves a great many functions, including these. Looking at the situation realistically, managers often do not or cannot afford to devote a sufficient amount of their time to these functions in order to carry them out at an optimal, or sometimes even satisfactory, level. For this reason, they revert to the complaint resolution method.

A final reason why the manager actually should not be the primary assessor/trainer/documentor is that once the program is set up, the actions needed to carry it out are routine in nature. The manager should be the conceptualizer. Routine daily implementation activities can be performed more cost effectively by other employees.

An Alternate System

The greatest degree of program integration can be obtained by utilizing the QA coordinator concept. In addition, such persons can be selected for their skill and expertise in assessment, training, and documentation. However, it often is difficult to obtain approval for such a position. An acceptable alternative is for the manager to conceptualize and coordinate the program while delegating specific functions to key subordinates. These people must be both knowledgeable and trustworthy because the manager will be relying on their skill and integrity.

For example, supervisors may be assigned to inspect work and follow up complaints. When this is done by more than one person, it is essential that a uniform method of documentation be used. Results can be submitted directly to the manager or can be collected and put into report form by a person assigned to the data collection/report writing function.

A particularly articulate employee with an interest in teaching may be assigned to develop, present, and document training programs. Finally, a well-organized clerical support person may be given the responsibility for coordinating the maintenance of the policy and procedure manuals.

To gain greater integration, these individuals can serve as a quality assessment committee, meeting on a scheduled basis to review the results of the program. By using this approach, more attention can be concentrated on QA functions than if they all were performed by the manager. In addition, the manager gains the full benefit from the particular interests, skills, and talents of key employees. The main objective is to keep conceptualization and program leadership flowing from the manager, and implementation and documentation flowing from the staff.

PROGRAM DEVELOPMENT

Identifying Objectives

Objectives can be as detailed as is desired or appropriate. However, the following four global objectives can serve as a starting point for all programs:

1. to assess quality of performance with the goal of maintaining a minimum level of 90 percent based upon measurement criteria (90 percent is an arbitrary average; some functions require 100 percent quality while others are adequate at lower levels)
2. to maintain complete, accurate, and current documentation of policies, procedures, and performance
3. to provide and document timely training programs necessary to achieve and maintain required performance levels
4. to establish and maintain a quality-conscious environment.

Defining Functions to Be Assessed

Quality can mean different things to different people. To make the program meaningful, it is necessary to define the specific subfunctions that comprise a service and the performance levels required to be considered acceptable. For example, a central sterile processing service may include decontamination, inspection, set-up, packaging, and sterilization. These subfunctions can be performed to produce a line of products, which might include surgical basin and instrument sets, surgical linen packs, special procedure trays, and so on. The quality of the total service is made up of the combined quality levels of each subfunction as applied to each product in the line.

Every service exhibits high quality in some subfunctions and relatively lower quality in others. It is impossible to talk about the quality of a service without first identifying component subfunctions, assigning them relative weights in the total service, and defining required performance levels.

Defining Characteristics for Measurement

Once the component subfunctions that make up a service have been identified, managers must define the individual characteristics of the products in the line. For example, a surgical instrument set might have to display the following characteristics in order to be rated acceptable:

- All correct instruments are in the set.
- All instruments are clean and function properly.
- Instruments are organized properly within the set.
- The set is correctly packaged and labelled.
- The set has been properly sterilized.

To make a decision about the acceptability of the set, managers must define standard methods for measuring the characteristics. In this example, these might be:

1. Check mixture of instruments against standard description of set.
2. Inspect each instrument according to defined criteria.
3. Inspect packaging and labelling against defined criteria.

4. Examine package for evidence of proper sterilizing procedure according to predetermined indicators.

Developing Inspection Documents

Standardized inspection documents must be developed to facilitate both the inspection and documentation processes. This helps ensure that inspection results are documented in a consistent way month after month, even if different people are involved in the process. This also makes it possible to develop trend analysis reports. Exhibit 8–1 is an example of a standard documentation sheet.

Defining Sample Sizes

A common problem in setting up a QA program is deciding how many samples of a particular product must be inspected in order to reach a statistically valid conclusion. In many cases, the required sample size will be so large that it will not be feasible to invest the time necessary to complete that many inspections. The general principle should be to inspect a statistically valid sample whenever possible. However, when this is not possible, the more important thing is to inspect a reasonable sample, in a standardized way, time after time.

In the early stages of setting up the program, it is helpful to enlist the aid of a management engineer or an internal auditor. These people can be particularly helpful in deciding upon sample sizes and frequency of inspections.

Determining Time Requirements

Once managers have identified the products and services to be monitored, have defined how acceptability is to be measured, and have decided upon sample sizes and frequency of inspections, they must calculate how much time will be required on a scheduled basis to carry out the program. It is at this point that two decisions have to be made. The first is whether the program will utilize a single coordinator or a decentralized approach. The second, and even

Exhibit 8–1 Quality Control Program for Central Sterile Reprocessing

Department		Checked by						Time		Date	

| | | | | | | | | | | Factor | |

Item	Cleanliness S	Cleanliness U	Assembly S	Assembly U	Package S	Package U	Label S	Label U	Sterility S	Sterility U	Storage S	Storage U	Observer comments
Issue activity (Check groups of items)													
Total ratings, supplies and equipment													

Key: 2 = Satisfactory; U = Unsatisfactory.

Source: Reprinted with permission of Marimargaret Reichert, Robinson Memorial Hospital, Ravenna, Ohio.

more important, is whether the manager is really willing to commit the resources necessary to maintain the program on a continuing basis. This is a vital decision. A program that receives only partial commitment will consume resources but will not provide an adequate return on investment. It is better to have no program than to have one that does not fulfill its purpose.

IMPLEMENTATION

Once the program has been designed and the commitment to proceed has been made, it is time to assign specific areas of responsibility. If a single coordinator will be used, that person must be selected. It is helpful to decide this early in the design phase so that the coordinator can assume primary responsibility for the development of the program. If this is not possible, it is vital that the coordinator be given complete information as soon as possible.

If the decentralized approach is chosen, this is the time to select team members who will be responsible for specific areas of the program. These persons must gain a complete grasp of all details. In addition, they must be given help in forming a cooperative team so that the QA committee can accomplish as much as possible in the time available.

No matter which approach is chosen, this is a time when the manager must fulfill the role of leader by establishing clear expectations for each team member and for the program as a whole. This means that all team members must know how much they are expected to produce, by when, and at what level of quality. They must develop a belief that if these standards are met, positive rewards will be given, and that failure to meet them will not be tolerated. Further, there must be confidence that information obtained by means of the program will be used to make appropriate adjustments to the operation of the department.

Once all participants have been trained, the initial monitoring can be completed and documented. The results should be reviewed in a timely manner by the group and corrections or adjustments made. This process should continue on a regular basis until the system has been stabilized. This may appear to be time consuming but it is a vital step. If it is completed successfully, the program gradually will be integrated into the participants' normal work routine and will be performed in a standardized and time-effective manner. If the step is not completed, the program may fall apart gradually.

PUBLICITY

A formal QA program is a tool to be used in establishing and maintaining a quality-conscious environment in the department. The ultimate goal of the program should be to provide routine, statistically valid testing that documents the fact that services are being provided at a satisfactory level as close to 100 percent of the time as possible. This will come about only when there is a combination of effective management and supervision, well-designed systems for performing work, and properly trained, motivated, and rewarded employees; in other words, when the manager is running a "quality" operation. The operational purpose of the program is to provide information that can be used to identify and positively reinforce particularly strong parts of the department (both employees and systems) and to identify and correct weaker parts.

It is important, therefore, to publicize the program to three distinct audiences: (1) employees, (2) other departments, and (3) upper management. It is important for employees to know the objectives and expectations of the department, their role in achieving them, and that their participation is being assessed. Employees should be kept informed of results; they should see positive results rewarded and negative ones corrected. If the program is perceived as having a negative focus, it will not receive employee support and can lead to problems in staff/management relations. If it is perceived as having a balanced focus, it can serve as a positive motivator and a stimulus to higher levels of performance.

Other departments need to know that the program exists and to be kept informed of results. This gives them confidence that the department is committed to quality performance and cares about customer concerns. In addition, customers often focus their attention on the relatively infrequent examples of poor performance and overlook the positive. Publicizing results is a way for managers to routinely reinforce their reputations for high-quality performance. This also can be a motivating element for employees because they like to think of themselves as being part of a well-respected organization.

Finally, it is vital to publish results to upper management. Beside the fact that it is always nice to look good for the boss, this is an excellent way to cultivate the support needed for future department requirements.

In some cases, those in upper management hear only about exceptions to routine operation, and these tend to relate to breakdowns in performance. Regularly sharing information about the routine proper performance of the material management department can help to establish a positive perception. In addition, it reinforces the manager's reputation as one who is committed to high-quality performance and who knows how to get it.

Having decided to publicize the results of the QA program, the manager is faced with the job of developing the publicity program itself. Most managers are not specifically trained in advertising techniques and should request assistance from the members of the public relations department in developing the publicity program.

Appropriate media must be selected for transmitting the information. These might include:

- monthly reports
- articles in the organizational newsletter
- posters
- special newsletters
- a section in the employee orientation program
- an agenda item at monthly nursing department staff meetings

In addition, particularly significant elements of information might be considered for inclusion in the hospital's overall marketing effort. These might prove helpful in recruiting physicians or nurses or in presenting an image of cost effectiveness to the general community.

Throughout this process, the public relations staff should serve as advisers and consultants. With their help, the material manager should be able to develop an informative and cost-effective publicity problem that will increase the value of the QA program.

PART II
PURCHASING

The purchasing function often is thought of as the cornerstone of the material management department. It often is the first function to be placed under centralized control. In addition, the purchasing agent is seen as the primary business representative of the organization.

The individual tasks of the purchasing department are repetitive in nature. They require technical and interpersonal skill in order to be carried out successfully. However, the key to an effective purchasing operation is organization. Component tasks, information support, and documentation systems must be highly organized in order to deal with the massive volume of transactions that must be handled.

This part, encompassing chapters 9 through 15, provides an overview and specific examples of how to complete the following objectives:

- designing an effective purchasing system
- establishing a proper legal foundation
- improving managers' negotiating ability
- selecting appropriate products
- selecting appropriate equipment.

9. Streamlining the Purchasing Process

RODGER E. ROURKE

Efficient purchasing—a key element of material management—requires a great amount of detailed information to be handled accurately, promptly, and smoothly. Much of this information is routine and repetitive. The key is to organize the routine so smoothly that primary attention can be concentrated on dealing with vendors to obtain needed items for timely delivery at the best price, or on situations or circumstances that are truly extraordinary and require personal attention outside the routine.

This chapter deals with organizing the purchasing process and covers the following nine major areas:

1. basic purchasing functions
2. ancillary purchasing functions
3. documentation and files
4. controls
5. purchasing office layout
6. computers in purchasing
7. purchasing special commodities
8. purchasing for special departments
9. special purchasing techniques.

BASIC FUNCTIONS AND TASKS

Ahead of anything else, the office must perform the basic purchasing functions well. The total operation is built around these basics.

Requirements Determination

In theory, the user departments determine needs and requirements but in reality purchasing must play an important role in such decisions. For repetitively used items, purchasing usually buys to inventory based on anticipated usage. Even for nonrepetitive items, purchasing often can provide valuable assistance to the user department in determining the actual demand and the requirements for equipment or supplies to meet that need.

Every purchasing action should be supported by an authorized requirements determination in one form or another. For special orders or capital item orders, this normally is in the form of a requisition or similar authorization. For repetitively used items purchased into inventory, there should be a procedure that delineates responsibility, authority, and control guidelines for determining stock levels. These replenishment decisions then are based on the authorized requirements determination to support purchase into inventory. Normally, material management will be authorized to replenish stock items based on authorized stock levels and actual usage.

Requisition Processing

Requisitions come in many different formats to meet the needs of a particular organization. The form should be as clear and uncluttered as possible. In a hospital setting especially, in the interest of expedience, requisitions should be filled out by hand rather than required to be typewritten. Whatever the format, requisitions need at least five elements of information:

1. Who is the requisitioner?
2. What account is to be charged for the purchase or issue?
3. What is needed?
4. When is it needed?
5. To what location is it to be delivered?

The requisition should follow a definite flow process that should be controlled so that both its status and the overall performance of the purchasing office in processing it will be known at all times. The process follows these steps.

1. The requisition should be stamped with date and time as soon as it is received in purchasing. This is a control measure and clearly delineates the time at which purchasing accepts processing responsibility.
2. The requisition, as soon as possible after being received, should be checked by a knowledgeable person for completeness and accuracy. If it does not contain sufficient information to complete purchasing action, the situation should be resolved with the requisitioner immediately.
3. Purchasing action should be taken as promptly as possible, consistent with effective buying practices.
4. The requisitioner should be notified, as soon as purchasing action is taken, by copy of the purchase order or by other means that the order has been placed and what the expected delivery date is.
5. Purchasing must have a system for prompt follow-up of promised delivery dates. Expediting is a purchasing service that the requisitioner has a right to expect. Vigorous expediting combined with regular vendor evaluation also serves to discipline sellers to meet promised dates.
6. Receiving is not a purchasing function but it is of great concern to purchasing. Purchasing needs to know that the item has been received and delivered promptly to the user department as specified.

Assisting Users to Prepare Requisitions

Determination of requirements and preparation of requisitions is essentially a responsibility of the user department but purchasing often can be helpful. Typical ways in which purchasing can assist users might include:

- identifying and defining particular items or options, accessories, sizing, capacity of equipment

- identifying potential vendors or sourcing of equipment to obtain competition and search out the best value in the market
- evaluating competitive pricing and helping to ensure that quotations are compared on an equivalent basis—"apples to apples"
- assisting, along with technical personnel, to evaluate particular items, including obtaining samples or loaner equipment for evaluation
- assisting in the development of financial justification to support the acquisition.

Forecasting for Regular Use Consumable Items

Regular use consumable items are brought into inventory according to an estimate of future need, based on past usage or some other criterion. This is more an inventory control function than a purchasing function but it is of great interest to purchasing. The more accurately requirements are forecast, the more precisely purchasing commitments can be made. In turn, purchasing commitments that are highly accurate in terms of quantity and delivery date are welcomed by vendors and provide leverage for lower prices or for other favorable terms.

The more precisely material management accounts for issuance of items (also called issues), the better will be the usage information upon which to forecast future requirements. (Chapter 19 presents information on cart exchange, par replenishment, and other issue control techniques that provide accurate day-by-day and unit-by-unit knowledge of usage.)

Purchase Actions and Competition

The objective of all purchasing should be to buy to value. Value is defined as the optimal combination of quality, service, and price. Unless quality is adequate, the purchase is useless; but if quality is excessive, then that is wasteful. There must be adequate service support for such factors as delivery, training, parts, and maintenance or the items will not be ready for use when needed. Subject to adequate quality and service, purchasing at lowest price provides the greatest value.

To measure quality accurately, the requirement must be well defined. Unless purchasing knows clearly what is needed, it is difficult to buy effectively. As noted earlier, it often is useful for purchasing to become involved in assisting the requisitioner to determine requirements so that the buying action may be more efficient.

The Bidding Process

The bidding process begins with a clear request for proposal (RFP) or request for bid (RFB). The materials or services required must be described in sufficient detail so that the vendor knows what is needed. If the bid is not clear, the vendor will tend to cushion the price to protect against uncertainty.

The bidding process may be formal or informal, public or not public. Unless there are regulatory requirements, the question is a matter of hospital policy. Formal bids are sent out in writing, usually are very detailed, and require an equally formal answer. Informal bidding may even be done over the telephone. Public bidding involves the submission of sealed bids that are opened at a public session with all vendors invited to attend; in that way, everyone hears all of the bids and knows exactly where they stand in the bidding. Private openings are done by the purchasing department and only the successful bidder may be announced. Unless there are regulatory requirements, there is no obligation to publicize bid prices or subsequent negotiations with particular vendors.

It often is appropriate to negotiate with one or more vendors before making the final award. If this is to be done, it should be stated in the RFP or RFB. If such negotiations are used, they should be for the purpose of clarifying and sharpening each vendor's proposal. The specific bid price of one vendor should not be used to force down another's bid. To do so is not ethical. Furthermore, it eventually will cause vendors to pad their prices in preparation for the squeeze that they have learned to anticipate. Finally,

particularly in for-profit hospitals, it could raise concerns about antitrust law violations.

However the process is structured, bidding must always be handled with a high degree of integrity. This means essentially that every vendor must be given an equal opportunity for the business. The buyer cannot disclose information to any vendor that will give that seller an advantage over another supplier. Such information might include prices or terms of competing vendors or special information concerning the purchase that is not generally available to all suppliers.

The hospital obviously should seek to buy the best value. Once the proposals are assembled, they must be analyzed carefully, including not only price but terms, conditions, the vendor's past performance and ability—in short, the total of all factors of quality, service, and price that make up the value.

As soon as possible after the choice is made and approved, the successful vendor should be notified formally and the actual purchase order completed and accepted by the supplier. The purchase order must contain the complete understanding of the transaction, including all terms and conditions. A little extra time spent in preparing the purchase order, and ensuring that it is complete and comprehensive, usually will save a great deal of time later in correcting mistakes and resolving misunderstandings.

The final step in the bidding process is to inform the unsuccessful vendors. This should be done with the same degree of formality or informality as the bidding. It should always be done, out of courtesy to the vendor for the time and effort spent in preparing a proposal.

Competition—Yes and No

Competition should be sought in all purchasing to obtain the best price. However, purchasing must be cost effective in seeking competition. In actions of low dollar value, the potential saving simply may not be worth the time and effort involved to obtain competition. In other cases, limited purchasing resources will dictate that they be applied where effective competition is likely to yield the greatest savings, even if that means forgoing competitive opportunities for small savings on other purchases.

Specific guidelines should be established on competitive purchasing. These usually involve establishing certain dollar values where competition will always be sought unless approval is given by administrative authority for noncompetitive purchase. There usually is a lower limit below which competition is deemed to be uneconomical. Between these two is an area that often is left to the buyer's judgment, with perhaps some general guidelines. In this connection, if the hospital is involved in group purchasing, the element of competition should be satisfied rigorously when the group agreement is established. Subsequent purchases under the agreement should be considered competitive even though the hospital does not seek competition for the particular transaction.

It is useful to keep a record of the percentage of purchases of various general categories that are made competitively. It should be a goal to increase the percentage of such purchases on the theory that that generally will result in better pricing.

One way to stretch purchasing resources is to establish competitive continuing contracts for items frequently ordered such as office accessories, physical therapy prostheses, and so on. Then, individual orders may be placed quickly and directly since competitive pricing already has been established for a specific time period.

Blanket Purchase Orders

Regularly used consumable supplies should almost always be bought on a periodic contract basis using a blanket purchase order (BPO) or similar technique. Competitive proposals should be obtained for estimated volume covering a significant period of time, usually one year; delivery orders then are placed from time to time as specific quantities are needed.

Items that lend themselves to this type of purchasing are those frequently ordered from the same vendor and where the items or services can be listed either specifically or within a clearly

defined category, such as sutures. It also is necessary that a specific price structure be reasonably defined. The facility should establish either specific prices with price protection for the duration of the agreement or a strictly controlled means of adjusting prices to inflation if necessary. If specific prices cannot be listed, then a specific discount percentage off a published price list or some other definitive means of determining pricing must be established. If prices are not defined, the term "contract" serves little purpose since prices would have to be negotiated each time an order is placed.

Advantages

The advantages of using blanket purchase orders or agreements are:

- Approval is given at an appropriate level for the term of the purchase agreement, usually one year, rather than a series of approvals for smaller disconnected actions from time to time without any view of the total purchase.
- The processing of delivery orders is simplified and therefore can be very responsive to requirements.
- Competition and negotiations in the purchasing process can be conducted with the vendor on the basis of total volume over the period of the agreement. This generally results in better prices than spot purchasing from time to time. It certainly results in better use of purchasing resources.
- The vendor can provide consolidated billing, which offers further efficiencies in accounts payable processing.

Disadvantages

The disadvantages of this means of purchasing are:

- It is necessary to make monthly reconciliation of consolidated invoices prior to payment.

- Order placement is decentralized once the overall agreement has been approved. While this can be controlled, it sometimes is unsettling to administrators who have been accustomed to approving each order transaction.

Controls

The disadvantages can be overcome if adequate controls are in place. Blanket purchase orders must never become blank checks. Specific controls must be imposed on each such agreement, as follows:

1. specific limitations on items, services, or categories of items or services that can be ordered under the agreement
2. specific designation by name or title of who can place delivery orders
3. specific limitation in dollar amount that can be ordered per month or per quarter; a further financial control is the hospital's budget system, which should not permit user departments to exceed authorized budget levels month by month
4. a definite expiration date for the agreement so that it does not remain in force indefinitely, and a provision that no orders be placed or accepted by the vendor after the expiration date
5. pricing control information that is sufficiently specific to determine the selling price for each item ordered during the duration of the agreement
6. specific procedures for processing receipts against the order and for validating physical receipt of items; where the agreement is for services, such as equipment maintenance, an invoice approval mechanism must be established to verify that billed services have in fact been provided satisfactorily. (For example, maintenance callbacks—a second visit to correct work not done on the first maintenance visit—sometimes may be billed separately in error when in fact there should be no charge. In the absence of adequate control, such erroneous charges may be paid routinely.)
7. prompt transmittal of copies of delivery orders issued under each agreement to purchasing for file so that it is possible to make periodic reviews of utilization of the agreements either in total dollar value or by line item
8. assignment of a maximum stock level quantity to be held for each item and the normal expected frequency of stock replenishment, if the agreement involves establishing a decentralized stock of items in a user department; when orders are placed too frequently, it is uneconomical for both the hospital and the vendor; on the other hand, orders placed too infrequently result in having too much inventory on hand.

Implementation Orders

The following types of orders may be used to implement these agreements.

Blanket purchase orders, as just discussed, are orders issued to cover requirements for a period of time but do not provide for specific delivery of products. Standing purchase orders are similar to blanket orders.

Sometimes the two terms are used interchangeably but more often a distinction is made: standing orders usually call for an established quantity to be delivered periodically—e.g., four cases every month or two dozen every week. The vendor then makes the shipments without further direction unless the hospital takes specific action to modify the quantity or scheduling of deliveries. This technique works well if usage is regular and predictable. The problem is that vendors fall into a well-established shipment pattern that can be hard to adjust if the hospital becomes overstocked or understocked on the items involved. In theory, the adjustment is easy; in practice, it can be surprisingly difficult to change the vendor's established routine.

Stockless purchasing or systems contracts are similar to blanket purchase orders or open orders but usually cover a wide category of items such as office supplies, plumbing repair parts, electrical parts, and so on. These usually involve setting up a charge account at the vendor for frequent small orders of a particular category of supplies. Systems contracting also frequently involves decentralized ordering. For example, every department in the hospital may be authorized to order office supplies directly from the vendor. The vendor then ships the requested supplies, marked for that department. Thus, the hospital carries little or no inventory. However, the facility loses detailed control of each order and must depend on after-the-fact review and budgetary controls to prevent overordering.

Other forms of periodic purchasing agreements may be established to meet particular needs. There is almost no limit to their variety and flexibility. It is extremely important, however, to be sure that adequate controls are in place on such an agreement to prevent abuse either by those authorized to issue delivery orders or by the vendor.

Processing Small Special Orders

Small special orders should be processed as expeditiously as possible. It still is important to seek competition. This may be obtained informally by telephone quotations. It also is possible to set up an add-on to a system contract so that noncontract items can be purchased at an established discount. For example, if there is a system contract or a blanket purchase order for office supplies it may be possible to include a provision to buy office accessories from the same vendor at substantial discount from list. Once the competitive price effectiveness of that arrangement has been established, routine orders can be placed for the contract period without need to seek competitive quotations on each.

Material managers should focus on efficiency and prompt processing. Forms should be kept as simple as possible and should be handwritten to avoid typing delay and to expedite processing.

The primary controls on this type of purchasing are budgetary limitations on the dollars available to a user department and an approval required on the requisition. Approval usually is established at various organizational levels, based on the dollar amount of the requisition.

A combined requisition and purchase order on a single form can be an efficient way to handle small, random, special orders. One section of the form is filled out by the requisitioner to indicate the items required, with the remaining section completed by the buyer who places the order with the vendor. This allows for rapid handling while maintaining adequate control.

The advantages of a combined requisition and purchase order include that it:

- is easy for the requisitioner to understand, fill out, and handle
- provides quick processing with minimum paper work
- eliminates typing
- provides for prompt distribution of copies
- ensures that the receiving copies are at the receiving area by the time the items are delivered, even with quick delivery
- provides a routine and prompt feedback to users on purchase order status
- permits effective follow-up on overdue orders
- maintains appropriate management control throughout the process
- provides a satisfactory audit trail.

A combined requisition and purchase order can be a six-part snap set to be filled out with ballpoint pen. One copy is retained by the requisitioner; it should be the last copy so that the requisitioner will be sure to press hard with the pen. One copy is returned to the requisitioner after the order is placed as notification that the order has been implemented and of the expected delivery date. One copy goes to accounts payable for accrual. One copy remains in purchasing, filed by delivery date, for expediting. The two other copies go to receiving to await delivery of the items.

One of these receiving copies eventually is processed to accounts payable to authorize payment of the invoice. The other is returned to purchasing as a record of the receipt and to close out the purchase order. There is no vendor copy. Nearly all such orders are placed by phone or to a vendor representative in person. The purchase order form serves no purpose and frequently results in duplicate shipments. If a vendor copy is needed, one can be made in a copier machine.

A few hospitals even use a combined purchase order and check for small orders. In such cases, a hospital check made out to the vendor is attached to the order, the vendor fills the order, fills in the amount due on the check and cashes it, returning the stub order with the items to the hospital. The check is printed with a maximum amount and the bank will not honor it beyond that level. Accounts payable then simply verifies that the order has been received, and no further processing is required. This requires careful controls, of course, and can be done only with vendors of demonstrated reliability. Under these special circumstances, however, this technique can be efficient and cost effective.

Buying Capital Equipment

Capital equipment generally has unique characteristics. It frequently is expensive to acquire, with high cost of maintenance and supplies over its life, so significant dollars are involved. To evaluate these costs properly requires consideration of cash flow over the expected life of the equipment. Since the equipment has a relatively long life span, there is a special concern to make a wise purchase.

In any case, it tends to be technically complex, which makes evaluation of competitive equipment more difficult. Finally, capital equipment may require extensive installation, special utility connections, or even new construction, which further complicates the acquisition process. In addition, it may have significant operational impact on staffing, maintenance costs, supply costs, clinical methods, productivity, or increase or decrease of workload in clinical or support areas.

For these reasons each purchase of capital equipment is unique. In order to work through the complexity and arrive at a wise purchasing decision it usually is best to consider a team approach. At a minimum the team should include the requisitioning user department,

maintenance, biomedical engineering, purchasing, and finance. The team also may include other areas that can contribute to an accurate evaluation and wise decision.

It is particularly important that a purchase order for capital equipment be complete and accurate, including detailed terms and conditions that, if carefully negotiated, can help to avoid later misunderstanding and protect the hospital. Examples of the sorts of terms and conditions that should be specified concern such matters as:

- warranty
- vendor-provided training for postwarranty in-house maintenance
- site preparation and responsibility for utility connections, environmental conditions, and so on
- maintenance support by the vendor during warranty
- maintenance response time and whether maintenance is available on a normal 40-hour week or around the clock
- vendor responsibility to interface with other equipment
- safety considerations
- payment terms.

Equipment or Supplies on Loan or Trial

All equipment or supplies brought into the hospital must be covered by a valid purchase order even if the items are only to be on loan or trial for a brief period. This formality is needed to protect the hospital from both a liability and an economic point of view. The institution is liable for all equipment and supplies used whether or not it has actual knowledge of these items. If it allows items to be introduced informally, it may be unknowingly accepting liability for articles that it has not evaluated properly. From an economic point of view there are numerous opportunities for backdoor selling, after-the-fact liability for supplies already used, or liability for damage to instruments while in hospital possession.

A certain degree of formality is fair to the vendor, too, in that it assures the seller that the equipment will in fact be evaluated while in possession of the hospital and will remain in its possession for only a stipulated period while under evaluation. It also clarifies the liability of the hospital for any damage that might occur during that period.

The purchase order for trial or loan should be authorized by the product evaluation and standardization committee if it is a new item to be evaluated. For equipment or similar items, authorization should come from the level of administrative authority required to purchase that same equipment. That helps ensure there is good faith to consider purchase of the equipment and avoids wasting everyone's time on frivolous evaluations.

Signature of Purchase Orders

Requisitions are the administrative authority to purchase. It is important to consider the authority for signature of a purchase order, which is a contract with the vendor on behalf of the hospital.

There should be a specific delegation from the top administrative authority to the material manager, the purchasing manager, or some other official to sign purchase orders on behalf of the hospital. That delegation also should provide for that official to redelegate limited authority to buyers to sign certain purchase orders, especially in a large hospital where one person cannot reasonably sign them all. This delegation should be based on dollar value and other circumstances, such as whether the items are for stock inventory or are capital equipment. The purchasing manager may be given authority to sign higher dollar value purchase orders for routine replenishment of inventory supplies than for capital equipment. In any case, the authority should be defined specifically so that the authorization for each person to act as an agent of the hospital is clear and unequivocal. This is for the protection of both the institution and the individuals involved.

Whenever any individual signs a purchase order it should be clear that that person is doing so on behalf of the facility. The signature line should show the name of the hospital, then the word "by," followed by the signature and title of the person signing. This makes it clear that that individual is signing on behalf of the hospital in accordance with approved authority.

Any signer also should be aware that the signature assigns full responsibility to that person on behalf of the hospital for total correctness of the purchase order, a legal contract. This is an important responsibility and should never be taken lightly

Expediting

Purchasing has the primary responsibility for expediting. Expediting should be done on the basis of vendor-promised delivery rather than waiting for the requisitioner to inquire or complain. Prompt expediting disciplines vendors to the importance of meeting promised delivery dates.

Expediting should be approached in a positive and constructive way. The two rules of expediting are: (1) never lose your temper and (2) never take no for an answer.

If the delivery is going to be delayed beyond the promised date, the user department should be informed of that fact and of the expediting status until the item is received.

Purchasing should maintain an informal but accurate record of expediting, follow-up, and telephone calls. This prevents the vendor from changing stories or providing inconsistent information. It maintains pressure on the vendor to complete the delivery on or as close to schedule as possible. This written record also is useful after the fact for vendor analysis. Reviewing the vendor's performance over a number of purchase orders gives a useful index of overall record.

Receipts Processing

Processing of receipts is not a purchasing function and in fact should not be under purchasing. The two should be separated for audit control purposes so that the person responsible for purchasing is not also the person responsible for checking the item into the hospital. Notwithstanding, receipt processing is a key area to the entire material control process and intimately related to purchasing. If the receiving procedure is not smooth and accurate, the purchasing function will suffer because the user departments will not be able to rely on delivery information provided by purchasing and vendors will not be paid promptly and accurately.

It is important to have positive control of material from the time it touches the receiving dock. Receipts must be processed at once, delivered promptly to the assigned area, and the record of processing must be certain and correct.

Receipts must be processed promptly because the receiving action is the legal acceptance by the hospital of the goods that have been delivered. This is important in relation to the condition of the goods upon receipt, liability for them subsequent to receipt (and insurance coverage), and time of receipt for payment terms. It also is important that goods be checked immediately upon receipt, at least for signs of exterior damage. If any exterior damage or possible damage is discovered, this should be noted on the bill of lading or delivery ticket before it is returned to the driver and a copy of the notation maintained with the receiving documents. Subsequently, goods have to be inspected promptly either on the receiving dock or in the user unit for internal or concealed damage. If any such damage is found, purchasing must be notified immediately so it can notify the vendor promptly. The vendor (or the shipping agent) will be responsible in most cases for concealed damage, but prompt notification is extremely important to press the claim.

Accurate receiving information keeps purchasing informed of the delivery status and provides information to pay invoices promptly. Prompt payment of invoices is important to take advantage of discounts and to maintain good vendor relations. If hospitals are known as slow payers, that will be reflected in vendors' future pricing. This does not mean, however, that invoices should be paid before they are due. Premature payment is not good cash management.

Two questions often asked about receiving do not have definitive answers. One is whether the receiving dock should have "quantity due in" information available. Auditors generally would prefer that this information not be available there so that the receiver is forced to count the items and record the number without being influenced by prior knowledge of what is expected. On the other hand, knowing what is expected gives the receiver the opportunity to cross-check the count and avoid reconciliation later. In any case, it is important that quantity counts on the receiving dock be accurate.

The second question deals with whether or not it is necessary to obtain signatures from user departments for items received and delivered directly to them. There is no question that it is more trouble to obtain signatures when items are delivered. However, this practice does document the delivery and avoids misunderstandings or futile searches for material that the user claims was never delivered.

ANCILLARY FUNCTIONS

In addition to its basic functions, every purchasing office performs a number of ancillary functions. Some of these, such as preparation of policies and procedures, interface with accounts payable, follow-up actions, and vendor relations, are common to almost every purchasing office. Other ancillary functions vary from hospital to hospital.

Policies and Procedures

Purchasing, with appropriate administrative approval, must publish guidelines for its own operation and for the entire hospital on buying matters. These guidelines may be in a book, in a series of individual policy and procedure papers, or in some other convenient form. They should be prepared formally, approved properly, and signed, dated, and distributed to all areas of the hospital that need to have knowledge of them. If individual policies and procedures are used, it is useful to divide them into those internal to the purchasing office and those external. Then, only the external procedures need to be distributed to the rest of the hospital. This saves considerable paper and makes it easier for user units to find the information that affects their interface with purchasing.

It also is important that policies and procedures be updated regularly. They should be reviewed at least annually. The master file copy of each should be stamped to indicate the date and the person who last reviewed it. If changes are necessary they should be prepared, approved, and distributed the same as the original policy or procedure.

Policies provide broad guidelines defining scope, authority, and responsibility. Policies may include:

- identification of who, specifically by title, is authorized to make purchases and the scope and limits of authority for each position
- a basic guideline for the product evaluation and value analysis program (this involves serious liability as well as economic questions)
- a requirement that purchases be made only by properly authorized order
- a prohibition against hospital employees' accepting gifts from actual or potential suppliers.

There are other policies but these serve to illustrate the sort of information that needs to be developed, approved, and published.

Procedures provide more detailed guidance for specific actions or processes. Typical procedures include:

- the requisitioning process for various categories of material such as stock items, non-stock special orders, capital equipment, services, etc.
- the product evaluation process
- the competitive purchasing process
- vendor evaluation
- purchase order preparation and processing.

As with the policies, there are many other procedures that need to be published but these illustrate the range of work to be done.

Procedures cannot cover every possible situation and any attempt to do so will result in a list that is overly detailed, cumbersome to use, and almost impossible to keep up to date. Proper procedures, however, can help ensure a smooth flow of routine, day-to-day matters so that special attention can be concentrated on the truly exceptional or unusual situations. Managers should use procedures to make 95 percent of the work run smoothly so that there is time for the other 5 percent to be handled personally on an exception basis.

Procedures are not complete unless they include controls to ensure that they are being followed properly. Such controls must be included as an integral part of any purchasing procedure.

Interface with Accounts Payable

The accounts payable unit in the accounting department must decide whether to pay or to challenge each invoice, based on comparing what was ordered, what was received, and what was billed by the vendor. This review is done in terms of item and quantity as well as unit price and total amount billed. It is up to purchasing to be sure that accounts payable knows clearly what was ordered, from whom, and the price and terms. If accounts payable is not fully aware of or does not fully understand the terms, then discounts will not be taken properly, extended payment terms may be missed, or the hospital in other ways may pay more for the items than it agreed to. For example, the terms of the purchase order may provide for 50 percent of payment on delivery and the remaining 50 percent upon completion of installation, testing, and acceptance by the hospital. If accounts payable pays the full price on delivery, then the hospital has lost the use of 50 percent of the purchase price during the installation period and has lost the leverage to ensure prompt and satisfactory installation by holding back the additional money due.

Accounts payable also must know accurately what items and quantities have been received against a particular purchase order. This is a receiving function and should not be done directly by purchasing. However, purchasing can be a great help in developing, or participating in the development of, effective procedures.

The question arises as to whether receiver documents go directly from receiving to accounts payable or via purchasing. Auditors generally prefer that they go directly to accounts payable for audit control and for prompt payment. On the other hand, if the receiving documents do not pass through purchasing, that department is not aware that the order has been received and may be pressing the vendor for delivery of items that already are in the hospital.

In some cases, receiving sends copies directly to both purchasing and accounts payable. This involves an additional piece of paper, however, and the ever-present possibility that the documents will not agree. As hospitals move toward the full use of computers to eliminate paper work, this question may simply disappear.

Some hospitals use a computer terminal on the receiving dock to enter receipts directly into the data bank. This eliminates a great deal of paper work and greatly speeds the receiving process. If the system is on line, both accounts payable and purchasing have immediate access to the information as soon as it is entered at the receiving terminal. The introduction of computers on the dock more than ever emphasizes the importance of the receiving function and the need to have qualified persons responsible for it. This function often is not fully appreciated but, if it is not well done, it creates a great deal of unnecessary confusion, error resolution, and follow-up work.

Purchasing also can help accounts payable by enforcing hospital procedures related to vendors—for example, by requiring that purchase order numbers appear on all invoices. Such conditions should be included in the standard terms of the order. It is up to purchasing to enforce these requirements because that department has the leverage with the sales representative.

Purchasing also must assist in resolving problems when discrepancies are found between purchase orders, receivers, and invoices, especially when these require vendor contact.

Follow-Up Actions

Purchasing must have means to follow up on actions or situations to be sure that things are done on a timely basis. Steps that routinely require follow-up include:

- the status of requisitions in process until the order is placed and the requisitioner is notified of the placement
- the status of purchase orders until completed, including expediting overdue deliveries (as discussed earlier)
- a reminder to initiate action to renew or cancel blanket purchase orders, standing orders, rentals, or leases; this reminder must come sufficiently in advance (perhaps 60 days or longer) to permit the situation to be evaluated, approvals obtained, and action completed before the expiration date of the existing agreement
- equipment on trial or loan, to be sure the evaluation report is completed and the equipment returned on schedule
- letters of intent to purchase that have an expiration date and must be either completed by a purchase order or be cancelled.

Various other items may require follow-up. The important point is that all such actions be under positive control and not left to chance or memory. In a busy purchasing office, something that is left to memory sooner or later will be overlooked. The result is likely to be at least embarrassing and may result in serious liability exposure or economic loss to the hospital. Various control devices can be used:

- A copy of the actual paper (requisition, letter of intent) can be filed in a series of folders by date. A file folder is prepared for each day of the month and for each succeeding month. At the begining of each month the papers filed for that month are spread into the daily files. This often is referred to as a follow-up or tickler file.
- A log book can be used with a checkoff column, with a routine follow-up on any items not checked off in the appropriate column or columns.
- A listing can be used, perhaps in a chronological or other convenient sequence. A list is useful in certain circumstances but as a routine operation in a large office it means another document to be prepared. In the preparation there is another chance for error by omitting something from the listing or putting it under the wrong date.
- The information for follow-up may be in a computer data base; if so, the computer can be programmed to pull out required information on a periodic or demand basis—for example, purchase orders overdue (for expediting with the vendor). This is useful and should be included in every computer program. In preparing this sort of listing from a computer, the printout must include only the exception data really needed to act upon rather than a long list of items that a human then has to scan to find exceptions. The computer can and should do the sorting.

These same follow-up techniques should be used for administrative activities in the purchasing office. Follow-up can be done on such things as reports due, projects in process, and due dates for the project or subelements, preparations for conferences, meetings, and so on. In scheduling projects, bar charts showing a time schedule for each element can be useful. A copy of the bar chart can be placed in the tickler file to follow up on each element as it is due for completion.

VENDOR RELATIONS

Maintaining a productive relationship with vendors is an important purchasing department responsibility. The relationship should be at arm's length and businesslike but not adversarial. It is to the hospital's benefit to develop efficient, dependable vendors. Effective suppliers similarly seek to develop a continuing relationship with the hospital. While it is entirely appropriate and useful to develop a friendly rapport with vendors, it should not be overdone, particularly in a social sense.

Purchasing personnel must recognize that vendors are representatives of organizations that may have a set of objectives different from those of the hospital. Vendor objectives can be in line with or at odds with hospital objectives. The purchasing office must be prepared to take a strong stand when appropriate. Even when there are disputes, the supplier should be treated with courtesy and tact. To do otherwise damages the image of the hospital, further complicates the problem at hand, and diminishes prospects for a useful and mutually satisfactory long-term relationship. The bottom line is that the hospital will have better success if it has a reputation for being a firm but fair and friendly place to do business.

Constructive feedback is one means to help vendors improve. Every purchasing office should arrange for this. It can be done informally in the normal course of business contacts between seller representatives and buyers or formally on a regular schedule involving not only the representative but also that individual's manager.

In planning for feedback meetings, managers must remember three things. First, they should use the session for communications, not recriminations. Second, they will need data to provide objective assessment of the vendor's performance. These data can be accumulated from purchase order files, on either a continuing or periodic basis, and should be collected and evaluated before the vendor visit. Such information should include on-time receipts, late receipts, number of errors in items delivered, and complete deliveries versus back orders and partial fills. The third point to remember is to give the vendor an opportunity to comment on the relationship from that person's point of view. There may be steps the hospital can take to make the vendor's operation more efficient and that should be reflected in better service and perhaps in lower prices.

There is value in maintaining a long-term relationship with a vendor, provided both parties are working to keep it productive and efficient. It is important for the hospital to maintain a competitive market but that does not necessarily mean constantly changing from one vendor to another. The hospital also must recognize the operational efficiencies of a continuing relationship. Personnel get used to working with one another and understand each other's systems. As a result, service should become more efficient over time. Nonetheless, the hospital must be prepared for a change if the current supplier is unwilling or unable to maintain a competitive price structure.

The purchasing office must establish policies with respect to vendor representatives' relationships with the hospital. For example, most facilities require that a vendor representative either deal with the buyer or, if the representative is to see someone else in the hospital, an appointment be made through the buyer. This helps the buyer keep up with what is going on and prevents a supplier from playing both ends against the middle by negotiating simultaneously with a buyer and with a person in the user department.

Another policy that should be stressed is that the vendor representative cannot leave samples or trial equipment in the hospital except with the authorization of a proper purchase order or other written document. There is danger that samples lying about unknown to hospital management could be used on a patient with poor results and the facility could face a serious liability problem.

It is useful to prepare a brief summary of hospital policies with respect to vendors and

their representatives and to incorporate them into a brochure to be made available to representatives and to their companies. This brochure should give a clear understanding of how the hospital purchasing office operates and what is expected of sellers.

INTERDEPARTMENTAL RELATIONSHIPS

It is vital that the purchasing office develop and maintain open communications with all departments in the hospital and with the medical staff. The material management department and the purchasing office must know what the various departments are trying to accomplish. They also must inform all departments as to what material management is trying to do in terms of service, cost containment, and so on.

It is important that communications be open so that problems are identified and resolved promptly. Purchasing and material management should seek to build a reputation for efficient service and a reservoir of good will that can be drawn on for support when needed. They should let others know of material management accomplishments in quantitative terms but in a low-key way. Again, this is part of creating an essential image of competency and performance.

Surveys of user departments can provide useful feedback. These can be responses to written questionnaires or can involve periodic visits to departments to discuss purchasing and material management support, problems, and other mutual concerns. This will result in some criticism, including, probably, some that is undeserved. The material management and purchasing offices must be prepared to handle that in a mature way. It does no good to get involved in a name-calling contest. It is especially important that any problems identified by users be followed up and resolved. Otherwise, the user departments that completed the survey will conclude that material management and purchasing are not listening and the potential positive effect will be reversed.

RETURNED GOODS

The purchasing office should be responsible for dealing with vendors concerning return of unsatisfactory or excess goods. If the situation involves unsatisfactory goods, these should be identified upon receipt and the supplier notified immediately. Time is of the essence. With prompt notification, there should be no problem in the vendor's either repairing or replacing the goods. The Uniform Commercial Code (see Chapter 10) covers the buyer well on this, provided that there is prompt notification to the vendor and that the hospital takes reasonable care to preserve the goods from further damage or deterioration pending return to the supplier.

A more ticklish problem arises when goods have been accepted by the hospital and later are discovered to have a latent defect or to be more than needed. In the case of latent defects, return or replacement of goods can be negotiated with most suppliers if they are notified promptly. After all, the vendor wants to retain the hospital business and usually is reasonably accommodating. Beyond that, most will even try to be accommodating in accepting back excessive satisfactory goods. In such cases there may be a restocking charge that compensates the vendor for the cost of return transportation and handling, or the hospital may be expected to pay for the return transportation. If the facility has had the goods for a long time, it is more difficult for both it and the supplier. This is another reason why there should be effective inventory control so that items do not lie fallow in the hospital for long periods.

Another question is whether the user department should be credited for excess goods returned. This is a matter of hospital policy and accounting practices. Generally, the most reasonable policy is that the user department will be credited to the extent that the hospital is able to obtain credit for, or to use, the items. If the goods can be utilized elsewhere in the facility, the user department should obtain full credit, and the charge moved to the department that now will use the goods. If the goods are returned to the vendor, then the department should get whatever credit is obtained. Otherwise, the user department will have to bear the charge for the wasted items.

Even if items cannot be sold or returned for credit, they sometimes can be donated for teaching purposes or to a charity. While that results in no dollar return to the hospital or to the user department, it may provide good will and—in the case of a for-profit hospital—a tax write-off.

OTHER PURCHASING FUNCTIONS

Various other functions may be assigned to purchasing; these vary from hospital to hospital. These may include:

- Control of movable equipment fixed assets: Hospitals must have a record of all equipment for accounting depreciation purposes, preventive maintenance, and in case of manufacturer's recall or other hazard notice. Sometimes the responsibility for maintaining such records is given to purchasing, although at other times it may be in maintenance or in accounting.
- Disposal of excess: This should be a purchasing function because that department is in the best position to know what other requirements may exist in the hospital and also has the best contacts with outside vendors. Excess to be disposed of may be equipment, supplies, or valuable byproducts such as silver recovered from film and film processing operations in radiology or other departments.
- Control of hazard warnings and manufacturer's recall: Some hospital entity must be responsible for acting as a point of control for hazard warnings or manufacturer's recall of medical equipment and supplies. This responsibility often is assigned to material management or purchasing, although in some cases it may be assigned elsewhere, such as biomedical engineering.

The important point is to be sure that whatever other functions are assigned, the authority and responsibilities are clearly defined and stated in a hospital policy document. Then it is up to the purchasing manager or material manager to develop and implement a clear, effective procedure to carry out the assigned function.

DOCUMENTATION AND FILES

Effective purchasing depends upon documentation and files of information derived from that record. A multitude of detailed information is processed daily in a purchasing office. That information must be readily available if the office is to function efficiently. It also is vital that it be readily accessible for legal protection of the hospital. The purchasing office deals with contractual relationships with vendors involving high dollar values, so the legal well-being of the hospital demands that information concerning orders placed, terms and conditions, items received, damaged goods, and similar activities be properly and accurately documented and filed for ready reference.

Documentation may be in the form of hard copy (paper), computer files, micrographics, or some combination of these. The basic documents used in a purchasing office are:

- requisitions or other authorizations to purchase and notation showing the status of each requisition at any time
- catalogs, price lists, and other documents containing vendor information
- requests for quotation or for bid, and vendor proposals
- purchase orders authorizing vendor delivery of goods and services and notation showing the status of each order at any point
- receiving documents showing evidence of receipt of goods and services in the hospital
- documents showing charges to operating departments arising out of purchasing actions; these may be processed simultaneously with receipts or later when issued to the user department; issues out of stock are not normally handled by purchasing but

it is important that it be sure that there is a system in place to record such issues accurately.

These documents come in various forms and may be separate or combined, such as a combined requisition and purchase order for small special-order items. In whatever form, they are the source documents for the operation of the basic functions in any purchasing office.

Basic Files and Access

In developing files it is important to determine their sequence and key, which depend on what information is needed. The file should be organized so that the most-needed information can be obtained most efficiently. This section discusses primary files and a recommended sequence. There is some flexibility to use other sequences as long as the necessary information can be obtained promptly from the file.

In the question of file sequence and file key, computers offer much more flexibility than manual files. If the computer file is properly programmed, far more information can be accessed more quickly than in manual files. In general, a manual file is in a particular sequence designed to facilitate the primary use. If other information is desired, it may be necessary to search the entire file. In a computer, one data file can have several keys. For example, a single requisition file may be accessed and sorted by vendor, by requisitioner, by requisition number, by date of requisition, or by other keys. To obtain similar flexibility in a manual file generally requires a cross-index log of some sort, which involves more effort.

Requisition File

The requisition file or log is essential to control processing and to provide the record of authority for purchase orders issued in response to properly approved requisitions. The file must work efficiently so that requisitions can be processed promptly. It also is important to be able to determine quickly the status of any requisition at any time. Finally, if the requisition files are maintained separately, they must be cross-referenced to a purchase order number.

Normally, requisitions initially are filed by vendor and chronologically within vendor until the order is placed. This facilitates order placement by grouping items for a single vendor. It also provides sufficient access for the short run, since placement must be done promptly.

After the order is placed, the requisition can be filed with the purchase order, by requisitioner, or by number if requisitions are numbered. The question of whether the requisition should be numbered is really a question of control. In a large system, it may be necessary to number requisitions in order to provide sufficient control. With a computer system, it may be useful to number requisitions as a file key and to have the computer automatically assign the numbers Unless dictated by a large system or a computer system, it probably is not necessary to number requisitions.

Since the most likely access to the requisition after the purchase order has been issued is a long-term audit requirement to justify the purchase order, the best filing probably is to attach it to the purchase order, where it is less likely to be lost and is readily accessible.

This leaves the problem of how to cross-reference the requisition to the department for status information. In a manual system this means either a requisition log or another copy of the requisition showing the purchase order number and filed by the requisitioner. Of these two, a requisition log probably is the easier and more effective. A requisition log is additional work but it provides ready reference and control. It should be a simple listing of requisitions in the order received and a series of checkoff columns showing the date when the order was placed, the vendor, and other information considered essential or useful.

For example, the log may show the purchase order number, in which case it will be necessary to go to the order file to get the delivery date. The latter is more work when a delivery question is asked but does not require that every delivery date be posted back to the requisition log and

also eliminates the danger of misposting the date to the log. The requisition log is useful only for control purposes and to answer questions. It should be as simple as possible and still meet the basic need. It should not include "nice to have" information unless the trouble of entering it can be justified by the value of having it readily accessible.

Purchase Order File

Purchase orders are contractual obligations of the hospital. The purchase order file may be in strict numeric sequence or divided by type of purchase order, for example: capital, noncapital, special orders, blanket purchase orders. If desired, each of these types may be assigned a different series of numbers.

The essential functions of this file are to provide a complete copy of every purchase order issued, since these are legal contracts, and a means of monitoring their status until received.

Every order should be numbered for positive reference, identification, and control. It is best to file orders by number because there is less chance of misfiling and it is easier to audit the files to be sure no orders are missing. It also provides an unmistakable key to find the order when needed.

This leaves the problem of cross-referencing orders by requisitioner and chronologically for follow-up of delivery date and expediting. Cross-reference to requisitioner can be best met by adding a "P.O. Number" column to the requisition log. Then there is a direct trail from the original requisition to the purchase order number.

The best way to handle the chronological file for follow-up on delivery date and expediting is to prepare an extra copy of the order. This copy needs only the basic order, not all of the supporting papers, terms, and conditions. These copies are filed chronologically by expected delivery date. This file is scanned daily and any items not received on time must be expedited with the vendor. Sometimes a log is used for this purpose but the chronological file works better. A log is another document that must be prepared, which means more work and more opportunity for error. It also is difficult to scan a log for items that are due on a particular day. In contrast, the file is specifically in chronological sequence so scanning is not necessary. Each day's expediting is in the file by that day.

A computer file makes this process much easier because the purchase order can be accessed, inquired, sorted, or listed by any of several keys. Follow-up file for expediting is easier because the computer can print out each day a listing of all purchase orders overdue delivery as of that day.

Receiving File

This file contains evidence of the receipt of goods and delivery to the proper place in the hospital. Once the purchasing office gets the document showing that the item has been received and delivered, it should be filed with the purchase order. If all action is complete on that order, it should be shown as such. At the same time, the expedite copy should be removed from the chronological file—and thrown away or used to document the performance of the vendor as to on-time delivery, quality of items furnished, and so on. It is handy to use the expedite copy for this purpose because it will already contain notations on any delivery problems.

A receiving log also should be maintained on the receiving dock. This is not a purchasing function but is related. This log should be kept so that there is unquestioned record of every item received on the dock on a particular day. Receiving documents can be lost. Furthermore, unusual receipts occur from time to time, sometimes without adequate paper work. When such events do arise, a supervisor should be involved to assist receiving personnel in handling the situation. Memories of such events dim within a few days and a receiving log that lists each receipt can be valuable in resolving questions that may arise later.

Follow-up Files

It is necessary to have appropriate logs or files to facilitate follow-up functions. For example,

there should be a chronological file or log in which blanket purchase orders or other continuing agreements are recorded by expiration date. This is to ensure that timely action is taken to consider renewing or extending such agreements before they expire. Other follow-up activities require similar supporting files.

Vendor File

The vendor file includes identification and often additional information such as terms and discounts normally offered by that seller.

This file is maintained by accounts payable rather than by purchasing for control purposes. From a control point of view it is not desirable to have purchasing introduce a new vendor without coordination with the accounting department. This control makes it far more difficult for an unscrupulous purchaser to create a "phantom" vendor. Even though it is an accounts payable file, purchasing does provide update information to be entered and uses the file extensively, particularly in computerized systems. If there is a computer interface between purchasing and accounts payable, purchasing can use the file for random inquiry about vendors. If the computer generates purchase orders, the system itself can draw information from the file, such as addresses and standard terms.

Other Documentation and Files

Other files maintained in the purchasing office will be dictated by particular functions assigned. Some examples are:

- items of equipment no longer needed, pending disposal
- product evaluation actions in process or previously completed
- a listing of acceptable products, both stock and nonstock items, based on product evaluation actions or other appropriate authorization.

In building such files it is important to sequence them to provide quick access to the information most likely to be needed. Managers should ask first what they want to get out of the file, then organize it to be able to get that information most quickly.

Responsibility for File Maintenance

Each file must be covered by an appropriate purchasing office procedure that must provide specific responsibility and accountability for maintaining and updating it. A file or log of any sort is worth little unless the information in it is up to date, accurate, and dependable. The procedure also should provide for periodic audit and/or reconciliation of each file. In the long run it is far more efficient to build accurate files in the first place than it is to correct mistakes and misunderstandings that result from inaccurate data.

CONTROLS

Purchasing must have control of the various processes in its office in order to ensure that work is done, schedules are maintained, documents are processed properly, accountability is maintained, and financial controls are observed, as well as to measure the office's workload, efficiency, and effectiveness.

Processing Controls

As a minimum, the following controls should be maintained:

- Requisitions in process to be sure they are properly documented and handled within acceptable time frames. Targets for processing times for each type of requisition should be established and reviewed weekly as to how well those deadlines were met.
- Blanket purchase orders due renewal so that action is timely. Part of the control for such orders is to be sure that they have a clearly understood expiration date. If a blanket purchase order is not renewed by that date and

the vendor is forbidden to make shipments under the old order after that date, there is a risk of interruption of supply support to the hospital.
- Receivers in process. Once an item has been received it is necessary to maintain control until the item has arrived at its proper destination in the hospital, and the receipt has been reconciled with the purchase order and has been processed to accounts payable for payment.
- Expediting of overdue deliveries. This must be done vigorously until the item is received. Users must be kept informed of the status of overdue orders and projected delivery dates.

Workload Measures

Typical workload measures in purchasing include:

- number of requisitions processed, which may be broken down by type of requisition
- number of purchase orders issued, which also may be broken down by type
- other workload measures, depending upon additional functions that may be assigned to the purchasing office in a particular hospital.

Effectiveness Controls

Effectiveness controls determine the degree to which the purchasing office is performing its assigned functions in support of the hospital. Typical effectiveness controls include:

- promptness in processing purchasing requisitions
- percentage of purchase orders placed competitively, as contrasted to single-source purchase orders
- promptness in processing receivers, for example, to obtain prompt payment discounts from vendors where offered.

Financial Controls

Financial controls may be established based on controls in the purchasing office or on data furnished from the hospital accounting department. Typical financial controls include:

- dollars chargeable to expense or to inventory
- total dollars' worth of purchases, which may be broken down into various categories
- total purchases per bed or per patient day, which also may be broken down by categories.

Simplicity in Reports

Most reports of purchasing office actions can and should be kept simple. It is neither necessary nor desirable to document every action in report form. That information is in the files, readily accessible if needed. Reports should cover only key indicators, the data elements that show whether functions are being performed efficiently and effectively. Routine reports should not contain the answer to every question that might be asked but merely an overview so that, if there is a problem, appropriate questions can be asked and more detailed answers obtained.

If reports are prepared manually, they should be handwritten in most cases and prepared as a normal byproduct of the routine work of the office, rather than as a special separate effort. If reports are prepared by computer, they should be tailored to meet the particular need and kept brief and simple. A computer should not be used to print out reams of information to be reviewed by a person. Rather, the computer should be programmed to select the key desired data elements and to list just that information.

Reports should be used, not just read and filed. They should go first to the decision maker or action taker. A report that contains information about blanket purchase orders due for renewal is of greatest value to the buyer responsible for the renewal. It should get to that buyer directly, not via the material manager and purchasing manager.

Reports should be used to track trends. An item that is below par one week may not be significant if the backlog is caught up promptly, but if it keeps reappearing there may be a more serious problem. Even in areas where goals are being met, the reports should be reviewed to see whether more challenging goals should be established to serve the hospital better or to reduce costs.

PURCHASING OFFICE LAYOUT

The physical layout of a purchasing office can do much to add to or detract from the efficiency of the operation. A number of ideal or typical layouts have been suggested but these do not usually fit in the space available. The purchasing manager must develop the best layout possible in the space available. The discussion in this section therefore focuses on needed or desirable features.

The overall atmosphere of the purchase office should be straightforward and businesslike. It should be neither plush nor shabby. A plush office suggests a lack of cost consciousness by purchasing—a highly undesirable impression to leave with vendors and other visitors. A shabby office, however, suggests that purchasing is not accorded an appropriate status by hospital management and may lead vendor representatives and others to think it lacks authority to conduct important business. First impressions are important. Visitors to the office, vendor or other, should be received graciously and as comfortably as possible.

Reception and Waiting Area

Company representatives should check in immediately upon arrival in the hospital. The waiting and check-in areas should be close together. The waiting area should be comfortable, provide for smoking if permitted, and be visible from the check-in point if possible so that the person responsible for vendor appointments can maintain visual contact.

It also is important to locate the waiting area so that it is not in the mainstream of office business and so that confidential information cannot be overheard accidentally. For the same reason, guests should not be allowed to wander outside the waiting area without authorization or escort.

It is a good idea to locate a bulletin board in the waiting area as a place to leave messages or other information of interest for company representatives. Vendor brochures containing hospital policies for representatives should be available. Messages and vendor brochures also may be left with the secretary or whoever is responsible for check-in and appointments.

Purchasing Officials or Buyer Offices

The primary requirements for these offices are privacy and reasonable comfort. Confidential negotiations must take place and information exchanged without fear of being overheard by competitors or other unauthorized persons. Since the buyer spends a good deal of time in the office, it should be reasonably comfortable and of adequate size to contain files, catalogs, and work space. It also should have side chairs for at least two or three visitors since the vendor representatives may bring a company manager and/or other hospital personnel may be present. For a larger group, a conference room would be more appropriate.

Clerical and Administrative Area

The clerical and administrative area where most of the routine processing takes place and most of the files are located should be away from the normal path of vendor representatives in order to preserve confidentiality. Casual traffic through this area may pick up confidential information from a glance at a piece of paper, a CRT screen, or a few words of overhead conversation.

As in other areas, this should be a reasonably comfortable place to work because the staff members have a busy day doing an important job. Although it usually is one large room, it should contain room dividers, filing cabinets, or modular work stations so that the individuals can do their jobs without being disturbed by conversations, telephones, or typing at other desks.

It also should include files and other equipment readily accessible to users. Finally, if computer equipment is used, the terminals should be so located that they are convenient and comfortable to work at and any tendency for eyestrain from heavy use of the CRT is minimized.

Catalog Files

Purchasing offices should have up-to-date catalog files from vendors with whom they are doing business or competitors with whom they may expect to do so in the near future. These should be located conveniently for buyers and others who need to use them. If, at the same time, they can be reasonably handy to the reception and waiting area, supplier representatives can be encouraged on each visit to check and be sure that their catalog is up to date. It is in the best interest of the vendor as well as the hospital that these catalogs be timely. Price lists that are public can be filed with the catalogs but confidential lists should be in the buyer's office or in the clerical and administrative area.

Conference Room

The purchasing office should have a conference room that will accommodate eight to ten people. This can be used for meetings with representatives of hospital departments on purchasing matters and with vendor representatives when the number of persons exceeds what can be comfortably accommodated in the buyer's office. It also can be used for internal meetings of purchasing office personnel and for inservice training. The value of the room is enhanced if it is equipped with a speakerphone so that everyone can participate simultaneously in a telephone conference, perhaps with an out-of-town vendor.

Lighting and Air

It is important that all areas of the purchasing office be properly lighted and have appropriate heating, ventilation, and air conditioning. The purchasing office is a busy place where important work is being done and where there is a premium on careful, thorough, and accurate work. Providing proper lighting and air handling permits persons there to do their best work without undue fatigue.

Co-Locating Material Management and Purchasing

There may be some advantage to co-locating the material management and purchasing offices. They can share certain facilities such as the waiting and reception areas, the conference room, or word processing equipment. They also can provide mutual support in such tasks as phone answering or unusually heavy typing workloads. Finally, the shared location facilitates coordination between these two closely related functions. There is one significant potential drawback, however: If they are located together, the material manager must be careful not to become overly involved in purchasing and thereby reduce the initiative of that manager and staff to do their own jobs.

COMPUTERS IN PURCHASING

There are three primary benefits to computer support of the purchasing function:

1. The computers provide a more effective medium for handling the tedious detail and file data that must be maintained in the purchasing office.
2. The information in the computer files is readily available to be accessed, screened, sorted, and displayed or printed in a variety of convenient formats to meet various functional needs of the office.
3. The computers can increasingly interface with other computers inside and outside

the hospital to exchange or process information.

For example, information on receipts and issues can be processed directly into the general ledger if the appropriate computer interfaces are made. Another example: the purchasing computer can interface with vendor computers so that orders may be processed directly to principal suppliers by electronic means. The vendor can provide return information on order status to the hospital through the same electronic channel.

In general, computers should not be used to print out masses of detail. Rather, they should be used to sort out detail and print only the selected information required for management or other purposes. For example, they can sort outstanding purchase orders by vendor for buyer follow-up during a representative's visit. The same data can be sorted by delivery date to expedite late deliveries or to schedule delivery and installation of major equipment.

Proper use of computers can make a purchasing operation more effective but it does not change the basic functions, files, and controls that must be in place if the office is to operate effectively. In other words, a computer can make a good purchasing office work better but it will not compensate for one that is poorly organized in the first place.

PURCHASING SPECIAL COMMODITIES

While general purchasing principles and procedures are applicable to most situations, there are special factors to be considered in acquiring certain categories of material or services.

Printed Forms and Printing

Purchasing forms and other printing work involves much design assistance and tailoring the job to the hospital need. Quality is an important consideration. It is increasingly important that printed forms be made to exact tolerances because they fit into computer equipment and other machines. Indeed, quality often is a major consideration—for example, the appearance and layout of marketing brochures. Vendor service is an important issue in terms of both quality and promptness. Achieving the required quality level involves close coordination and follow-up between supplier and ultimate user. Since printing often is done with short lead times, this coordination is even more challenging.

These somewhat intangible questions of quality and service, together with typically short lead times, make it difficult to buy printing work on a straight price comparison basis, job by job. The question of comparison pricing is made more difficult by the well-established relationship between quantity purchased at one time (which determines length of print run) and unit price. Almost without exception, the larger the print run, the lower the unit price per item; however, large runs result in large inventories that create offsetting holding costs. (This is discussed in more detail later.)

One other aspect of purchasing printing deserves special mention: the importance of thorough and accurate proofreading, both before the job is submitted to the printer and when the proofs are returned. Before the job is submitted, the text and layout should be reviewed carefully because printer's errors are corrected at the printer's expense but mistakes by the hospital can result in added cost to the hospital. On final proofs, errors identified by the hospital are corrected by the printer. However, if the hospital approves the proof and does not detect errors, they will appear in the final product. At that point, corrections can be made only at great expense that usually must be born by the hospital.

Purchasing Printed Forms

In printing work there is an important distinction between setup costs and run costs. Certain costs associated with the setup of presses generally are irrespective of the length of the run; other costs are directly related to the length of the run (such as the cost of paper). Since the setup cost must be spread over the length of the run, the longer the run the lower the price per item for setup. Therefore, the best unit price results from long runs; however, these create the problem of large inventories of forms.

The way to achieve long runs without correspondingly large inventories is by grouping similar sizes and types of forms to be run together. For example, if all 8½" by 11" snap sets are printed at the same time at the same printer, setup costs are reduced significantly because the printer need only change plates for the different forms. This achieves good economy and a relatively low unit price per form. The length of the run comes from combining a number of forms, rather than a large number of one. Therefore, it is possible to print as low as three to four months' supply of high-volume usage forms at each run and keep inventories correspondingly low.

Prime Vendor for Printed Forms

The primary advantage of using a single or prime supplier to provide all forms (other than those printed in-house) are:

- The prime vendor can assist in developing and implementing a forms management program. Major printers have programs already established and considerable expertise in implementing them.
- The prime vendor can assist in forms design and redesign, a service usually offered as part of a package.
- The prime vendor representative works continuously and closely with the hospital, acquiring an ability to quickly design effective forms.
- A single vendor allows grouping of similar sized forms to be printed in a single run.
- A prime vendor eliminates the need for bidding each individual job and considerably expedites the processing and delivery of printed forms. This is particularly important since new forms frequently are ordered with short delivery deadlines and it is desirable to keep inventories as low as possible.

• The prime vendor, in cases where relatively long print runs are required for a particular form (in spite of grouping like forms for consolidating runs), usually can warehouse the forms and deliver them to the hospital as needed. The vendor will expect a fee for this service, of course, but it does take pressure off the hospital storage facilities and has a cash-flow benefit in that the forms normally are not paid for until delivered. While the hospital does not pay until delivery, it does have a liability to buy out, within a reasonable or stipulated time, the entire inventory of forms—the hospital, not the vendor, is at risk for obsolescence. The inventory thus should be kept as small as possible, even if some of it is going to be held by the printer.

A prime vendor relationship for printed forms should be entered into with extreme caution, as with any other prime vendor. Such a prospective prime supplier is expected to have a close and complex relationship with the hospital over an extended period. Therefore, a great deal of care is necessary in developing the proposed agreement and in choosing the seller. In selecting the prime vendor the hospital should:

• inquire carefully into the quality of the supplier's work, in both design and execution
• consider the particular individual who will represent the vendor to the hospital; this is the person who will do much of the actual work and design and the hospital's satisfaction will depend a great deal upon that person's effort and success
• establish measures to verify that the vendor's prices are competitive in the market; this can be done by comparing overall costs or prices for specific segments against those with earlier suppliers and those of other similar hospitals
• solicit references from each of the proposing vendors and fully check their level of quality and service as well as whether their

prices have remained competitive over a period of time
• meet with key officials of the prospective vendor and clearly delineate the hospital's objectives and the seller's plans to meet them
• schedule periodic meetings, perhaps quarterly, to evaluate progress in achieving the stated objectives.

Other Printing Work

Depending upon the in-house capability, some or most printing work may be done outside the hospital. This may involve marketing brochures, patient booklets, administrative material on employee benefits, or training materials. It may be useful to obtain some of this work through the prime vendor for printed forms. In general, however, the volume of these jobs is such that the work is handled more efficiently by smaller local companies.

The question again arises whether to bid this work on a job-by-job basis or establish some sort of prime vendor relationship with one or two local shops. From a purely economic point of view, bidding each job is superficially attractive and probably yields greater price competition.

There are disadvantages, however. In theory, each job is a complete package ready for layout and printing at the time it is given to the job shop. In actuality, it is more likely a partially completed idea with many questions yet to be resolved and many revisions yet to be made. In that event, the ultimate price can vary considerably from what was quoted originally and the value of the competitive quotation process is reduced correspondingly.

These jobs also tend to be required on short deadlines. If the hospital does a great deal of work with a particular vendor, that printer is more likely to adjust schedules and make a special effort to meet short deadlines than one that gets only occasional work. Finally, as noted with respect to prime forms vendors, a particular supplier that works closely with the hospital over a period of time comes to understand its requirements and ways of doing things and can serve its needs more effectively and efficiently. Over time this benefits both the vendor and the hospital.

For these reasons it is worthwhile to consider evaluating local printing concerns and developing a prime relationship with one or two of them, depending on the normal volume and type of work.

Radiology Film

Radiology film is noted for its extremely high price, perishability, susceptibility to damage, and the importance of vendor service beyond furnishing it.

Since the film is costly, there is a great advantage to competitive purchasing. However, the ability to develop competition is reduced because of radiologists' tendency toward strong brand preferences and because of the technical complexity of comparing competitive brands of film. Nonetheless, every effort should be made to develop price competition. One way this can be achieved is by participating in a group purchasing program with other hospitals.

A key element in evaluating and purchasing radiology film is the technical services offered by the supplier, beyond furnishing of film. These usually are important to the radiology department and require careful evaluation and coordination with that unit.

Perhaps the single most important contribution material management can make in connection with radiology film is to establish a system that provides a high inventory turnover. Since radiology film is perishable, and susceptible to damage if handled or stored poorly, there is good reason to turn inventory quickly.

By working closely with radiology to establish a single inventory point and monitor it carefully, it should be possible to achieve a turnover rate of 26 times a year or more—that is, to average only about 2 weeks of film on hand. It still is important to purchase at the best price possible but dramatic savings can be achieved by applying rigorous inventory control.

Maintenance and Repair Supplies

Many maintenance and repair supplies are bought on an as-needed basis by workers in the maintenance department from local building, plumbing, and electrical supply houses. If this is done on a purchase-by-purchase basis, the paper work becomes cumbersome and annoying to everyone involved: maintenance department, vendor, purchasing, and accounts payable.

It is better to set up a controlled trade charge account. This can be done with a blanket purchase order with selected local supply houses. The order delineates the categories of items and who may make purchases. The workers return the individual purchase tickets to the maintenance department. The vendor sends a monthly billing much the same as with an individual credit card account. This billing is validated and approved by the director of maintenance before payment.

This process can reduce purchase costs. When the blanket order is being established, purchasing can arrange for a trade discount that normally ranges in the area of 30 percent to 50 percent. This is the same discount given to local tradespeople and there is no reason why the hospital should not get it also. There are additional savings from the reduction in paper work all along the line. In general, this approach provides entirely adequate control and probably better control than the item-by-item purchase order. Certainly everybody involved will be happier with the simpler system.

Gas Cylinders

The principal concerns in purchasing gas cylinders are the quality of the product and the demurrage or rent that may be charged. In such purchases, the gas in the cylinders is bought but the cylinder is rented and is returned to the vendor. The vendor allows a period of free use, normally 30 days, but if the hospital keeps the cylinder beyond that point, there is an additional charge called demurrage for rental.

The primary consideration in purchasing gas is its quality and purity and the cleanliness and proper marking of the cylinder. Therefore, it is extremely important to evaluate the vendor carefully to be sure that a quality product will be furnished consistently. Demurrage charges can be kept low by a tight central inventory control with either a one-for-one or a par level replacement policy.

Construction Work

When hospitals are involved in construction work, material management may be responsible for the entire project, but that is the exception rather than the rule. In general, material management and purchasing normally are responsible only for interior furnishings and other movable equipment. The degree of involvement of material management can vary considerably and therefore needs to be well defined with respect to other responsibilities concerning the project.

Early Involvement of Purchasing

There are several reasons for purchasing and material management to be involved in the early planning for construction projects. Many involve areas where there will be material storage or material movement when the project is finished. Material management can be helpful in planning for efficient storage and movement of supplies, even during the schematic phase. As the project develops, purchasing should be involved early in developing terms and conditions to be included in the bidding documents. Terms and conditions such as safety tolerances for medical surgical equipment may be more familiar to in-house purchasing than to the architect. Purchasing also may be useful as a liaison between the user department and the architect and in developing cost estimates for some of the equipment and possibly for the furnishings.

Early involvement of purchasing may have direct cost savings benefits as well. Purchasing may suggest item designs or manufacturers that will enhance standardization of equipment and/or permit cost-effective buying through group purchasing contracts or similar means.

If purchasing is involved early, it may be possible to follow through (soon after bidding) with actual buying of furnishings and equipment to be delivered later. Properly done, this can avoid price increases that may occur between the time of order and delivery some months later.

"Owner Furnished/Contractor Installed"

In some cases, the hospital purchasing office can acquire fixed equipment (sterilizers, operating room lights, radiology equipment) at a better price than the contractor can. Furthermore, if the contractor buys the equipment, its cost is then included in the base price of the entire project. The fees of the contractor, construction manager, and architect all are usually calculated on a percentage of the base price. It thus is wise to show this equipment on the construction document as "owner furnished/contractor installed." This means that the owner will furnish the equipment on site but it is the contractor's obligation to make all preparations and arrangements to install it.

If this is to be done, however, the items must be deleted before the construction documents are sent out for bidding. If the hospital waits until after the bids have been received, then tries to delete certain equipment to be "owner furnished," bidders must allow a credit for its deletion. The problem is that the credit will be significantly less than the amount that would have been allowed if the equipment had not been in the bid in the first place.

Early Changes

It is a well-established rule that the further a construction project proceeds, the more difficult and expensive it is to make changes. Changes are relatively cheap, easy, and frequent during the early planning. However, as this progresses, and especially as construction gets under way, changes become more difficult and more expensive. This is another argument for early involvement of purchasing and material management so that their contributions can be incorporated into the process while changes still can be made at relatively insignificant cost.

Computer Equipment

Acquisition of computer equipment is another area where it is important that purchasing be involved early. Too often, a comparative analysis is finished and the successful vendor is notified, and only then is the package turned over to purchasing to "negotiate a good price." By that time, of course, the competition is over and negotiating leverage is gone.

This situation seems to arise from a sort of mystique that computers are so different from other equipment that normal purchasing procedures should not apply. Nothing could be further from the truth. All of the procedures and techniques normally involved in the acquisition of capital equipment apply equally to computer equipment. As is true with other specialized equipment, of course, some special considerations need to be taken into account.

It is important to have a good ad hoc acquisition team (in some cases, computers are rented, not bought) consisting of at least the prospective user department, data processing people, and business and financial representatives. It also is essential to begin with a clear set of functional requirements and a clear understanding of what the system is expected to do.

In evaluating proposals, hospitals should be wary of vendor-planned demonstrations of equipment. It is much better to require that the hospital's own work be done on the machine. The hospital representatives should take examples of work to the demonstration, or furnish them in advance, have the vendor run them on the computer, and, if possible, have hospital people actually run their work.

This hands-on testing with the hospital's work documents will provide a far better evaluation of the real capability of the equipment to meet the need. It also is important to obtain references from the vendor and to check them thoroughly. It frequently is advisable to supplement the reference checks with onsite visits to see how the equipment is operating in another similar organization.

Vendors should be required to inspect the proposed installation site, or the drawings and specifications for it if it is not yet built, to be sure that the area, the environment, the utility connections, the air conditioning, the electrical power, and all other physical and environmental factors are satisfactory. It is important that this be done before purchase so that there are no surprises requiring extensive air conditioning, utility inputs, or similar expensive site preparation work not identified in the original package.

Most of these considerations apply to the purchase of any major capital equipment, especially expensive and complex items, but these points are particularly important with computer equipment. If the ad hoc purchasing team members work closely together and do their homework well, it is unlikely that any significant points will be overlooked.

PURCHASING FOR SPECIAL DEPARTMENTS

Most of the problems or concerns that may arise in the course of purchasing for special departments such as radiology, laboratory, food service, or operating room can be overcome by developing rapport and teamwork. This requires that purchasing recognize the special needs of these departments. The essence of effective buying for such departments is not to win the debate over whether purchasing cost considerations or department operational considerations will prevail but rather to work together so that all of these priorities are reasonably satisfied. If that is done, it is possible to acquire specialized material using good competitive purchasing techniques that produce good values while still satisfying the technical and operational requirements of the department.

The user is concerned primarily about:

• Technical control and flexibility in selection of items: Users may feel that nobody understands these particular items sufficiently to make an appropriate selection and they are properly concerned that they maintain control in this area.

- Consistent product quality: It may be necessary to discuss with users whether they are ordering excessive quality. In most cases that can be resolved, but only if the users are assured that they will maintain control over the quality of product furnished.
- Ready availability: Users are concerned that supplies be available and usually equate that with large stocks on hand. As users gain confidence in simple and effective ordering procedures, they are likely to be more receptive to efforts to wean them away from the concept of large stocks on hand.

Material management also is concerned about obtaining reliable usage information for projection of future needs to assist in maintaining low inventories.

While these concerns may appear to be in conflict, they all can be satisfied reasonably. The following basic approach can be used whether the hospital is large or small and whether the purchasing operation is manual or computerized. It is not a detailed procedure but rather a basic approach to reconcile the potentially conflicting goals of specialized departments and purchasing when buying materials for them:

- Periodic contracts, usually annual, should be established. An annual contract puts enough business on the table for everyone to feel it worthwhile to be involved. The user department probably will be willing to be involved to assure that its technical and clinical requirements will be fully met and that the supply procedures provide adequate service. There are sufficient dollars involved on an annual basis for purchasing to establish a fully competitive bidding process and there are enough dollars in the annual package to ensure vendor attention and competitive proposals.
- A blanket purchase order or a similar technique should be used to establish a term

agreement (usually annual) with the vendor. Once the contract is set, authority can be delegated to the user department to place delivery orders as provided under the agreement and subject to the controls incorporated into it.

These delivery orders (or blanket purchase order releases) involve only a question of timing and quantity. They cover all other terms, conditions, prices, and so on. Since they involve only items already arranged for purchase, reordering can be delegated to the specialized department, subject to appropriate controls. This gives the department more confidence in the ordering process because it has more control. At the same time it provides records of orders so that purchasing has clear documentation of usage for estimates of future requirements.

This approach also helps keep inventories low. Since it generates accurate usage information (or at least order information that is an approximation of usage) and since good practice requires that a physical count of the inventory be taken at least annually, material management can compute turnover for the specialized items held in the user department. That turnover figure provides a factual basis for discussion with the department concerning inventory levels. The order placement procedure that delegates control of timing and quantity to the user department should help that unit gain enough confidence in the system to be willing to work to lower inventory levels.

The accumulation of accurate order data on a line-by-line basis over a year or more can provide better usage information. This will improve the accuracy of the request for proposal on the next round of competitive bidding, should sharpen the vendor's bidding, and should result in further improvement of pricing.

SPECIAL PURCHASING TECHNIQUES

Special purchasing techniques are applied not in lieu of but in addition to the general procedures and practices discussed so far. Part of the challenge of an effective program is applying the appropriate techniques to specific cases. This involves considering the commodity to be acquired, the requirement for it, the magnitude of the purchase, and the method of distribution in the hospital. Some modification of routine techniques or application of special techniques may provide particular benefits in terms of more effective competition and better pricing, lower inventories, or reduced operating costs. Two of the most commonly used techniques are "consignment buying" and "stockless purchasing."

Buying on Consignment

In a consignment purchase the vendor places inventory at the hospital but the facility does not actually buy or pay for items until used. The inventory on hand in the hospital actually belongs to the vendor; the institution has physical possession (and responsibility) but not ownership. As the stock is used, the vendor replaces the items and bills the hospital for those consumed.

This usually involves a vendor representative who inventories the stock monthly (in some cases more frequently). From the inventory and intervening shipments it is calculated how much has been drawn from the stock and presumably used. Obviously, the hospital must pay for all items removed from stock whether they were in fact used, misplaced, stolen, or whatever. The vendor then bills the hospital accordingly.

Advantages

The principal advantage of consignment purchasing is cash flow, because the material is paid for only as it actually is used. The other advantage is that the vendor becomes a partner in the hospital's effort to reduce inventory. It no longer is to the supplier's advantage to have a great deal of inventory on hand at the hospital (at hospital expense); rather, it now is to the vendor's advantage to keep inventories lean, which is what the institution wanted all along.

Dangers

Consignment buying arrangements must be entered into cautiously and carefully to be sure that the following potential dangers do not become problems:

- Tight control must be kept on consignment material. Even though the hospital does not actually "own" the material, it still is liable for it.
- Prices must be watched carefully to be sure they remain competitive. A vendor who has a great deal of consignment inventory in place in the hospital may feel free to edge prices up more than would be done in a more openly competitive situation.
- Vendors may not be enthusiastic about consignment purchasing and may seek other ways, such as pricing, to compensate for the cost and trouble of setting up such an arrangement.
- The supplier may not position enough inventory and the hospital may suffer stock-outs and back orders. Clearly, this is not acceptable.
- The vendor, in spite of the cash flow consequences, may overstock the hospital, using its "free storage" as the seller's warehouse.
- The intimate arrangement established with a consignment vendor makes it more difficult to change from one seller to another.
- It may be necessary to buy out the inventory on hand, especially items custom-made for the hospital, if a change in vendor is required at the end of a consignment arrangement. Such an arrangement should always anticipate the possibility of a future termination and should include specific provisions for return of inventory to the vendor or buyout by the hospital.

Consignment is best used when expensive items are involved, when brand changes are not likely, when the inventory involves brand-differentiated items that the hospital will have to carry in any case, and especially when the vendor has a well-established track record for reliability and dependability.

Stockless Purchasing

In a stockless purchasing system all stocks are held by the vendor—none are on hand in the hospital. Clearly, this is not applicable to critical items that must be on hand but is more applicable to such items as office supplies. The vendor agrees to hold inventory on a complete line of items and prepares a tailored catalog of them for distribution in the hospital. Departments then place orders directly to the vendor. These orders may be accumulated in the purchasing department and turned over to the vendor once or twice a week, but that department does no consolidation or review of the orders.

The vendor pulls, packages, and addresses the orders by hospital department. These are delivered directly to the ordering department with no item-by-item receiving action by the hospital. The supplier's invoice shows charges by department. This invoice is received and checked only for overall size and general accuracy. Particular receipts may be spot-checked but it generally is assumed that departments have received items ordered unless they complain about nonreceipt. The invoice is paid accordingly.

There is, of course, the risk that some items will not be delivered yet will be paid for. In a properly designed system this risk should be small, however, and more than compensated for by the saving in operating costs from the simplified system. The ordering process, the receiving process, and the invoice reconciliation all are simpler and less costly.

Advantages

The principal advantages of a stockless purchasing system are minimum paper work, minimum handling of items in the hospital, consolidated billing (usually on a monthly basis), and, of course, the elimination of inventory in the hospital and consequent cash flow benefit.

Dangers

As in consignment purchasing, there are cautions to be considered carefully in establishing a stockless purchasing system. The system should be designed to avoid the following:

- There may be no emergency stocks on site in the hospital.

- The hospital is tied rather closely to one vendor for a prolonged period, so the choice of supplier must be made carefully. As in consignment purchasing, it is important that the chosen vendor have an established track record for reliability and dependability.

- The vendor must be efficient and accurate so that stock picks made on a department-by-department basis are accurate and do not create subsequent distribution problems in the hospital.

- Pricing and price increases must be controlled carefully. Being tied to one vendor always raises the specter of prices creeping to noncompetitive levels. The system must be designed carefully so that this does not occur.

- The hospital must have good budget and expense controls because the primary rein on department overordering is that the charges appear directly against each department's budget. If department heads are responsible for staying within budget allocations and this is monitored on a monthly or quarterly basis, the risk of overordering should be minimal. If controls are lacking, there is a corresponding lack of motivation in the department to control ordering and a stockless purchasing system under such circumstances could get out of hand.

- The departmental staff must be reasonably responsible and mature so that it can handle the delegation and relative autonomy this system provides.

GROUP PURCHASING

Larger volume purchases should result in lower prices. If several hospitals combine buying from a single vendor, then volume increases and, all things being equal, prices should be lower. The basic idea of group purchasing is as simple as that. There are complications, however, and these may diminish or even negate advantages of group purchasing.

The Vendor View

Vendors look for volume and savings in operating expenses. Assured volume means revenue and also an opportunity to plan and schedule workload and inventory more efficiently. Sales representatives' time, transportation, and warehouse operations can be used more efficiently. The added volume and increased efficiency mean the supplier can make an acceptable profit while still charging lower prices.

Vendors are understandably concerned about how much they can depend on the promised volume of group purchases. In some groups, this volume is highly committed and dependable, in others it is uncertain because group member hospitals may go off on their own.

Vendors also are concerned about timely payment. Working on a narrower margin, the time cost of money becomes even more important than usual.

The Purchasing Group View

Purchasing groups justify their existence by offering lower prices than member hospitals could obtain otherwise. Therefore, groups want a large membership (measured in beds and purchase volume) of highly committed hospitals to participate.

As groups become larger, the challenge of maintaining cohesiveness and commitment becomes greater. The more hospitals in the group and the more widely scattered their locations, the more difficult this coordination is likely to be.

Vendors unsuccessful in a group award often will test the commitment of group hospitals by offering to meet, or beat, the group price and/or by challenging the quality of the products covered by the agreement. If this ploy is successful, the successful vendor loses volume, the group is weakened, and the next round of bidding to that group is likely to be less competitive.

Sometimes groups are reluctant to press hospitals to maintain disciplined commitment for fear of losing members and purchasing volume. This may have an ironic result. The lack of commitment usually means less dependable volume and therefore higher prices than other, more committed, groups enjoy. These poorer prices may lead the more committed hospitals to seek membership in a stronger group. The group might better have lost the weaker hospitals in the first place by insisting on commitment.

The Hospital View

Hospitals join groups for low prices they hope can be obtained with minimum offsetting operating expenses. Groups have operating expenses, however, and these ultimately are paid by the member hospitals, one way or another, directly or indirectly. Group membership also requires some effort by member hospitals, such as participation in product selection, evaluation of vendors and their proposals, keeping track of current group agreements, and, usually, participation in periodic group or committee meetings.

Should a Hospital Belong to a Purchasing Group?

Group membership, from a purely purchasing point of view, is an economic matter. If the improved prices, less the offsetting administrative costs, result in a probable net saving to the hospital, group membership should be considered.

The question of product evaluation and standardization is a major consideration. There must be a significant effort to standardize products. Member hospitals also must work to agree on the acceptability of more than one brand of competitive product so as to provide effective competition for group business.

Group membership sometimes involves factors beyond purchasing. In such cases, purchasing may have to make the best of a decision dictated largely by other considerations.

In any case, purchasing should carefully investigate any group in which a hospital is considering membership so that it goes in with its eyes wide open.

What to Look For in a Purchasing Group

Pricing is the primary consideration. The group should offer substantially better prices than otherwise available or there is no reason to consider group membership.

These are considerations to be studied involving the group itself:

- How well do group goals and objectives correlate with those of the institution?
- Is the group program well focused and mature or does the group still have to get its program fully organized?
- What are the administrative costs of the group? How efficiently does the group operate?
- How skilled is the group at negotiation? The group is going to negotiate major contracts on the hospital's behalf; is the institution satisfied that the group can do that job well?
- How does the group handle product evaluation and standardization? Since product standardization is an essential element of group purchasing, is the hospital sure it can participate effectively in that process?
- How does the group track record overall compare with other groups—or with what the hospital can do on its own?

As for the vendors who hold agreements with the group, are the products, quality, and service they offer generally acceptable to the hospital? As for the other hospitals in the group:

- Are they larger or smaller than the hospital? Generally, smaller hospitals benefit most from being in groups with larger ones.
- What is the level of commitment of the member hospitals? More committed groups generally produce lower prices.
- How well managed are the other hospitals in the group? Are they institutions with which the hospital will be comfortable working closely?
- Has thought been given to the competitive position of the hospital vis-à-vis others in the group?

Other hospitals, including members, should be asked about the group. So, too, with other hospitals that might have belonged to the group but do not. Why not? And hospitals that once belonged to the group but left—why did they?

PRIME VENDORS*

A prime vendor relationship can be advantageous to both the hospital and the supplier but the advantages must be weighed against the disadvantages in any particular application.

It is up to the purchasing manager of the hospital to see that prime vendor agreements are used only where appropriate, that they are structured to gain the maximum benefits while adequately protecting the hospital against potential risks, and that once in effect they are monitored carefully to ensure that the hospital continues to enjoy the benefits and to be free of adverse effects.

The scope of the agreement may range from a narrowly defined and homogeneous class of items (e.g., printed forms or parenteral products) to a broad category such as all medical and surgical items needed by the hospital. The length of the agreement may range from periods as short as one year (though two- and three-year

---

*This section is adapted from an article by the author in *Hospital Materiel Management Quarterly*, vol. 5, no. 4, May 1984, published by Aspen Systems Corporation, © 1984.

agreements also are common) to an indefinite period that may extend over many years.

In general, the broader the scope of a prime vendor agreement and the longer its duration, the greater the potential disadvantages that must be weighed carefully. The larger the dollar value involved, the greater will be the difficulty in making alternative purchasing arrangements if the agreement fails.

The potential benefits of a prime vendor agreement do not accrue automatically. They must be carefully negotiated, then monitored to ensure that they actually are realized. Likewise, the negotiator must do everything possible to minimize potential disadvantages. If the hospital is unable to protect itself adequately against significant potential risks, this in itself may be sufficient grounds to reject the agreement and look to another prime vendor or to an alternative purchasing technique.

Potential Benefits

The hospital should expect to realize all or most of the following benefits from a well-structured prime vendor agreement:

- The hospital should enjoy a highly dependable source for the products specified. Back orders should be few or nonexistent.
- The hospital should be able to reduce inventory levels. With a dependable source and prompt shipments, safety levels in inventory should be low.
- Purchasing should be simplified. After careful and thorough periodic competition and negotiation, there should be no further need for a competitive sourcing evaluation or for decisions about each purchase.
- Ordering and receiving also should be simplified. The paper work and processing become routine, standardized, and well understood by all involved. In some cases, the vendor can produce shipping forms that can be used for processing in the hospital, thereby reducing the institution's paper work burden.

- Standardization in the hospital may be facilitated by its commitment to a single-vendor line of products.
- The hospital should enjoy an economic advantage in terms of lower prices and extended price protection. When a prime vendor agreement is out for competitive bids, the bidders recognize that it is an all-or-nothing proposition. The process should result in tight competitive pricing.
- The hospital purchaser should receive excellent service and careful attention from the vendor because of the volume of business involved. The supplier often offers special services, such as computerized inventory accounting, that are helpful to the hospital in inventory control. These services are not really free as they are considered part of overhead and are included in the pricing for each of the items bought. Of course, the special service should be of value to the hospital and not duplicate one of its existing resources.

The vendor should be prepared to react with considerable vigor to emergencies or to special needs of the hospital.

Potential Disadvantages and Risks

Notwithstanding the potential attractive advantages, potential disadvantages also are involved. A poorly structured prime vendor agreement or one that is not faithfully executed carries risks that can have extremely serious consequences in terms of expense to the hospital or disruption of its operations. The primary potential disadvantages and risks are:

- The hospital may be committed to a broad line of products that are not of consistently high quality. For example, a vendor with an excellent line of dressings may not have catheters of equal quality.
- The opportunity for evaluation of competitive items by clinical units is more restricted. Thus, standardization within the

hospital could have an adverse impact on the clinical quality of products used.

- Economic competition may eventually be reduced. Especially with broad-line agreements of long duration, the tendency, and in many cases the intent, is for the hospital to buy new items added to the line from the same vendor. The hospital is less likely to obtain competitive prices for these add-on items. In fact, other suppliers probably will consider their chances of selling the new item to be too slim to warrant the effort of competing with the prime vendor.

- Opportunities for other competitors to enter the market may be reduced. These may lose interest in the hospital because they feel they have no real opportunity to compete. This is particularly true of narrow-line suppliers who may offer excellent values in their particular line but are not prepared to compete with a broad-line prime vendor. If smaller and newer vendors are driven out, all purchasers in the market will suffer eventually.

- Prices may rise at a slow but steady rate to unacceptable levels unless the agreement includes stringent controls that are exercised rigorously. Price escalation controls must be monitored scrupulously to be sure that they are observed.

- The hospital may become overly dependent on the prime vendor, particularly if its internal ordering, receiving, and invoice payment functions are highly integrated with the supplier's internal systems.

- A change of vendors may involve changes in internal hospital systems, realignment of employees, the teaching of new procedures, or investment in additional inventory to discontinue a consignment arrangement. All these changes are difficult and may tempt the hospital to endure increasing prices, deteriorating service, or reduced quality of product, all of which it would not tolerate if it were in an openly competitive situation.

Sales and service attention may fall to unacceptable levels if the vendor is shortsighted and regards the account as "in the bag" for the next year or two. Provisions should always be included to protect the hospital from this danger, even to the extent of cancelling the agreement if necessary.

KEY POINTS

Purchasing requires that a great deal of accurate and detailed information be handled so smoothly that primary attention can be concentrated on obtaining needed items for timely delivery at the best price.

Routine functions should be organized into standard procedures with adequate controls. Then managers will have time to deal with exception situations, handle special projects, and plan for improvements in effectiveness and productivity.

The purchasing process must give first priority to the basic functions of requirements determination, purchase actions, and competition, expediting, and receipts processing.

Ancillary functions also are important and must be well organized. These include:

- development of policies and procedures to guide and control operations
- interface with accounts payable to be sure questionable invoices are challenged and proper invoices are paid promptly
- timely follow-up on items pending or in process
- vendor relations to get best performance from each vendor
- medical staff and interdepartmental relations
- return of goods to suppliers for various reasons
- other ancillary functions that may be assigned.

Documentation and files contain the detailed information upon which the purchasing operation depends. This information must be maintained accurately and kept up to date.

Controls must be established to be sure that routine functions are performed promptly and effectively and that exception situations are identified quickly for special attention.

The layout of the purchasing office will affect efficiency of operations. The overall layout and furnishings should be efficient, maintain confidentiality, provide a businesslike atmosphere, and be neither plush nor shabby.

Computers can be helpful in a well-organized purchasing operation but adding computers will not straighten out a poorly organized operation. Computers also must be properly applied with well-designed software to have a positive effect.

There are special considerations in purchasing certain commodities such as printed forms,

maintenance and repair supplies, or construction work, and in buying for certain departments.

Special techniques, such as stockless purchasing and consignment, should be considered where these techniques can be used to advantage.

Purchasing groups are visible and growing. Whether or not to join a group, and if so which one, are questions that require careful and thoughtful evaluation.

Prime vendor relationships may offer a net advantage to the hospital but these also have to be evaluated carefully.

Above all, it must be remembered that the efficiency and effectiveness of the purchasing operation will have a significant impact on both the operations and the costs of the hospital.

10. Legal Aspects of Hospital Purchasing

Michael K. Gire and Diane M. Signoracci

A material manager must bring many skills to the job of making purchasing decisions. Among these is an understanding of the legal issues of entering into contractual relationships for the provision of goods and services. This chapter explores these legal issues and how they should be addressed in the context of making purchases on behalf of a hospital.

FUNDAMENTALS OF CONTRACTS

A contract is a promissory agreement between two or more persons that creates, modifies, or destroys a legal relationship.[1] The elements of this definition can be broken down into its component parts. As each is examined, the concept of a "contract" takes on a clearer definition.

The first element is that there must be a "promissory agreement." This means that there must be a promise on the part of the parties to do something, and the parties must reach an agreement as to what it is that is to be done.

The second element is that two or more "persons" must enter into a contract. "Persons" in this context is defined generically as individuals, corporations, partnerships, or other types of unincorporated organizations. The essential element is that there must be at least two parties in order to create a contract.

The last element is that the promissory agreement must create, modify, or destroy a legal relationship. It is not enough that the parties have an agreement; it must be one that creates, modifies, or ends some legal rights so that there will be a remedy in the event of a breach of the contract.

To form a contract, there must be an offer and an acceptance of that offer. "Offer" is a promise, a commitment to do or refrain from doing some specified thing in the future. The offer creates a power of acceptance permitting the offeree by accepting the offer to transform the offeror's promise into a contractual obligation.[2] An offer differs from preliminary negotiations or mere advertisements. An offer represents a firm commitment on the part of the offeror to sell or do something in return for some payment or performance by the offeree.

In order to create a binding contract the offer must be accepted by the offeree. If this acceptance is qualified or conditioned by the offeree so that it does not conform with the terms of the offer, then this "acceptance" may be considered as a counteroffer of the original offer.

THE PURCHASE ORDER

The purchase order represents the type of contract that normally is used to enter into a contractual relationship between a purchasing agent and a supplier of goods. A purchase order is typically a written form document, drawn up by the prospective buyer of goods and sent by that buyer to a prospective seller of the goods. A written purchase order is preferred to an oral order because the writing memorializes the substance of the agreement sought by the buyer. It protects the buyer from unbargained-for terms in the event of misunderstandings and disputes under that agreement. The typed or written information on the purchase order describes the goods and specific terms of the bargain sought by the buyer on that particular purchase; the printed information sets forth the general terms sought by the buyer on all of its standard purchases.

In legal terms, a purchase order often represents the buyer's "offer" to purchase goods from the seller, giving the seller the power of "acceptance." If the seller accepts the offer by either sending the buyer a confirming acknowledgment or by shipping goods that conform to the buyer's offer, then a contract is formed. Therefore, because a purchase order may ripen into a contract upon its acceptance by the seller, it is important that it be complete in all contract terms.

The face of the purchase order should provide the specific information relevant to the purchase: the name and address of the seller and the buyer, description of the merchandise, shipping instructions, delivery terms, and payment terms. A sample face sheet of a hospital purchase order is presented in Appendix 10–A.

The sample purchase order in Appendix 10–A contains terms and conditions favorable to the hospital-buyer. Consequently it is not unlikely that, on receipt of such a probuyer purchase order, a hospital supplier would either ship the goods ordered or acknowledge the order without adopting its prohospital terms. Instead, the supplier's documents are likely to contain terms and conditions favorable to the seller, and one of those terms may provide, as did the hospital's purchase order, that the supplier's invoice or acknowledgment is the complete and final agreement between the parties. Given the likelihood of competing forms, questions arise as to (1) which form will control transactions under the purchase agreement and (2) how the hospital can draft a purchase order to guarantee that its terms and not the terms of its suppliers will control the purchase agreement.

In common law, any response to the hospital's offer to purchase goods, other than a "mirror image" of that offer (accepting all terms and conditions), would not have constituted acceptance of the hospital's offer. A supplier's invoice or acknowledgment that contained terms different from or in addition to the hospital's terms would have represented a counteroffer by the supplier to the hospital, which the hospital would have been free either to accept or reject. However, if the hospital accepted the goods (even without expressly accepting the supplier's terms), the hospital would have been deemed to

have accepted the goods subject to the terms of the supplier's "counteroffer."

The common-law approach to competing forms presented significant problems. The time of contract formation was unrealistic. By delaying contract formation until the buyer's acceptance of the seller's counteroffer, the common law allowed the buyer to back out of the agreement for reasons other than conflicting contract terms, e.g., lower prices elsewhere. However, if the buyer accepted the goods, the common-law approach was significantly proseller, imposing the terms of the seller on the buyer.

PURCHASING CONTRACTS UNDER THE U.C.C.

The Uniform Commercial Code

Under the federal system of government, the individual states traditionally have had broad discretion in enacting legislation governing commercial transactions. Because of this autonomy, over time the various states adopted laws that often were inconsistent or in conflict with those of other states. These inconsistent or conflicting laws created an impediment to the growth of interstate commercial transactions.

The Uniform Commercial Code (U.C.C.) represents an effort by the National Conference of Commissioners on Uniform State Laws to introduce uniformity into the laws governing certain types of commercial transactions. The official text of the U.C.C. was promulgated in 1951 and has been enacted by 49 states (Louisiana being the exception), the District of Columbia, and the Virgin Islands. Because the U.C.C. is enacted locally, there may be some variations among jurisdictions as to exact wording. Accordingly, it is important when working with the U.C.C. to consult the local codification.

The U.C.C. replaces any number of often-conflicting state statutes on commercial transactions, including the Uniform Sales Act, the Negotiable Instruments Law, and a number of so-called "uniform" acts concerning bills of lading, warehouse receipts, conditional sales, and statutes dealing with the financing of commercial transactions. Hospital purchasers of goods are governed by article 2 of the U.C.C., which deals with transactions in goods.

For purposes of this analysis, it is assumed that the hospital is the "buyer" for U.C.C. purposes.

Contract Formation

Under U.C.C. § 2–204, a contract for the sale of goods may be made in any manner sufficient to show agreement, including conduct by both parties that recognizes the existence of such a contract. This is so even if the amount when the agreement is made is undetermined, or if there are terms that have been left open, so long as the parties intended to make a contract and there is a reasonable basis for giving an appropriate remedy.

To accept an offer, the U.C.C. provides that unless it is otherwise unambiguously indicated by the language or circumstances, the acceptance can be in any manner and by any medium reasonable under the circumstances. When an order or other offer to buy goods is for prompt or current shipment, acceptance can be by either a prompt promise to ship or by prompt or current shipment of the goods. If the seller ships nonconforming goods, § 2–206 provides that this is not an acceptance of the buyer's offer if the seller seasonably notifies the buyer that the shipment is offered only as an accommodation to the buyer.

Competing Forms

The drafters of the U.C.C. attempted to resolve the problems of the common-law approach to competing forms in § 2–207, which reads in full:

(1) A definite and reasonable expression of acceptance or a written confirmation which is sent within a reasonable time operates as an acceptance even though it states terms additional to or different from those offered or agreed upon, unless acceptance is expressly made conditional on assent to the additional or different terms.

(2) The additional terms are to be construed as proposals for addition to the contract. Between merchants such terms become part of the contract unless:
   (a) the offer expressly limits acceptance to the terms of the offer;
   (b) they materially alter it; or
   (c) notification of objection to them has already been given or is given within a reasonable time after notice of them is received.

(3) Conduct by both parties which recognizes the existence of a contract is sufficient to establish a contract for sale although the writings of the parties do not otherwise establish a contract. In such case, the terms of the particular contract consist of those terms on which the writings of the parties agree, together with any supplementary terms incorporated under any other provision of this Act.

U.C.C. § 2–207 cuts into the common-law mirror image or counteroffer approach to competing forms. It provides for contract formation on the exchange of forms, regardless of the presence of competing terms. Between nonmerchants the terms of the buyer's offer become the terms of the contract, and the additional terms of the seller become proposals for additions to the contract, which require the buyer's assent for inclusion in the contract.

Between merchants, such additional terms automatically become part of the contract unless: (1) the offer expressly limits acceptance to its terms; (2) the additional terms materially alter the contract; or (3) the buyer objects to the terms within a reasonable time. The operation and purpose of § 2–207 may become confused when either or both parties include a clause in their respective documents that insists on all its terms for contract formation.

As relevant to hospital purchases, the operation of § 2–207 can best be explained by the use of a hypothetical situation. Assume that the hospital offers to purchase goods from a supplier. The order provides for a warranty that the goods will be free from defects; the purchase order is silent on arbitration. Assume that the supplier responds with an acknowledgment that disclaims any warranty for the quality of the goods and provides that all disputes under the contract be submitted for arbitration. The supplier ships the goods, which the hospital accepts and pays for. Assume further that a dispute concerning the quality of the goods arises. Does a contract exist between the hospital and the supplier? If so, which terms under the contract are controlling?

If the bargained-for terms—price, quantity, description of goods, delivery terms, and payment terms—appearing on the face of the hospital's purchase order and the seller's acknowledgment agree, then a contract is formed on exchange of these documents. However, if the bargained-for terms do not agree, no contract is formed under § 2–207(1) because the supplier's acknowledgment would not be a "definite and reasonable expression of acceptance" of the hospital's offer. Generally the typed or written terms of the printed form documents must agree for contract formation on exchange of forms.

Under § 2–207, regardless of the competing terms, the supplier's acknowledgment represents an acceptance of the hospital's offer, at which time a contract is formed on the hospital's terms. But what about the supplier's disclaimer and arbitration provisions? Subsection § 2–207(2) provides that "additional" terms are to be construed as proposals for addition to the contract. However, only the supplier's arbitration provision literally represents an "additional" term because the hospital's purchase order was silent on this point. The supplier's disclaimer is not an "additional" term but a "different" term because it conflicts with the hospital's warranty provision. Although

§ 2–207(1) permits contract formation in the presence of both "additional" and "different" terms, § 2–207(2) provides that only "additional" terms are to be construed as proposals for addition to the contract.

The use of the words "different" and "additional" in § 2–207(1) and the use of only the word "additional" in subsection 2 have given rise to a variety of interpretations from the courts and commentators. One view is that only additional terms will be considered as proposals for addition to the contract and that different terms will be excised from the agreement. The rationale of this approach is that subsection 2 literally applies to only "additional" terms and that the offerer cannot be expected to assent to conflicting terms.[3] In the hypothetical situation, under this approach, the supplier's disclaimer provision would be dropped from the agreement and the hospital's warranty provision would control future negotiations and actions under the contract.

Another approach to the different/additional dichotomy is that the different terms will be cancelled out. The contract then consists of terms on which the parties are in agreement, and standard U.C.C. provisions replace the conflicting terms.[4,5] The supporters of this approach emphasize the language of comment 6 to § 2–207, which reads in part:

> Where clauses on confirming forms sent by both parties conflict each party must be assumed to object to a clause of the other. . . .

As a result the requirement that there be notice of objection found in subsection 2 is satisfied and the conflicting terms do not become part of the contract. The contract then consists of the terms originally expressly agreed to, terms on which the confirmations agree, and terms supplied by the U.C.C., including subsection 2 .

Under this theory the hospital's warranty provision and the supplier's disclaimer clause would cancel out and the code's implied warranties of merchantability and fitness for a particular purpose would control.

Some courts and commentators urge that subsection 2 is appropriately applied to different terms as well as additional terms, pointing to the language of comment 3 as support for their position.[6] Comment 3 to U.C.C. § 2–207 provides that "[w]hether or not additional *or different* terms will become part of the agreement depends upon the provision of subsection (2). . . ." If this approach is adopted, the fate of the supplier's disclaimer provision as well as its arbitration provision will be determined under subsection 2.

Under subsection 2 of § 2–207, the supplier's disclaimer provision and arbitration provision may become additions to the contract automatically if the hospital and its supplier are considered to be "merchants." The U.C.C. defines "merchant" in § 2–104(1) as: "a person who deals in goods of the kind or otherwise by his occupation holds himself out as having knowledge or skill peculiar to the practices or goods involved in the transaction."

Comment 2 to § 2–104 further states that:

> Section . . . 2–207 . . . dealing with . . . confirmatory memoranda . . . rest[s] on normal business practices which are or ought to be typical of and familiar to any person in business. For purposes of [U.C.C. § 2–207] almost every person in business would, therefore, be deemed to be a "merchant" under the language "when . . . by his occupation holds himself out as having knowledge or skill peculiar to the practices . . . involved in the transaction . . ." since the practices involved in the transaction are nonspecialized business practices such as answering mail.

Given the language of the U.C.C. and its comment, hospitals and their suppliers would be considered merchants for purposes of § 2–207. Therefore, in the hypothetical situation, unless one of the three exceptions to subsection 2 applies, the supplier's disclaimer and arbitration clauses would become part of the contract.

Exceptions

Expressed Limits

The first exception to the general rule of subsection 2 is found in paragraph a, which bars additional terms from becoming part of the bargain if "the offer expressly limits acceptance to the terms of the offer." If the hospital's purchase order expressly limits acceptance to the terms of that order, then the supplier's disclaimer and arbitration clauses would not become additions to the contract under subsection 2.

Materiality

Paragraph b, subsection 2, excludes additional terms that "materially alter" the contract from becoming part of that document. Although the U.C.C. does not define "material," comment 4 to § 2–207 lists examples of typical clauses that would materially alter a contract. Among these examples is a clause negating standard warranties. Therefore, under § 2–207(2)(b), the supplier's disclaimer provision would not become part of the contract because it would be considered to materially alter the contract.

Neither the U.C.C. nor its comments indicates whether the addition of an arbitration clause would be considered a material alteration of the contract. Some courts have held that an arbitration clause in a seller's form is not a material alteration[7]; other courts have reached the opposite conclusion.[8,9] One court noted that whether or not an arbitration clause constitutes a material alteration in § 2–207 is a question of fact to be determined in light of the circumstances of each particular case.[10]

Prior custom within an industry and course of dealing between parties also are considered in deciding this issue.[11,12] Therefore, whether the supplier's arbitration clause would be excluded from the contract as a material alteration under § 2–207(2)(b) might depend on the jurisdiction in which the action is brought, the circumstances of the transaction, the arbitration custom in the hospital supply industry, and previous dealings between the hospital and supplier.

Reasonable Notification

Paragraph c of subsection 2 excludes additional terms from the contract when "notification of objection to them has already been given or is given within a reasonable time after notice of them is received." Because paragraph c allows for objection before the fact, the hospital could guarantee exclusion of the supplier's disclaimer and arbitration provisions by a clause in its purchase order that provides that "Buyer objects to any terms in addition to or different from the terms of this order."

If that clause is omitted from the purchase order, the hospital still may bar the disclaimer and arbitration provisions by notifying the supplier of the hospital's objection to those provisions. However, this notification must be given within a reasonable time after the supplier's document containing the objectionable terms is delivered to the hospital or after such terms otherwise come to the hospital's attention. U.C.C. § 2–204(2) provides that "a reasonable time for taking any action depends on the nature, purpose and circumstances of such action." However the provision of notice within a reasonable time does not require immediate action, and what is a reasonable time is ordinarily a question of fact.[13]

As with the question of materiality, the hospital must look at the surrounding circumstances, the custom in the hospital supply industry, and its prior dealings with this vendor to determine what is notice of objection within a "reasonable time." It is in the hospital's best interests to notify the supplier of its objection to the disclaimer and to arbitration provisions as promptly as possible.

To the proposed hypothetical situation add the assumption that either the hospital's purchase order or the supplier's acknowledgment contains a provision that insists on acceptance of or assent to all its terms and only its terms. The addition of such provision throws the agreement into analysis under the "expressly conditional" clause of subsection 1 of § 2–207, which states in part that: "A definite and reasonable expression of acceptance . . . operates as an acceptance even though it states terms additional to or different

from those offered . . . *unless acceptance is expressly made conditional on assent to the additional or different terms*" (emphasis added). The "expressly conditional" clause of subsection 1 precludes contract formation on the exchange of documents with conflicting or additional terms in which the documents of at least one party expressly insist on assent to or acceptance of all of its terms.

If the hospital's purchase order states: "This order can be accepted only by a document that consists of all the terms of this order and contains neither additional nor different terms," a contract under § 2–207(1) would be formed only if the terms of the supplier's acknowledgment "mirrored" the buyer's terms. In the hypothetical situation no contract would be formed because the supplier adds an arbitration provision and disclaims the warranties provided by the hospital's purchase order.

If the supplier's acknowledgment provides that: "Seller's acceptance is expressly conditioned on buyer's assent to the additional or different terms and conditions set forth herein," a contract would be formed on the exchange of documents only if the hospital agreed to the supplier's disclaimer and arbitration provisions. It is reasonable to assume that the hospital would not assent to such provisions, so no contract would be formed.

Because no contract has been formed on the exchange of documents in these situations, both the hospital and supplier would be free to back out of the agreement. However if each party chooses to perform under the agreement (i.e., if the supplier ships the goods ordered and the hospital accepts and pays for them) a contract would be formed. The issue would remain, however, as to what terms govern future actions under the contract. Assume, as before, a dispute develops over the quality of the goods. The hospital claims breach of the purchase order's warranty provision and seeks standard judicial remedies. The supplier contends all warranties are disclaimed by its acknowledgment and that disputes are to be settled by arbitration.

The courts on various occasions have addressed actual patterns similar to those of this hypothetical situation. In *Roto-Lith Ltd. v. F.P. Bartlett & Co.,*[14] the First Circuit Court of Appeals addressed a situation in which the seller's acknowledgment contained a disclaimer that conflicted with the buyer's warranty provision and in which the seller's acknowledgment was "expressly conditioned" on assent to all its terms.

Reverting to the common-law approach, the court held that the seller's acknowledgment was not an acceptance of the buyer's offer but, instead, was a counteroffer to the buyer, which was accepted by the buyer upon its receipt and use of the goods. Because the buyer was held to have accepted the seller's counteroffer on the seller's terms, the seller in *Roto-Lith* was given the benefit of its disclaimer. If this approach were adopted in the hypothetical situation, the supplier's acknowledgment would be characterized as a counteroffer. The hospital's acceptance of the goods ordered would be deemed an acceptance of the supplier's counteroffer and an assent to the counteroffer's terms, including disclaimer and arbitration provisions.

The common-law approach to competing forms with "expressly conditional" clauses, as adopted in *Roto-Lith,* has been subjected to severe criticism by commentators.[15] More importantly the approach has not been followed in numerous decisions involving the battle of the forms under § 2–207.

The decision of the Seventh Circuit Court in *C. Itoh & Co. v. Jordan International Co.* represents the more widely accepted approach to cases involving competing forms with "expressly conditional" clauses.[16] The court found that no contract arose on exchange of documents by virtue of § 2–207(1) because the seller had conditioned acceptance on the buyer's consent to an arbitration clause. The Seventh Circuit rejected the *Roto-Lith* decision, however, and refused to find the buyer's acceptance of the goods tantamount to acceptance of the seller's counteroffer. The court based its opinion on the language of U.C.C. § 2–207(3):

> Conduct by both parties which recognizes the existence of a contract is sufficient to establish a contract for sale although the writings . . . do not.
> . . . In such case the terms of the particular contract consist of those terms on which the writings of the parties agree, together with any supplementary terms incorporated under any other provisions of [the U.C.C.].

The court found that under subsection 3 a contract arose when both parties proceeded with performance as though there were a contract. However the court, quoting subsection 3, held that the contract did not include the additional terms of the seller but was limited to "those terms in which the writings of the parties agreed, together with any supplementary terms incorporated under any other provision of [the Code]."[17]

It is important to note that contract formation under § 2–207(3) gives neither the buyer nor the seller the disputed terms in its document; subsection 3 instead fills out the contract with standardized provisions of the code. As a practical matter, however, contract formation under § 2–207(3) may put the seller at a disadvantage because the vendor often will wish to undertake less responsibility for the quality of its goods than the standard provisions of the U.C.C. impose.

In the hypothetical situation posed, contract formation under § 2–207(3) would result in the excision of the supplier's arbitration provision. Because the code does not provide for standard arbitration terms, no U.C.C. provision would replace the excised term and disputes under the hypothetical contract would not be subject to arbitration. Furthermore, both the hospital's warranty and the supplier's disclaimer would drop out of the agreement and be replaced by the implied warranty provisions of the code.

Hospital management can use the U.C.C. to provide itself with a more favorable purchasing agreement than was available under common law. However, it must structure its purchasing procedure to take full advantage of U.C.C. provisions. All purchases should be documented by a written order. The purchase order itself should consist of terms that are favorable as well as necessary to the hospital's interests as the buyer of goods. Hospital management, however, should not expect that in every purchase the supplier will agree to all the terms of the purchase order and should anticipate a prosupplier form document in response to its probuyer purchase order.

U.C.C. § 2–207's approach to the battle of the forms is more favorable to the buyer. However, there probably is no language that can be inserted in an order that will guarantee the hospital—as purchaser—in forming a contract on its terms if the supplier responds to that order with a form acknowledgment that requires assent to all of the vendor's terms. However, language can be inserted that will ensure the hospital of not forming a contract on the supplier's terms: "the buyer objects to any terms in addition to or different from the terms of this order."

This language, while protecting the hospital from unfavorable terms of the supplier, may result in contract formation under subsection 3, in which case neither party will receive the disputed terms of its forms. Still, under U.C.C. § 2–207(3), the standard code provisions that replace the cancelled competing terms of the buyer's and seller's forms are more likely to favor the hospital as buyer. If, however, the hospital demands a particular term, it should try to make it a "written-in" or "dickered" part of the agreement. If the supplier refuses to negotiate on the term, the hospital may have to decide whether it is more advantageous to forget the entire agreement or to live without the disputed term.[18]

PERFORMANCE OF THE CONTRACT

Once a contract has been formed under U.C.C. § 2–301 the seller is obligated to transfer and deliver the goods and the hospital is obligated to accept them and pay in accordance with the terms of the contract. There are, however, a number of legal issues that can arise in the implementation of these obligations.

Seller's Obligations

Delivery

Although the seller's obligation is to "deliver" the goods, where delivery is to be made depends on the contract terms or, in the absence of express terms, the operation of the U.C.C. If no place of delivery is specified, it is the seller's place of business. Where the seller is required or authorized to send the goods to the hospital and the contract does not require the vendor to deliver the goods at a particular destination, then unless otherwise agreed § 2–504 requires that the seller must:

- put the goods in the possession of such a carrier and make such a contract for their transportation as may be reasonable having regard to the nature of the goods and other circumstances of the case; and
- obtain and promptly deliver or tender in due form any document necessary to enable the buyer to obtain possession of the goods or otherwise required by the agreement or by usage of trade; and
- promptly notify the buyer of the shipment.

This means, therefore, that if the hospital wants to include any specific delivery terms, it should expressly include them in the purchase order. For example, if a specific type of carrier is to be used, or if the hospital wants the shipment to be at the seller's expense, the purchase order should make specific reference to these types of special delivery terms.

Definition of Delivery Terms

Certain terms are used in describing delivery obligations of the seller that can have material impact upon the vendor's duties to the hospital. "F.O.B." means "free on board" and when used with the following language can affect the obligations of the seller:

- *"F.O.B. place of shipment"* means that the seller must bear the expense and risk of delivering the goods into the possession of the carriers.
- *"F.O.B. place of destination"* means that the seller must bear the expense and risk of transporting the goods to the place of destination specified in the contract.
- *"F.O.B. vessel, car, or other vehicle"* means the seller must bear the expense and risk of delivering and loading the goods onto the carrier.

Tender of delivery by the seller is made by putting and holding conforming goods at the hospital's disposition. Upon tender of delivery by the seller, the hospital becomes obligated to accept the goods and to pay for them in accordance with the contract terms.

Hospital's Obligations

Right of Inspection

Once the seller has tendered delivery in accordance with the purchase order specifications or the U.C.C. requirements, if the contract requires payment before inspection the hospital is obligated to do so unless nonconformity of goods appears without inspection. Payment before inspection does not, however, constitute acceptance by the hospital. If the contract is silent on the hospital's right to inspect the goods, the facility (with certain limited exceptions such as C.O.D. shipments) has the right to inspect the goods before payment or acceptance. The expense of any such inspection must be borne by the hospital, but it can recover the cost if the goods do not conform and are rejected.

Acceptance

Acceptance of the goods occurs under § 2–606 when the hospital-buyer:

- after a reasonable opportunity to inspect the goods signifies to the seller that the goods are conforming

or that he will take or retain them in spite of their nonconformity; or

- fails to make an effective rejection (subsection (1) of U.C.C. § 2–602), but such acceptance does not occur until the buyer has had a reasonable opportunity to inspect them; or
- does any act inconsistent with the seller's ownership; but if such act is wrongful as against the seller it is an acceptance only if ratified by him.

Further, under § 2–606(2) acceptance of a part of any "commercial unit" constitutes acceptance of the entire unit.

Acceptance of goods has definite legal consequences: (1) The hospital must pay the contract price for goods accepted. (2) The action precludes rejection of the goods (except if there is a reservation of the acceptance). (3) The hospital must notify the seller of any breach within a reasonable time after it is or should have been discovered. (4) The burden is on the hospital to establish any breach with respect to the goods accepted. Thus, it is incumbent upon a buyer, whenever possible, to inspect and in a timely fashion reject nonconforming goods in order to place the hospital in the most advantageous position.

Although acceptance does preclude rejection of the goods in question, the hospital retains the right to seek damages for those that are not in conformance with the contract. For example, if a vendor were to ship nonconforming medical supplies and the hospital, out of necessity, used them, it could sue for damages or assert such damages as a "set-off" in any action by the seller to recover the purchase price. In a set-off, the value of the amount of such supplies used is deducted from the total dollar amount of any legal action arising from the transaction.

Revocation of Acceptance

If the hospital has accepted goods from the seller, under § 2–608 it can revoke the acceptance of a lot or commercial unit whose nonconformity substantially impairs the value if the acceptance was made:

- on the reasonable assumption that its nonconformity would be cured and it has not been seasonally cured; or
- without discovery of such nonconformity if his acceptance was reasonably induced either by the difficulty of discovery before acceptance or by the seller's assurances.

Any such revocation of acceptance must occur within a reasonable time after the hospital discovers or should have discovered the ground for it and before any substantial change in condition of the goods that is not caused by defects (U.C.C. § 2–608(2)).

BREACH OF CONTRACT AND REMEDIES

Hospital's Rejection

If the goods or the seller's tender of delivery fails in any respect to conform to the purchase contract, the hospital may (1) reject the whole, (2) accept the whole, or (3) accept any commercial unit or units and reject the rest (U.C.C. § 2–601). To determine what constitutes a "commercial unit" for partial acceptance, § 2–105(b) states:

> "Commercial unit" means such a unit of goods as by commercial usage is a single whole for purposes of sale and division of which materially impairs its character or value on the market or in use. A commercial unit may be a single article (as a machine) or a set of articles (as a suite of furniture or an assortment of sizes) or a quantity (as a bale, gross or carload) or another unit treated in use or in the relevant market as a single whole.

If the hospital intends to reject the goods tendered by the seller, the rejection must be within a reasonable time after delivery or tender and the hospital must notify the vendor of the rejection. The hospital has continuing obligations after a rightful rejection; specifically, it must not exercise ownership rights over the rejected goods and should hold them with reasonable care at the seller's disposition for a time sufficient to permit the vendor to remove the rejected goods (§ 2–602).

Hospital's Obligations

Since a hospital is a "merchant" for purposes of the U.C.C., when it rightfully rejects goods it is under a duty to follow reasonable instructions from the seller with respect to the items and, in the absence of such instructions, to make reasonable efforts to sell the goods for the vendor's account if they are perishable or threaten to decline in value rapidly.

The hospital is entitled to be indemnified for any expenses incurred on behalf of the seller, and a reasonable commission if it sells the items on the vendor's behalf. In any event, the hospital is held to a good-faith standard only in caring for the goods after a rightful rejection, and its resell obligations apply only if the seller does not have an agent or place of business in the hospital's market (§ 2–603(1) and (3)).

Reasons for Rejection

In general, a hospital is not required to state in detail the reasons when giving a notice of rejection. Under § 2–605, however, there are two circumstances when it must state the particular defect that justifies rejection:

- where the seller could have cured it if stated seasonally; or
- between merchants when the seller has after rejection made a request in writing for a full and final written statement of all defects on which the buyer proposes to rely.

The explanatory comments associated with this section of the U.C.C. describe the reason for this requirement of particularity in the statement of the alleged defect:

> 1. The present section rests upon a policy of permitting the buyer to give a quick and informal notice of defects in a tender without penalizing him for omissions in his statement, while at the same time protecting a seller who is reasonably misled by the buyer's failure to state curable defects.

> 2. Where the defect in a tender is one which could have been cured by the seller, a buyer who merely rejects the delivery without stating his objections to it is probably acting in commercial bad faith and seeking to get out of a deal which has become unprofitable. Subsection (1)(a), following the general policy of this Article which looks to preserving the deal wherever possible, therefore insists that the seller's right to correct his tender in such circumstance be protected.

Actions Anticipatory of Repudiation

Before the time the seller is obligated to perform under the contract, the vendor may repudiate its obligations to the buyer. In such a case, § 2–610 provides that a hospital can wait a commercially reasonable time for the seller to perform or proceed to undertake other remedies provided for in the U.C.C. (and discussed later). In either event the hospital can suspend its performance under the purchase contract.

If a hospital has reasonable grounds to be insecure about the ability of the seller to perform its obligations, under § 2–609 it can in writing demand adequate assurance of due performance. If the vendor does not provide adequate assurance of due performance within 30 days of such a demand, the hospital can treat the failure as a repudiation of the contract.

Failure of Presupposed Conditions

Under § 2–615 there are instances when the seller's performance will be excused because it has been made impractical by the occurrence of a contingency, the nonoccurrence of which was a basic assumption on which the contract was made, or by compliance in good faith with any applicable foreign or domestic governmental regulation or order. The explanatory comment on this section clearly indicates that this excuse of performance is limited to unforeseen supervening circumstances that were not contemplated when the contract was written and is not intended to cover increased costs or market fluctuations:

> . . . for that is exactly the type of business risk which business contracts made at fixed prices are intended to cover. But a severe shortage of raw materials or of supplies due to a contingency such as war, embargo, local crop failure, unforeseen shutdown of major sources of supply or the like, which either causes a marked increase in cost or altogether prevents the seller from securing supplies necessary to his performance, is within the contemplation of this section.

If a seller relies upon this excuse from performance, timely notification must be given to the hospital, and if the ability to perform is impaired only partially, the vendor must allocate production and deliveries among its customers.

Where it receives such a notice under § 2–616, if the proposed lack of performance substantially impairs the value of the contract, the hospital can:

(1) terminate and thereby discharge any unexecuted portion of the contract; or

(2) modify the contract by agreeing to take its available quota in substitution.

Cure by Seller

If the tender or delivery is rejected because of nonconformity and the time for the seller's performance has not yet expired, § 2–508 gives the vendor the right to notify the hospital of its intention to cure the nonconformity and proceed to make a conforming delivery within the time specified for performance in the contract. If the hospital has rejected as nonconforming a delivery that the seller had reasonable grounds to believe was acceptable, the vendor can have additional reasonable time to substitute a conforming tender if it gives timely notice.

Hospital's Remedies for Seller's Breach

If it has accepted the seller's tender, § 2–607 provides that a hospital must, within a reasonable time after it discovers or should have discovered any breach, notify the seller or be barred from seeking any remedy. Thus, for a hospital to avail itself of any of the remedies listed, it must make a timely rejection or, if the goods have been accepted, a timely notice of the breach.

U.C.C. § 2–711 provides that where the seller fails to make delivery or repudiates the agreement or the hospital rightfully rejects or justifiably revokes acceptance, the hospital has the right to cancel the contract and recover as much of the price as it has paid and also can seek additional remedies:

(1) the buyer can "cover" by purchasing goods in substitution for those due from the seller and recover as damages the difference between the cost of the cover and the contract price together with incidental or consequential damages (less expenses saved in consequence of the seller's breach) (U.C.C. § 2–712); or

(2) the buyer can recover as damages the difference between the market price at the time the buyer learned of the breach and the contract price, together with incidental and consequential damages (less expenses saved in consequence of the seller's breach) (U.C.C. § 2–713).

In certain instances, the hospital also may have the right to proceed against the seller to obtain the actual goods in question if the vendor has failed to make delivery or repudiates its obligations under the purchase contract (§ 2–502, § 2–716).

Where there has been a breach of contract by the seller, the U.C.C. permits the hospital to deduct all or any part of its damages resulting from the breach from any part of the price still due. For this provision to apply (§ 2–717) the breach must involve the same contract as the price in question is to be paid, and the hospital must notify the seller of its intention to deduct the damages in question.

Where the hospital has paid a part of the price or incurred expenses for inspection, receipt, transportation, care, and custody of the goods, if it has made a rightful rejection or justifiable revocation of acceptance it has a security interest in the items for all such payments. If the hospital offers to restore the goods to the seller upon such payments and the vendor refuses, the hospital also has the right to sell the goods. The proceeds from such a sale must be given to the seller after the hospital has deducted the amount it previously paid.

The U.C.C. also specifies remedies that are available in the event of litigation, but for a hospital to avail itself of these remedies the law of the state in which it is located will govern the filing of the action.

Liquidated Damages

There are instances when parties may seek to stipulate at the time of contract formation what the damages will be in the event of a breach. U.C.C. § 2–718 recognizes this principle of predetermined damages but only if the amount is reasonable in light of the anticipated or actual harm caused by the breach, the difficulties of proof of loss, and the inconvenience or non-feasibility of otherwise obtaining an adequate remedy. An unreasonably large liquidated damages provision will be considered void because it serves as a penalty rather than an attempt to fix a reasonable level of damages.

OTHER CONSIDERATIONS

Legal Role of the Material Manager

In addition to understanding the basics of contracting for goods, a material manager must be cognizant of the legal relationship with the hospital. This section presents general guidelines for a material manager functioning in a purchasing capacity on behalf of a hospital.

An essential element to any successful purchasing program is to ascertain the authority given to the material manager, specifically: (1) What is the authorization and approval process for contracts? (2) What are the limits on the material manager's authority to enter into contracts? (3) Whom should the material manager report to for authorization above the specified limits? The material manager also should determine what factors might impose additional restrictions on purchasing authority such as competitive bidding requirements imposed by law, bond documents, grants, or governmental financing programs.

Once the limits of the material manager's authority are known, those limits should not be exceeded. If a purchasing agent exceeds the authority granted by the hospital, the institution may have a right to seek damages against that individual for actions outside the scope of authority.

When representing the hospital in contractual negotiations with suppliers, the material manager should make known to the supplier that all agreements are being made on behalf of the institution. Suppliers have a right to know the entity with which they are contracting, and a vendor who is not told that the material manager is acting as an agent for the hospital may have a right to seek enforcement of the contract against that manager personally. Thus, in all correspondence and in all purchase orders and other contracts, the material manager's position and relationship to the hospital should be identified.

Conflicts of Interest

When entering into contractual relationship on behalf of the hospital, the material manager is acting in a fiduciary capacity. This means that the manager has a position of trust that requires the individual to act in the best interests of the hospital. Accordingly, the material manager must scrupulously avoid situations where there may be divided or competing loyalties that cause purchasing decisions to be based on matters that may not be in the best interests of the hospital.

The most fundamental type of conflict of interest in the purchasing context arises when the material manager is entering into an agreement with a supplier in which the manager has a personal interest. Regardless of how fair the transaction is to the hospital, this gives the appearance of impropriety because of the material manager's personal interest in the supplier. If, in addition, the transaction is not fair to the hospital, then the material manager may be in breach of fiduciary obligations.

Other conflicts of interest may arise under varying circumstances and to varying degrees. For example, a relative of the material manager may have an ownership interest in a supplier that might influence the manager to acquire goods or services from that vendor. Or a supplier offers gifts or other inducements to the material manager.

There are several steps that can be taken to protect the material manager and other hospital employees from allegations of breach of fiduciary duty because of improper purchasing arrangements. The hospital should adopt policies:

1. prohibiting suppliers from offering and hospital employees from accepting gifts or other inducements

2. prohibiting employees from participating in contractual arrangements with any suppliers in which they or a relative have a financial interest; this does not mean that the hospital cannot contract with any such supplier, only that an employee having a direct or indirect personal interest in the vendor cannot participate in arranging such an agreement
3. requiring employees involved in purchasing to protectively disclose potential conflicts of interest and to give notice whenever a potential or actual conflict arises.

A written policy on procurement practices will help to ensure that situations in which a potential conflict of interest may arise are brought to the attention of the proper hospital authorities. Any such policy also should be coordinated with other conflict-of-interest policies governing the hospital's board of trustees, administrator, etc. Some areas of disclosure that should be considered in such a policy are the following:

• any positions or financial interests held in any concern from which the hospital purchases goods or services
• any positions or financial interests held in any concern that is in competition with the hospital
• any governing body memberships or managerial or consultative relations with any outside concern that does business with or competes with the hospital
• any gifts, excessive entertainment, or funds received from any outside concern that either provides goods or services to the hospital, seeks to do so, or does business with or is in competition with the hospital
• any disclosure or use of information relating to the hospital for the personal profit of the employee or to the advantage of any business entity in which the employee holds a position or has a financial interest
• any other matter in which the employee's ability to act in the best interest of the hospi-

tal may be compromised by a competing outside interest.

In the event that a conflict of interest occurs, the written policy also should address the specific actions to be taken. Specific policies that should be considered include the following:

• to whom the employee should report the conflict of interest
• whether the employee will be permitted to participate in any transactions on behalf of the hospital in which the person has a conflict of interest
• what the role of an employee should be in an instance where such individual has a conflict of interest
• who should have authority to act on behalf of an employee who has a conflict of interest.

By adopting policies governing these issues, a material manager can ensure not only that the hospital's contractual relationships are entered into in a manner that is in the facility's best interests but also that the persons making purchases on its behalf are cognizant of and insulated from potential conflicts of interest.

KEY POINTS

To implement an effective hospital purchasing plan that incorporates due regard for the legal implications of contractual relationships, the critical first step is to review the contracts currently in use. In most instances this will be the purchase order form, and the hospital should incorporate into its form the U.C.C. provisions that favor its purchases.

Once a well-drafted purchase order has been adopted, the hospital should announce procedures to manage purchasing in accordance with the provisions of the U.C.C., specifically:

• Communications from sellers should be reviewed to determine whether there are contract formation problems because of competing forms.

- Procedures should be adopted for the timely inspection and, when necessary, rejection of nonconforming goods.

- Procedures should be adopted to preserve the hospital's legal right in the event of a breach of the purchase contract by the seller.

Since the U.C.C. is adopted at the state level, the codification for the state in which the hospital is located should be copied and used as a reference for the development and maintenance of a program that protects the hospital's legal rights when entering into purchasing contracts.

Finally, the hospital should adopt policies defining the authority of persons making purchases on its behalf and defining how conflict-of-interest problems will be resolved.

NOTES

1. BLACK's LAW DICTIONARY, 394 (4th ed. 1968).

2. J. CALAMARI & J. PERILLO, CONTRACTS, § 15 (1970).

3. *Air Prods. & Chem., Inc. v. Fairbanks, Morse, Inc.*, 58 Wis. 2d 193, 106 N.W. 2d 414 (1973).

4. *Idaho Pipe & Steel Co. v. Cal-Cut Pipe & Supply, Inc.*, 98 Idaho 495, 567 P.2d 1246 (1977).

5. *Lea Tai Textile Co. v. Manning Fabrics, Inc.*, 411 F. Supp. 1404 (S.D.N.Y. 1975).

6. *Ebasco Serv., Inc. v. Pennsylvania Power & Light Co.*, 402 F. Supp. 421 (E.D. Pa. 1975).

7. *Gaynor-Stafford Indus., Inc. v. Mafco Textured Fibers*, 52 A.D.2d 481, 384 N.Y.S.2d 788 (1976).

8. *Marlene Indus. Corp. v. Carnac Textiles, Inc.*, 45 N.Y.2d 327, 408 N.Y.S.2d 410 (1978).

9. *Valmont Indus., Inc. v. Mitsui & Co. (U.S.A.), Inc.*, 419 F.Supp. 1238 (D.Neb. 1976).

10. *N & D Fashions, Inc. v. DHJ Indus., Inc.*, 548 F.2d 722 (8th Cir. 1976).

11. *S. Kornblum Metals Co. v. Intsel Corp.*, 38 N.Y.2d 376, 379 N.Y.S.2nd 826 (1976).

12. *Gaynor-Stafford Indus., Inc. v. Mafco Textures Fibers*, 52 A.D.2d 481, 384 N.Y.S.2d 788 (1976).

13. *Trailmobile Div. of Pullman, Inc. v. Jones*, 118 Ga. App. 472, 164 S.E.2d 346 (1968).

14. 297 F.2d 497 (1st Cir. 1962).

15. J. WHITE & R. SUMMERS, UNIFORM COMMERCIAL CODE, at 28–32 (2d ed. 1979).

16. *C. Itoh v. Jordan Int'l Co.*, 552 F.2d 1228 (7th Cir. 1977).

17. Ibid., 1236.

18. WHITE & SUMMERS, at 38.

Appendix 10–A

General Terms and Conditions on Purchase Order*

Exhibit 10–A1 A Sample Purchase Order

Name of Hospital-Vendee _____

Purchase Order No. _____

To

[   ]

(Vendor Name
and Address)

[   ]

Important
This Purchase Order number must appear on
all correspondence, invoices, packing slips,
shipping papers, and packaging.

Ship to:

[   ]   (Please mail   Date _____
                                          3 copies of
(Receiving Dept.   Invoice)   Invoice To:
of Vendee)   [   ]

[   ]   (Accounts Payable
                                                          of Vendee)

                                                          [   ]

Ship Via:	F.O.B.:	Payment Terms:	Delivery Required:

Dept:	Account No:	Notify:	Requisition No:

Furnish The Following Upon And Subject To All Conditions And Instructions Stated On Reverse Side.

Quantity	Description	Buyer Code	Price	Total

This order is not binding until accepted.

This order, including the terms and conditions on the face and reverse side hereof, contains the complete and final agreement between Buyer and Seller and no other agreement in any way modifying any of said terms and conditions will be binding upon Buyer unless made in writing and signed by Buyer's authorized representative.

Hospital/Vendee

By _____

Purchase Order is accepted (*Name of vendor*), by _____

*Reprinted from *Hospital Materiel Management Quarterly*, vol. 2, no. 3, February 1981, pp. 11–16, published by Aspen Systems Corporation, © 1981.

11. Improving Negotiating Skills

WILLIAM L. SCHEYER

Discussions about negotiation tend to focus on situations involving the working out of business contracts. While they certainly are negotiating situations, they are not the only ones. Everyone negotiates daily on issues such as how the family will spend time together, obtaining coverage for an undesirable work shift, or lowering the contract price of an important supply item. How can material and purchasing managers go about systematically improving their effectiveness in negotiation?

Attempts to improve any acquired skill involve two essential elements: planning and practice.

PLANNING

It is easy to get caught up in the crush of daily affairs and fail to allow sufficient time for planning. That is a sure-fire way of reducing effectiveness in any activity, but particularly in negotiation. However, it does take time to do proper planning. Therefore, a wise approach is to identify issues or items directly related to managers' primary operating objectives or, in the case of purchasing, items that have the greatest dollar impact, and concentrate their efforts on them.

An effective strategy might be for the material manager to handle key negotiations personally, delegate others to the director of purchasing, some others to specific buyers, and some to related department heads such as the pharmacy or stores, processing, and distribution (SPD). The material manager then can provide overall coordination of the total effort without having to conduct all negotiations personally. It really does not matter how the plan is organized just as long as there is a well-thought-out plan to follow.

Identify Objectives

Before managers can increase the frequency with which they achieve objectives, they must have a clear understanding of what they are. For example, it is not sufficient to seek "a better price" for IV solutions; it is necessary to decide what price the hospital will be willing to pay as well as what other items are needed. These might include price protection, local warehousing, frequent delivery, and so on. Managers also should identify for themselves how important each of these items is to their plan. In addition, they should determine what they have to offer in return.

Identify the Other Party's Objectives

It also is important to determine the other party's objectives. This usually is more difficult to do. Obviously, the other's primary objective is to obtain all of the hospital's business at the vendor's most favorable price. However, there usually are additional elements that are important to the representative and to current circumstances in the seller's company. Having some idea of what these are can be helpful in setting up a strategy.

The best way to determine these is to establish a positive and open relationship with the other party well in advance of the time of formal negotiation. Additional sources of this information are other managers who have dealt with the vendor, company documents such as annual reports, and general information from newspapers, trade journals, and so on. The idea is to establish a clear picture of the "total event" in establishing a consistent and effective strategy.

Plan Strategy

The first decision involves whether to plan to adopt a "win-lose" or a "win-win" approach. In general, the latter approach provides the best long-term results. When both sides can come away feeling that their key objectives have been met, and that neither has been taken advantage of, the stage is set for a mutually beneficial relationship. However, it is vital to be able to recognize a situation in which the other party is stating a "win-win" philosophy while trying to take the hospital to the cleaners. If this should occur, the manager will have to decide whether to adopt a "win-lose" approach or simply not to do business with that party.

Next, the managers should work out the details of how to conduct the actual negotiation sessions. This includes when and where meetings will take place, whether to meet one-on-one or to use a team approach, and so on. The managers also must decide how to organize the points to be discussed and what items of lesser importance to their overall objectives they will be willing to concede, if necessary, for those of higher importance.

Numerous books have been written on this subject. It will be helpful, in developing strategies, to read some of them and select the suggestions most relevant to one's individual style and circumstances. The following list of steps, though certainly not all-inclusive, may serve as a starter for managers. They should:

- establish a sense of their own power and legitimacy—in other words, believe that they have something that the other side wants and that they have every right to negotiate assertively
- make the other persons feel important and they will be more likely to respond to the hospital's needs
- establish a positive relationship in which each side invests time and energy
- not feel it necessary to control the transaction—let the other person help meet their objectives

- offer multiple alternatives, keep trying out options until points of agreement are discovered
- be persistent
- not rush or allow themselves to be rushed
- always try to meet the other person's needs but make sure that the hospital's needs are being met, as well
- take notes and follow up meetings with a letter of agreement.

PRACTICE

Practice comes in three forms. First is rehearsal. For major negotiations, managers should plan their strategy in detail, then rehearse key elements either alone or with a team member. Practicing behavior in a nonthreatening or reduced stress environment makes it easier to carry out the conduct successfully under increased pressure. For extremely important negotiations, this step is definitely worthwhile.

The second form of practice comes through actual experience. The more often managers do something, the better they will become. This is particularly true if they take the time to analyze their performance, build upon their strengths, and take steps to correct their weaknesses.

Finally, practice comes from seeking out new information and incorporating it into their own performance. This can come from finding a particularly effective negotiator and observing such an individual in action. It also can come from reading some of the many books on the subject, selecting the ideas that work, and building them into their behavioral repertoire. (See Suggested Readings at the end of this chapter for some of the books about negotiation.)

KEY POINTS

It sometimes is difficult to admit, even to oneself, that negotiating skill can stand improvement. However, this is true for even the most experienced manager. The ineffective negotiator is one who becomes locked into a set style, who cannot remain open to new options, and who cannot break out of this pattern of inflexibility.

Negotiation is a dynamic activity. Each event is unique as it brings together a new combination of people and circumstances. The keys to effective negotiation are to:

- allow sufficient time to plan for and carry out important negotiations

- develop a detailed plan
- rehearse the key elements
- adjust performance according to what works.

By adopting these steps, managers should be able to increase the effectiveness of their negotiations.

SUGGESTED READINGS

Charell, Ralph. 1978. *How to get the upper hand*. New York: Stein and Day.

Cohen, Herb. 1980. *You can negotiate anything*. Secaucus, N.J.: L. Stuart.

DeVille, Jard. 1979. *Nice guys finish first*. New York: William Morrow & Co.

Fensterheim, Herbert, and Jean Baer. 1975. *Don't say yes when you want to say no*. New York: David McKay Co., Inc.

Fisher, Roger, and William Ury. 1981. *Getting to yes*. Boston: Houghton Mifflin.

Levin, Edward. 1980. *Levin's laws: Tactics for winning without intimidation*. New York: M. Evans.

Nierenberg, Gerard I. 1968. *The art of negotiating: Psychological strategies for gaining advantageous bargains*. New York: Hawthorn Books.

Richardson, Jerry, and Joel Margulis. 1981. *The magic of rapport: The business of negotiation*. New York: Avon Books.

Warschaw, Tessa Albert. 1980. *Winning by negotiation*. New York: McGraw-Hill.

Winkler, Jon. 1984. *Bargaining for results*. New York: Facts on File Publications.

12. Selecting Optimal Products

JOEL J. NOBEL AND ROBERT MOSENKIS

Selecting and purchasing products of optimal quality and cost-effectiveness to fulfill specific patient care or institutional objectives from a myriad of vendor offerings can be a difficult challenge. It can be confusing, frustrating, and time consuming. This process is further confused by the frequent assumptions that there is a single best answer, that there is an inherent conflict between quality and cost, and that the use of the "highest" quality product provides the best patient care. In fact, there frequently is more than one "right" answer, good (rather than highest) quality products often have lower true costs, and the primary determinant of quality of patient care is far more often human skills than products used. What, then, is optimal quality?

It is defined, for purposes here, as the mix of product attributes that achieves the most reasonable balance between safety, performance, efficacy, reliability, and cost effectiveness in fulfilling the specific intended clinical purposes over the prescribed time or frequency of use. Under this definition, quality is understood in a relationship to specific need as well as its cost effectiveness in meeting that need. It is not an abstract concept of perfection that exceeds mission requirements, nor does it exist in some isolated, pristine state unrelated to cost.

Selecting a product for which the material manager has primary responsibility for choice is relatively simple. It merely requires gathering all relevant significant information and using good judgment. The primary pitfall is being sure that the end-users' requirements are well understood and kept in mind during the decision-making process.

Shared decision making is a far greater challenge in which the role of the material manager will vary in different institutions, at different times, and for different types of products. In the ultimate analysis, the decision-making process is facilitated by having good information; conflicts about decisions are best resolved by sharing and accepting information.

OBSTACLES TO RATIONAL CHOICE

There are many obstacles to rational choice. Some are self-imposed and others are difficult to control. What are these obstacles and how can they be overcome?

Confusion sometimes starts with failure to understand clearly the specific diagnostic, therapeutic, or patient-support objectives and needs. Clear, direct, and frequent communication with product users, and taking the time to thoroughly understand their needs through visits to their working environment, is obligatory continuing education for the material manager.

Sometimes the gap in logical selection lies in the thinking process of the individuals or departments expressing need for a product. They may define their needs in terms of a specific type or even brand and model, instead of in a manner that allows the material manager to help optimize product quality and cost effectiveness. While many clinical and support staff members, through education, experience, and research, may make specific requests that already are optimized for their needs and even those of the institution, others may express suboptimal or even poor choices for many reasons.

They may have a poorly conceived concept of need or have taken far too narrow a view of their objectives. They may simply be unfamiliar with alternative products and suppliers. They may be compulsive fad or trend followers seeking change for the sake of newness or in response to the latest advertisement or convention exhibit. They may be afflicted with fear of legal consequences because a sales representative has convinced them that a currently used product is associated with excessive risks, or believe that failure to adopt a new product or concept denotes technical backwardness and failure to meet a new standard of care or competition.

When fear of liability is raised by sales representatives (or even attorneys) as the primary reason for adopting a new technology, it suggests the offering of a product that is scientifically or clinically unproved; therefore, it should not be purchased. Good technology stands exclusively on its technical and clinical merits.

When economic gain for the hospital or department is cited by a sales representative as the primary reason for adopting a new technology, it raises two questions. First, is the probability of financial gain real, subject to rational expense and revenue analysis by a disinterested party (e.g., a reimbursement specialist or cost analyst)? Second, and more important, regardless of a positive cost and revenue study, is use of the technology truly in the best interest of patients? If the answer to both questions is not unequivocally yes, the issue of relative quality between competing products is moot.

When asked to purchase a specific product that is not already in routine use in the institution, the material manager should determine whether there are competitive items and whether the requester is aware of other sources and the relative benefits of competing goods. Offers by the material manager to obtain additional information to help the requester make the best decision are rarely turned down, especially if the offers are posed in terms of best products, rather than best prices. Having the requester agree on two or three good products then permits the material manager to negotiate with vendors for best prices.

Disagreement about product selection may arise from hidden agendas as well as legitimately different views. Hidden agendas usually arise from very human characteristics, such as power struggles and economic or psychological competition between clinical and administrative personnel, among departments, and among disciplines with different perspectives, needs, and experience (e.g., physicians vs. biomedical engineers, nurses vs. physicians, surgeons vs. anesthesiologists). While it usually is helpful to perceive the hidden agendas, it is not always necessary to confront them directly to make the best choice of products. It usually is most constructive to treat all differences in views and stated needs as legitimate, even when they are not, and springing from real differences in experience, need, or information available to the various parties.

This type of conflict usually is resolved most easily by first agreeing on a broad goal because it pursues an objective that is clearly recognized as desirable. (For example, the goal might be standardization of monitoring equipment throughout the hospital, which will result in less costly training and maintenance, possible cost savings in a larger purchase, and common cables and connections to simplify and speed patient care during transfers between operating room, recovery room, and critical care units.) Getting agreement to even a qualified common goal, such as "common monitoring equipment *if* an excellent vendor can really supply good equipment which meets *all* of *our* needs" (as opposed to "yours" and "mine") is a good start. Acceptance of such a broad, even qualified, goal then enables the material manager, working with other key support staff (e.g., the clinical engineer), to gather, organize, and present all pertinent information to the other decision makers for their review.

Legitimate differences of opinion about products and product selection criteria, even with access to common data, may persist because of differences in experience, education, training, and professional responsibilities. For example, in selecting an electrosurgical unit, a clinical engineer is more likely to give greater weight to safety than is a surgeon. The latter, while concerned about safety, may give a greater emphasis to power output or ease of use. The ultimate factor that usually resolves such differences of opinion should not be superior political power or weight of authority but comprehensive, objective data and rational analysis that can be accepted comfortably by all participants in the decision-making process (admittedly at the risk of appearing irrational and foolish if they reject such information).

OVERCOMING THE OBSTACLES

Overcoming the obstacles to decision making about product selection is growing easier in some respects and harder in others. Proliferation of products, their trend toward sameness, and competition make the job more difficult. The improving quality and availability of reliable information make it easier. In a very real sense, assessing quality, after the data-gathering phase, is primarily a matter of examining the quality and reliability of data about products and organizing them as useful information to support decision making. Part of the process of evaluating such data is understanding their limitations and maintaining a high level of consciousness about how people perceive or distort facts.

The broad issues are straightforward. Invalid information derives from ignorance, misinterpretation, self-delusion, unbalanced selectivity, or outright distortion and deception. Neither vendors nor hospitals are immune to any of these faults, although institutions more often suffer from ignorance and tunnel vision and vendors more often are guilty of self-delusion and unbalanced self-interest than is either party guilty of conscious dishonesty or deception.

The Role of Intuition and Experience

Despite the struggle for objectivity in gathering and assimilating data, and despite increasingly sophisticated analytical tools, intuition and experience are invaluable. While intuition and experience sometimes serve in lieu of data (sometimes, but not always a dangerous posture), they are especially useful when brought to bear on well-organized and comprehensive data. The material manager's experience, intuition, and judgment and that of the product users are vital.

When new information is inconsistent with experience, and a decision or conclusion is imminent that is counterintuitive, the information is more likely wrong than is intuition. While it is possible to make the right decision for the wrong reasons, or the right decision on an intuitive basis, or the right decision with a limited amount of information, the probability that it will be the best one obviously is much improved if the information is drawn from a broad base of experienced and objective sources.

Questions That Must Be Answered

A number of questions must be answered to assess product quality objectively:

1. What is needed and why? What is its function? What alternative technology also fulfills the objective (e.g., single vs. multichannel ECG machines)?
2. Who produces and sells the acceptable alternatives?
3. What are the characteristics of the competing products and which ones will meet the general requirements (i.e., what are the general characteristics of the competitors' models and brands under consideration, and which ones can be excluded quickly because their attributes do not match user needs)? While manufacturers' literature is the obvious and most common source, side-by-side comparison of product characteristics based on vendors' literature usually is limited by inconsistencies in terminology, measurement methods, and descriptions.
4. What has been the experience of other users of these products (e.g., delivery, safety, reliability, maintainability, accuracy, service response)?
5. Is unbiased information based on independent, objective, third-party testing of the products available?

The answers to the first question have been discussed. Standard hospital purchasing directories or data bases, if kept up to date by their publishers and replaced frequently, will quickly provide the answer to the second question. With regard to question 3, some purchasing directories provide only very general product characteristics and the information itself is of highly variable quality and accuracy.

It usually is necessary to develop a detailed chart to compare product characteristics. Unfortunately, it is difficult for individuals who lack a strong, relevant technical background to construct such tables because considerable experience and judgment are needed to know which characteristics are vital in making valid comparisons. Size and weight and price are obvious, but accuracy, resolution, noice rejection, and other technical characteristics, often expressed differently by various vendors, are another matter and often are at the heart of decision making about the quality of technical products. The validity of the information is directly proportional to the experience of the information specialist and the amount of time spent in gathering and organizing the data.

Recently introduced systematic product comparisons for capital equipment and some specialized disposable products do provide reliable up-to-date information, are protected against inappropriate influence by device and supply manufacturers and distributors, and deal effectively with the many variations of how manufacturers describe their products (see Exhibit 12–1). Hundreds of comparisons are available covering thousands of products. They save considerable time in gathering data. In addition, custom comparisons for items not yet incorporated in these information services are available as part of the membership benefits accorded to participating institutions.

While user experience often is regarded as the ultimate means of determining product quality, utility, and cost-effectiveness, it has a number of significant practical limitations:

1. Who has the experience? Customer lists supplied by vendors may be selective, emphasizing users with positive views of the product.

2. How many users constitute a reasonable sample?
3. How long is their experience?
4. Are they typical users?
5. Are there hidden commercial interests?
6. What questions should be asked?
7. Will other users respond honestly?

On the other hand, relying exclusively on problem reporting systems for assessing user experience obviously emphasizes negative experiences that, while unbalanced (after all, products with problems generally have positive attributes as well), are essential pointers to critical safety and reliability issues. A review of problem reporting systems' data banks for pertinent information is essential to wise product selection. Clearly, however, user experience has limitations. It rarely encompasses more than a limited number of competing products in any given institution. Also, given equal quality, the brand in widest use is likely to have the most reported problems. Hospitals rarely set up structured data-gathering systems to capture such experience in a consistent manner.

Pooled user data for many institutions are becoming increasingly available but currently are limited largely to capital equipment. The Emergency Care Research Institute (ECRI) Hazard Reporting and User Experience Network, developed with grant funding, is the most extensive system, with more than 30,000 reports from the government and the private sector. It is a systematically organized body of knowledge developed to facilitate computer searching. It encompasses extensive reports from the medical, nursing, hospital, engineering and legal literature, problems reports from ECRI's international problem reporting network, the U.S. Food and Drug Administration's Device Experience Network, and data from questionnaires and interviews with clinical product users. It uses a standardized nomenclature and coding system to index all reports.

Some of these reports are selected and provided in specialized ECRI publications. Customized data base searches also are available to

Exhibit 12–1 Emergency Care Research Institute (ECRI) Product Research and Selection Systems

Questions	References
*What is it called? *Who makes it? *Who sells it? *Where do we contact the vendor?	*Health Devices Sourcebook* (issued annually with free custom updates at any time) *ECRI/McGraw-Hill Hospital Product Comparison System* (issued monthly) *ECRI/McGraw-Hill Clinical Laboratory Product Comparison System* (issued monthly) *ECRI/McGraw-Hill Diagnostic Imaging and Radiology Product Comparison System* (issued monthly)
*How do they work? *What are the specifications of these products? *How do product characteristics and specifications compare among available brands and models?	*Health Devices* (issued monthly) *ECRI/McGraw-Hill Hospital Product Comparison System* *ECRI/McGraw-Hill Clinical Laboratory Product Comparison System* *ECRI/McGraw-Hill Diagnostic Imaging and Radiology Product Comparison System*
*What risks and reported problems and recalls are associated with the general class of products and with specific models?	*Health Devices Alerts* (issued biweekly) and *Action Items* (issued weekly)
*What broad factors impact our decision to buy a newly emergent technology (e.g., economic, legal, ethical, regulatory, staffing)? *Which is the best brand and model to meet our needs and why, based on objective tests and evaluations?	*Issues in Health Care Technology* (issued bimonthly) *Journal of Health Care Technology: Assessment, Planning, and Value Analysis* (issued quarterly) *Health Devices* *Health Devices* telephone consultation services (free to members)
*How do we meet the challenge of planning, selecting, and assimilating a major new technology?	*All previous references *Health Devices* telephone consultation services *ECRI consulting group and field assistance
*How do we resolve significant disagreement about which product or system to acquire?	*All previous references *Health Devices* telephone consultation services *ECRI consulting group and field assistance
*What shall we do about an existing product that we believe may be defective or dangerous? *What shall we do if a device appears associated with injury to patient or staff?	*Advise ECRI's Hazard Reporting and User Experience Network (215) 825-6000 *Preserve and sequester the equipment and all associated disposables *Notify ECRI's Accident Investigation Group (215) 825-6000

member hospitals; ultimately, the entire system will be available via computer network.

Formal testing of performance, reliability, safety, and clinical effectiveness of products is undertaken, of course, to a greater or lesser degree by manufacturers but usually is limited to their own products. It therefore fails to provide the comparative data about a class of products necessary for decision making by hospitals. While premarket testing of some products may be required by the FDA, questioning the objectivity or validity of such tests by manufacturers has become a minor industry for government, prudent users, and consumer activists. These types of data rarely can contribute to the purchasing decision because they are hard to obtain, rarely are organized in a way to help compare competing products, and carry the stigma of self-interest, regardless of their validity.

The only dedicated, systematic, independent medical product testing program in North America was implemented in 1971 by ECRI to provide objective data to support product selection and decision making. ECRI's Health Devices Program has evaluated a wide range of capital equipment and disposable products based on detailed laboratory and clinical testing. It provides ratings of brand-named competing products. To assure objectivity, ECRI and its staff accept no financial support from the medical device industry. However, because of the cost of such intensive testing—typically $40,000 to $60,000 for a class of devices (e.g., disposable syringes, or gloves, or capital equipment such as patient monitoring systems or mobile x-ray machines), the number of classes of products tested is necessarily limited. To date, 140 classes have been tested in great detail.

Where can a material manager get demonstrably reliable, up-to-date, and cost-effective data on clinical products that are organized coherently to support effective decision making when assessing products? Reliable data usually are difficult and costly to produce and organize. High-quality data sources, however, are the essential tools of the competent material manager and are far less expensive than in-house staff assigned to produce similar information because the cost is pooled among thousands of hospitals, and the cost of suboptimal decisions is so high.

REAL VS. APPARENT QUALITY

Product quality must be defined within the general framework of cost, inventory, storage, deployment, disposal or reprocessing, user training, and patient charges, as well as specific clinical needs. Selection of quality cost-effective products obviously is related to the growing cost per case or prospective payment environment.

In this economic environment, purchasing disposable supplies on a cost-per-unit basis, as opposed to a cost-per-use or cost-per-case basis, is sometimes self-defeating. While, at first glance, it may be difficult to distinguish between unit cost and cost per case, there often is a close and adverse connection. It is critical to distinguish between true and apparent costs. Supplies with a high defect rate, for example, may be used in greater quantity, with excessive consumption perceived as a pilferage problem rather than one of quality.

For example, the authors' study of one hospital's purchasing practices for scalp vein needles proved revealing. A relatively high-quality scalp vein needle had long been in use there. The material management department arbitrarily, without consulting users, changed products. It obtained another manufacturer's needle at a unit cost 40 percent lower, obviously believing that needles were needles and a 40 percent saving was highly desirable. Even the most cursory observation of house staff and IV teams, however, would have demonstrated that the less expensive unit was harder to use and needle sharpness was decidedly inferior.

Physicians and IV team members had to make three and four times as many attempts to place needles, causing great pain and tissue damage in both infants and debilitated adults. They also used two to three times the number of scalp vein sets, throwing them away as an act of frustration as well as an effort to preserve sterile technique, when they failed to enter veins successfully. Ignoring the cost of their time and lowered productivity, far more of these needles were used per case than with the superior brand. While the unit cost may have been 40 percent lower, the usage and throwaway rate climbed so rapidly that the actual cost of needles consumed to achieve successful placement increased by more than 50 percent.

In an institution that charged for administration of intravenous fluids but did not charge the patients specifically for the number of scalp vein needles used, this clearly was a losing proposition. Had the patients been charged for each needle used, this increased expense would have been recovered in a cost-reimbursement environment but there still would have been a net loss because of the increased time of placement, the greater investment in inventory, and the higher cost of storage and deployment. In a diagnosis related group (DRG) cost-per-case environment, the hospital would have lost even more from the change. The lesson is clear in this case: Higher quality meant lower true cost.

Purchase price often is not the best index of cost. In a sense, then, the concept of life cycle cost analysis should be applied, in principle if not detail, to single-use items as well as to capital equipment in order to understand true cost. This, in turn, requires an understanding of how a product is used, by whom, and under what conditions.

Understanding true cost is a challenge to analytical thinking. It requires sharing information and perspectives on a continuing basis among all participants, ranging from the purchasing and material management and central supply departments to the clinical users. Communication about quality should not stop with the purchase but only well after the new product has been placed in service.

Because the impact of purchasing decisions is not always obvious to material managers, it is essential that follow-up analyses be undertaken when vendors, models, or types of supplies are changed. While detailed analysis before decision making may be common in some institutions, evaluation of the long-term consequences of those changes is rare.

Selecting the optimal product clearly involves more than simply comparing prices, and purchasers choose between products based on their needs and budgets. Similarly, the material manager must match the hospital's needs for performance, safety, and reliability with cost considerations against the available products.

This chapter has presented methods for gathering such information and has portrayed some pitfalls to objective decision making. Exhibit 12–1 describes a number of information sources. Armed with these techniques and tools, the material manager can provide the hospital with the optimal product with less investment in time and with a far greater level of confidence that the best choice has been made.

13. Product Standardization

Donald B. Rhoad

Individual freedom may be an important influence on many human activities but it has no place in the selection of supplies and equipment in a hospital setting. Indeed, the selection process in any business must be intentional and controlled. The objective of each selection decision must be to obtain the greatest total value for the organization. This value is based upon an objective assessment of specific needs that must be satisfied and an evaluation of items that may meet those needs.

This chapter examines the most effective approach to managing the selection of supplies and equipment in a hospital. Known variously as a product standards committee, product evaluation committee, standardization and evaluation committee, product review committee, and as many other variations as imagination and creativity will allow, the entity is referred to here as a product standards committee.

CURRENT PRACTICES

The truth is that there is a wide variety of standards committees. They are different in every possible way, including:

- philosophy
- size
- composition
- status within the formal organization
- status within the informal organization
- procedure
- scope.

And, of course, some hospitals have no product standards committee at all. Presumably living in the nineteenth century, these institutions apparently prefer haphazard product selection and frequent surprises.

OBJECTIVES OF A STANDARDIZATION PROGRAM

The objectives of an effective product standardization program include maintaining an appropriate measure of control over what items are used in a hospital and seeking optimum values in the interest of cost containment while providing quality health care.

Control

Too much control, of course, can be a negative factor stifling a healthy questioning process. Those questions need to come from all levels of the organization. Questions, ideas, and suggestions may deal with either product or procedure; they may arise from an advertisement seen in a journal, an employee's own work experience, or even just inspiration.

However, there must be a measure of control so that a suggested change follows a logical course during a process of consideration that is balanced and objective. The process must permit an opportunity for a full explanation of the change followed by appropriate questioning by individuals representing such corporate interests as patient care, cost of operations, and institutional liability. Expressed another way, the control must be open enough to encourage new ideas but disciplined enough to subject them to impartial challenge.

Other Values

The standardization process offers several important benefits to the institution over and above control.

Standardization contributes to a common denominator of patient care by discouraging a profusion of different products performing a similar function. This makes for fewer surprises for doctors. Products used and the manner of treatment are more predictable.

A product standards committee can be a staff development director's best friend. Inservice training is simpler when supplies and equipment are standardized, and as a result is likely to be more thorough. With the planned adoption of new products, inservice training can be scheduled in a logical sequence and its importance becomes more apparent. In addition, a sales representative's assistance is more likely to be made available when that person's product has just been approved for hospitalwide use. This can enhance the training process, add credibility to the particular inservice effort, and take some of the teaching burden off staff development personnel.

Efficient use of hospital staff places a premium on the ability to reassign employees, most commonly nurses, from one unit to another as needs change. If orthopedic admissions drop and oncology patients increase, staffing adjustments may have to be made to ensure that the nurses are where the patients are. Standardization of IV administration sets, dressings, or other related products simplifies immeasurably the process of staff transfers.

It should be obvious that product standardization facilitates and streamlines the material management functions of ordering supplies, maintaining inventories, and distributing goods to the various users. Suppliers are more willing to establish and maintain stocks of items for a hospital when the volumes are large. When a product is used throughout an institution, the storeroom supervisor is in a better position to adjust to changes in individual units' demands thanks to the broad base of usage within which shifts in supply allocation can be made. With

regard to distribution, standardization contributes to more efficient par stocking or exchange cart makeup.

Product standardization also is an ally of the purchasing department. Negotiations based upon committed volumes of business should result in lower prices and more reliable delivery performance. Most suppliers respect the hospital management that controls the selection of supplies; doing business with such an institution is attractive because it is more predictable and easier for the vendor itself to manage profitably.

It also is true that when a hospital demonstrates that it can control the selection of its supplies through standardization, each vendor will recognize that this same control enables the institution to award or withdraw business in response to changing price and service values. This contributes significantly to the purchasing department's success in attracting competitive prices and responsive service.

ORGANIZATION

As noted earlier, there are quite a few approaches to product standards committees. In part this results from differing philosophies of management—participative on one hand and directive on the other. Another contributing factor is the role that efficiency plays in a hospital's management style; the use of ad hoc or other standing committees for specific investigations contribute to the more efficient use of the product standards committee's meeting time.

Membership

Some product standards committees are small and rather tightly controlled by material management personnel. While nursing is represented on the committee, the panel normally is dominated by material management when the group is small. Decisions are reached fairly easily and committee actions are implemented efficiently. When controversy arises, it is typically after-the-fact and outside of the committee.

Paradoxically, the standards committee that is small in the interest of control is often on the defensive in its relationship with the users of supplies and equipment—users who have likely had inadequate input into selection decisions.

From the long-term viewpoint, a larger product standards committee providing for more broad-based representation can implement the standardization process more effectively. Such a committee might include the following members:

- purchasing director
- SPD (stores, processing, and distribution) director
- nursing directors
- surgery director
- infection control director
- staff development director
- clinical (biomedical) engineering representative
- medical staff representative
- accounting representative.

Others may be invited for specific discussions.

It should be noted that more than one nursing representative is indicated. The goal in designing a committee of broad membership is to provide for representation from the variety of disciplines likely to be affected by the panel's decisions. Since the decisions deal with goods used in different settings throughout the hospital, there must be variety in the membership representing those areas most frequently affected. It is desirable, for example, to have nursing members and physicians who represent pediatric, oncology, and orthopedic specialties. Their needs may be different, and these differences need to be heard.

Admittedly, the bigger the group, the harder it is to reach a consensus. Yet when each member is genuinely sensitive to the needs of the others, compromises are reached surprisingly easily. When people do not feel threatened and know that their opinions will be considered, they are more willing to listen to others and perhaps gain new perspectives as a result. Furthermore, when a variety of interest areas are involved in the evaluation process, there is less likelihood of disenchantment with the resultant decision for there is less chance for a feeling of disenfranchisement.

Clearly, many dynamics are at work on a broad-based product standards committee. The chairperson, therefore, must be competent at conducting meetings. It is important to draw out pertinent comments to ensure a balanced discussion, yet the chair must also know how to bring that discussion to a close at the right time and how to guide the debate to a consensus.

The purchasing director often serves as chairperson, having developed substantial experience conducting meetings involving groups of varied sizes. In addition, it is convenient because of the heavy purchasing involvement in the standardization process. On the other hand, if another individual clearly is a more competent chair, it is to everyone's benefit to have that person conduct the meetings.

The most effective product standards committees make extensive use of other committees. For detailed information, additional opinions, or evaluation coordination, it can be helpful to draw upon the resources of surgery, linen, safety, procedures, or some other similar standing committee. On the other hand, the chair may choose to appoint an ad hoc committee to deal with a specific task. While the standards committee must make the final decisions, these other standing or ad hoc groups are ideal for gathering information and making recommendations. In essence, total membership can be expanded dramatically without having to convene all these people in one meeting room at one time.

One final important feature of a successful standardization process is top-management support. It is absolutely essential that a product standards committee be given, unequivocally and in writing, lines of authority. If there are exceptions, such as highly specialized equipment, they should be spelled out. A corporate policy document, signed by the chief executive officer, is one of the best mechanisms to show this administration support. It should be circulated, of course, to all hospital management. Further, it should be cited, when necessary, judiciously yet unhesitatingly, in order to establish clearly the credibility of the committee.

OPERATIONS

The product standards committee has been introduced, justified, created, and staffed; now, the discussion changes to how it functions as a key decision-making group in the organization.

Product Referrals

As might be expected, items appear on the committee's agenda because of any one of several different actions. Some are planned and can be anticipated; many are not, however, and are caused by some external influence.

Many supplies are purchased under the terms and conditions of contracts negotiated by the hospital's purchasing department or by a purchasing group with which the hospital is affiliated. The contract expiration dates are established, of course, and provide logical time frames for committee considerations. These should be scheduled in advance; indeed, the committee's annual calendar can begin to take shape with the inclusion, month by month, of commodities whose contracts expire at given times. The normal procedure provides for a product review as soon as details of the new contracts become available. Such contracts rarely run more than three years, and often for only one year.

In the case of noncontract items, the purchasing department may learn of an attractive product from a sales representative, from advertisements or printed articles, or even from other hospitals. In representing a better value than the product currently used, the proposed item may be less expensive, more convenient, safer, more durable, more available, or in some way more attractive to the hospital.

Similarly, a user of the current product may learn of a new product and wish to have it considered by the committee. The apparent attraction can be any of those just mentioned. Progressive hospitals encourage their employees to be alert for "a better idea," and that includes new products.

If the clinical engineering or risk management staff learn of potential problems with a currently used product, consideration of alternate products may be requested. While this does not happen frequently, the product standards committee is an excellent forum for such expressions of concern.

Documentation

Records of meetings are essential. Whether they are ordinary meeting minutes or forms, they provide a written representation of the discussion, information gathered, or action taken. Documentation records must be filed carefully so they are easily accessed at a later date.

Value Analysis

While product evaluation establishes the extent to which a product can do a particular job, value analysis focuses on the function and seeks the most economical and efficient method to perform that function. Well-managed standardization programs use value analysis to look beyond the product to the procedure. For example, instead of conducting only a product evaluation of different brands of IV infusion pumps, the committee may wish to conduct a value analysis to determine what method or methods best accomplish the function of controlling flow during IV therapy.

Value analysis is a more basic and thorough study and, once done, it need not be repeated for the same function for some time unless factors influencing the function should change significantly. Regrettably, this method of assessment still is viewed by many with a measure of mystery and cynicism. When that ignorance is dispelled, value analysis becomes an important tool in a product standards committee's cost-containment efforts.

From time to time, a question may be raised about a product as to whether it would be better to make it or continue buying it. Hospitals sometimes tend to promote self-sufficiency to unreasonable extremes: Is it better to buy sterilized special procedure trays or assemble and sterilize them in the hospital?

A rule of thumb for such make-or-buy issues is that if a vendor is doing the same function for many customers, that company probably can do it at a lower unit cost than one hospital by itself. The emphasis is on the words "same function"; special hospital requirements may make in-house production the best approach. Nevertheless, the tendency to do it in-house should be challenged and the real costs scrutinized, remembering that the hospital's primary raison d'être is to provide health care, not make products.

Product Analysis

When undertaking a product assessment, the committee must ensure that the process includes a number of steps, each of which contributes to an informed and objective final decision. To overlook one or more phases of the review increases the risk of an invalid conclusion and, thus, a waste of time and effort.

First, an informational profile must be developed about the product: usage and cost information, not just overall usage data, and which departments use it. Cost information should include any recent record of price increases. The object is to learn as much as possible about the product currently in use in the hospital, even if the review is to consider its replacement by a different item. To this end, it often is valuable to request a literature search by the hospital's library, by a municipal library, or perhaps by someone in a knowledgeable department such as infection control or risk management. The purchasing department normally is best suited to assemble product knowledge information.

One important but often overlooked aspect of building a profile of a product is its status as a revenue producer. Is it a specific patient charge item and, if so, what is the charge? When was that charge amount last reviewed? On the other hand, the item may be one component factor in a composite patient charge. If that is the case, it is helpful to know how important a factor the product is.

Objectivity in evaluating alternate products is greatly enhanced by the development of a well-written specification. The specification should be prepared to meet the following needs:

1. It should identify criteria that are important in the evaluation of the item. These criteria may be classified as mandatory or desirable. A product that does not satisfy a mandatory criterion should not be considered further. Desirable criteria may be weighted to indicate the user's level of interest.
2. It should include only information that can be shared with potential vendors. Confidential information must not be included.
3. It should identify previously qualified manufacturers and, where appropriate, brand designations.

Utilizing the product specification and other product information such as estimated usage, the purchasing department may request quotations from prospective suppliers. All quotations should be in written form, rather than verbal, for two important reasons: (1) A written quote protects each party from misunderstandings on the part of the other. (2) Such a request gives this step in the product standardization process the significance it deserves.

When quotations are requested, it is advisable to ask for additional material such as descriptive literature, clinical data sheets, and even samples if practical. After all proposals are in, the purchasing department can record the results in a bid summary, or spread sheet, so that the strengths and weaknesses of each quotation may be seen easily.

PRODUCT EVALUATION

As noted earlier, one objective of an effective product standardization program is the seeking of optimum values in the interest of cost containment while providing quality health care. If it is consistent with this objective, the committee will proceed with evaluation of a new product only if there are clear indications that it represents a better value than that available in the product currently in use. That better value may be in the form of a lower price, more convenience in use, greater availability, or better product performance.

The last factor, performance, can lead to a bad product selection decision, however, unless it is always judged within the parameters of how much performance the hospital actually needs. For example, an item that is guaranteed to be sterile is of no special value in an application where sterility is not needed; two gloves instead of one in a tray are of no value if only one glove is used in the procedure.

In the final analysis, the product standards committee must consider all the information available to it, then decide whether or not an evaluation of a new product is warranted. That information will include product knowledge, revenue status, the hospital's product specification, and the bid summary. If a better value is available in a new product, that item should be evaluated.

When it has been decided that a product should be evaluated, a test plan must be prepared. If an item is noncontroversial, the simplest evaluation is quite adequate. Users often view such products as generic items and place little or no significance on the brand or manufacturer. In such a case, sending some samples to a single representative user department for prompt approval normally is sufficient. Indeed, certain product standards committee members may represent user departments and thus may be able to approve the item at the meeting itself.

Frequently, however, a proposed product change requires more extensive evaluation, such as when brand allegiance is significant or there are apparent differences between products. In that situation, product evaluation will serve several key objectives.

First, it will allow those who are trying the product to become familiar with it and possibly develop confidence in it. This often is critical to a successful change of products. For example, nurses should be comfortable with a new brand of dressing before its introduction will be totally successful—they must believe it to be effective, safe, and convenient to use.

The second objective is to prove objectively the suitability of a product. The preferred approach is to have identified the least expensive item that meets the criteria in the product specification, then evaluate it. In this approach, evaluation will simply determine that the product does or does not satisfy the criteria. The single-product evaluation is simple and straightforward; more complex is the multiproduct evaluation, in which two or more brands are analyzed to determine which one is preferred. Implicit in this approach is the fact that the institution's real needs are not known and that the committee is looking around to see what is available. The danger here is that what is really needed can become distorted by what would be "nice to have." While the multiproduct evaluation does serve a useful purpose when a general survey of differing items is desired, the single-product approach normally is much more advisable.

Among the considerations in preparing any evaluation plan are the following:

- Users: It is best to use no more participants than are really necessary to determine the product's acceptability in its most typical applications. In most cases, one or two departments should be sufficient.

- Evaluation sheet: The format identifies the product and lists yes-no questions. The criteria in the product specification are addressed, for they are the basic determiners of acceptance. There also is room for comments.

- Timing: It is wise to give some thought to the evaluation schedule to ensure that no external factors adversely affect the trial results. A holiday season, major construction work, a new department director, or preparation for a Joint Commission on Accreditation of Hospitals inspection can disrupt an otherwise normal evaluation. Also important is the duration of the test.

Several weeks or a month normally are long enough although certain situations may warrant exceptions.

- Product test: Enough product must be available to ensure continuity during the evaluation and those participating need adequate instruction in proper product use. Inservice testing may be conducted by a sales representative or the institution's staff education personnel. For evaluations of short duration, sample products often can be obtained from manufacturers at no cost. Longer trial periods, however, normally consume so much product that an institution should be prepared to pay for it. Finally, evaluation product should be clearly marked and set aside to prevent accidental nontest use.

- Test supervision: There must be a test coordinator or contact person for each department participating in the evaluation. The coordination may be by a single person or by several, but either way it must be clear to the evaluators to whom they can turn with questions or concerns. Timely follow-up by the coordinator will confirm that the right items are being used and that the evaluation forms are being completed. An active, enthusiastic role by a coordinator says to a test participant, "This is an important evaluation that deserves the best effort from everyone involved."

- Data analysis: At the conclusion of the product's trial period, the evaluation forms are collected and analyzed. When yes-no questions have been used, the analysis can include the actual answers compared with the desired ones. For example, suppose that an evaluation form has ten questions and, of the desired answers, seven would be "yes" and three "no." If one evaluator responded with the desired answers in nine of the questions, the item has received a 90 percent rating from that individual. User comments are meaningful if they are shared by a number of users; the number of repetitions of a comment is an important piece of the total analysis.

COMMITTEE DECISION

For the product standards committee to make an intelligent decision regarding the possible adoption of a product as a new "standard," it must be presented with both cost and performance information. The committee must know how the new item compares in cost with the one it may replace. It also must know whether the item performs in a satisfactory manner. Given this information, its decision should be a relatively obvious one.

On occasion, however, the decision may not be as easy as the facts would indicate. For one thing, people often have brand preferences that stem from long experience with a product, an especially helpful sales representative, nursing school training, friends' testimony, or the manufacturer's reputation. In such cases, adopting a different product as hospital standard because the facts indicate its superiority can be difficult and even emotionally troublesome. Some committee members may require more time than others to get acquainted to relying on the facts from an evaluation instead of the more subjective influences that previously had been adequate for product decisions. These members need to be reminded patiently of the absolute necessity of reliance upon objectivity.

When one committee has the kind of power that the product standards committee possesses, communication within the institution becomes very important. Without good communication, the committee may be distrusted, viewed as a bureaucratic obstacle to be circumvented whenever possible, and otherwise misunderstood. If several channels of communication are kept open, however, misunderstandings can be avoided.

It is important to inform the person who initiates a product evaluation request as to the action taken or planned. This tells the individual that the request has been received and is receiving consideration. Those who participate in an evaluation test deserve a word of thanks for their efforts promptly after their involvement has ended. The personal touch is best because it usually makes "thanks" seem more genuine, and a note is better than a phone call because it can be shared, perhaps by being posted on a bulletin board.

In addition to these personal contacts, committee news should be shared with the rest of the hospital, perhaps through a nursing newsletter or general employee bulletin. A particularly positive feature is to play up the participation of others in the request initiation, product inspection and evaluation, and other consulting roles.

IMPLEMENTATION OF PRODUCT CHANGES

The introduction of a new product as hospital standard must be thorough; problems can arise if steps are omitted. Storeroom, distribution, purchasing, and staff education people normally must be involved.

Most products will be ordered by the storeroom staff, although some may be purchased directly by user departments. In most cases, the new standard product should not be used until the remaining inventory of the displaced product has been eliminated. Upon introducing the new product, all users should be notified accordingly.

It is the purchasing department's responsibility to advise vendors involved in a product standardization change. The "old" product's supplier must be informed; if the hospital had authorized the vendor to set aside inventory to ensure uninterrupted supply, that stock must be used or returned. There will be negotiations with the new product's supplier to establish the level of service that is necessary.

The institution's staff education people must determine what methods, if any, will be used to familiarize employees with the new product. It may be that no special orientation is necessary. Often, however, specific training is desirable and this is done by either vendor representatives or staff education personnel. Inservice instruction is time consuming, but a great deal of learning normally takes place, often by people who think they have all the answers already. Inservice training should be an investment in time for improved performance.

An audit or review of the degree of success experienced after adoption of each new product standard is an easily overlooked final step in the process. Six months after each standardization action, the hospital's experience should be assessed. Is the conversion complete or are there still some holdout departments? If some departments still are not using the product, why not? Sometimes lessons are learned in these follow-up audits that help to improve future implementation plans for newly adopted products.

14. Capital Equipment Purchasing

JOSEPH A. DATTILO AND GIL MEREDITH

Since the late 1960s, health care material managers have made significant progress in improving the effectiveness of their methods of purchasing, storing, reprocessing, and distributing supplies throughout their facilities.

However, much slower progress has been made in controlling the capital equipment purchasing process. Although a substantial segment of health care dollars is expended for these purchases, material managers have been hesitant to exert influence in this area. Control has been maintained by clinical and other department managers. It is vital that material management professionals develop a system through which the material manager and the requesting department manager can work together to obtain the appropriate equipment at the best possible price.

JUSTIFICATION PHASE

Establishing the Need

Creating a corporate culture and a capital approval process through which appropriate justification of capital equipment purchases is expected and produced is a major duty of the material manager.

All capital purchases are initiated from a perceived need—for a new service, for up-to-date technology, for a solution to a problem, to replace obsolete or worn-out equipment. It no longer is acceptable to purchase expensive equipment based on the unjustified, perceived needs of a physician or department manager. The first duty of the requester of such equipment is to justify this need and the expenditure of limited capital for that purpose.

The requester, the purchasing manager or material manager, material staff, the capital equip-

ment committee, and administration all must work cooperatively to determine the need for such a purchase, the alternatives, and the impact of not making it. The requester must feel obligated to provide an appropriately detailed justification, and must be instructed on the type and extent of analysis needed. Administration must make available information and the use of staff to assist the requester in attempting to justify the need. And the capital equipment committee must react professionally, without bias and without reservation, in reviewing the justification and subsequent questioning of the requester.

The Initial Justification Process

The justification and review process should be formalized so that all requesters know the requirements at the outset. The process should be consistent so that favoritism is not perceived and it should be as simple, yet as detailed, as appropriate for the type and dollar amount of the equipment being requested.

The first step is to describe the need for the equipment. A few short paragraphs normally are sufficient. The benefits of purchase then should be described. Again, a few paragraphs should normally suffice. Some potential benefits are:

- improved patient care
- improved patient safety
- reduction in length of stay
- reduction in operating expenses
- improved revenue collection.

Next should be an estimate of the costs associated with the purchase. Costs should include those for:

141

- equipment purchase
- associated installation
- associated labor
- associated utility
- associated supply
- training
- service contract.

All alternatives should be listed, showing the advantages, disadvantages, and reasons for not choosing the alternative. Next is a description of the impact if the capital purchase is not approved. Once again, a few paragraphs would suffice.

More Detailed Justification

With the completion of the initial phase, the request is forwarded to the committee chair, who determines what further justification should be necessary before presentation to the capital equipment committee. The chair also decides whether an investigator should be assigned to assist the requester with completion of justification and to provide an unbiased viewpoint. This investigator can be a staff member of the hospital, perhaps a management engineer, or possibly a member of the capital equipment committee.

Depending upon the type and dollar amount of the equipment or project being requested, the chairman can choose from among the following options:

- Initial justification is complete, no further investigation or justification is needed.
- Additional justification by the requester is required, an investigator is not needed.
- Additional justification is required, an investigator will be assigned to assist the requester.

Further justification of the request can involve many areas. Some of the major topics are:

1. How does the request fit with the hospital's long-range plan?

2. How does the request fit with the local health regulatory agency's plans?
3. Will approval be needed from the local health regulatory agency?
4. What is the current competitive situation in the hospital service area as it pertains to this project? How would this expenditure impact on this situation?
5. How will this project impact on other services in the hospital:

- within a department
- other clinical departments
- support services
- quality of care
- occupancy
- length of stay
- physician referrals or physician recruitment?

6. Does the medical staff support this project?
7. What is the effect on staffing?
8. What training will be required?
9. What promotion will be required:

- to the medical staff
- to employees
- to the community?

10. What are the options for shared services?
11. Can the hospital market this service to other facilities? What is the potential?

Financial Justification

In all likelihood, a detailed financial justification will be required. Again, the amount of detail will be dependent upon the complexity and the size of the project. Exhibit 14–1 presents a typical detailed financial justification.

Section I involves costs associated with the project. The collection of these figures is necessary to determine the total cost of the project and the amount that will be expensed for each year throughout the life of the equipment or project.

Exhibit 14–1 Detailed Financial Justification

I. Costs

A. Estimated cost of equipment (including shipping) $ _____

_____
Dept. Manager
Purchasing

B. Estimated cost of installation, building
modifications (please attach details) $ _____

_____
Dept. Manager
Maintenance

C. Depreciable life of project   _____ yrs.

_____
Department Manager
Accounting

D. Equipment to be replaced:
1. Description _____

_____

_____

2. Fixed asset number   _____

3. Present age   _____

4. Assigned useful life   _____

5. Current book value $ _____

_____
Dept. Manager
Accounting

6. Current market value $ _____

_____
Dept. Manager
Purchasing

E. Associated Increase in Expenses

	Year 1	Year 2	Year 3	Year 4	Year 5	Year 6	Year 7	Year 8	Year 9	Year 10
Training										
Labor										
Utilities										
Supplies										
Other										
Total Increase in Expenses										

Exhibit 14–1 continued

II. Revenue and Decrease of Expenses	Year 1	Year 2	Year 3	Year 4	Year 5	Year 6	Year 7	Year 8	Year 9	Year 10
A. Increases in Revenue										
1. Revenue increases from additional inpatients										
a. Medicare										
b. Medicaid										
c. Others										
2. Revenue increases from additional list of current inpatients										
a. Medicare										
b. Medicaid										
c. Others										
3. Revenue increases from additional outpatient testing										
a. Medicare										
b. Medicaid										
c. Others										
B. Decreases in Revenue										
1. Revenue decrease from reduced length of stay										
a. Medicare										
b. Medicaid										
c. Others										
2. Revenue decrease from reduced number of inpatients										
a. Medicare										
b. Medicaid										
c. Others										
C. Net Increase or Decrease in Revenue										
D. Decrease of Expenses										
1. Reduction in expenses from reduced length of stay										
a. labor										
b. supplies										
c. utilities										
d. other										
2. Reduction in expenses from reduced number of inpatients										
a. labor										
b. supplies										
c. utilities										
d. other										

Exhibit 14–1 continued

	Year 1	Year 2	Year 3	Year 4	Year 5	Year 6	Year 7	Year 8	Year 9	Year 10
3. Reduction in expenses from new technology										
a. labor										
b. supplies										
c. utilities										
d. other										
4. Total reduction in expenses										

Source: Departmental document, reprinted with permission of St. Francis-St. George Hospital, Inc., Cincinnati, Ohio.

Section II covers increases in revenue or decreases in expenses. This section is much more difficult to determine. It requires forecasts regarding increases and/or decreases in admissions, patient days and/or tests, and the resultant effect on revenues and expenses.

The calculation of revenue was much simpler before the advent of prospective payment reimbursement systems. Because of the subsequent variations of reimbursement techniques, it now is necessary to determine the effects of the projects based upon the various methods affected. The requesting department will need considerable assistance from the finance department to determine the effect on revenues and costs.

The point of this analysis is to determine the financial payoff of the investment. In and of itself, the financial analysis does not consider issues such as improved patient care and patient safety. It can provide only one piece of the puzzle, which must be completed to obtain the entire picture.

There are many methods for evaluating investment proposals. The two discussed here are payback and net present value (NPV).

The Payback Method

The payback method or payback period is the number of years it will take the facility to repay the original investment from the net cash flows resulting from the use of the newly purchased equipment.

In the comparison in Table 14–1, the payback period for Project A is three years, that for Project B is two years. Based on this method, Project B would seem the better investment. However, this method has a few flaws. It does not take into account the income beyond the payback period. As illustrated in Table 14–1, over the five-year life of both projects, Project A would return $2,000, Project B only $1,400. This method also does not take into effect the time value of money. Although a simple method, the payback system can lead to significant errors if used as the only way of determining the financial effectiveness of equipment investment.

Net Present Value Method

Taking into account the fact that a dollar received today is preferable to a dollar received

---

Table 14–1 Payback Method

Project A		Project B	
Investment $1,000		Investment $1,000	
Year	Net Cash Flow	Year	Net Cash Flow
1	$200	1	$500
2	300	2	500
3	500	3	200
4	500	4	100
5	500	5	100

tomorrow, the net present value (NPV) method was designed. To determine the NPV of the investment, the net cash flows must be discounted at the facilities' cost of capital, or the present value interest factor (PVIF), which can be found in the appendixes of most accounting or finance texts. The result is known as the net present value of net cash flows. The original investment is then subtracted from the net present value of net cash flows to determine the net present value of the investment.

The net present value in Table 14–2 indicates that both projects would be financially advantageous. It also is evident that Project A, with a return of $457.34 or 45.7 percent on the original $1,000 investment, is considerably more attractive than Project B, which has a return of $148.40, or 14.8 percent.

THE PURCHASING PHASE

Following the formal approval, the purchasing phase begins. It is important to note at this time that all of the steps in the process described need not and should not occur for all capital purchases. Just as in the justification phase, the complexity and dollar amount of equipment to be acquired will determine the appropriate steps to be utilized in the purchasing phase.

Material Management Responsibilities

A primary function of a purchasing agent in equipment decisions is to serve as a naive questioner in the initial steps. As an outsider, the purchaser can attempt to focus the user department manager's attention on the broad perspective of what need the equipment is to fill. It can be useful to have an unbiased reminder of the goal to be served.

A more traditional and still appropriate position of the purchasing manager is to encourage a climate of competition among potential vendors. If the purchaser can handle the negotiations with vendors and give them the knowledge that the user department's subjective perceptions will

Table 14–2 Net Present Value Method

Project A

Yr.	Net Cash Flow	PVIF 10%	NPV of Cash Flow
1	$200	0.9091	$181.82
2	300	0.8264	247.92
3	500	0.7513	375.65
4	500	0.6830	341.50
5	500	0.6209	310.45
		NPV of Net Cash Flows	1,457.34
		Less Investment	1,000.00
		NPV of Project A	457.34

Project B

Yr.	Net Cash Flow	PVIF 10%	NPV of Cash Flow
1	$500	0.9091	$454.55
2	500	0.8264	413.20
3	200	0.7513	150.26
4	100	0.6830	68.30
5	100	0.6209	62.09
		NPV of Net Cash Flows	1,148.40
		Less Investment	1,000.00
		NPV of Project B	148.40

not be the total basis of the decision, an aura of objectivity and true competition can be developed. Suppliers need to know that there are some checks and balances on the department and to understand that financial restraint is an important consideration.

Material management personnel also are the most qualified to develop actual purchase terms and conditions. This is an area that certainly should not be left to the user department. The conditions of payment, delivery, and other aspects of vendor compliance with requirements must be established by the material management representative.

It is possible to implement a step-by-step process by which purchasing departments can approach the accomplishment of these goals. Without technical expertise, purchasers can assist the user department in developing and implementing timely competitive bid specification procedures.

The Purchasing Process

This process seeks to provide a hospital with objective bases for:

1. evaluating appropriate vendors
2. defining functional needs of the equipment to be purchased
3. translating the functional needs into detailed and measurable specifications
4. finding a dollar basis for objective comparison of different vendor proposals
5. providing a basis for consensus among the clinical or other user department, the material management department, and hospital financial administration.

What is desirable is to create a structure in which all parties concerned can have faith. The hospital's need is to buy the best equipment for its intended function at the lowest possible total cost. It needs to be emphasized that buying the best equipment for the function should precede and define expectations of what the appropriate price is.

Inherent in devising a process that ensures accountability is the need to involve multiple segments of the hospital management team in the decision process. Purchasing cannot decide what equipment the requesting department needs and the latter should not assume the function of a purchasing agent.

Organizational and reporting structures vary from institution to institution but the basic sequence of decision making and the concept of shared accountability can be applied regardless of the particular organizational structure.

In instituting a systematic purchase process, it has to be recognized that decisions will take longer than if one individual or department controlled the system. The most time-efficient method for purchasing capital equipment is to give the department managers carte blanche to select what they feel they need. There is reason to believe, however, that that inevitably will be the most expensive. Planning purchases several months in advance of need will enable a hospital to choose among the widest range of vendors, define its requirements more precisely, and ensure that no opportunities for function enhancement or cost savings have been overlooked.

Generic Functional Specifications

The key to encouraging price competition and ensuring the appropriateness of purchases is the development of generic functional specifications. These allow multiple vendors to compete, although the details of any company's offerings may make each appear to be a unique product.

Most equipment is composed of some necessary features, some desirable features, and some irrelevant or even undesired characteristics. A bid system must be developed that accounts for this and includes identification of absolute requirements while quantifying the importance of potentially desirable enhancements. Only by defining these parameters will it be possible to make accurate and equivalent price comparisons.

Purchasing must encourage user departments to develop specifications from a functional standpoint, and as generically as possible. What is specified should be able to be supplied by more than one vendor and reflect criteria that can be applied to each seller fairly.

Requiring the requester to provide explicit functional requirements will assist the department manager in refining the needs. There may be instances where this process will make it clear that the initial estimate of the type of equipment required should be modified. Identifying requirements in detail makes it clear that the equipment specifiers will be held accountable for their recommendations.

Throughout the process of developing the technical specification details, it is essential that the goals of consensus between the user department and the purchasing department be kept in view. The very fact of establishing a systematic joint process for specification development will aid this. Making it clear to requesters that they are required to be very precise in their requests will encourage them to take purchasing's role more seriously than they might have done traditionally.

The delineation of requirements and preferences and the quantification of preference should result in a high degree of accord between material management and the user department. Clinical departments, in particular, have viewed "interference" from purchasing skeptically. As they become convinced that purchasing is trying first and foremost to arrange for the acquisition of the appropriate system, their degree of faith in the process should increase.

Specification Writing

The most generic method for presenting specifications to bidders is in terms of the performance expected from the capital equipment. Encouraging the clinical or other user department to put its specifications into a performance format is a step toward eliminating brand prejudice influence on the eventual award.

The purchasing agent should keep in mind throughout the process of reviewing technical specifications that the greater the physical detail specified, the less likely multiple bidders will be able to meet the specifications. Some components may have to be specified in explicit detail but each function needs to be described first in terms of its performance, then in physical detail only when absolutely necessary.

Preference Point System

The following preference point system has been designed based on the fact that no two vendors offer identical equipment. It should be noted that this preference point system is not the only useful method of specification, nor should it be used for all capital equipment purchases. It is, however, valuable in the purchase of radiology and nuclear medicine equipment, some computer systems, and so on. In these cases, each article is uniquely configured according to the manufacturer's perception of its potential market. All proposed packages will deviate in some details from the minimal required system.

This does not imply that those deviations are not significant. The fact is that there are both minimal requirements and preferred characteristics. In a fair competitive quotation process, it is unlikely that any vendor would meet all of the preferences, particularly if they are expressed in terms of performance. Detailing which characteristics are absolute requirements and which are preferences does provide a framework, however, for financial comparisons.

Narrowing down the department's thinking to the point where it can determine the difference between a requirement and a preference is a matter of in-person group negotiations. Armed with a complete shopping list of equipment characteristics, the negotiator of this process (either the requesting department manager or the purchasing manager) conducts a session to evaluate each feature in terms of its requirement or preference and further define exactly how strong each preference is.

Once degree of preference for each given enhancement is established, a simple point scale of one to ten is sufficient to identify this to vendors. This will alert them that the institution is willing to pay ten times as much for a ten-point option as it is for a one-point option. It should be emphasized that internally the institution will assign points on the degree of functional utility of the options and not necessarily in accord with their prevailing prices. Even though this is not in strict concordance with expected price, the institution still will establish that it is willing to pay a specified dollar amount per point. However, the dollar value of each point is not identified to the vendors. They will be aware only of the relative value the hospital places on each preference (Exhibit 14–2). It should be noted that some specifications are rigidly detailed, others are in broad, functional terms.

The problem then becomes one of assigning the dollar-per-point basis by which preferences will be judged. Ideally, this would be decided on the basis of the return on investment that each

preferred option would yield but in practice this is difficult to determine. A more feasible approach is to survey the market for the expected expense of a range of options. For example, when the most preferred option is identified, vendors can be surveyed informally to determine their expected cost of that option. Similarly, the least preferred option (a one-point feature) can be investigated as to its cost. Once the range is known, a simple averaging process can yield a dollar figure to be used as a basis of per-point assignment.

The dollar-per-point average obtained this way should be agreed upon internally before the detailed specifications are put out as requests for bids. It must be understood that the institution has agreed internally in advance to pay this pre-

Exhibit 14–2 Technical Specifications

Request for Proposal—Specification, Department of Radiology

Component/ Function	Item (Fully Describe Alternates)	Comments (Check Off, Fill In, List or Describe)	Yes	No	Buyer Preference	Points
IV. cont'd	1. cont'd	10:1 105 Line, Aluminum Interspaced, Approx. 36–44″ Focus Grid .... _____			. Required, or .	
		10:1 150 Line, Al. Interspaced, Stationary .... _____			...Preferred...	4
		Table Top to Film Distance _____cm			...Smallest...	4
		Tray to Accommodate All Customary Cassette Sizes .... _____			...Required...	
		Tray Range Equal _____cm			.110 minimum.	
	Top	Material _____..................			.Carbon Fiber.	4
		_____mm Al equivalent @ 70 kVp .				
		Shape _____ Curved _____ Flat .. _____			.Flat Required.	
	Accessories & Other Features	Compression Band .... _____			...Required...	
		Foot Support, Detachable .... _____			...Required...	
		Patient Hand Grips................			...Preferred...	1
		Retractable Step for Mounting .... _____			...Required...	
Tube Support (Overhead)		Telescoping O.T. Support _____			...Required...	
		Longitudinal & Transverse Motion To Allow For: Cross Table Hip Radiography, Either Side of Table.......... _____			...Required...	
		Radiography of Any Anatomy of Patient on Care With Walk Room Around Cart .... _____			...Required...	

Source: Excerpt of departmental document (p. 21), reprinted with permission of St. Francis-St. George Hospital, Inc., Cincinnati, Ohio.

determined dollar per point for the options identified as preferred.

Acceptance Standards

As each of these specifications is developed, a standard for judging them in the final analysis should be established. When these acceptance parameters are included in the final request for quotation, the vendors are provided with a clear standard by which to present their proposal. The other purpose of establishing acceptance tests is, of course, to judge whether the delivered product has met the terms and conditions specified. If these tests are detailed in advance, there is little room for discord at the time of installation.

The degree of specificity and sophistication of the testing will depend, to a large degree, on the resources of the purchasing institution. Even in the absence of internal engineering support, however, consulting firms are available that can perform acceptance testing procedures for a reasonable fee. If an institution plans to use such consultants, they should be engaged before distribution of the specifications to ensure that their testing methodologies are understood by the vendors.

Engineering Checklist

Once the technical details have been agreed upon, there needs to be assurance that the physical facility is able to accommodate such equipment or plans for modification of existing structures need to be developed. One method for assuring that there will be no surprises in this area is to provide each of the vendors with a form similar to the one developed by the American Hospital Association in its TEAM (Technology Evaluation and Acquisition Methods) program.[1]

In most cases of replacement equipment, there probably will be few problems with existing facilities. When purchasing new types, however, extensive modifications may be required and the new units incompatible with existing power supply, air conditioning, water requirements, and so on. These potential sources of problems must be identified before purchase so

that their costs can be included in the final proposal comparison.

If, for example, the equipment being purchased requires temperature-controlled conditions, the degree of required precision of that control may vary among vendors. This variability may well have a large impact on the total cost of one vendor's system versus another's. The engineering checklist will enable the institution to specify those costs while the suppliers are providing their purchase costs through the bidding process.

Instructions to Bidders

Once again, the instructions to and requirements of the bidders will depend on the size and complexity of the project. Appendix 14–A presents typical bidding instructions and requirements applicable for most types of equipment purchases and small projects. Appendix 14–B details more complex instructions to and requirements of bidders. These types of requirements would be utilized for large dollar expenditures or projects of major complexity.

Certain government-financed institutions or projects require more stringent public bidding procedures. It is the responsibility of the purchasing manager or material manager to determine the overall extent of the bidding instructions and requirements.

There may be circumstances in which delivery and installation times are relatively critical to an institution: the replacement of an emergency department x-ray or an angiographic suite. Similarly, the installation of a new type of technology may be very important to an institution in order to maintain its market position. In those cases, the speed with which the system can be delivered and installed may be quite significant financially.

When dollar value can be assigned to speed and efficiency of installation, it may be appropriate to inform vendors that bonuses will be paid for early delivery and/or efficient installation. Such bonuses should be identified in advance and should be applied regardless of the eventual vendor. It also is appropriate in this context to specify financial penalties for poor delivery and installation. The two incentives—bonuses and penalties—need to be applied equally and equitably. It is not appropriate merely to award bonuses for good performance without having financial recourse in the case of poor performance.

The initial basis for identifying vendors from which to solicit bids will be a subjective listing of those in the area known to the clinical department to be able to provide the equipment needed. The purchasing department can supplement this first list by market research, providing the user department with additional vendors that may be considered. This can be done as simply as saying, "Is there any reason we can't solicit a bid from brand Z?" This simple initial market survey usually is adequate to identify enough potential bidders to continue the process of refining the bid list.

Vendor Performance History

Vendor performance history, particularly in providing service support, is a critical issue in purchasing capital equipment. Combined with the subjective perceptions that the requesting department will provide, documentation of the performance of particular suppliers in the institution or in the service area should be considered, if available. Obvious deficiencies such as defaulting on bid bonds and failure to support equipment with adequate service may eliminate some vendors from the initial list. This history need not come from the individual institution alone but also may be the result of an informal survey of other using departments or purchasing agents in the area.

These current user contacts can be helpful in identifying any functional problems that may have emerged with particular equipment configurations. For example, it will be helpful for the hospital to know whether the kind of radiology system it has in mind has some limitations on the kind of patient that can be conveniently examined using it. A particular product might meet rigorous technical specifications, yet have design limitations that make efficiency of use a

problem. Contacting current users of each vendor's particular equipment will bring out considerations like this. New information discovered in this way can thus affect the development of the final specifications.

A preliminary vendor evaluation form similar to the one in Exhibit 14–3 can be useful in refining the bid list. This assists in providing the hospital's capital approval committee with accurate estimates of the level of expenditure to be expected. It also can identify differences among vendors that may require further clarification in the formal specifications.

Prebid Conference

Once a preliminary bid list is established, a useful device for further clarifying system requirements is to arrange for a conference in which all potential vendors and representatives of the requesting and purchasing departments are involved. The purpose is to discuss the general perceived requirements of the equipment to be purchased and to solicit advice and possible new ideas from the vendors. Doing this with all suppliers represented simultaneously is a way of ensuring that all have heard the same information, perceptions, and needs from the requesting department.

A final technique for evaluating vendors and the equipment proposed is for representatives of the clinical department to visit a range of users. Purchasing managers may or may not find this useful to them, but users characteristically put great faith in their perceptions of a system viewed in its working environment. This again is an opportunity for new ideas or refinement of characteristics to affect the eventual specification form.

EVALUATION PHASE

Once the bids have been returned, the first step in evaluating them is to review their compliance with essential required characteristics. Ideally, all vendors would meet all required characteristics. In many circumstances, however, there will be some deviations by some or all of the

Exhibit 14–3 Example of Preliminary Vendor Evaluation

Digital Radiography Modification

1. Estimated cost of standard digital radiography system to be retrofitted to buyer's existing special procedures room. $_____.
2. Estimated cost of special procedures equipment modifications required for effective digital radiography use. (For Q. 1, 2, consult Cincinnati office, Xonics Medical Systems.) $_____.
3. Note standard warranty terms; items covered, not covered, length, hours of service, response time, etc. Note price for one-year warranty option if not standard.
4. Detail supplies needed for digital venous angiography applications. Quantities, sources, price estimates. Use 1,000 procedures/year as volume estimate.
5. Provide complete listing of Radiology/Ultrasound/Nuclear Medicine installations by your company in Greater Cincinnati. Include purchase dates with system descriptions.
6. Provide complete user list of D.V.I. equipment currently operational, noting installation dates.
7. Provide list of service personnel living in and working out of the Cincinnati area. Detail experience and training of each individual.
8. Detail service response terms and conditions, noting penalties your company is willing to accept for noncompliance with promised response terms.
9. Attach most recent corporate annual report, including Standard & Poor's abstract and any other pertinent data substantiating corporate stability.
10. Complete the attached Form 7–3 Engineering Checklist [omitted here]. Consult with Radiology Department Manager to obtain any needed facility information. Attach supplemental sheets as appropriate.
11. Provide complete information (including costs) regarding operator and hospital maintenance training available.

Source: Departmental document, reprinted with permission of St. Francis-St. George Hospital, Inc., Cincinnati, Ohio.

---

suppliers. Even though characteristics have been identified as absolute requirements, some minor deviations still may be accepted at this point. These characteristics should be reviewed and a decision made immediately as to whether the proposal will be considered in further detail. This is the one point in the evaluation process where subjective factors may enter and caution needs to be exercised to ensure fairness to all vendors while avoiding undue rigidity.

Preference Weighting

Once the number of bids has been narrowed down by a summary appraisal, the number of options proposed should have their preference points totaled. The extension of this number of preference points by the predetermined dollar value per point yields a figure to be discounted from the total quoted price.

Table 14–3 is an example of discounting preference dollar value from total price. This example also illustrates that the lowest price may not be the greatest value. Following this process will yield instances in which the highest quoted price actually turns out to be lower when weighted for the enhancements. In other circumstances, however, the discounting of preference points still may show the lowest total price to be the best

---

Table 14–3 Preference Weighting Work Sheet

	System A	System B
Total bid price	$145,000	$160,000
Preference points	14	76
One point value	× 250	× 250
Enhancement value	3,500	19,000
	145,000	160,000
Adjustment	−3,500	−19,000
Comparison price	141,500	141,000

Decision: Buy System B

Source: Departmental document, reprinted with permission of St. Francis-St. George Hospital, Inc., Cincinnati, Ohio.

buy. The key is to award the contract on the basis of highest value as opposed to merely comparing initial bottom lines.

Other Weightings

The final step in determining the award is to derive the total cost of the equipment over its expected lifetime by weighting for service and/or installation costs. The ideal comparison basis would be a long history of expected service costs for particular types of systems from the various vendors. If it is known, for example, that a particular supplier's equipment generally will require $1,000 more a year in service support, and the equipment has a life of eight years, $8,000 should be added to this vendor's equated price. Similarly, the previously identified installation costs need to be added at this time.

While installation of facility modification costs should be fully known for each vendor, service expense weightings may not be available for all bids. An average weight may be assigned to vendors whose service record is unknown or further research conducted at other using hospitals. To avoid the problem of subjectivity, comparable cost weightings need to be applied to all proposals or to none.

When all these calculations have been completed, the result should be a price comparison basis that enables the institution to choose the best equipment for its dollar.

RECEIPT AND INSTALLATION

The most appropriate time to coordinate the receipt and installation of equipment is before the purchase. This takes considerable planning and coordination to ensure an expeditious and smooth installation process.

The requesting department manager, the purchasing manager, the maintenance/engineering manager, the receiving manager, and the vendor all should know their respective roles and how they fit into the overall scheme of the project long before it arrives on the receiving dock. It is the purchasing or material manager's responsi-

bility to coordinate this process, to build the appropriate requirements into the bidding process, and to inform all parties of their responsibilities.

Fixed Asset Controls

On receipt of a piece of capital equipment or completion of a capital project, the accounting department normally assigns a fixed asset number and lists the item or improvement as a depreciable asset. At the same time, material managers should take this opportunity to gather the following information they will need to utilize throughout the life of the equipment:

- description of asset
- category of asset (office equipment, diagnostic equipment, furnishings, etc.)
- fixed asset number
- building and room location
- acquisition date
- acquisition price
- manufacturer
- manufacturer's catalog number
- model number
- distributor
- purchase order number
- quantity
- warranty expiration date
- service contract cost
- service contract vendor
- service contract expiration date
- estimated useful life (for accounting purposes)
- estimated replacement date
- next preventive maintenance date.

This information, if kept and sorted properly, can supply the purchasing or material manager with a data base of valuable information. It also can be of significant help to the maintenance, clinical engineering, or medical departments in maintaining the equipment. It can be of significant help to the finance department when trying to forecast replacement equipment requirements one to five years hence. And it can be of significant help to the purchasing manager or material manager in keeping track of vendor history and service information.

Many hospitals have the ability to tie this type of information to their financial computer system. If this is not available, there are numerous software packages that provide for this type of recordkeeping. An appropriate sorting software package on a minicomputer could be customized to provide the needed detail. If all else fails, a well-controlled manual system still would suffice.

It is important to keep this information up to date. Equipment must be tracked as it is transferred throughout the organization. Proper accounting of changes in warranty and in the service contracts, as well as information regarding the liquidation of the asset, also can be controlled in this manner.

Training

The requesting department is responsible for coordinating appropriate personnel for training on the new equipment. This should be planned well before the installation. Possibilities include the hospital's sending the involved individuals to the manufacturer's facility for training, sending them to other hospitals utilizing the vendor's equipment, the seller's sending technical representatives to the hospital to train the staff, and training on the equipment after installation. Whatever is most appropriate and most beneficial to the hospital should be pursued. The vendor's responsibility should be spelled out carefully in the bid and the purchase order. It is the responsibility of the purchasing or material manager to see that this vitally important area is not overlooked in the purchase of equipment.

Service Contracts

The purchase of equipment is not complete until arrangements have been made to service it after the warranty period has expired. The best time to negotiate a service contract is before the purchase.

Obviously, price is not the only issue to be considered. The American Hospital Association has prepared a checklist that could be valuable when preparing to negotiate service contracts. This checklist appears in the *AHA Guideline Report*, "How to Evaluate Equipment Service Contracts."[2]

Insurance underwriters have instituted an alternative to purchasing service contracts: they will insure major pieces of equipment at rates that often are below the cost of the service contract. The underwriters agree to reimburse the hospital for any costs incurred when breakdowns occur. The hospital still can utilize the services of the manufacturer to accomplish the repairs, knowing that these costs are reimbursable by the insurers.

OTHER CONSIDERATIONS

The purchase of a piece of equipment is not complete after receipt. All parties impacted by it need to be cognizant of its receipt and the part they will play in its successful implementation. Although in most cases the responsibility for spreading this information lies with the requesting department, it is important that the purchasing or material manager be aware of this requirement.

In addition, if this equipment is new or provides a new service, it almost certainly will be beneficial to market this service to the medical staff, the community, and the employees. The marketing department is an obvious resource in this endeavor.

The first time through this process, a fringe benefit will be the education of both the purchasing and the requesting departments to each other's goals and perspectives. This can only make coordination of future purchases of capital and supply equipment more effective. The requesting department needs to be made more aware of the legitimate concerns of purchasing in regard to price and accountability; purchasing needs to learn more of the technical requirements that the user department considers so essential.

The net result of this entire process is to create an atmosphere of cooperative endeavor with the institution's goals as its primary focus. Clinical or other user departments should not operate as though they were entities separate from the hospital as a whole. The overall position of the institution both financially and in the marketplace needs to become part of each department's awareness and basis for decision making.

Purchasing departments in general have a need to assume a more cooperative posture with clinical or other user departments. In the past there often has been conflict between departments or abdication of responsibility by purchasing managers for the actions of other departments. Neither is an appropriate response to an institution's overall requirements. Getting purchasing managers involved in learning the functional and technical details of equipment will improve their perspective on the demands placed on them by other departments. The bottom line should always be the acquisition of appropriate equipment at the lowest possible costs.

NOTES

1. American Hospital Association, "Case Study Digital Subtraction Angiography Evaluation and Acquisition at St. Francis-St. George Hospital, Inc., Cincinnati, Ohio," *Technology Evaluation and Acquisition Methods for Hospitals*, September 1983.

2. American Hospital Association, "How to Evaluate Equipment Service Contracts," *Guideline Report*.

BIBLIOGRAPHY

Boergadine, L. "Defining CP's Role in Capital Acquisition," *Purchasing Administration* (April 1, 1981).

Bradley, B. "Is Your Equipment Out of Control?" *Hospital Purchasing Management* (February 1980).

Campbell, S.R. "Procurement of Major Equipment," *Hospital Materials Management Quarterly* (February 1981).

Holmgren, John H. *Material Management & Purchasing for the Health Care Facility*. Ann Arbor, Mich.: AUPHA Press, 1982.

Meredith, Gil. "Generic Functional Specifications," *Medical Imaging Administrator* (December 1982): 11.

National Research Corporation. "Equipment Planning Survey; Formal Equipment Buying Plans are Common, But Not at Small Hospitals," *Modern Health Care* (October 1983): 118–20.

Pauley, W.E. "Equipment Acquisition," *Purchasing Administration* (March 1980).

Teselsky, R.P. "Expanding on Product and Equipment Evaluation Procedures," *Hospital Materials Management Quarterly* (May 1981).

Appendix 14–A

Bidding Instructions (Simple Format)

ITEMS BELOW APPLY TO AND BECOME A PART OF TERMS AND CONDITIONS OF BID. ANY EXCEPTIONS THERETO MUST BE IN WRITING.

1. Bidding Requirements:

   a. Late bids properly identified will be returned to bidder unopened. Late bids will not be considered under any circumstances.

   b. Bid prices must be firm for acceptance for thirty (30) days from bid opening date. Cash discount will not be considered in determining the low bid. All cash discounts offered will be taken if earned.

   c. Bids must give full firm name and address of bidder. Failure to manually sign bid will disqualify it. Person signing bid should show title or authority to bind his firm in a contract. Firm name should appear on each page of a bid, in the space provided in the upper right-hand corner.

   d. Bid cannot be altered or amended after opening time. Any alterations made before opening time must be initialed by bidder or his authorized agent. No bid can be withdrawn after opening time without approval by the Hospital, based on an acceptable written reason.

   e. Telegraphic response to any bid invitation must show: price bid, requisition number, opening date, description (brand, model, etc.) of product offered, and delivery promise. Confirmation on bid form should be postmarked on or before opening day and/or received within forty-eight (48) hours after opening day. Show regular information on envelope and add the word: "Confirmation." Telephone bids are not acceptable when in response to this invitation to bid.

   f. Engineering checklist must be completed and returned with this bid.

2. Specifications:

   a. All items bid shall be new, in first-class condition, including containers suitable for shipment and storage, unless otherwise indicated in invitation. Verbal agreements to the contract will not be recognized.

   b. Samples, when requested, must be furnished free of expense. If not destroyed in examination, they will be returned to the bidder, on request, at his expense. Each sample should be marked with bidder's name, address, and requisition number. Do not enclose in or attach bid to sample.

   c. All quotations must be accompanied by descriptive literature giving full description or details as to type of material and equipment that is to be furnished under this contract. Samples, where required, shall be delivered to the purchasing department before the opening of quotations, unless otherwise stated in the specifications; failure of the bidder to either submit literature or supply samples may be considered sufficient reason for rejection of the quote. All deliveries under the contract shall conform in all respects with samples, catalog cuts, etc., as submitted and accepted as the basis for the award.

   d. In addition to the requirements of paragraph C, all deviations from the specifications must be noted in detail by the bidder in writing at the time of submittal of the quote. The absence of a written list of specification deviations at the time of submittal of the quote will hold the bidders strictly accountable to the Hospital to the specifications as written. Any deviation from the specifications as written not previously submitted, as required by the above, will be grounds for rejection of the material and/or equipment when delivered.

3. Award:

Award of bid will be based on the information provided by the bidder. The award will be made consistent with PRUDENT BUYER POLICY of the Hospital. Considerations to this award will be:

1. Price   4. Delivery
2. Quality   5. Design
3. Service

(Not necessarily listed according to priority)

a. Cash discounts will not be taken into consideration in determining an award.
b. With regard to differences between unit prices and extensions, unit prices will govern and extensions will be modified accordingly.
c. Freight charges may be a determining factor only when all price, quality, and service specifications are equal.

4. Delivery:

a. Failure to state delivery time obligates bidder to complete delivery in fourteen (14) calendar days. A five- (5)-day difference in delivery promise may break a tie bid. Unrealistically short or long delivery promises may cause bid to be disregarded. Consistent failure to meet delivery promises without valid reason may cause removal from bid list.
b. No substitutions or cancellations will be permitted without written approval of the Hospital.
c. Delivery shall be made during normal working hours only, 8:30 a.m. to 4 p.m., unless prior approval for late delivery has been obtained from Agency.
d. Any freight charges applicable to this quotation must appear on the quotation. All freight agreed to by the Hospital must be prepaid and added to the Hospital's invoice.

e. In all cases, seller will be responsible for filing damaged freight claims with the transporter of the merchandise.

5. Patents and Copyrights:

The contractor agrees to protect the Hospital from claims involving infringement of patents or copyrights.

TEFRA STATEMENT

Section 1861 (v)(1) of the Social Security Act (42 U.S.C.Sec. 1395x) as amended, requires us, as Medicare providers, to obtain the agreement of persons who contract with us for services with a value or cost of $10,000 or more in any twelve-month period, that the books, documents, and records of such contractors must remain available for verification of cost by the Comptroller General for a period of four years following completion of the contract. Seller acknowledges and expressly agrees to this requirement, on its behalf and on behalf of any subcontractor who shall perform any part or all of this contract for Seller having a value or cost of $10,000 or more.

OSHA STATEMENT

Seller represents and warrants that all articles and services covered by this purchase order meet or exceed the safety standards established and promulgated under the Federal Occupational Safety and Health Law (Public Law 91–596) and its regulations in effect or proposed as of the date of this order. Seller will submit OSHA Form 20, material safety data sheet, upon request.

SUBMITTAL OF QUOTE CONSTITUTES ACKNOWLEDGEMENT AND ACCEPTANCE OF THE TERMS AND CONDITIONS AS OUTLINED ABOVE.

INQUIRIES PERTAINING TO BID INVITATIONS MUST BE DIRECTED TO DEPARTMENT MANAGER, PURCHASING.

Authorized Signature

Source: Departmental document, reprinted with permission of St. Francis-St. George Hosp., Cincinnati, Ohio.

Appendix 14–B

Bidding Instructions (Complex Format)

A. INSTRUCTIONS TO BIDDERS

In accordance with the contract documents set forth herein, proposals will be received by Hospital through _____, 19____, at the (describe location).

1. *PROJECT SCHEDULE*

Schedule installation to be completed by _____.

2. *PREPARATION OF PROPOSALS*

a. The bidder shall submit his proposal on the attached proposal forms and specification sheets. No other forms will be accepted. A unit price and extended price shall be stated on the specification sheets for each item either typed or written in ink.
b. Each bidder is to bid on all items that he manufactures or supplies.

3. *SUBMISSION OF PROPOSALS*

a. All bidders shall submit _____proposals enclosed in a sealed envelope marked "Bid Document Equipment" on or before ____, 19____.
b. The proposals with all literature and the Bond shall be delivered to:
      (address and designate)
c. Where proposals are sent by mail, the bidders shall be responsible for their delivery before the date set for the receipt of proposals. Late proposals will not be considered and will be returned unopened.

4. *WITHDRAWAL OF BIDS*

a. Bids may be withdrawn on written request received from bidders *prior to date fixed for opening bids*.
b. Negligence on the part of the bidder in preparing the bid confers no right for the withdrawal of the bid after it has been opened.

5. *COMPETENCY OF BIDDER*

a. A contract will not be awarded to any person, firm, or corporation that has failed to perform faithfully any previous contract with the Hospital.

6. *CONSIDERATION OF PROPOSALS*

a. The Hospital reserves the right to reject any or all quotations or to waive any informalities or technicalities in any quotations in the interest of the Hospital.

7. *BID GUARANTEE*

a. Each proposal shall be accompanied by a bid guarantee for five percent (5%) of the amount of the total bid. Bid guarantees shall be a Bond made on the Proposal Bond Form or a cashier's check.

b. The Proposal Bond shall guarantee that the bidder will not withdraw, cancel or modify his bid for a period of sixty (60) days after the scheduled closing date for receipt of bids. The Proposal Bond shall further guarantee that, if his bid is accepted, the bidder will enter into a formal contract in accordance with the method of contracting hereinafter specified.

c. In the event the bidder withdraws his bid within the sixty (60)-day period or fails to enter into a contract if his bid is accepted, he shall be liable to the Hospital for the full amount of the bid guarantee.

d. The Proposal Bond shall be returned to all unsuccessful bidders after the successful bidder has executed the Performance Bond and the bid has been accepted by the Hospital.

e. The Proposal Bond must be endorsed by surety or sureties, and names of endorsers must be typed immediately below signature.

8. *METHOD OF CONTRACTING*

a. Award of contracts will be in the form of a Purchase Order made by the Hospital on the basis of the *best* bid from a qualified contractor.

b. The successful bidder shall deliver to the Hospital a Performance Bond with sureties satisfactory to the Hospital in the amount of one hundred percent (100%) of the total accepted bid.

c. The agent of the surety bonding company must be able to furnish on demand:

   a) Credentials showing his power of attorney.
   b) Certificate showing the legal right of the company to do business in the state of the Hospital.

9. *INTERPRETATION OF CONTRACT DOCUMENTS*

a. Discrepancies, omissions, or doubts as to the meaning of the specifications should be communicated in writing to the Hospital for interpretation. Bidders should act promptly and allow sufficient time for a reply to reach them before the submission of bids. Any interpretation made will be in the form of an addendum to the specifications, which will be forwarded to all bidders and its receipt by the bidder must be acknowledged on the Form of Proposal.

10. *RESPONSIBILITY OF THE BIDDERS*

a. Bidders shall visit the site and note local pertinent field conditions such as availability of loading docks, elevators, and all other receiving and inspecting facilities.

b. Bidders are responsible for the installation and start-up of their equipment including the following:

c. Bidders are to include with this quotation complete information on the local service center including:

d. Bidders are to include with this quotation all warranty information concerning the system components outlined in Bidder's Proposal.

e. Bidders shall provide an annual price for manufacturer's recommended preventive maintenance program to be provided by factory-trained and qualified personnel, after the warranty period.

11. *SALES TAX*

  a. The Hospital is a tax-exempt institution.
  b. Copies of the exemption certificate will be furnished upon request.

12. *METHOD OF PAYMENT*

  a. Requests for payments (invoices) must include the following information for processing:

    1) Purchase order number
    2) Manufacturer name and catalog item number
    3) Dollar amount.

  b. Payment for equipment shall be made according to the following schedule:

    1) Ten percent (10%) of contract price as down payment shall be made within ten (10) days of acknowledgement of order.
    2) Eighty percent (80%) of contract price shall be due and payable within ten (10) days of delivery, installation (to include field assembly, interconnection, equipment calibration to manufacturer's specification, and checkout), and acceptance by the Hospital of all system components as outlined in Bidder's Proposal.
    3) Ten percent (10%) shall be payable six (6) days after acceptance by the Hospital.

  c. The Hospital reserves the right to refuse payment on an invoice due to damaged item(s), quantity variance, model variance, or any failure to comply with the contract documents.

B. FORM OF PROPOSAL

Submitted by: Date:

_____   _____

TO: HOSPITAL

We, the undersigned, have familiarized ourselves with the local conditions affecting the cost of the work, and with all contract documents for this work, including:

       INSTRUCTIONS TO BIDDERS   PROPOSAL BOND

       PROPOSAL FORM   BID SPECIFICATIONS

And also have received and incorporated into the makeup of the specifications the following addenda:

Addendum No. _____ Dated _____ Addendum No. _____ Dated _____

Hereby propose to furnish all labor, equipment, and transportation to deliver and install all materials, and to perform and supervise all work as required.

TIME OF COMPLETION: Installation must be complete by _____, 19_____.

EXECUTION OF CONTRACT: If written notice of acceptance of this bid is mailed, telegraphed, or delivered to the undersigned within sixty (60) days after date required for the receipt of the bid, or any time thereafter before this bid is withdrawn, the undersigned will, within ten (10) days after date of such notice, execute and deliver a Performance Bond.

NOTE A: Bids submitted by virtue of the proposal hereby acknowledged by the Hospital to be made under the assumption that the successful bidder will not be prevented, on account of strikes or other disruptions affecting sources of supply or affecting normal progress of the work, from obtaining the materials necessary to carry out this contract to complete the work covered thereby.

NOTE B: It is understood and agreed by the undersigned that the Hospital reserves the right to reject any or all bids, or to accept the bid that embraces such combination of proposal that will promote the best interest of the Hospital.

NOTE C: It is agreed that this proposal shall be irrevocable for a period of sixty (60) days after the date set for the receipt of proposals.

NOTE D: It is understood and agreed by the undersigned that they will cooperate and coordinate their work with the contractor who will be in the final stage of work at the Hospital.

The undersigned hereby designates the office to which such notice may be mailed, telegraphed, or delivered:

_____

_____

_____

Enter here the service information requested in 10-D of "INSTRUCTIONS TO BIDDERS": __

_____   _____

_____

SIGNATURE OF BIDDER

SEAL (if a corporation)   Date _____
                                        Name of Firm _____
                                                     _____
                                                  By _____
                                               Title _____
                                    Business Address _____
                                                     _____
                                                     _____
                                    Telephone Number _____
                               State of Incorporation _____

NOTE 1:   If bidder is a corporation, write state of incorporation, and if a partnership, give full name of all partners.

NOTE 2:   Any deviation from the specifications must be specifically stated. Include also an explanation where the bidder's project exceeds the above specifications.

NOTE 3:   Alternatives, where presented in addition to the base bid, will be considered but must follow the instructions above, listing deviations to the specifications, and include complete descriptions and literature.

C. PROPOSAL BOND

KNOW ALL MEN BY THESE PRESENTS, THAT WE, _____

_____, (hereinafter called the Principal), as principal, and

_____, (hereinafter called the Surety), as surety, are

firmly bound unto the Hospital in the amount of _____
(amount not less than five percent (5%) of the accompanying bid plus the sum of all additive alternates) in lawful money of the United States for payment of which said Principal and Surety bind themselves, their heirs, executors, successors, administrators, and assigns, jointly and severally.

WHEREAS, said Principal has submitted to the Hospital a written proposal for certain work in connection with the (describe project), a copy of which is hereto attached.

NOW THEREFORE, the condition of this obligation is such that if said Proposal be accepted, the Principal shall, within ten (10) days of written notice thereof, enter into proper contract for the work covered by the Proposal, and shall furnish a Performance Bond satisfactory to said Hospital. If there is a difference between the amount of the Proposal and the amount accepted then, this obligation shall be reduced to five percent (5%) of the value of the Proposal accepted. This Proposal Bond shall be valid for a period of sixty (60) days from the date set for the receipt of the Proposal attached thereto.

Signed and sealed this _____day of _____, 19_____

Witness: _____(SEAL)

_____,   _____
                                        Principal

Countersigned at _____(SEAL)

By _____

D. SPECIFICATIONS

PART 1—GENERAL

1. *RELATED DOCUMENTS*

    a. Contract Documents, including General and Supplementary conditions and General Requirement, and contract drawings for the Hospital, apply to the work specified in this section.

2. *DESCRIPTION OF WORK*

    a. Successful bidder shall furnish, deliver F.O.B. jobsite, and install, all equipment specified herein, including all necessary attachment devices and all incidentals and accessories required for a complete and operable installation. Any omissions of the details in specifications does not relieve the bidder from furnishing a complete functioning installation of highest quality for all purposes intended.

b. The work shall be coordinated with the mechanical and electrical trades where services and connections are required for proper installation and operation of equipment.

c. It shall be noted that all interconnecting cabling throughout the installation shall be furnished by the bidder at no additional cost to the Hospital.

d. The Bidder is required to clean up, remove, and dispose of all debris resulting from work hereunder.

3. *QUALITY ASSURANCE*

   a. Manufacturer's Qualifications:

      1) Only manufacturers having a minimum of five (5) years experience in the manufacture and installation of the quality and type of the respective items of equipment specified herein shall be considered qualified.

      2) Manufacturer shall be able to demonstrate to the Hospital's satisfaction, proximity of spare parts and availability of experienced, competent maintenance service.

      3) Should the manufacturer find at any time during the progress of the work that, in his opinion, existing design or conditions require a modification of any particular part or assembly, he shall promptly report in writing such matter to the Hospital.

   b. Substitutions

      1) The following specifications are to establish a standard of quality and performance and are not intended to exclude any manufacturer or company from bidding quality equipment that can be proven to meet functional standards as set forth. The equipment to be furnished must meet the highest standards of the profession.

4. *CODE COMPLIANCE*

   a. All equipment furnished and installed under this section shall comply with all requirements of local, state, and federal building, health, sanitary, and NFPA Codes.

5. *STANDARDS*

   a. In addition to the above, the following standard shall apply to the extent referenced herein:

      1) Underwriters Laboratories, Incorporated (UL): Listings and approvals as required.

      2) Electrical components and wiring: Furnish and wire electrical components of equipment in this section to conform to NFPA 70 (National Fire Protection Association).

      3) All new equipment must be HHS certified.

6. *SUBMITTALS*

   a. Roughing-in Drawings:

      1) The Bidder will provide rough-in drawings and will coordinate and verify the dimensions and required services with the architect.

      2) Roughing-in drawings must be supplied within two weeks after receiving notice of the award, to provide information to other contractors performing the roughing-in.

   b. Shop Drawings:

      1) Submit shop drawings and catalog cuts of standard manufactured items. Indicate in detail the methods of installation, connections, and all pertinent data relating to each item of equipment.

2) Catalog cuts shall indicate the specified model and characteristics of the item being furnished.

c. Operating and Maintenance Instructions:

1) The Bidder shall furnish the Hospital with four (4) bound copies of written instructions, giving detailed information as to how the equipment is to be operated and maintained. Maintenance manuals shall include appropriate parts list and the name of the service representative.

2) In addition, a representative from the equipment manufacturer shall visit the project and instruct the Hospital personnel on the proper operation and maintenance of the equipment. The instruction period consists of not less than two (2) separate sessions, to be scheduled by the Hospital after occupancy.

d. Guarantee and Preventive Maintenance:

1) Upon completion, and as a condition for acceptance of the work, the Bidder shall submit written guarantee(s) covering each item included in this section for a period one (1) year from date of beneficial use. The guarantee shall cover all workmanship and materials and the Bidder agrees to repair or replace all faulty work and defective materials and equipment, including labor.

2) The Bidder shall be responsible for maintenance of the equipment for the first six (6) months, with all costs for parts, labor, and trips to and from the hospital covered by the warranty.

Source: Departmental document, reprinted with permission of St. Francis-St. George Hospital, Inc., Cincinnati, Ohio.

15. Capital Equipment Purchasing in Radiology

GIL MEREDITH

No manager of a health care facility would miss an opportunity to save 15 percent a year on a supply item whose cost ran into the hundreds of thousands of dollars annually. In a radiology department, for example, competitive quotation processes for film purchasing are taken for granted. Indeed, much effort is spent in such departments finding ways to trim film utilization by a few percentage points. The need to save is obvious yet opportunities for greater savings in radiology purchasing often are ignored or missed.

The purchase of major capital equipment for radiology may be an annual event even in moderate-sized hospitals. The 300-bed community hospital, for example, might typically have $2.5 million in replacement value of radiology equipment that needs upgrading and replacement at a rate of $300,000 a year. At today's prices this means that this hospital has eight x-ray rooms, one of which is due for replacement each year. In many cases, of course, the purchasing is more sporadic and clustered than this but the opportunity is clear in any event.

Above the replacement capital level are the costs of adding new and innovative technology. This process has been going on for years and shows little sign of abating even in the cost-per-case environment. The wave of new, first-time CT scanner purchasing has largely passed, succeeded by the age of magnetic resonance imaging (MRI). Many hospitals also have added digital angiography equipment, cardiac catheterization facilities, complex tomography machines, and so on. It is clear from all this that expectations for radiology capital expenditures cannot be limited to the replacement cycle alone.

Before discussing effective control of capital expenditures in radiology, the cost/benefit issue needs study. While this is a particularly acute question in regard to new technology, routine replacement costs need to be viewed in a similar light. All equipment must be analyzed from the perspective of what it produces, diagnosis related group (DRG) as well as procedure, while exploring the cost effectiveness of options such as overhaul, upgrade, refurbishment, and new purchase, which is the last resort.

Even with stringent cost/benefit analyses, there still will remain a significant volume of new radiology equipment purchasing. What is needed is a process by which material managers and purchasing agents can gain some control over those expenditures. Such major capital funds decisions should not be left to the clinical department alone.

RADIOLOGY PRICING

The potential for savings in radiology capital equipment is not as easy to identify as it is in some other purchasing situations. Most radiology equipment manufacturers and vendors do not publish complete price lists as bench marks against which the success of a purchasing effort can be judged. Even when list prices are identified for some items, the package of equipment typically bought by radiology is configured uniquely for each facility, and identifying the true list price of the final package is nearly impossible.

Group purchasing organizations have negotiated contracts with x-ray equipment vendors that specify a percentage reduction from list price for their members. Since that price is almost never identifiable, these contracts are of limited use and indeed, in some circumstances, have limited the hospital's ability to negotiate effective terms and conditions. For example, these group contracts may invalidate performance bonuses and penalties. For these reasons, reliance on group purchasing organizations to save capital costs may not be prudent practice. Radiology capital purchasing is one circumstance in which the individual institution can conduct its own negotiations and achieve the best results on a local level (see Appendix 15-A).

CAPITAL PURCHASING TRADITIONS

The degree of formality in radiology purchasing generally increases as hospital size grows. The most formal processes usually are in public, tax-supported institutions that are required to solicit formal competitive bids. The least formal and most flexible situation would be that of a small rural hospital whose area is serviced by only one vendor. In that circumstance, competitive bidding probably would be a futile exercise, so a purchasing group might be of real use.

Most hospitals lie between these extremes. Traditionally, radiologist preference has played the strongest and sometimes the only role in the decision. Hospital administrations and boards have been loath to accept nonphysician judgment on diagnostic equipment. The result is that radiologists develop or maintain brand preferences, sometimes out of proportion to an objective analysis of the utility of various manufacturers' equipment. This is one reason why capital equipment purchasing in radiology has been a difficult area for administrations to come to grips with.

In recent times, most hospitals of intermediate size have been shifting away from this absolute prerogative. In general, the rise in the educational level and sophistication of radiology managers and the increasingly systematic approach of material management departments have together exercised restraint. However, the radiologists' input is necessary and desirable, particularly on equipment they will use, such as fluoroscopic systems. Hospitals should assure themselves that their radiologists are not unmindful of the prudent buyer principle. Radiology departments need, especially, to recognize the value of encouraging price competition among multiple suppliers.

Special Circumstances

Consideration of multiple vendors for each purchase needs to be amended somewhat in the case of an institution involved in research and innovation. There may be good reasons for their deciding that a particular vendor's system is what is desired. Consideration must be given to the specialists and physicists involved in setting the design parameters. Based on the institution's research commitment, the details these individuals specify may need to be taken as absolutes.

For hospitals that do not have trained radiological engineers or physicists and with management personnel unskilled in the specification process, the use of consultants should be considered. Ideally, an institution should use consultants infrequently, such as for the purchase of extremely specialized equipment, or on a one-time basis to train hospital personnel in the process.

Action Plans

An effective methodology for organizing a system of shared responsibility is to develop a detailed action plan delineating the responsibilities of each segment of the organization (Exhibit 15–1). This can serve as a perspective framework to understand all the individual steps involved.

It should be noted that the action plan specifies not only what is to be done but also who is responsible for ensuring that each step is carried out, and establishes a timetable for each phase. Exhibit 15–1 is a part of the methodology developed by the American Hospital Association in its Technology Evaluation and Acquisition Methods (TEAM) program.[1] Depending upon the complexity of the purchase, steps in evaluating technology may be deleted or expanded.

Formal systems can create a frustratingly slow process but the potential savings justify the time commitment. For even a simple radiographic

Exhibit 15–1 Excerpt from an Action Plan

Action Plan
Digital Subtraction Angiography (DSA)
Page Two

Item #	Steps	Person Resp.	Results	Dates Start/Due
9.	Conduct needs assessment (historical/demographic)	Dept. Mgr. Planning	Trend analysis and activity projections	10/25/82– 11/30/82
10.	Survey physician demand	VP Med. Aff.	Information campaign conducted and DSA utilization questionnaire returned by physician	11/8/82– 11/22/82
11.	Conduct financial assessment based on several activity level projections.	Budget Dir.	Thorough return on investment projections.	11/16/82– 11/23/82
12.	Preliminary vendor evaluation and engineering checklist.	Dept. Mgr. Rad.	Vendor evaluation and engineering checklist information submitted to Dept. Mgr. Purchasing	11/17/82– 11/30/82
13.	Conduct impact assessment.	Dept. Mgr. Planning	Completed impact statement.	11/23/82– 11/30/82
14.	Capital budget approval	Exec. VP	Board of Trustees approval of project for fiscal 1983.	11/30/82– 11/31/82
15.	Conduct vendor screening	Dept. Mgr. Purch.	Vendor screening work sheet and vendor checklist complete.	12/6/82– 12/20/82
16.	Develop detailed technical specifications.	Dept. Mgr. Rad.	Specifications to be included in requests for proposal.	12/6/82– 12/20/82
17.	Distribute requests for proposal identifying purchase terms and conditions.	Dept. Mgr. Purch.	RFPs sent to qualified vendors.	12/20/82

Total time frame for this project was nine months.

Source: Departmental document, reprinted with permission of St. Francis-St. George Hospital, Inc., Cincinnati, Ohio.

room, it would not be uncommon to allocate four to six months to the process, with delivery and installation time extending that even longer.

Policy Requirements

In initiating any bid system, the capital equipment committee or similar authority should establish overall hospital policy requirements.

The details of how the policies are expressed will, of course, be different in each institution but there are certain policy requirements (discussed in Chapter 14 and later in this chapter). The following factors also need special attention in radiology equipment purchasing:

- Functional analysis: This would include a listing of procedures to be performed on the particular equipment, anticipated volumes, revenue and expense projections, and an analysis of an alternative method of achieving the same or similar results without the requested purchase.

- Performance and service documentation: The best information for judging the quality of vendor proposals is a thorough history of performance of similar equipment. If this documentation has not been maintained previously, it should be required in the future. It is important to have planned in advance to document a machine's performance.

- Site planning: Radiology systems are custom designed for the site of installation. Both new services and replacements require especially close cooperation among the radiology and building services departments and the supplier. Space and utilities modifications may add substantially to the total costs of any package.

Radiology/Purchasing Cooperation

There are appropriate and achievable goals for purchasing departments that can help build a cooperative relationship with radiology. The first is to act as a hospital financial management representative to radiology. The purchaser serves as a reminder of the overall goals and position of the hospital with regard to accountability and appropriateness of expenditures.

A second function is to provide third-party negotiating assistance. This go-between role can deemphasize some of the subjective and emotional issues that can intrude into purchasing decisions. A third function is to facilitate the accomplishment of purchasing objectives by developing formal procedures and documents that detail the legal and financial obligations of the hospital and the vendor. This is not to say that the purchaser actually writes the technical portions of the specifications but rather ensures that they are provided fairly to all vendors and in such a way as to promote the development of enforceable contractual obligations on both parties.

THE EQUIPMENT

With minimal prior knowledge, a technological system can be evaluated if it is broken down into small enough component units. In the most simplistic terms, functions and components almost always fall into categories that can be evaluated on the basis of: (1) presence or absence of a specific function, (2) larger or smaller measurable units, and (3) a small sequence of discrete material, construction, or function options.

The level of detail a purchaser can participate in is well demonstrated by looking at the personal computer market. While few understand exactly what goes on in the computer's internal information processing unit, everyone is aware of some parameters that characterize it. For example, a familiar term is K and it is known that in general, the more K a computer has, the more powerful it is; floppy discs handle more information storage faster than magnetic tape systems; and the line rate of printers is a useful objective method of comparison. A look at print samples from various companies can help decide the particular type that is appropriate to a hospital's use.

Radiologic System Characteristics

Radiology systems generally have more components than a personal computer but the same process can be followed in becoming familiar with their characteristics.

With the exception of self-contained systems, such as mobile radiographic instruments, most radiology purchases are uniquely configured packages of components. While the predesigned systems offered by various vendors differ, all major sellers can put together comparable packages that will meet a hospital's functional goals. Because of this, it is important to define with the radiology department the functional system required. In few circumstances is a recommended package the ideal for any particular application. Radiology's tendency to push for a single supplier comes from its having dealt with a vendor that presents what the department ought to want.

The major functional subsystems of a radiology package are: (1) the x-ray table with its motion controls and image receptor accessories, (2) the x-ray generator or control unit with its power supply and high-voltage transformer interfaces, (3) the fluoroscopic image receptor and filming devices with their attachment either to the ceiling or to the table, (4) the x-ray tube with its ceiling suspension and beam limitation attachments. Specialized systems need additional components or unusual modifications (Appendix 15-B).

The specification development process begins by outlining these major subsystems, then breaking them down into identifiable components. The purchasing manager helps radiology representatives define their requirements for each subsystem, then each component.

Generic Functional Specifications

Chapter 14 described a system to distinguish between requirements and preferences in defining equipment specifications. This process is particularly valuable in radiology purchases.[2]

The role of the purchasing manager in this effort is to act as a critical, naive questioner and continuously interpret financial management's goals to radiology. The more rigid a specification the department develops, the more appropriate are the questions: "Is this absolutely necessary?" "Are there alternative ways of achieving the same function?" "What are the financial benefits of this particular preference?" This point-by-point analysis helps focus on critical function requirements and defines needs in terms that will allow the widest possible range of vendor competition. The key is to keep this goal in mind and develop specifications that are function-oriented (as opposed to hardware-oriented) and as generically applicable as possible.

Sources of Information

When system needs have been broken down to the component level, sources of technical specification are available for comparisons among vendors. *The Imaging Equipment Compendium* developed by the American College of Radiology is probably the most useful source for identifying measurable characteristics of equipment components.[3] (Other sources are cited in the bibliography of this chapter.) The American Hospital Radiology Administrators also has developed prototype specification formats.[4] Another American College of Radiology publication, *Acceptance Testing Protocols,* can further refine specifications.[5] It is important to consider the inclusion only of specifications that can be checked and evaluated in the delivered product. If a hospital has no method for determining whether it has purchased what has been specified, there is little reason to include such specifications. Even without sophisticated engineering resources, acceptance testing is essential to ensure vendor accountability. This can be as simple as measuring the degree of tilt of a table or as rigorous as repeated testing to ensure linearity of generator output.

ESTABLISHING GOALS

Before initiating any capital purchase at the level of expenditure typical of radiology systems, the institution must have its specific goals in mind. A functional analysis of the required performance is essential before beginning the process. Return on investment calculations need to be as precise as possible, especially in terms of the type of patient upon whom the equipment will be used and the marketing position of the institution as it relates to this type of client.

Other essential goals at the outset are to ensure internal agreement on the course of action to be followed and to establish procedures to monitor the effectiveness not only of the purchase but of the equipment as well. These also entail predetermination of acceptable expenditures for system enhancements.

The first time through this process produces a fringe benefit: the education of both the purchasing and radiology departments to each other's goals and perspectives. This can only make coordination of future purchases more effective. Radiology must be made more aware of purchasing's legitimate concerns on price and account-

ability. Purchasing needs to learn more of the technical requirements that radiology considers so essential.

NOTES

1. American Hospital Association, "Case Study: Digital Subtraction Angiography Evaluation and Acquisition at St. Francis-St. George Hospital, Inc., Cincinnati, Ohio, *Technology Evaluation and Acquisition Methods for Hospitals* (Chicago: Author, September 1983).

2. Gil Meredith, "Generic Functional Specifications," *Medical Imaging Administrator* 1, no. 11 (December 1982).

3. American College of Radiology, *Imaging Equipment Compendium: A Comparative Reference of Equipment Characteristics* (1983).

4. American Hospital Radiology Association, "Equipment Specifications and Performance Standards," *Radiology Management* 2, no. 5 (Summer 1980): 27–34.

5. American College of Radiology, *Acceptance Testing Protocols: A Systematic Approach to Evaluating Radiologic Equipment* (1983).

BIBLIOGRAPHY

Berry, Gary C., et al. "Objective Equipment Selection and Performance Evaluation." *Radiology Management* 2, no. 5 (Summer 1980): 14–26.

diMonda, Richard. "Keeping Abreast of Technology: Sources of Data on New Developments." *Hospitals, JAHA* (January 16, 1984): 85–90.

Grossman, Richard. "Leasing Versus Buying Equipment." *Applied Radiology* (November/December 1983): 69–72.

Hamilton, Betty, ed. *Medical Diagnostic Imaging Systems.* New York: F. and S. Press, 1982.

Hendee, William R. "Managing the Procurement Process." *Administrative Radiology* (December 1983): 29–31.

Hendee, William R., and Rossi, R.P. "Performance Specification for Diagnostic X-ray Equipment." *Radiology* 120 (August 1976): 409–412.

Horan, John J., Jr. "Purchasing a CT Scanner Through the Quotation Process." *Hospital Purchasing Management* (September 1980).

Kirschner, Larry. "Format for Comparing Equipment Specifications." *Radiology Management* 2, no. 5 (Summer 1980): 35–42.

Meredith, Gil. "Equipment Purchasing: The Impact of DRGs." *Administrative Radiology* 3, no. 1 (January 1984): 16–20.

Robb, W.L. "Buying Diagnostic Imaging Equipment: Points to Ponder, Pitfalls to Avoid." *Hospital Materials Management Quarterly* (February 1981).

Siedband, Melvin P. "Purchasing Dilemma: Replace or Refurbish." *Radiology Management* 4, no. 1 (December 1981): 2–3.

Appendix 15–A

The Vendors

NATIONAL PERSPECTIVE

The national position of a vendor may be of only minor interest in any specific purchase situation. At this writing there are six major vendors with wide geographic representation (CGR, Elscint, General Electric, Philips, Picker, and Siemens.) The field is evolving with new entrants that may be strong locally, such as Fisher, Hitachi, Raytheon, and Toshiba. Specialized equipment such as CT, digital imaging (DSA or DVI), heart monitoring equipment for cardiac catheterization, and others may involve an even wider range of vendors. (In addition to these manufacturers, a number of nonmanufacturer vendors may be strong in a given area.)

LOCAL CONSIDERATIONS

A major consideration in any purchase situation is the ability of a particular vendor to provide adequate local service, including local availability of parts and, in some cases, the need for local commitment to stock consumable supplies for a piece of equipment.

The primary local variable may be the perception by sales representatives of the competitive climate in a given market. The ability of local sales personnel and the perspective of the local district sales manager may well influence the ability of any health care facility to negotiate effective terms, conditions, components, and price. Subjective judgments on the degree of cooperation the hospital is likely to be able to elicit from a particular supplier are vital considerations in purchase decisions. These factors can determine what vendors will be contacted to submit bids, particularly where numerous sellers are represented locally.

VENDOR MARGINS AND DISCOUNTS

The difficulty in identifying the list price of radiology equipment (as noted) does not negate the fact that the vendors have established those prices, usually internally and secretly. In this industry, gross margin is up to 40 percent of this unofficial list price. Vendors usually begin negotiations somewhat below what they would consider to be list price, presenting this as a budgetary quotation. Percentage reductions from this generally should not be expected to exceed 20 or 25 percent. A local salesman may be given the authority to discount 10 percent below list price, with a further 5 or 10 percent cut approvable by the district manager. Beyond this reduction of 15 to 20 percent, the district manager typically would have to seek approval from regional or national sales executives.

Occasionally a hospital can motivate a vendor to seek approval for greater than typical discount—a factor usually determined by the local market position of the particular seller. Circumstances such as the need to penetrate a previously slow market or to showcase a particular system provide incentives for additional discounts.

RADIOLOGY/VENDOR RELATIONSHIPS

In some circumstances, a radiology department develops a virtually exclusive relationship with one vendor—an appropriate situation when only one supplier can provide service. Prudent purchasing in such circumstances should be limited to ensuring that radiology systems do not exceed the facility's functional requirements.

Where there are numerous vendors to consider, radiology departments tend to form preferential relationships with one of them. These relationships often are based on reasoned evaluation of the quality of equipment and service but also on personal preferences for the sales representative or the equipment. In encouraging radiology to consider several vendors, the hospital purchasing manager should explore the history of the department's relationships with local suppliers.

Aside from historically acquired brand preference (which can come from the radiologists or managers who have trained on a particular brand of equipment) the primary basis by which vendors are judged is the quality of the service support they provide. This critical element generally is judged on the performance of the local service office. This is the reason why in particular areas of the country one brand of x-ray equipment predominates over all others. Radiologists and managers in an area may say that brand X is the only reliable equipment, whereas their counterparts from another area may specify brand Y. If they are being honest in their assessments, the geographical variation in service support quality provides an explanation for this bias.

Since several x-ray companies have regional pockets of strength, it is clear that local support is as important as the actual quality of the equipment. That is not to say that there are not differences in components or types of systems but there is less variation in manufacturing quality than most radiologists perceive.

It is important to be aware that service quality can change or be negotiated to change. Service organizations wax and wane in a region, and any vendor increasing market share is likely to improve the quality of the service support. For these reasons, even vendors with previously less-than-excellent service reputations often can be considered in purchase decisions. What needs to be confronted is not so much the facts of the situation but the halo effect of a vendor's reputation.

INDUSTRY CHANGES AND TRENDS

Experiences in the computer field are reflected to some degree in the x-ray industry. In the late 1970s and early 1980s, a number of vendors proved unable to compete. On the other hand, some suppliers have developed solid market positions. In general, the newer vendors often can offer their product at competitive pricing levels, so the difficult judgment is whether they have enough financial and technological stability to continue to support their product after sale.

X-ray equipment has a life span of five to ten years, requiring service, parts, and upgrade support throughout that period. A searching appraisal of the probable corporate stability of each vendor is necessary before the purchasing department overenthusiastically responds to exciting new technology or attractive price proposals.

Radiologic Equipment

SUBSYSTEMS AND COMPONENTS

The following are brief outlines of the major subsystems and components of common radiology systems.

Radiographic

A basic radiographic system consists of the generator and control; the x-ray table, which may be stationary or tilting; and the x-ray tube and its support, which may be fixed to the table, based on the floor, or suspended from the ceiling. Working with a radiology representative, the purchasing manager can break each of these three major subsystems down into half a dozen components or performance characteristics.

Fluoroscopic

Fluoroscopic systems generally are composed of the essential components of a radiographic system plus an image intensification and television display system. Generally this image-intensifying system also includes some way of recording stop-motion images that may include a spot-film device or some other method of serial permanent imaging.

For a system to function well in a fluoroscopic mode, there will be elaborations of the basic systems used for radiography. For two examples, the simplest generators cannot handle the fluoroscopic room configuration of two x-ray tubes and normally tilting tables are a necessity for fluoroscopy.

Tomographic

There are dedicated tomographic systems that in simplest terms represent a radiographic system in which the image receptor and x-ray tube move in coordinated fashion during the x-ray exposure. This motion may be simple, in one direction (linear), or may represent a number of complex motion types.

Tomography can be included as an enhancement to a system that also functions as a basic radiographic facility. It is a major question for radiology departments whether a dedicated tomographic system is appropriate or whether the add-on hybrid apparatus is more appropriate. These decisions will depend on the type of workload that the equipment is likely to experience.

Mobile

There are two basic types of mobile x-ray equipment. The first generally is called a portable and is a combination x-ray generator and exposure system that can be wheeled to the patient's bedside. These systems often have unique generation and x-ray production methods adapted to the demands of mobile work, and may include battery systems for exposure and/or power motion.

The second type is a mobile fluoroscope, often called a C-arm. This is an x-ray generator combined with the image intensifier used in fluoroscopy for live, real-time imaging. Most of these systems also are capable of producing radiographs, although such use often is limited by low generator capacity. These systems are used most often in surgical applications where physicians must monitor the course of surgery on an intermittent basis.

Angiographic

Angiographic suites are x-ray systems that incorporate all the characteristics of radiographic and fluoroscopic systems, with specialized design of some components. For example, the image intensifier may be somewhat different in an angiographic room, and the angiographic table sometimes will have quite different design requirements (such as raising and lowering its table top) than a normal fluoroscopic table.

The major addition to angiographic purchases involves systems for rapid sequence x-ray filming. These often are arranged in pairs so that simultaneous or alternating imaging can go on from two directions. These film-changers and associated controls greatly complicate the physical design of such rooms and the requirements of the generator and x-ray tube systems.

An angiographic subset is the type used for imaging the arteries of the heart and heart chambers. These cardiac catheterization facilities generally are the most expensive x-ray systems the hospital will purchase (outside of computed tomography) and have function and design criteria at high levels of sophistication and performance. Various angiographic facilities, especially cardiac catheterization units, also involve patient monitoring gear similar to that used in a cardiac care facility or surgical suite.

Computed Tomographic

Computed tomography (CT) systems are generally an exception to the uniquely configured x-ray facilities. Most computed tomography manufacturers allow few options in design.

However, there are add-ons that become a major issue because of their high price. For example, remote image viewing consoles for radiologists to monitor the exam at a distance are a costly but often necessary addition to a CT unit. Other options may include larger computer information storage systems such as disc drives and magnetic tape recorders and additional image-processing capabilities such as radiation therapy planning software.

Because of the high price of CT systems and the limited number of manufacturers, purchasers have only limited discretion. Serviceability is an essential characteristic for all x-ray vendors but it is particularly crucial for CT. For example, if only two vendors offer local CT service, it may be a mistake for a hospital to solicit bids from other manufacturers. Because of the critical nature of the procedure, the imperative concern in CT may be the response and technical ability of local service personnel. Just a few days of downtime on a CT scanner can cost the hospital more than it would be likely to save through any rigorous competitive bidding process.

Major Accessories

Image-processing equipment constitutes the bulk of major accessories that may be included in a radiology system—for example, television camera setups that impress images in a small format on x-ray film. Systems such as these multiformat cameras may be used in angiographic, fluoroscopic, and CT systems. They also are finding wider application for mobile fluoroscopic systems, providing more convenient and faster methods of documenting surgical procedures.

X-ray film processors themselves may be components of these systems. More frequently, however, they are located in centralized darkrooms and often are a separate purchase. Noteworthy is the "daylight" or "room light" system in which x-ray films are dispensed into cassettes (the imaging filmholder) from machines outside the darkroom. These films then are released automatically into the film processing equipment without the need for any staff person to enter a darkroom. These systems have particular use in emergency departments and have been designed as integral parts of some new hospital construction (eliminating or reducing the number of darkrooms) to reduce space and associated building costs.

This chapter has not addressed the associated disciplines of nuclear medicine and ultrasound. Such equipment has its own unique characteristics but can be approached in a similar way by breaking the purchases down into subsystems and components.

CRITICAL PERFORMANCE PARAMETERS

There is yet another way to approach the specification process: Hardware often needs additional qualifications such as those described next.

Radiation Output

Generators, x-ray tube systems, and fluoroscopic systems all need to be described in terms of the energy level (voltage) and current (milliamperage) that determines their radiation output. The exposure times and number of exposures possible in a given time also may be critical.

With increasing sophistication of technical support available to a hospital, the actual x-ray beam characteristics may be measurable and definable. These could involve measurement of the effective energy level of the beam (half-value layer) and measurement of the geometric properties of the beam exiting the x-ray tube (effective focal spot size). The choice of how tightly to specify radiation output depends upon the sophistication available. At a minimum, though, radiation output must be specified, at least to the level of generator power requirements and x-ray tube output limitations.

Image Conspicuity

The final product of any radiographic system is the image to be interpreted. This image generally is thought to be composed of three separate but complexly interacting elements: film density, film contrast range, and adjacent small structure resolution. The sum of these three interacting variables produces what has been called image conspicuity.

The components most closely associated with this are the geometric characteristics of the x-ray tube focal spot and the characteristics of the image receptor systems, be they television image amplification systems or x-ray cassettes with associated film.

The actual emphasis on performance of a system in any one of these regards will vary, depending upon the system. The purchaser need only be assured that radiology representatives have not neglected these issues or, contrariwise, set performance goals that are unrealistically high.

Functional Flexibility

In subjective judgment of equipment, the flexibility and ease with which it can be manipulated is a major concern. It is difficult to develop objectively quantifiable standards in this area but it is a real and legitimate concern.

One way of helping quantify this characteristic is for a purchasing agent to arrange for site visits with a representative of radiology to look at and physically handle several kinds of equipment. From this a scale of preference can be established that, while noting which equipment the department thinks is best, still can allow it to consider purchasing other units that may be acceptable if other factors are equal or superior.

Serviceability and Service Cost

The best possible method of judging serviceability and service costs is a thorough history of equipment service and associated cost. If a system for keeping track of service history has not been developed, the hospital should do so.

Once such a history is established, the differential cost of service can be evaluated in subsequent purchases. For example, if one vendor proposes a product with a $20,000 lower price but has shown a history of $4,000 a year in extra service costs, the total expense over the lifetime of the equipment can be used as a basis of comparison rather than just the purchase price alone.

In the absence of in-house records sufficient to detail expected service costs, the experience of other institutions can be used. Larger, teaching type hospitals are likely to have maintained a history of equipment service costs and may serve as a valuable resource to a community hospital.

The American Hospital Association maintains a data base of equipment function nationwide and can provide a hospital with the names of institutions that in the past have purchased the items under consideration. While such reports may be anecdotal and unquantified, they still can provide some basis for comparison.

Warranties

Throughout the x-ray industry six-month warranties covering parts and service are the standard—but they typically exclude x-ray tubes and other vacuum glassware such as image intensifier tubes and television camera tubes.

If standard six-month warranties are used as a comparison, there is no price variance between vendors. If, however, a supplier offers longer warranties, some cost formulation is necessary for comparison. A simple methodology is to ask vendors to quote as a supplemental option the cost of their one-year service contract, which begins at the expiration of warranty. Dividing this by the term of the warranty will give some estimate of the dollar value the vendor assigns to warranty extension.

Of course, terms and conditions of warranties must be examined to ensure comparability. Guaranteed service response time may be one item where vendors will differ. And while x-ray tubes are not generally included in the warranty terms, vendors may offer different prorations for their return during warranty.

PART III
SUPPLY, PROCESSING, AND DISTRIBUTION

More and more, health care facilities are coming to realize that controlling the initial purchase price of supplies, equipment, and services is not the only approach to improving their bottom line. Finding methods to receive, store, process, and distribute material more effectively can have an equal, and often greater, impact on financial performance. Institutions also are broadening their concept of material to include food, linen, pharmaceuticals, mail, information, and even people.

This part identifies the expanding scope of the supply, processing, and distribution (SPD) department and provides specific details of a number of its components.

Chapters 16 through 20 discuss the core functions of receiving, storing, and distributing material, including often overlooked functions such as mail services and both interfacility and patient transportation. It concludes with a discussion of the emerging phenomenon of off-site central distribution centers.

The final portion, Chapters 22–25, provides information on how to operate and control central processing, often known as central service. Much has been written about this but it often is not included in material management texts. As more material managers assume direct responsibility for this function, it will be imperative that they become familiar with these concepts. This section also includes detailed information on controlling the use of ethylene oxide, which is a major responsibility from an employee safety and legal liability standpoint.

16. Managing the Receiving and Transportation Department

William L. Scheyer

The purchasing department is the foundation of the material management division because it visibly represents the health care facility's interests to the business community. The receiving department, however, is a vital and often overlooked link in the material management chain because it is the entry point for all goods coming into the organization. It serves as a control element in the hospital/vendor relationship by ensuring that the proper goods arrive in appropriate condition and by coordinating with the accounts payable department to make sure payment is made only for items that actually arrived.

The design of this department can range from that of the basic receiving office that handles only the receipt of incoming goods to that of the receiving and transportation entity that also provides internal transport of goods between locations in a multisite health care organization. In addition, a number of related ancillary functions, such as mail service, can be attached to this department.

PHYSICAL DESIGN

The Ideal Arrangement

If a manager has the option of designing a new facility, the following elements must be provided:

1. Truck space: This must include an adequate number of receiving bays to meet the anticipated volume of deliveries. This will vary from organization to organization but must be based upon both the historical and anticipated number of daily deliveries from different vendors. In general, except in extremely high-volume operations, three bays will suffice.

2. Adequate turnaround space for incoming trucks: It is relatively expensive to dedicate space for this function as it sits empty most of the time. However, if it is not done, the result is a chronic pattern of traffic jams as trucks maneuver in the street. This is irritating for the drivers, slows the flow of deliveries, and can be a traffic hazard.

3. Adequate area for queuing of trucks: If receiving bays and turnaround space are provided, and if scheduling is effective, the need for this will be minimized. However, there inevitably will be times when more deliveries arrive than can be handled at one time. The only alternatives are to send trucks away or have them wait their turns. If no space is available in the dock area, the trucks will line up on the street. This is not an effective solution and can be avoided by providing a reasonable amount of queuing space.

When possible, the dock itself should be enclosed so that goods can be unloaded directly from the truck into the building. When this is not possible, an overhang should be provided so that materials are not exposed unnecessarily to inclement weather. This also helps the receiving employees, who then do not have to continually move from an inside to an outside environment.

Internal Areas

Once items have been taken from the truck, a number of internal areas are important in facilitating proper material handling:

1. A holding area for inspecting the incoming goods: If sufficient space is not allowed for this, constant confusion results. This leads

179

to rushed and inaccurate counting and inspecting. This must not be allowed to happen because accurate inspecting and counting are the two reasons this department exists so adequate space must be provided.

2. A holding area for materials awaiting delivery: Shipments should be cleared out of the receiving area as quickly as possible but there will always be some delay. Adequate space must be provided to keep items from being mixed into other incoming or outgoing shipments and from being damaged while awaiting in-house delivery.

3. Another holding area for items awaiting return to the vendor, or other outgoing shipment: The same rule applies—clear them as soon as possible but while they are in the area, keep them separate and safe. By its nature, a receiving department is a high-traffic area. Large quantities of material are constantly moving in and out. To manage this function effectively, it is imperative that adequate space be allocated for handling various types of shipments and that the space be kept uncluttered and not be used for any purpose not related to the basic functions of the department.

Office space often is considered a luxury but it is not. The department must have a control center. This should be large enough to hold the supervisor, receiving control clerk, and all files and records. In addition, it should be able to accommodate future expansion, such as a dispatcher for ancillary transportation functions.

Unloading and Delivery

The basic work of this department involves a mixture of heavy labor and detail work. The receiving clerks must be able to unload heavy shipments from the delivery trucks, then accurately inspect, count, and record them onto standard documents. To do this, work surfaces must be provided for doing paper work. These can be fixed or fold-down types, depending upon space availability. In general, fold-downs are more flexible.

To facilitate unloading and delivery, material handling equipment is required. This generally is of three types: (1) pallet trucks, (2) four-wheel flat-bed delivery trucks, and (3) two-wheel dollies. The last two types are fairly simple to select. They must be sturdy and able to be kept clean. Purchase price is the main determinant in selection. Pallet trucks are a different matter. These can be either electrically driven or manually powered hydraulic trucks. In general, when the average loads that must be handled approach 1,500 pounds, electrically driven units should be considered seriously. These will speed up the work, reduce the risk of employee injury, and generally improve morale.

When selecting this type of equipment, optimal balance should be sought between purchase price and factors such as safety features, capacity, space required to operate, and service support from the manufacturer. The important point is that when material handling equipment is out of service, the receiving department is drastically slowed down, if not out of service. Therefore, it is vital to select and maintain proper equipment.

In terms of location, the receiving department should be adjacent to or immediately above or below the official inventory section of the hospital. This is because a high percentage of goods received will go to the inventory area. It is most effective to place these two areas on the same level. However, if this is not possible, a dependable elevator must be available for moving material between these departments. Elevator downtime (time spent out of service) can have a dramatic effect on departmental productivity. If an elevator is used, it is important to have a written back-up plan outlining exactly how functions will be performed, and what routes will be used, if it is out of service.

To recap, when designing a receiving area, the main points to remember are to allow adequate space for the following functions:

- truck movement
- unloading

- counting
- inspecting
- documentation
- temporary holding
- office activity.

The area also must be kept clean and uncluttered. Clutter is anathema to an effective receiving department.

Alternatives

Many times, particularly in older facilities, the manager will have to find ways to function despite poor design. The following ideas may be helpful in meeting this challenge. Limited truck space can be compensated for by enforcing a strict delivery schedule. All primary vendors should be given specific days and times for making deliveries. This can be part of the hospital/vendor relationship stipulated by the purchasing agent. The schedule must be enforced strictly. Variances cannot be tolerated or daily chaos will result.

The lack of adequate temporary holding areas can be compensated for by making the system for scheduling internal deliveries as effective as possible. Moving materials out of the area should be a daily priority of the receiving supervisor. It may be best to implement a policy of clearing all of the day's incoming orders by the end of the day, even if it requires overtime. The purchasing agent should help by making sure that when large orders are placed for departments outside material management, the ordering manager has made provision for accepting and storing the goods.

In some facilities, the primary trash disposal location is near the receiving department because it often is the only location with adequate space for the trash collection truck to maneuver when coming to clear out the dumpster. This is not a good design because it means that clean material coming into the hospital is placed in close proximity to grossly soiled material. This is a poor infection control situation. If it is unavoidable, the only solution is to keep the trash contained, keep the collection site

and pathway to it as clean as possible, and reduce cross-traffic whenever possible.

In general, the approach to take in compensating for less than optimal facilities is to define the basic required functional characteristics of the area, be creative in looking for ways to provide them, and be assertive in enforcing solutions once they have been identified.

POLICIES AND PROCEDURES

Unloading, Counting, and Inspecting

In an ideal system, all shipments would be completely counted and inspected before the delivery truck is allowed to leave. This usually is unrealistic. The answer is to inspect for obvious external damage and to ensure that the facility's bulk piece count agrees with that on the vendor's packing slip before signing for the shipment. As soon as possible after unloading, the shipment should be completely counted and inspected. Any discrepancies must be documented immediately and reported to the receiving supervisor. The supervisor must notify the purchasing agent to coordinate resolution of the problem.

There are two schools of thought as to whether the receiving documents that are sent to the receiving department awaiting arrival of a shipment should show quantities. The author's feeling is that they should not. This provides an additional internal control to ensure that orders actually are counted. Receiving clerks must be given an understanding of the importance of their role in controlling the flow of material into the hospital and must pay close attention to detail in verifying descriptions, quantities, and correct units of measure. These are probably the most common sources of errors in receiving departments.

In bulk orders, closed cases of standard type do not have to be opened and inspected. However, periodic spot checks are advisable, particularly if there is reason to suspect that a vendor is sending incomplete orders.

Because accurate counting and inspecting are so important, and because such a wide variety of material passes through this area, employees must receive adequate training. It takes time to develop a competent employee in this area so every effort should be made to keep the turnover rate low.

Another effective internal check involves the use of a receiving control clerk, who reconciles the documents completed by the other receiving clerks against the open purchase order log. This person can identify and correct discrepancies, usually involving count errors or unit-of-measure errors, before they reach the accounts payable department. This reduces the delay that results when the vendor invoice does not match the receiving document, affecting prompt payment discounts. It also helps to prevent incorrect receiving information from leading to erroneous payments to vendors.

The receiving control clerk is the person who sends completed receiving documents to either the computer room for keypunching or directly to the accounts payable department. This person also maintains all receiving document files and runs the clerical side of the office.

Deliveries

Once shipments have been officially received by the hospital, it is important that they be delivered to inventory or to other ordering departments as quickly as possible. This can be done by the receiving clerks after the counting/inspecting is done. This approach has two advantages: (1) Deliveries are made by people familiar with the orders because they counted them. (2) It gives the receiving clerks a break in the routine of the regular job, which can have a positive effect in terms of morale.

Another approach is to have deliveries made by a separate group. This is particularly effective if these deliveries are combined with those of other departments. The use of such a delivery pool can increase the efficiency of this function. Deliveries can be done on a fixed schedule or whenever an order has been completely counted and inspected.

The process of delivering orders can be too easily taken for granted. However, it also can be an excellent source of positive public relations

for the material management department. Delivery personnel must always be clean, well groomed, and in proper uniform. They should receive training in basic customer relations techniques. A representative from the ordering department must sign for receipt of the shipment. A copy of the receiving document should be left for their records.

A common problem involves departments that order large amounts of material, or capital items, and do not make adequate provision for accepting them when they arrive. This presents the receiving department with the dilemma of what to do with the shipment until the ordering department is ready to accept it. Whenever possible, the purchasing agent should coordinate the total transaction in advance, including making arrangements for installation of new equipment, disposition of the old, and provision for storing large stocks of supplies. When this cannot be accomplished, it may be necessary to maintain a short-term holding area and to resolve problems as they arise.

Return Goods and Overshipments

The receiving department should serve only as the shipping point for items being returned to vendors and should not be involved in coordinating the transaction. The original ordering department must be responsible for initiating the transaction, and purchasing must work out the terms with the vendor. This includes obtaining a return goods authorization, making arrangements for pickup or shipment, generating the paper work, and notifying both the originating and receiving departments of the details.

Receiving department personnel should refuse to accept items for return unless the completed paper work is attached. Once the documentation is in order, the item should be placed in the outgoing holding area. Holding areas should be monitored routinely by the supervisor to ensure that items are not allowed to sit for long periods of time. If an item is found in this category, it must be expedited.

The receiving control clerk usually will be the person to identify an overshipment. This can involve individual line items that show receipts greater than the amount ordered or entire orders that have been shipped twice. In general, excess shipments should be refused and returned at the vendor's expense. Acceptance may cause a vendor to decide to increase sales by simply shipping extra items. At the least, it violates the hospital's inventory replenishment plan.

However, there are circumstances where it does make sense to accept items. For example, a frequently ordered storeroom item may be less costly to keep than to return if the hospital will have to reorder immediately. This is particularly true if the inventory turnover rate is high. The decision to accept or reject an overshipment must be made by a representative from the ordering department. If a shipment is to be accepted, a purchase order must be provided to document the receipt.

TRANSPORTATION SERVICES

Vehicle Acquisition

Transportation services usually are operated by multisite health care facilities where there is a need to move materials between related operating sites. However, with the current trend toward diversification, there may be occasions when single-site hospitals have a need for these services. The first step in developing such a service is to identify the specific needs to be met and to determine whether an internal transportation service represents the least costly method of meeting the needs. It may be less expensive, depending on the volume and frequency of deliveries, to buy the service from a private company.

If a health care facility chooses to develop an in-house service, it must decide on how many vehicles will be needed and what functional specifications must be met. Data must be collected concerning the type of material to be carried, the volume in terms of cubic feet, how the material will be packaged and contained, whether there will be special handling requirements, and so on. Once these data have been analyzed, a decision can be made as to what type and size truck will be required. Throughout this process, it will be helpful to call upon the assistance of a management engineer. Truck rental companies also can help; however, it must be kept in mind that the representative's objective will be to sell or lease a vehicle to the hospital.

Once specifications have been established, the decision must be made whether to buy or lease the vehicle either by, or with the assistance of, the hospital's financial officer. If the decision is to buy, provision must be made for servicing the vehicle. If in-house automotive maintenance is available, this must be negotiated and documented in detail with the manager of that department. If the service must be obtained outside the hospital, specifications must be developed and competitive bids obtained. If the vehicle is to be leased, service may be included under the terms of the lease or may be provided under a separate service contract. Maintenance of the vehicle is at least as important a factor in the decision as is the purchase price.

Once the vehicle is in operation, it is necessary to keep detailed records of service performed, both routine preventive maintenance and unplanned special service. A system must be set up to obtain fuel at the lowest price and to document fuel consumption. This is important in budgeting for future years as well as for an internal check in determining whether the vehicle is meeting performance expectations. Adequacy of routine maintenance, as well as fuel efficiency of the drivers, can be monitored by documenting fuel consumption patterns.

Driver Training

Operation of a hospital-based transportation service involves a heavy responsibility. The drivers are representing the institution every minute they are on the road in terms of their appearance and their driving techniques. A traffic accident involving a hospital vehicle not only is expensive, it also can lead to a negative image in the community. In addition, a history of safe operation can lead to lower insurance costs.

It is important to select experienced drivers with safe records. Each driver should have a chauffeur's license. Before hiring, the hospital security officer should check the potential employee's record with the state's department of motor vehicles. Once employed, a driver must undergo a thorough course of training for the specific vehicles to be operated. If the vehicles are leased, this training should be part of the agreement with the vendor. Even if they are purchased, this training usually can be provided by a reputable company for a reasonable price.

The drivers also should be given training in hospital policies and procedures and in customer relations techniques. As with delivery people, truck drivers can be an excellent source of positive customer relations. They must understand that this is as much a part of the job as is safe driving.

The files of individual driving records and training documentation should be kept up to date and reviewed at least annually. If training is provided by an outside company, it may offer special programs, such as safe-driving competitions and driver appreciation events. These are worthwhile and should be utilized. A crew of safe and dependable drivers is one of the most valuable assets of the department, and efforts to support the group will always provide a positive return on investment.

Policies and Procedures

A comprehensive set of concise policies and procedures is important to ensure that the department routinely performs according to standard expectations. The following list is not all-inclusive but gives an idea of the types of information that will need to be covered:

- published schedule, listing arrival and departure times
- daily start-up checklist, including fuel, tires, lights, brakes
- procedure for reporting and responding to breakdowns on the road
- plan of alternate coverage in the event of a breakdown
- plan for notifying customer departments of disruptions in service

- procedure for ensuring that all items to be transported have been loaded onto the truck
- procedure for securing items properly within the truck
- procedure for checking items in at the destination and for obtaining signatures documenting their receipt
- procedure for cleaning the truck
- procedure for securing the vehicle at the end of the day.

Accountability for who is to perform a procedure should be assigned clearly. For example, the driver should be responsible for completing the daily start-up checklist. If a truck runs out of gas, the responsible person can be identified easily and the breakdown in performance reviewed and documented.

MAIL SERVICES

Every large organization generates mail and must have at least some centralized control over it. This is because the U.S. mail personnel will not make pickup and delivery rounds to every operating department. The management of the mail service often is overlooked as a potential source of significant cost reduction. This service lends itself to direct supervision by material management personnel because it is generic in nature, involves high volume, and relates with every operating department in the organization.

The mailroom can be located wherever space is available. However, when possible, it makes sense to place it near the receiving department, as this puts the mail in line with the daily flow of incoming and outgoing material. The room must be large enough to accommodate mail-handling equipment, sorting bins, mailroom employees, and the expected volume of mail. The latter is easy to underestimate as the mail itself takes up more space than might be expected. It is important that the room be large enough to be kept uncluttered. With a high volume of mail passing through each day, it is vital that pieces of different type and destination not be intermingled. In terms of room configuration, mail must be able to flow in, undergo handling processes, and flow out in as linear a manner as possible.

Equipment

Four types of equipment generally are required to support a mail service operation:

1. mail-processing units
2. postage meters
3. scales
4. sorting bins and tables.

The mail-processing units are capital items. All of the normal steps for selecting such equipment must be completed. These include determination of functional requirements, writing of specifications, competitive bidding with major companies, and lease-or-buy analysis. The decision process should answer the following questions in this order:

1. What type and capacity machine is required?
2. Which company can best serve the facility's needs?
3. Should the unit be bought or leased?

In general, electronic equipment is preferable to mechanical because of reduced downtime and ease of repair. Availability of local service and guaranteed response time are important elements. When possible, provision should be made for a loaner unit to cover instances when the equipment must be out of service for longer than a day. As with all capital equipment, preventive maintenance and complete documentation of service history are important in both managing the service and in planning for future needs.

Postage meters must be rented from a company licensed by the U.S. Postal Service. Money is then put into a postage account at the post office and entered by post office personnel onto the meter. As mail is processed, the amount on the meter decreases. When the amount remaining reaches a predetermined level, additional money must be paid to bring the meter back up to par. It is vital that an internal system be developed for monitoring this, so that the money is controlled and the meter does not run out while mail is being processed.

Systems are available in which money is kept in a central account and when the meter needs replenishment, a special telephone number is dialed and the meter is replenished electronically. This is of significant benefit only when the meter must be replenished frequently and it is inconvenient to go to the post office to handle the transaction manually.

Mail scales can be manual or electronic. In any high-volume operation, electronic scales are a must. In fact, almost any operation can justify an investment in an electronic scale. This is based upon savings gained through more accurate weighing and calculating of required postage. The companies that sell this equipment will provide cost-justification studies. However, it is not difficult for a hospital to conduct its own analysis. The department supervisor should have a representative day's mail weighed by the clerk on a manual scale, then reweighed by the supervisor on the electronic scale. Unless the facility has an extremely accurate manual scale and clerk, the postage cost should be less using the electronic scale. A percentage saving for that day's mail can be calculated then extended for a month. The payback period in months thus can be determined easily.

Sorting bins and tables are generic in nature. It is necessary to determine the number of each required to support the operation, then provide adequate space. Price should be the major determinant in selection.

U.S. and interoffice mail should flow into the mailroom and be sorted. All pieces should be distributed to hospital departments via scheduled rounds throughout the day. Outgoing mail from the departments should be picked up on the rounds and returned to the mailroom for sorting and distribution. The goal should be to have all mail cleared by the end of the day except for interoffice pieces that came in on the last round. Whenever possible, pieces should be handled only once. Outgoing U.S. mail should be picked up or taken to the post office at the end of the day.

Special Services

The U.S. Postal Service provides a number of special programs, some of which can result in significant cost savings. Bulk mail, for example, can provide savings of up to 75 percent per piece. There are specific requirements in sorting and bundling these mailings, and these can appear time consuming. This mail also receives lower priority handling by post office personnel than does first-class mail. However, for large mailings of standard pieces that can be planned in advance, such as promotions of new services, bulk or third-class mail not only is adequate, but also is far less expensive. The mail supervisor should publicize this service to all sending departments and should be responsible for monitoring all outgoing mail so that any large mailings that qualify for this program can be handled in this way.

Another source of potential saving is the incentive discount provided to companies that presort their mail by zip code. Under the rate structure that was implemented early in 1985, this amounts to a three-cent saving on each piece of first-class mail. Again, specific requirements must be met to qualify but the savings from this program alone can be thousands of dollars a year.

Presorting mail is time consuming and requires additional space for sorting bins. As a result, companies exist that will presort the mail in return for part of the discount. The decision as to whether to obtain the total discount by doing the work in-house or to split the discount and avoid the additional processing expense should be based on which approach affords the greater total saving. In any event, hospitals should take advantage of this program.

Guaranteed overnight delivery of mail and small parcels is a service offered by the U.S. Postal Service as well as private companies. Additional services, such as electronic transmission of mail via telephone lines, are becoming available. Mail supervisors must stay informed about the various services on the market to fully meet the hospital's need for timely and cost-effective mail services.

Policies and Procedures

Written policies and procedures should be in place for all functions. These include:

- procedure (and who is accountable) for replenishing the postage meter
- procedures for keeping track of all categories of postal expense
- controls over who is authorized to obtain and submit monies to the Postal Service
- procedure for handling improperly or incompletely addressed mail
- documentation of equipment performance and service
- backup procedure for processing mail when the postage equipment is out of service
- published schedule of delivery rounds.

Training

Everyone is familiar with stories of persons who started out in the mailroom and rose to be president of the company. The idea is that the mailroom is the bottom rung of the ladder. This perception should not be allowed to persist. The ability to process a large volume of mail accurately on a daily basis, understand and comply with postal regulations, and obtain maximum savings in postage expense while at the same time serving as a customer relations representative for the material management department requires more than an entry-level person. This job should be viewed as a staff specialist position. If it is not, the supervisor responsible for the mail service will spend an inordinate amount of time monitoring the function and following up problems. Even worse, the hospital will not receive high-quality mail service at the least possible cost.

Once the mail clerk has been selected, training must be provided in the operation of the equipment, postal regulations, location of departments throughout the organization, systems to use in handling the mail, and customer relations techniques. The supervisor should be the primary trainer. However, valuable assistance can be provided by the U.S. Postal Service and by the company that sells the mail-processing equipment. In addition, it is necessary to select and train replacements. This is critical in order to maintain proper service during periods when the full-time person is off duty.

The mail service is one that is visible to administration and to the medical staff. It can either enhance or detract from the reputation of the material management department. For this reason, every effort should be made to provide service that not only is high quality but is visibly so.

Chargeback Systems

Mail service in some ways is a hidden cost in the organization. Most managers do not recognize how expensive this is to the hospital. One way of identifying this for managers, and thereby reducing overconsumption of the service, is to charge postage expense back to originating departments. Equipment is available to perform this function automatically. However, workflow must be rearranged somewhat to make use of it. This is an alternative that should be considered. The most important element in containing postage expense is having a knowledgeable supervisor who monitors mail flow and who is backed up by a competent and dedicated staff.

Periodically, complaints are heard about rising prices and poor service from the U.S. Postal Service. These sometimes are legitimate. However, they can be minimized if the hospital supervisor maintains open lines of communication with Postal Service representatives. The local postmaster usually is willing to share information about operations and customer service specialists are available in most locations. Finally, staff specialists for specific programs are available regionally. The supervisor should make it a point to know and rely upon these people in order to obtain the greatest value for the postage dollars spent.

Quality Assessment

Because mail is one service that visibly affects every department, it is important to provide and maintain a reputation for an operation that is both high quality and cost effective. Two mechanisms may be used to help ensure this: (1) Test mailings should be sent routinely and the results documented. These involve sending items to designated people and recording the dates and times received. This can be done for both inter-office and U.S. mail. (2) The supervisor should maintain frequent contact with all departments, particularly those that have large volumes of mail. The customers' levels of satisfaction with the service should be documented routinely.

The receiving and transportation department is a vital link in the chain of effective material management. Its functions, such as counting, sorting, inspecting, recording, and delivering all are fairly basic in nature. However, they must be performed accurately time after time. This requires the selection of competent employees, adequate and continuing training, and routine quality assessment by a knowledgeable and dedicated supervisor. When all of these elements are provided, the needs of the hospital and its patients can be served properly.

17. Inventory Control

JERRY W. RAYBURN

Inventory is defined here as materials that have been acquired based upon an anticipated future use but at the time of review are awaiting use. Accountants use the term inventory to refer to the asset accounts that contain the values of materials awaiting use. Inventories are an integral part of any business involved in production of goods and services.

There are obvious similarities between inventories in health care and in any other industry. Inputs of labor, materials, and technology are combined to provide a service (i.e., patient care). But there also are some basic dissimilarities. A variety of influences have had an impact on the way health care organizations have accounted for and managed inventories. There have been pressures, caused by the rising cost of capital, to reduce inventories. These pressures have become particularly intense in hospitals where cash flow is a problem.

The increasing cost of space and the growing number of alternative uses for existing space have further intensified these pressures to reduce inventories. In distinct contrast, the cost-based system of reimbursement has promoted the expensing of inventories at the time of purchase so the costs are reportable immediately. When this has occurred, it often has resulted in excessive and poorly managed inventories, leading to increased costs.

OFFICIAL AND UNOFFICIAL INVENTORIES

Inventories booked as an asset often are referred to in health care as official inventory. This is where most of the reduction effort has been applied in the past. Materials expensed at the time of purchase are those that comprise unofficial inventory. Although the materials were purchased in anticipation of future use, until they actually are used they represent dollars that have been expended while the expected value from the expenditure has not yet been received. Efforts to manage and reduce unofficial inventories can be well rewarded through a short-term drop in materials costs and improved cash flow.

With the advent of prospective payment systems in health care, still more pressure is rising to reduce both official and unofficial inventories. It makes good business sense to keep inventories to a minimum level but it is critical that as they are reduced this be done in a methodical manner based on all available information, rather than in a haphazard fashion. A nonscientific approach will result in increased stock-outs and a continuation of excessive dollars in inventory.

Management of inventories means to control the resources consumed in anticipation of future material use. The resources subject to control include space allocated to inventories, labor used in their storage and control, dollars invested, technology, and equipment used in storage and control (e.g., computers, forklifts, shelving).

Inventory Control Definitions

Six main terms are used in inventory management that need to be defined because they are used throughout this chapter.

1. Usage

This refers to the quantity of a given item that is expected to be used (based upon historical data or projections) for a specific period of time.

2. Lead Time

This is the total of both internal and external lead times. Internal lead time is the time required for a requisition to be processed, a purchase order typed and signed, and the order placed with the vendor. External lead time is the time required for the vendor to receive the order, enter it, pick and ship the goods, to the time it arrives at the requesting facility.

3. Safety Factor

This is the factor by which the expected lead time will be modified to provide a margin of safety to cover potential variations in and/or usage during lead time. Safety factors typically are established through the addition of a percentage of the expected usage during lead time or through the use of statistically derived K-factors.[1]

4. Reorder Point

This is the level at which a reorder of an item is initiated as inventory is consumed. Reorder points often are determined informally but the author advocates scientific determination as follows:

$$\frac{\text{Reorder}}{\text{Point}} = \frac{\text{Usage}}{\text{per day}} \times \frac{\text{Lead Time}}{\text{(in days)}} + \frac{\text{Safety}}{\text{factor}}$$

5. Economic Order Quantity (EOQ)

This concept often is simplistically misapplied in practice. The formula includes all costs associated with acquisition of materials, including these elements:

1. Order cost is the expense of placing an order for a given item. If an item normally is ordered along with many others, the total order cost should be divided by the number of items normally on that order. In the health care industry, order cost typically ranges between $20 and $50 (see Appendix 17–A for a detailed discussion on determination of order cost).

2. Holding cost is the expense of keeping materials in storage awaiting use, including cost of capital (typically 9 to 15 percent), insurance, space, handling, building depreciation (or rent, if offsite), taxes, obsolescence, shrinkage. Total handling costs normally range from 20 to 40 percent (see Appendix 17–B for a discussion on determining holding costs).

3. Unit cost is the cost of one of the items for which economic order quantity is being determined. This cost must be for the same unit of measure upon which usage is based.

$$\frac{\text{Economic}}{\text{Order}} = \sqrt{\frac{\text{Annual usage} \times 2 \times \text{Order cost}}{\text{Unit cost} \times \text{Holding cost (\%/100)}}}$$

Application of the EOQ formula is simple. The results are subject to review and revision, based upon other relevant factors such as space limitations or a short-term cash shortage, but most cost-related factors are included in the formula.

6. Reorder Quantity

It is desirable to differentiate between economic order quantity, which is mathematically determined, and reorder quantity, which is the actual amount that will be reordered following considerations of judgment and common sense. For example, economic order quantities for items known to be used sporadically in large quantities (e.g., burn care supplies and dialysis solutions) should be adjusted. Here the importance of patient care must override the economic factors that constitute the calculated economic order quantity.

METHODS FOR REDUCING INVENTORIES

Prerequisites to Reduction

This background is preparation for discussing specific techniques of management and reduction of inventories. Inventory reductions must occur in a methodical manner. To do so, a reasonable understanding is required of the following four areas, as they relate to each product:

1. Product information

    - What is the use of the product?
    - How critical is the product to patient care?
    - Can substitutions be made for the product?
    - Is there a range of similar sizes?

2. Product availability

    - What is the normal lead time?
    - How predictable (consistent) is the lead time?
    - Are there multiple sources for the product?
    - How is the product shipped?
    - Is the product available on an emergency basis?
    - Do other area hospitals use the product?

3. Usage patterns

    - What is the usage per year?
    - Is usage seasonal or cyclical?
    - Is usage sporadic?
    - How much does usage vary from month to month?

4. User information

    - How many different users are there?
    - What are the types of users?

Obviously, it would be extremely time consuming to formally detail such information for each product in inventory but it is important that a general understanding exist among those preparing to undertake the task. Many products can be categorized by vendor or by product type and treated similarly, thereby simplifying this process.

Once the products are understood, along with their use and the relevant variabilities to be expected, hospitals can consider how to go about reducing inventories. It is important that a plan be developed so that the process will become a continuing philosophy, not just a one-time project.

Review of Existing Inventory

The first task is to determine a starting point. It is useful to calculate turnover for each area for which an inventory account exists. To maximize the use of resources, it is desirable to identify where the greatest dollars are (and/or where the poorest turnover is) for incorporation into the reduction plan.

The next step is to identify the highest dollar items within each inventory. This requires an itemized listing of the previous physical inventory. It is suggested that a dollar cutoff be established to make it easier to focus on the right items. One way to do this is to divide the total value of the inventory by the number of items. This results in an average value per item. Managers then can look for items that represent more than two times the average and above. This group of items will be the focus of initial attention. By comparing the counted quantity on hand with the calculated reorder point plus economic order quantity, the theoretical maximum is defined. If it is found that the physical inventory count exceeds the calculated maximum, the item is a candidate for reduction.

It then is necessary to review the existing inventory for excess items. The approach taken depends on the quality of usage information available. Unless a perpetual inventory system is in use, this can be a difficult task. Items that are grossly overstocked often are apparent but multiple items that are slightly overstocked will not be so obvious. It is useful to review first items known to be stored in more than one location. As those that appear to be excessive are found, a review of their usage history will permit a determination of whether there is, in fact, an excess.

The final step in this process is to identify nonmoving items. Again, unless a perpetual inventory is in use, this may be difficult. A periodic review of usage histories, in relation to quantity of each item on hand, is the best way to locate nonmoving items. If such history is unavailable, a review of item purchase histories should reveal those that have not been reordered since the last review. These items are likely nonmoving. In addition, items found to be out of date should be compared with usage. The fact that they became outdated indicates that usage is falling or that they were ordered in too large a quantity.

Implementation

The existence of excess and nonmoving inventories usually implies that the items have not been controlled as they should. As such items are found, it is most important that controls be put into place to prevent such situations from recurring. This is best done through the implementation of mathematically determined reorder points and economic order quantities for them. This makes it possible to quantify the inventory reduction to be expected. A record should be kept so that a summary report can be generated. This step often is overlooked even though it is vital in measuring results.

Formal reorder points and economic order quantities should be put into use through a mechanism that allows continuous collection of usage data. For manual systems, this purpose is served well by traveling requisitions—cards that contain all descriptive and vendor information along with the historical usage patterns about a particular repetitively purchased item. The card is filed in the using department until the item needs to be ordered. At that time it is sent to purchasing for reorder. There the order is placed and the details are documented on the card. It then is returned to the department, to be refiled until the inventory of the item again falls to the reorder point. However, if available, a computerized system offers even greater flexibility in collecting usage data as well as the capability of automating the generation of purchase orders based upon these data.

Inventory reductions should be made through evolution rather than through drastic cuts. This lends itself to the inventory reduction plan discussed earlier. To maintain confidence and support from users, they should be provided with a basic understanding as to why it is important that inventories be reduced, how the task is being implemented through a scientific approach, and reviewed with common sense. User input should be solicited to help ensure that reduction efforts are focused on the right items.

Techniques for Inventory Reduction

There are a number of specific techniques available for reducing excessive inventories. Here are four of them:

1. Excess and/or nonmoving materials can be returned to vendors for refund, credit, or exchange for items that are being used routinely. It may be possible to use leverage with vendors to get them to take these items back. For example, a vendor who is anxious to increase volume of business may be willing to make concessions of exchange or credit for excess inventories in conjunction with a greater commitment of sales from the hospital. Caution should be exercised to ensure that such an arrangement is mutually advantageous (as opposed to "blackmail").

2. Excess materials should be consumed before reordering. A reorder point should be calculated and adhered to for future reorders. The question of whether or not to consume existing excess inventory will be based, in large part, on judgment. It may be preferable to use the materials if the vendor will not take them back or if a significant restocking fee is charged.

3. Excess and/or nonmoving materials can be sold to other hospitals. It is quite possible that another hospital in the area is using the product(s) that are in excess. These very likely can be sold or traded for items that are used regularly.

4. Excess and/or nonmoving materials can be sold to a salvage dealer. This can be expected to result in a loss but if the items are in significant excess or are not expected

to be used again, it probably is better to take the loss and be rid of them.

The overall goal should be to minimize any losses associated with excess or nonmoving inventories. But if none of these alternatives is reasonable, managers must decide whether the value of the items and the possibility that they may one day be used more than offsets the value of the space they are occupying. It may be prudent in certain circumstances to simply discard the nonmoving items.

The following five options are oriented toward preventing recurrences of excessive and/or nonmoving inventories:

1. Product standardization is one of the key tools. If multiple users standardize on the same product, the chances of its becoming obsolete are greatly reduced. Standardized products also are easier to keep in inventory because vendors are more willing to stock them, and in justifiably larger quantities. A strong product standardization committee can be valuable in achieving a high degree of standardization.

2. Par level/exchange cart distribution systems greatly reduce the need for inventories in user departments. This has a dramatic impact on inventory reduction efforts. The user department no longer need be concerned with whether or not an item was ordered; it can simply depend upon having the article there when needed. Material management no longer need be concerned over rush orders from the department. The workload is far easier to schedule, resulting in other labor efficiencies. In addition, the inventory is known and routinely monitored and controlled, ensuring that it does not become excessive. It is a simple task to review usage of each item periodically to avoid nonmoving items.

3. Consignment inventories are a reasonable alternative for many specialty items. Under this concept, the vendor agrees to keep materials at the hospital at no charge until they actually are used. The advantage for the hospital is that a range of product styles and sizes is always available without having dollars tied up in inventory. It is important to have a clear mutual understanding with the vendor on liability for lost and/or damaged items as well as how usage will be documented. Managers also should conduct a comparison study to ensure that the reduced inventory costs are not more than offset by higher product costs.

4. Requests for purchase of supplies must be routinely analyzed by purchasing personnel to ensure that quantities requested are reasonable. Traveling requisitions or a computerized history of past purchases are invaluable so this analysis can be based upon fact rather than guesswork. If the determination of order quantities is left to the discretion of users, there will be no control of inventories. It was this nonsystem that allowed inventories to become excessive in the first place.

5. Material management personnel cannot maintain expertise in the use of all supplies within each specialized function. But they are responsible for control of the supplies, regardless of their physical location. For this control to be achievable, users must be educated in basic inventory control practices. This promotes teamwork and a mutual understanding of the process of maintaining inventories at a level that meets the needs of users while minimizing their costs. The working relationship between material management and the user departments has to be one of cooperation and communication if the inventory management effort is to be successful.

With knowledge of how excessive inventories can be reduced and prevented from recurring, other considerations can be examined. It should be evident that the ability to manage inventories well is directly related to the accessibility and accuracy of information about their component items. One common approach to improving the quality of information is the perpetual inventory system.

PERPETUAL INVENTORY SYSTEMS

The term perpetual inventory system describes a process that tracks levels of items through routine documentation of receipts and issuance (or use). In simple terms, the quantity on hand, plus receipts, minus issues equals the new quantity on hand. It is helpful first to review the other alternative—the nonperpetual inventory.

Nonperpetual inventories are those controlled without routine updating of balances for each item. In practice, such a system may provide varying degrees of control, depending upon the formality and understanding that exists. The nonperpetual system is referred to as the "eye-balling" method because it depends upon control by sight. This visual review may be simple or sophisticated. Ideally, a nonperpetual system includes at minimum: traveling requisitions or bin cards for each item (including a record of past orders, dates of order, purchase order numbers, vendor information, and record of receipts and receipt dates), mathematically determined reorder points based upon actual lead times, and mathematically determined order quantities.

The basic input of the nonperpetual inventory control system is the recognition that it is time to reorder and initiation of the reorder. This approach to inventory control has four distinct advantages:

1. The system requires the persons doing the stock picking to be involved, which results in many opportunities for input of judgment. For example, if a given item is being used more quickly than usual, the person who recognizes this can bring it to the attention of the individual who reorders.
2. The system is simple, easy to learn and to teach to others. Traveling requisitions provide a simple method for controlling unofficial inventories and at the same time offer

an opportunity for material management to exert a positive control influence.
3. The system can be flexible. Adjustments to reorder point and reorder quantities can be made immediately without additional communication.
4. The system is inexpensive. There is no need for an elaborate file or a computer.

There are, however, two primary disadvantages in a nonperpetual control system:

1. Information about the inventory is not readily available. The only way to find out whether a given item is in stock or needs to be reordered is to go look at it. This is inconvenient and requires additional time to go check.
2. It is excessively people-dependent. People sometimes forget to compare the quantity on hand with the reorder point. People do not always notice that an item is being issued faster or slower than usual.

In contrast to the informality permissible in a nonperpetual inventory, a perpetual system mandates formality. There are significantly more variables in the process of making sure that each item is reordered at the right time. The primary additional information required is the routine subtraction of all issues from, and the addition of all receipts to, the inventory balances for each item.

There are two primary advantages in a perpetual inventory system:

1. Information is more readily accessible. In purchasing, it may be easier to group orders for items from each vendor. This improved information can contribute to the reduction of supply costs.
2. Timeliness and convenience are much greater. Those involved in purchasing have access to all inventory balances without having to go look at the items. This can improve service levels provided to users.

Two potential disadvantages of a perpetual inventory system are:

1. All issues and receipts must be documented and subtracted or added to the inventory balance. This is a labor-intensive task in a busy facility. It is easy for the updating task to receive a low priority when crises arise. This can lead to future crises because the inventory balances were not current, leading to orders' not being placed at the proper time. As data entry is increasingly performed using bar-code readers, this disadvantage is becoming less significant.
2. Accuracy of the inventory balances is dependent upon people. It is often said that perpetual inventories are perpetually wrong. This is because the accuracy of the system relies upon people, who often do not understand the need for complete accuracy and timely updating.

In establishing a perpetual inventory system, there are two basic choices. First, the information can be maintained on a manual basis. This typically takes the form of a visible record file, with each inventory item listed on a card in a central file. Starting with a beginning inventory balance for each item, all issues are entered and subtracted, resulting in a new inventory balance. Similarly, all receipts are entered and added to the inventory balance. Periodically, all items purchased from a given vendor, or all items in a given category, are reviewed and the inventory balances compared with the reorder points (usually indicated on the visible record). Items at or below the reorder point are then reordered.

The second alternative to a perpetual inventory system is to use a computer. Options as to what type of computerized system to use include the following:

- An in-house system operating on the hospital's mainframe computer. This usually is a very cost-effective approach but it is not uncommon for priority for development and/or enhancement to be far below business office and financial applications.
- A time-sharing service in which users must connect to a mainframe computer to update data or to request reports. Such a system may be expensive unless it is a component of a total hospital shared system.
- A combination of time-shared service and an onsite microcomputer, where users may enter data off-line and periodically connect to the mainframe for actual update of inventory balances. This is intended to be a more cost-effective alternative than time-sharing alone because connection time is reduced.
- A dedicated in-house microcomputer, a more recent alternative. With the advent of relatively inexpensive mass storage and with increasing computing power and speed, this appears to be quickly becoming the most cost-effective and the most flexible concept available.

Most computerized purchasing and/or inventory control systems incorporate a perpetual inventory system. This makes good sense because computers can perform the addition and subtraction functions quickly and accurately. Along with the mathematical capability, computers can rearrange the data and produce reports about such information in an almost unlimited number of ways.

The advantages of using a computer in maintaining a perpetual inventory include the following:

- It promotes management of inventories because it makes information readily available. It should be noted that this is not automatic. A computer does not manage the inventory, it only provides information that facilitates management by people. This information includes:

1. timely updates of usage and lead time information so safety stocks can be minimized

2. increased awareness of nonmoving inventory items
3. inventory value and turnover analysis information, by item category.

- It automates mathematical activities, thereby removing the opportunity for human error from this aspect of the system.
- It imposes a more systematic workflow. A well-designed system does not permit inventory to be issued until a sufficient quantity of the item has been entered as received. By requiring certain input sequences, the system can promote consistent workflow patterns, which may reduce other types of human errors.
- It allows significant flexibility in reporting. Production of inventory catalogs—alphabetic, numeric, or by location, for example—are simple and quick tasks for a computer. These same tasks are major undertakings when the input data must be organized and typed manually. Many of these types of tasks simply cannot be performed in a cost-effective manner until a computerized system is available.

The disadvantages of a computerized perpetual inventory system include the following:

- Cost is a major factor. Although costs have been falling as microcomputers have become more powerful and less expensive, systems still range in price from $500 to $4,000 a month on a software lease basis. When this cost is expressed as a percentage of the inventory value being controlled, it may range as high as 5 percent of the inventory value per month. Obviously, these kinds of dollars would necessitate a personnel reduction in order to justify the cost.
- Automation of a nonworking manual system is likely to result in a nonworking computerized system. People working with the computerized system tend to attribute everything that goes wrong to the computer. This may get in the way of their

recognizing the need to work in a disciplined and systematic manner because it is so easy to blame problems on the computer and avoid responsibility for their actions (or lack of actions).

- Computerization often is viewed as a labor-saving opportunity but this rarely is the case. Computers are looked upon as possessing the ability to eliminate jobs. This is unusual, especially in hospitals. Instead, existing jobs are redefined. It is typical to see a single person assigned to perform all the computer interface functions.
- Computers are capable of offering almost unlimited flexibility but most systems fall far short of this and instead require input and output functions to follow very defined, and therefore limiting, procedures.
- Computerized systems, because they require input in such a defined manner, need considerably more traininng of personnel in how to use the system than do manual systems.

Because computerized perpetual inventory systems are becoming less expensive, and therefore it is easier to justify their cost, an increasing number of hospitals are likely to choose this alternative. It then becomes useful to review features to consider in computerized systems. This checklist is by no means exhaustive but is intended to provide a basis for discussion with potential providers of inventory management software. Features can be categorized as follows:

Inventory Control

- Does the system reject attempted issuance of items when there is insufficient inventory?
- Does the system calculate revised reorder points based upon actual lead times or are such points simply minimums based upon guesswork?
- Does the system calculate economic order quantities based upon the EOQ formula or

are reorder quantities numbers based on historical experience and guesswork?

- Can the system classify the inventory based upon annual cost per item? (This is known as ABC analysis and is discussed later in this chapter and in Chapter 18.)
- Does the system provide for inventory value summaries by product category upon request?
- Does the system perform inventory turnover analysis?
- How does the system facilitate physical inventories?
- Does the system contain provisions for cycle counting? (This is discussed later in this chapter.)

Purchasing

- Does the system print purchase order documents? If so, is the format flexible enough to meet the hospital's needs?
- Does the system provide recommended purchase orders for review and revision before actual printing of the documents?
- Does the system provide for alternate vendors for each product?
- What capabilities are available for monitoring vendor performance?
- How does the system provide for nonstock ordering? Are nonstock items maintained on file by department? What reporting options exist for these data?
- What capabilities does the system offer in the following types of specialized purchase orders?

  - capital equipment?
  - standing orders (automatic shipments)?
  - blanket orders?
  - rentals and/or leases?
  - preventive maintenance contracts?

- Does the system tie into automated order entry systems for major vendors?
- Does the system provide vendor bid lists?

- How does the system facilitate or relate to group purchasing contracts?
- What other special functions are available?

Receiving

- Does the system require receipts to be entered in order units or in issue units?
- How are partial shipments handled?
- How is expediting facilitated?
- Does the system maintain an open order file for all purchase orders?

Distribution Systems

- How does the system relate to existing distribution systems within the hospital? Does it necessitate any changes?
- Does the system include the capability of producing exchange cart and/or par level replenishment inventory recording sheets?
- Does the system perform analysis of appropriateness of existing par levels and recommend revised pars based upon actual issues to each area?
- Does the system utilize streamlined data entry of these issues (e.g., prompted screens which lead the operator through a routine sequence of steps, bar code entry, or optical character recognition reader)?
- Does the system offer pick lists printed in item storage location sequence for exchange carts and/or par level restocked areas?
- What support does the system offer for a surgical case cart system?

Financial/Accounting

- What inventory accounting method(s) are available?

  1. LIFO—last in, first out?
  2. FIFO—first in, first out?
  3. average cost—how many previous order costs are calculated into the average?
  4. replacement cost?

- Are the following cost distribution reporting capabilities offered?

  1. value and detail of issues by department?
  2. value and detail of issues by category?
  3. detail of issues by item, by requesting department?

- Does the system provide all necessary information for Medicare cost reporting?
- Does the system accommodate the existing general ledger account and subaccount codes?
- How does the system relate to the hospital's accounts payable function? Does it offer improved information?
- How will data be transferred between the system and the hospital's general ledger?
- Does the system offer any enhancements in control of revenue derived from patient chargeable supplies?
- Does the system automate reconciliation of lost charges?
- Does the system offer any capabilities for analysis of rate formulation for supplies?
- What capabilities does the system offer that will help the facility to better react to diagnosis related groups (DRGs) and the current prospective payment environment?
- How does supply charge input relate to this system versus the financial system? Is input duplicated? Can the two functions communicate data?

Storage

- What types of stock catalogs are available?
- Is a catalog by storage location available?
- Is a catalog by item category and/or user department available?
- Does the system permit factoring product size/density into the economic order quantity formula?
- Does the system include generation of pre-printed requisitions for major departments?

- Does the system allow more than one unit of issue (e.g., case, box)?
- Does the system offer capabilities for tracking more than one storage location for each product?
- How does the system handle internal back orders? Does it keep track of departments that have ordered an item that is out of stock so these issues can be made when the article is entered as received?

Data Processing

- What provisions for data security are incorporated into the system?
- What error detection and error handling routines exist in the program? Are these sufficient to ensure data integrity?
- What is the data backup procedure? Is data backup mandated by the system or is it simply advocated in the user manual?
- Will the system be able to accommodate the number of daily transactions generated now? Is it expandable to accommodate future increases if required?
- What interfaces will be required between the material management system and the hospital data processing system? Do these exist or will they have to be developed?

General

- What is the cost of the system? What are the variables in this cost? How controllable are they?
- How will the introduction of the system affect current staffing and/or organization?
- Is it possible to negotiate a maximum cost per month?
- What is the minimum contract term? What is the required cancellation notice?
- What is the minimum hardware configuration? Does it fit in with the existing workflow? What options are likely to be needed and at what additional cost?

- What are the support capabilities offered by the vendor?
- Is there a complete user's manual for the system?
- How will training of personnel be performed?
- How are issues and receipts transaction journals maintained? Does this permit easy error detection?
- What error prevention features are built into the system?
- What level of flexibility and/or adaptability is built into the system?
- Does the system include present or future interdepartmental communication capabilities?
- Is the vendor for the system financially strong? Will the supplier continue to offer the system along with enhancements for the foreseeable future?

Related Capabilities

- Does the system allow dual use of the hardware for word processing and other functions?
- Are any of the following applications feasible?

  1. equipment/asset control?
  2. linen utilization monitoring and reporting?
  3. preventive maintenance scheduling?
  4. operating room scheduling?
  5. quality control monitoring?

- Does the system operate on a batch mode, an on-line mode, or on a real-time basis?

These questions should provide a reasonably good understanding of the capabilities and limitations of any computerized inventory systems being considered. This is a rapidly developing aspect of material management, and therefore what was nearly impossible a few years ago may be commonplace now. Features that would be desirable but are unavailable now may become available soon. It is useful for managers to make contact with a few of the leading vendors in this industry and update their knowledge from time to time. This also is an excellent opportunity to share with the vendors ideas on the features that should be incorporated into their systems.

Most computerized inventory systems have some provision for maintaining a reorder point and a reorder quantity for each item. Determining economic order quantity was discussed earlier; now the concept is analyzed in more detail, along with other possible methods for establishing reorder quantities.

ALTERNATIVES TO ECONOMIC ORDER QUANTITY

The use of economic order quantities (EOQs) (advocated earlier in this chapter) offers significant advantages but it is essential to understand the assumptions underlying the concept and to consider alternative approaches.

The EOQ formula is derived through the application of calculus to the problem of finding the minimum total cost of ordering and holding a specific item. It should be remembered that ordering more at a time results in lower annual ordering costs while minimum inventories result in lower carrying costs. The formula considers these contrasting goals and mathematically determines the minimum juncture point.

The limitations on using the economic order quantity in the real world include the following:

- The formula is based upon the fact that usage must be known and fairly constant over time. In a hospital, usage can be sporadic but fortunately the need for most items is predictable.
- Use of the formula requires assigning specific numerical values to factors that, in the real world, can be difficult to determine. Pinning down true ordering costs and true carrying costs is difficult because they involve both fixed and incremental elements. It is easy to say that the ordering cost

is $10, which includes forms, postage, labor, and such, but if the number of orders increases or decreases it is unlikely that the labor component will vary much. Unfortunately, the labor component accounts for most of the dollars. Similarly, carrying costs are based, in part, on cost of storage. Again, the cost of space used for storage does not vary much because, even though less may be needed, the cost of the building does not change.

• Quantity discounts are not included in the economic order quantity formula. Realistically, it is not uncommon for a vendor to offer incentive discounts for ordering in larger quantities or to impose additional charges for failure to meet a minimum order quantity. It is relatively easy, though, to take these issues into consideration after the economic order quantity is determined.

In spite of these limitations, the economic order quantity continues to be one of the best tools available. This is because, although it is difficult to determine exact ordering and carrying costs, these can be reasonably approximated and then considered in the determination of the quantity to be used. In addition, the total cost curve (ordering and carrying costs) is quite flat,[2] and therefore a moderate deviation (e.g., plus or minus 25 percent) from the calculated economic order quantity does not increase or decrease total cost significantly. Other methods of determining order quantities result in far more arbitrary results and fail to consider underlying cost factors. Alternative methods of determining reorder quantities are described next.

Variations in the EOQ Formula

Each of the factors in the economic order quantity formula has an impact on the calculated result. The formula assumes that each component behaves as a variable cost. If it is known that certain of these behave as fixed rather than variable costs, it is reasonable to modify the formula to reflect this fact. For example, if order costs are fixed, the order cost variable should be

deleted from the formula, a change that will result in increased frequency of orders. Such manipulations of the formula should be implemented with care because few costs are truly fixed; rather, they are fixed for only a certain range of activity.

Economic Review Period

This method is based directly on the economic order quantity formula, utilizing the same input factors; however, instead of deriving a reorder quantity, it determines the period (expressed in weeks) between reviews. The reorder quantity then is calculated based on the expected usage during the time between reviews. The formula for determination of the review period is as follows:

$$\text{Review period (weeks)} = \sqrt{\frac{5{,}408 \times \text{Order cost}}{\text{Annual usage} \times \text{Unit cost} \times \text{Holding (\%/100) cost}}}$$

Note: 5,408 is derived by multiplying 288 (constant) times 52 weeks/12 months (or 4.33)^2.*

This method offers advantages for primary or major vendors from whom a large number of line items are routinely ordered. Typical categories that lend themselves to this approach include intravenous solutions and administration sets, sutures, housekeeping supplies, and forms. Instead of each item's reaching its predetermined reorder point, at which time an order would be generated, all items in the category, or from a specific vendor, are ordered at regular intervals.

The advantages are that fewer orders are generated and fewer deliveries from that vendor are required. Formal reorder points are recommended for these items, though, because unusual or sporadic usage may necessitate reor-

---

*Adapted from *Purchasing and Materials Management for Health Care Institutions* by Dean S. Ammer, published by Lexington Books, D.C. Heath & Co., Lexington, Mass., p.127. © 1975 D.C. Heath & Co.

dering an item before its next scheduled review. Of course, the determination of the reorder points would follow the formula stated previously, considering usage during lead time and adding the calculated safety factor.

Minimum/Maximum and Target Turnover

The minimum/maximum reorder method consists of establishing the level at which each item is to be reordered and the level to which it is to be reordered back up to the maximum. Although simple in concept, this approach usually oversimplifies the inventory control process. In use, cost factors seldom are considered properly and minimums, which should equate to reorder points, usually are guesses and thus promote poor service levels. The one advantage of using a minimum/maximum reorder method is that space constraints for each item can easily be built into the maximums.

Each item, by category or annual dollar cost, has a reorder quantity established based on the turnover goal for items of a similar annual cost or category. It can be decided, for example, that because IV solutions and sets represent a high annual cost and usage, a turnover of 26 times will be the goal, which will help to make up for items for which it is more difficult and/or less practical to increase turnover. Therefore, the reorder quantity for items in the IV solution and set category will be a two-week supply. This method, although not common, offers advantages when trying to reduce inventories. It lends itself to use in conjunction with fill-rate management (maximizing the likelihood that items are in stock each time they are requested) or finding the optimal balance between fill rates and inventory turnover rate.

The limitation of this method is that initial turnover goals are arbitrary unless they can be based on good dollar usage information. Such information may not be readily available.

None of the methods of determining appropriate reorder quantity provides the best result in every situation. But a review of the advantages and disadvantages of each provides a basis for deciding which approach to use for various products and situations. The combined use of economic order quantity and economic review period should result in a practical and cost-effective reorder system. The other methods can be incorporated when specific pressures necessitate their use.

Another area for consideration is how best to prioritize efforts in inventory management. One of the best ways is through determining where the greatest dollars are invested, and which products are most critical to patient care.

ABC AND CRITICALITY INDEXING

These topics are covered in detail in Chapter 18 but it is useful to discuss them briefly here. ABC analysis is a concept frequently advocated in the control of inventories. Its purpose is to identify items in the inventory that represent both the highest dollar impact and the highest utilization. The process of ABC analysis is worthwhile because it points out items that need to be focused upon, and improved control of these items can have the most impact on both inventory value and service levels.

Application of ABC analysis first requires that the annual usage be determined for each item in inventory. The annual usage is then multiplied by the unit cost to derive the annual cost. When annual cost for all items has been determined, the items are ranked from highest to lowest.

Normally, the first 10 percent of the items account for 70 percent of the total annual cost, the next 20 percent of the items for 20 percent, and the remaining 70 percent of the items for only 10 percent. Obviously, the inventory reduction efforts should focus initially on the 10 percent of the items that account for 70 percent of the dollars. This prioritization is an essential step in the inventory control process.

As a practical application of ABC analysis, it is useful to establish target turnovers for each classification. For example, a target of 15 turns for A items, nine turns for B items and four turns for C items will average out to nearly 13 turns in aggregate. These goals are readily achievable.

Recognizing that the A items represent 70 percent of the total dollars, it should be apparent that improper control will result quickly in serious service problems that will affect their users. This does not have to occur if common sense is applied and there is proper communication with users.

It may be useful to go beyond this informal approach and develop an index as to the criticality of each product. (This also is covered in detail in Chapter 18.) It is useful here to understand that the objective of a criticality indexing system is to consider each product in terms of how essential it is to patient care and whether or not there exists an acceptable substitute for the item should it be out of stock. There are several approaches that attempt to quantify the criticality of each item and include this factor in the determination of reorder points and economic order quantities.

INVENTORY PERFORMANCE MEASUREMENT

Alternative methods exist for monitoring the effectiveness of inventory management efforts and determining the level of inventory performance. Ways of measuring inventory performance are reviewed next, along with their advantages and disadvantages.

Trended Value

Trended inventory value is a useful measure when historical data are known. It is easy to compare current and past values following the application of an inflation factor. The shortcoming of this measure is that it presupposes that the value was reasonable to begin with. If it was, in fact, too high or too low, the trended value will indicate only whether it remained too high or too low.

Turnover Analysis

Turnover is a useful measure. It is determined as follows:

$$\text{Inventory Turnover} = \frac{\text{Annual dollar value of issues}}{\text{Average inventory value}}$$

This provides an indication as to how effectively the dollars invested in inventory are being used. Reasonable turnover rates vary by department; for example, an engineering department inventory often turns only twice a year whereas a dietary departmental inventory may turn 20 to 30 times a year.

It is reasonable to aim for a total hospital inventory turnover of 10 to 12 times a year. Higher turnovers tend to require too much intensity and lower ones need a higher investment than is desirable. Turnover is a useful measure in comparing one inventory to another, both within a hospital in comparing departments, or in comparing like departments in other hospitals.

Space Allocation

Given costs of construction, it may be desirable to measure inventory performance based on the amount of space used for storage of materials awaiting use. This cannot be used as an exclusive measure but if space for additional services can be made available through better inventory management, it certainly results in cost savings.

Inventory Dollars per Bed

Inventories in hospitals frequently are measured in terms of dollars invested, usually by category, divided by the number of beds. This is a useful gross measure. Typical aggregate values range from $500 to $6,000 per bed. Obviously this wide range limits the full usefulness of the measure. The reason for the wide range is that different hospitals use different measures. For example, the value at one facility may represent only official inventory while at another facility it is the total of unofficial and official inventories. The bed figure may represent licensed beds or occupied beds.

This measure is most useful when it is used for comparing progress over time within a facility (adjusting, of course, for changes in scope of services and/or utilization), or when comparing hospitals that are known to be similar, in activity levels and specialties. Simplistic comparisons of inventory dollars per bed totally ignore related but critical issues such as inventory service levels and fill rates.

To manage an inventory properly, it first is necessary to determine the starting point. This usually necessitates taking a physical inventory. The process is discussed next, along with a possible alternative if the inventory is tracked on a perpetual system.

PHYSICAL INVENTORIES VS. CYCLE COUNTS

Physical Inventories

Simply defined, a physical inventory is a method of visually checking and documenting items, the quantity of each, and the dollar value of each and of the total. It is necessary to know the value of the inventory for management purposes but it is essential that these values be determined for accounting purposes because inventories are accounted for as assets.

Since physical inventories are taken to determine the dollars invested in unused materials, it is worthwhile to give consideration to what inventory locations are included. It is common in hospital accounting to maintain inventory accounts in the general ledger for a limited number of storage areas—for example, general stores, pharmacy, and dietary. But in reality, these areas may account for only 50 to 60 percent of the total dollars. In failing to quantify the inventories in surgery, radiology, laboratory, engineering, nursing, and other supply-intensive areas, it is assumed that these are not significant enough to control or cannot be controlled. Both assumptions are incorrect. These are the areas that typically represent the greatest opportunities for reducing inventory costs. Therefore, at some point they will have to be counted in order to establish the starting point.

There are numerous methods of taking physical inventories. These vary widely in level of sophistication and labor intensity.

The simplest method is to take a pad and pencil to the storage location and write down the description and quantity of each item. The cost of each item is determined, multiplied by the quantity counted, and the values totalled. Obviously there are some pitfalls even in this simple approach.

To determine costs for each item later, it is necessary to write the unit of measure (case, box, each), the manufacturer or vendor, and the product catalog number. The counting itself, especially if for accounting purposes, needs to follow a systematic procedure to ensure that each item is counted accurately and only once. This usually necessitates a counting team, with one person counting and calling out and the other writing what has been called out.

Another approach, which is not much more sophisticated, is the use of preprinted inventory sheets. These can be generated manually by typing up count sheets based upon the prior physical inventory. It is even better if each item, by location, is listed on a count sheet before the inventory. The inventory then is just a process of filling in the quantities.

It should be noted that physical inventories are very time consuming. It is important that the material manager invest the necessary time in planning the inventory, including the selection of the most capable employees to be involved and making sure that they understand the process to ensure accuracy and timely completion.

In analyzing the results of the physical inventory, it is important that an appropriate review take place to ensure that the final values reflect reality. There should be a conscious effort to avoid focusing on just the net inventory adjustment. Instead, consideration needs to be given to individual variances, their significance, and possible explanations for their occurrence. It is through this type of review that future inventories will be still more efficient and variances will be minimized.

In view of the volume of data involved in a physical count, the process lends itself to computerization. The computer can be used to generate the preprinted count sheets as well as to maintain the file of items, locations, and prices so that when counts are entered, the extensions are made immediately and the value determined. Even a simple word processing system can facilitate this approach.

Most perpetual inventory systems include a module for taking physical inventories because they are required for the initial starting balance for each item. It also is necessary to take periodic physical inventories to validate the asset account for accounting purposes and because over time counts may 'become incorrect and need to be corrected. This is particularly important when using computerized systems because incorrect quantities lead to increased stock-outs, which in turn lead to decreased service levels and increased expediting.

Cycle Counts

In the cycle count method, inventory balances are verified and corrected through routine partial physical inventories. Typical approaches include weekly random selection of items to be counted, of a specific category of items to be counted, or simply of a certain percentage of the items based on a location or other type of listing.

Each of these approaches has its advantages and disadvantages. The choice must be based on the specific need. If the inventory system is generally running smoothly, with a minimum of stock-outs, then random selection makes sense because it provides a continuing index of overall accuracy. For example, if there are 1,000 items, each week 20 items might be sampled randomly. The overall accuracy of the method can be gauged by how many of the sampled item counts exactly match the balance stated by the system. It then is possible to establish an acceptable range and say, for example, that although one (5 percent) or 2 (10 percent) of these sample counts do not match, the integrity of the system still is acceptable.

If there are known incorrect inventory balances in a specific category, then it makes sense to recount those products so orders will be based on accurate data. This approach to cycle counting should supplement, rather than replace, the random or percentage selection procedure.

It is a good practice to review all inventory balance corrections and determine how the errors arose. Most computerized systems depend upon several different people adhering to very defined procedures. As a result, there is implicit opportunity for error and it can be difficult to identify responsibility for mistakes in input. Cycle counting offers an excellent opportunity for monitoring adherence to proper procedures as people interface with the system.

A proper procedure and well-documented routine of performing cycle counts may be accepted by the financial officer and outside auditors in lieu of periodic physical inventories. This obviously is worth aiming for even if it only reduces the frequency of physical counts. Such a procedure should spell out how cycle counts are performed, how items to be counted are selected, and the documented record of the counts. It is not reasonable to expect to reduce the error rate to zero but as that level is lowered, this option should be discussed with the controller.

It usually is understood that there are numerous opportunities for error in counting, pricing, and extending values in a traditional physical inventory. Using cycle counts, it should be possible to reduce the errors to a level below that of physical inventories.

INVENTORY REDUCTION CHECKLIST

This information was presented in the sequence that best lends itself to long-term inventory reduction. It is useful now to review a summary of this process:

- Material managers must clearly understand the current health care market in order to be effective in marketing and gaining acceptance for the process within a hospital.
- Considerable information must be collected before a systematic and planned reduction of inventories can begin. This includes:

1. product information
2. product availability

3. usage patterns
4. information about users.

- Specific techniques must be implemented to reduce inventories. These include:

1. identification of nonmoving inventory items
2. exchange, consumption, or sale of excess inventories.

- Excess inventories can be prevented from recurring through:

1. product standardization
2. implementation of distribution systems that facilitate reduced inventory levels
3. utilization of consignment inventories where possible
4. routine monitoring of purchase requests for nonstock items
5. education of user departments in basic inventory control practices in order to utilize their input and expertise.

- Perpetual inventory systems and computerized systems add greater sophistication and resulting management information for controlling inventories.
- The extensive checklist for comparing and selecting a computerized inventory control system should be reviewed by those considering such a system.
- A computer used in the management of inventories can be enhanced by additional refinements, including:

1. alternative methods of refining the economic order quantity formula
2. economic review period for items ordered from major vendors
3. managing inventory turnover
4. ABC analysis
5. criticality indexing.

- The effectiveness of inventory control efforts must be monitored by such methods as:

1. trended value over time
2. turnover analysis
3. space allocated to inventories
4. inventory dollars per bed.

- Cycle counting offers potential labor savings in traditional physical inventory while improving accuracy at the same time.

MATERIAL MANAGEMENT ACCOUNTABILITY

The continuing implications of this information on hospital material managers are considered next.

As material managers have gained more acceptance in hospitals in recent years, greater realization has been gained of the results possible in cost control. In this era of prospective payment, even greater demands will be made. Inventory reduction represents one of the key opportunities in reducing costs of operation.

Material management clearly is the most logical function upon which to place responsibility and accountability for inventory, yet few such managers are taking the necessary steps to control inventories throughout their facilities. Purchasing managers see the unnecessary duplication resulting from lack of standardization. Central supply employees see the hoarding and squirreling that take place in operating units. Storeroom personnel observe the lack of planning because patient care departments have priorities more important than controlling supplies.

Although dollars expended for supplies vary greatly from hospital to hospital, it has been the author's experience that these costs typically range between 10 and 30 percent of the operating budget. Material managers need to assume inventory control responsibility to see that these dollars are expended for the right items, and only when they need to be spent. It is only through accountability for all inventories throughout the organization that the necessary improvements will be brought about.

Through a planned and systematic review of all inventories, and through a prioritized reduction effort, significant dollars can be saved. Finally, through routine monitoring of purchases, inventory can be kept at an optimal level and can maximize service levels while minimizing the invested dollars and labor expenses in material management.

NOTES

1. Dean S. Ammer, *Purchasing and Materials Management for Health Care Institutions* (Lexington, Mass.: Lexington Books, D.C. Heath and Company, 1975), 121–23.

2. Charles T. Horngren, *Introduction to Management Accounting*, 4th ed. (Englewood Cliffs, N.J.: Prentice-Hall, Inc., 1978), 504.

BIBLIOGRAPHY

Ammer, Dean S. *Purchasing and Materials Management for Health Care Institutions*. Lexington, Mass.: Lexington Books, D.C. Heath and Company, 1975.

Housley, Charles E. *Hospital Materiel Management*. Rockville, Md.: Aspen Systems Corporation, 1978.
———— *Controlling Hospital Supply Inventories*. Rockville, Md.: Aspen Systems Corporation, 1983.

Appendix 17–A

Calculating Order Costs

There are at least two approaches to calculating the cost of placing an order. All costs associated with placing, receiving, and paying for an order should be included. These ordinarily include:

- cost of completing a requisition
- cost of reviewing the requisition
- cost of discussing the item with potential vendor(s), including pricing
- cost of purchase order form
- cost of preparing the order (e.g., typing)
- cost of placing the order with vendor (e.g., telephone call and/or mailing)
- cost of disbursing and filing the document
- cost of expediting the order, if required
- cost of receiving the item(s) ordered, including checking in, documenting, and forwarding the paper work to accounts payable
- cost of receiving and filing the invoice for the item
- cost of moving items from point of receipt to point of storage or use
- cost of matching the invoice to the receiving documentation
- cost of follow-up between accounts payable and receiving, if required
- cost of follow-up between accounts payable and purchasing, if pricing does not match
- cost of issuing a check once invoice and receipt documentation match
- cost of check
- overhead costs associated with all of the above, including offices, typewriters, and computer(s), if used.

Average order costs are calculated by determining the total annual costs for purchasing, receiving, and accounts payable functions and dividing this amount by the number of orders issued per year. The weakness of this approach is that it fails to consider the variability in the cost of placing orders. The number of items ordered per purchase order may vary dramatically. In addition, the costs just outlined combine both fixed and variable elements. To facilitate decisions, managers need to know how much it costs to place an additional order or whether anything can be saved if fewer orders are placed.

The alternative to basing decisions on average cost per order is to base them on the incremental order cost. This means that the decision as to whether to order more or less frequently will be based upon what it will cost to place each additional order and what it will save by reducing the number of orders by one.

To take this step, it is necessary to analyze each of the cost factors to determine which are fixed and which are variable. For example, the costs of equipment (depreciation) tend to be fixed and thus can be ignored until the increasing number of orders would require the purchase of another typewriter. Labor costs behave similarly. But in today's market, care needs to be exercised to avoid the assumption that labor costs are fixed when they should be viewed as variable. It is possible to perform time studies to determine labor costs for each element.

In application, it is helpful to determine the average number of line items on each purchase order. The total average cost per order should be divided by this number to derive the average cost per line item. This information then needs to be incorporated into the economic order quantity formula so the calculated results will be based upon factors that are as accurate as possible.

Appendix 17–B

Calculating Holding Costs

It is difficult to quantify inventory holding costs precisely. Any costs related to storage and handling of the goods, along with all those involving the dollars invested in inventory, are to be included. This analysis must include the following cost factors:

- Cost of capital invested in the inventory: This usually is the most significant of all.

- Cost of space used for storing the inventory: This usually is assigned on the basis of the number of square feet assigned to the function. Historical costs may be used for existing space but replacement cost is required when considering additions or off site storage.

- Cost of handling: This should account for labor used in moving materials from point of storage to point of use.

- Cost of material-handling equipment: This includes shelving, carts, hand trucks, and fork lifts.

- Cost of insurance coverage: This should protect the inventory in case of fire, water, or wind damage, or theft.

- Cost of security services: This should be isolated for inventory.

- Cost of housekeeping services: This, too, should be spelled out specifically for the storage area.

- Opportunity costs: This covers both the space and dollars invested in the inventory.

- Costs of obsolescence, loss, and pilferage: These are related in part to the cost of security service.

- Taxes: These should be identified where applicable.

- Costs of keeping inventory records: This includes computerized control, if used.

- Costs of stock-outs and emergency orders: These apply where inventory is not available.

- Costs of periodic physical inventories: These go back to the old, familiar eyeballing count.

Inventory holding costs are calculated by first quantifying as many of these factors as possible. Many will have to be extrapolated from total costs and prorated, based on the inventory value and/or space. For example, insurance costs are not likely to be specifically identified with the inventory; rather, the total premium will have to be allocated based on the proportion of the total assets that inventory constitutes. This also is true for security and housekeeping costs.

Costs related to handling of inventory can be determined by identifying the proportion of labor dollars in material management used to perform these functions. It is much more difficult to define these costs for inventories outside the direct control of material management. Costs of material handling equipment consist of the acquisition cost divided by the expected useful life (depreciation).

The cost of space should be based on the historical cost of the building. This figure, often expressed on a per-square-foot basis, should be available from the financial officer. Replacement cost should be used when a building addition or an offsite warehouse is under consideration. It should be recognized that an opportunity cost also may be associated with space occupied by inventories. If the option of placing a revenue-producing service into the space used for inventories is under considera-

208

tion, the cost of continuing such use of the space is increased to the expense of additional space for the service.

The remaining costs are related to investment. There are many alternative uses for capital, including the purchase of operating inventories. If the dollars were not invested in inventory, they could be invested in adding revenue-producing services or, at a minimum, with a bank to draw interest. In view of these alternatives, this cost of capital must be assigned to the inventory. The amount to be assigned obviously will vary as interest rates and alternative uses for the capital vary. The financial officer should be consulted for determination of the present capital cost, along with trends.

Once these factors have been quantified to the degree possible, the next step is to summarize them. This involves a combination of dollar amounts and percentages. The dollars must be divided by the current inventory value to convert them to percentages. The percentages then are added, resulting in the total holding cost percentage. This value is used in the calculation of economic order quantities and economic review periods.

18. ABC and Criticality Indexing

Gary L. Calhoun and Karen A. Campbell

Although industry has long been involved in the search for and implementation of new and improved approaches to inventory control, health care facilities have been slow to recognize the value of such control.

This failure has not been without costs but frequently they have not been quantified. Nursing staff members in almost any hospital could tell numerous stories about the unavailability of supplies; on the other hand, finance directors in some institutions probably have a less tangible understanding of the dollar costs related to supply shortages.

In a cost-based reimbursement environment, there were few incentives for institutions to be concerned with the costs of inventory. The changes in reimbursement mechanisms in the last few years, however, have made it imperative that these costs be managed.

Where inventory control has been practiced, there have been two primary objectives:

1. Cost control: Industry probably has been much quicker than hospitals to embrace this objective because a profit margin has always been essential to its continuing existence.
2. Assurance of timely availability of supplies: Hospitals have a more compelling incentive to achieve this objective than most other industries because health facilities use supplies to take care of patients rather than to manufacture items.

For any set of circumstances, there is always the potential that the two objectives, cost control and assurance of available supplies, may be in conflict: that is, in order to ensure the timely availability of supplies, it sometimes is necessary to pay a premium. The likelihood of experiencing high costs is increased significantly by the absence of controls on inventories. Thus, effective control mechanisms not only must achieve those two objectives but also must resolve the potential conflict between them.

Mechanisms for controlling inventories have two components: (1) analysis and categorization of supply items and (2) selection and application of the appropriate management control model for each category. This section focuses on the first component, although some introductory material on the second also is provided.

TRADITIONAL METHOD OF ANALYSIS

Historically, when material managers identified which inventory items required close monitoring and control, their action was based on the volume purchased or the dollar cost. The criticality of an item for either a manufacturing process or patient care has not been a consideration in traditional analyses such as the ABC inventory control system.

Inventory control methods that do not consider criticality run the risk of not identifying other types of costly stock-outs. Such costs are both tangible and intangible. In hospitals, certain items are essential to ensure high-quality patient care. The intangible costs involve jeopardizing the quality of the health care delivered and being unable to predict the unavailability of a critical item. The tangible costs resulting from a critical item stock-out involve the increasing importance of inventory expense control.

Today, controlling nonlabor expense is crucial to meeting a hospital's operating cost objectives. Inventory cost is the single largest component of nonlabor expense. Identifying the items in a hospital's inventory that are the most important to manage is an essential strategy in controlling their expense and in evaluating the performance of the material management department.

Hospitals should consider a variation of ABC inventory control that rates all inventory items not only according to volume and cost but also according to criticality to patient care. An index number can be derived that can then be used in the ABC allocation process to determine the placement of the item within inventory categories and provide better control and management information in analyzing stock-outs.

REVIEW OF TRADITIONAL ABC ANALYSIS

The traditional ABC inventory system separates stock items into various categories in order to ascertain which ones require close control. The criterion for the categorization, historically, has been a measurement that combines both the cost and quantity of the items used.[1] Thus, if 15 percent of the items represent 60 to 70 percent of the total inventory value, these high-value items typically are allocated to the A classification. Similarly, a middle range of 10 percent to 15 percent of all items may represent 15 percent to 30 percent of the total inventory value. These are put in the B category. The remaining 70 to 75 percent of the items are to the C category.[2] Table 18–1 shows an ABC categorization of a sample inventory.

INTRODUCTION TO ABC CRITICALITY INDEXING

There is an apparent inadequacy in the traditional ABC inventory control method, especially as it relates to hospitals. Items that may have been relegated to the C category because of low-cost or low-volume characteristics may in fact be critical for patient care or extremely difficult to acquire, and thus costly in terms of the consequences of a stock-out.

To address the inadequacy of the traditional ABC inventory control system, the University of Michigan Hospitals developed an ABC criticality indexing method that consolidates the inventory item characteristics of volume, cost investment, and criticality into one index number. This index number is then used to assign the inventory items to the ABC categories, thus ensuring close monitoring and control for all three factors.

The indexing process involves both the user departments and the material management department. The criticality component of the index must be derived from the input of a variety of users. These can be selected on the basis of a representative cross-section of the user population or the list can be more inclusive. Depending on the size and complexity of both the hospital and its inventory, the initial effort to identify criticality can incorporate the entire inventory of patient care supplies or focus on some smaller portion of it. For example, a hospital could begin its analysis with exchange cart items or medical/surgical supplies.

Table 18–1 ABC Categorization of a Sample Inventory

Category	Items	Value	% of Total Value	% of Total Items
A	217 items, value $700 to $9,400	$430,289	70	15
B	175 items, $250 to $699	100,606	16	12
C	1,065 items, below $250	84,396	14	73
Totals		615,291	100%	100%

DEVELOPING THE CRITICALITY COMPONENT

At the University of Michigan Hospitals, the first attempt to develop a criticality index included all patient care items and input from a cross-section of users. A list of the 1,207 patient care items stocked in hospital stores was distributed to material management, representatives from nursing (general medical/surgical, pediatric, and intensive care), the operating rooms, and the physician staff. The items were grouped into similar categories to facilitate the reviewers' task. The reviewers were asked to evaluate and classify each item according to its criticality to patient care.

In the first project the list of items was distributed by mail, with only written instructions. For the second attempt, the list was distributed at group meetings that provided an opportunity for the reviewers to ask questions.

The classification criteria were as follows:

1. Group X: The item has no acceptable substitutes. Stock-outs are not tolerated in the patient care process.
2. Group Y: The item has readily available substitutes but these are not as satisfactory as the original product and a stock-out lasting longer than 48 hours could compromise the patient care process.
3. Group Z: The item has readily available substitutes that are acceptable. Stock-outs lasting longer than 48 hours could be tolerated well by the patient care process.

4. Group O: The item was not familiar enough to the reviewers to be classified.[3]

Each group was assigned a number value (X = 3, Y = 2, Z = 1). Using the classification criteria, reviewers categorized each of the items as an X, Y, or Z. These categories were converted to numerical values by material management. For example, all Xs were given a value of 3. These values were summed (by item for all reviewers) and divided by the number of reviewers familiar with the items (those giving nonzero ratings) to obtain an average criticality value for each item. An example of this process is shown in Table 18–2.

To ensure the dependability and predictability of the ranking system, a statistical test of reliability was performed on the scores of a 10 percent random sample of the items. An analysis of variance yielded a correlation, or reliability, coefficient of .83, which is significant at the .001 level of confidence. The relative importance of the items did not vary across individual evaluators but remained consistent. In other words, the ranking process yielded scores from individuals that reflected the relative importance of the ranked items on a consistent basis.

The criticality component identified by the ranking process was used by the hospitals in their efforts to control inventory. Even with the assistance of the criticality index, however, the hospitals continued to experience stock-outs of items termed critical by specific patient care units.

Table 18–2 Process for Obtaining Average Criticality Values

	Item 1	Item 2	Item 3	Item 4
Nurse A	X = 3	Z = 1	Z = 1	Y = 2
Nurse B	X = 3	Z = 1	Y = 2	X = 3
Nurse C	Y = 2	Z = 1	Z = 1	Y = 2
Nurse D	X = 3	Z = 1	Z = 1	Y = 2
Nurse E	X = 2	Z = 1	Y = 2	Y = 2
Total	13	5	7	11
Total ÷ 5 or Average Criticality	2.6	1	1.4	2.2

Source: Reprinted from *Hospital Materiel Management Quarterly*, Aspen Systems Corporation, © 1982.

It was not clear whether the continuing stock-out problem was the result of too vague a measurement of criticality or of some other problem in the inventory control system. To determine whether critical items could be identified more accurately, a new process was developed that incorporated a unit-by-unit review of items for criticality. Only nursing units were involved in this new process, thus excluding some of the departments that had been involved in the original index method.

The hospitals use an exchange cart system to supply the inpatient nursing units with all medical and surgical and some pharmaceutical supplies. Exchange cart items thus served as a well-defined and highly pertinent category of supplies for purposes of criticality indexing. The list that stockkeepers used to inventory each cart provided a base list for classifying items.

The list for each nursing unit was given to its head nurses, who were asked to evaluate and classify each item according to its criticality to patient care on the unit. The classification criteria were the same as those from the first review except that Group O was eliminated because each reviewer was familiar with all items to be classified.

One other modification was added: a constraint was placed on the number of items that could be placed in the A category; that is, each head nurse was allowed to identify only 10 percent of the items in Group A.

There were a number of reasons for this. In discussions with head nurses before the review, it became obvious that the definition of what constituted an A item could be interpreted broadly and that the majority of items might be so categorized. A large number of items in the A category would have defeated the purpose of using the ABC system. Furthermore, the inventory control systems, which still are predominantly manual and time-consuming, were inadequate for management of more than 10 percent as A items.

Any head nurse who had difficulty complying with this limit was encouraged to contact material management and after discussion an agreement was reached as to which should be assigned

to the A category. As a result of the discussion and negotiation process, the reviewers were allowed to exceed the 10 percent constraint to a limited extent.

Next, the lists were analyzed to identify items that appeared to be critical for only one or a small number of nursing units. The head nurses there were interviewed to ensure that these items did conform with the definition for the A category. Items that conformed were given a weighted value of 3 even though only a few units had designated them as A items. This value assignment differed from the process described earlier for developing the criticality component. The need for special treatment of items categorized as A by only a few units is the result of the averaging process used to obtain the criticality index.

To illustrate: If 30 reviewers categorize an item as C and two reviewers as A, its average value would be 1.1. If the average value of 1.1 is used, it should be treated as in category C even though there are a few units for which the item is, indeed, critical.

The process for deriving the criticality measure for the remaining items was the same as in the original study. The values assigned to each item by all head nurses evaluating that item (not all rated all items since articles used varied from unit to unit) were summed and divided by the number of reviewers for that item to obtain an average criticality value for each.

The advantage of expanding the number of users queried, while limiting their evaluation to only items with which they are most familiar, is that the measure of criticality obtained should be more concrete and more accurate than that resulting from an assessment by a more limited group of users with only partial familiarity with the items. The disadvantage of this new approach is that it is somewhat more complicated and can be very time consuming if users require much interaction with material management to arrive at a final categorization.

To a great extent, the type of process used by a hospital will depend on variables such as the degree to which supplies vary among patient care units and the resources available to conduct the evaluation. Any hospital interested in developing a criticality index should weigh the advantages and disadvantages of the two approaches in terms of its own characteristics.

CRITICALITY, COST, AND VOLUME

To develop an ABC criticality index, values had to be generated for cost and volume as well as for criticality. The cost characteristic of each item was reduced to one number by assigning each current ABC inventory category a value, as was the volume characteristic for each. The ABC inventory analysis ranked by cost (in accordance with the process identified earlier for the traditional ABC analysis) had a value of 3 assigned to the A category items, 2 to the B, and 1 to the C. The ABC inventory analysis ranked by volume had the same value assignments $(A=3, B=2, C=1)$.

Each inventory item then had three number values associated with it, representing criticality, cost, and volume. These characteristics were consolidated into one index by weighting each characteristic and summing the values as follows:

$$\text{item index} = W_1 \text{ (criticality value)} + W_2 \text{ (cost value)} + W_3 \text{ (volume value)}$$

The weights assigned were $W_1 = 2$, $W_2 = 1$, $W_3 = 1$. Criticality was deemed the most important characteristic when categorizing the items into the ABC classifications; therefore, it was given a higher relative value. Following is

an example of the calculation of an index value for a specific inventory article, Item #43 (Infusion Set):

$$\text{index} = \underset{\text{(criticality value)}}{W_1} + \underset{\text{(cost value)}}{W_2} + \underset{\text{(volume value)}}{W_3}$$
$$9 = \underset{5}{2(2.5)} + \underset{3}{1(3)} + \underset{1}{1(1)}$$

The index values ranged from 12 to 4. The higher values reflected items that were either deemed critical by a majority of the reviewers or had been confirmed as being critical for one or a few units and also had high dollar values and high turnover. Any items with index values between 12 and 9.5 were placed in the A category of inventory control. The distribution of scores had a natural break at 9.5. (Break points will vary among hospitals.) Items with index values between 9.4 and 6.5 were assigned to the B category, 6.4 to 4 to the C. The effect on the item distribution is shown in Table 18–3.

OLD REPORT VS. NEW

Originally, two stock-out reports were generated at the University of Michigan Hospitals, both based on ABC rankings: one by monetary value, and the other by number of issues. Information provided for each inventory category included:

- the stock-out rate
- the number of stock-outs for all items
- the number of items that reach stock-out level
- a listing of A items stocked out during that month.

Table 18–3 Effect on Item Distribution

Critical ABC category	Index value range	% of total inventory	Traditional ABC category	% of total by value	% of total by no. of issues
A	12.0–9.5	18	A	14	16
B	9.4–6.5	54	B	35	17
C	6.4–4.0	28	C	51	67

Source: Reprinted from *Hospital Materiel Management Quarterly*, vol. 3, no. 4, May 1982, published by Aspen Systems Corporation, © 1982.

The new ABC criticality indexing method report lists the number of stock-outs, the number of items that reached stock-out level, the stock-out rate by A, B, and C categories, and all articles stocked out during the month that are categorized as A items. The new index-ranked inventory produces only one report.

An example of the information and statistics that the two types of stock-out reports yield for a typical month is presented in Tables 18–4 and 18–5.

Another column, to provide total stock-out statistics, could be added to the criticality report. Sufficient information also is available to generate reports for all four possible indexes:

1. criticality index
2. volume index
3. cost index
4. combined index.

An alternative to the indexing system, which a hospital may want to consider, is a nonweighted inventory ranking, strictly by criticality, that does not incorporate monetary value or issue volume. The result would be similar to traditional reports but would review stock-outs by the third category of criticality (Table 18–6).

MANAGEMENT CONTROL MODELS

The categorization of items accomplishes nothing by itself. Its value is as a guideline for application of different management and control techniques. The costlier it is to an institution to not manage an item effectively, the greater the effort should be to ensure its appropriate management.

Typically, the A category items are subjected to such management control models as economic order quantity (EOQ) and reorder points (ROP), with probabilities assigned to the calculated demand units. The B category is managed through the use of the EOQ model but ROPs usually are estimated. The C category is managed through item standardization and subjectively determined EOQs and ROPs.[4]

In addition to control models used to quantify the material acquisition process more accurately and thus reduce the number of stock-outs resulting from internal processes, provision must be made for external factors beyond the material manager's control. For example, if the manufacturer or distributor has a stock-out, a hospital must have established procedures for obtaining the item in question (or a substitute) from a different source.

The procedures for rectifying stock-outs when they do occur can be varied to ensure that efforts made are commensurate with the category to which an item has been assigned. Such procedures are particularly important for items that are critical to patient care. The criticality index allows a hospital to identify critical items that require special procedures and thereby to limit the number of those for which it must take extraordinary measures.

BENEFITS AND COSTS

The ABC inventory control method reflecting item criticality has several benefits:

Table 18–4 Traditional ABC Stock-Out Report for a Typical Month

| | A category | | | B category | | | C category | | |
| | | No. | | | No. | | | No. | |
	No. of stock-outs	of items	% of stock-outs	No. of stock-outs	of items	% of stock-outs	No. of stock-outs	of items	% of stock-outs
By $ value	9	8	0	27	27	6.0	37	34	5.4
By no. of issues	2	2	1.6	19	19	4.2	33	32	4.8

Source: Reprinted from *Hospital Materiel Management Quarterly,* vol. 3, no. 4, May 1982, published by Aspen Systems Corporation, © 1982.

Table 18–5 New ABC Stock-Out Report for Same Month Using Criticality Index Statistics

| | A category No. | | | B category No. | | | C category No. | | |
	No. of stock-outs	No. of items	% of stock-outs	No. of stock-outs	No. of items	% of stock-outs	No. of stock-outs	No. of items	% of stock-outs
By criticality index	11	10	5.0	39	39	6.0	23	20	6.7

Source: Reprinted from *Hospital Materiel Management Quarterly,* vol. 3, no. 4, May 1982, published by Aspen Systems Corporation, © 1982.

- The process of ranking the stock items involves the input of a variety of users. These people appreciate the opportunity to contribute their specific knowledge and expertise to a project that can increase the quality of patient care and the efficiency of operations. The project is perceived as an active step toward ameliorating the stock-out problem. In addition, the project facilitates communication between users and the material management department.

- The system provides both the administrator and material management director with a means of evaluating the performance of the material manager and the department. Once a stock-out standard has been agreed upon for each category, acceptable and unacceptable performance objectives can be set.

- The system may need only periodic updating, once the hospital inventory has been reclassified using the criticality indexes. At University Hospitals, new items added to the inventory must be approved by a multidisciplinary standardization and product evaluation committee. The item's index value is identified at the same time it is added to the hospital inventory.

- The patient care process benefits from the enhanced managerial control of inventory items classified as critical and their consequent availability. Thus, the ABC criticality index provides an opportunity for hospitals to optimize the quality of patient care while minimizing the cost.

The costs of the system are basically the reviewers' time and some possible loss of validity as a result of reviewer biases. Reviewing the large number of items in hospital stores is a tedious task and the time it requires may discourage many qualified persons. Once the review is completed, there is the task of calculating the index numbers and recategorizing the items. This is particularly cumbersome in an institution that does not have access to a computer.

The alternative of a report identifying stock-outs based only on criticality and not the weighted index value would provide the criticality information with less effort but management then would have three reports to analyze instead of one.

Some degree of validity is lost in the bias of the reviewers. For example, it was discovered that when reviewers were given the option of

Table 18–6 New ABC Stock-Out Report for Same Month Using Criticality Statistics

| | A category No. | | | B category No. | | | C category No. | | |
	No. of stock-outs	No. of items	% of stock-outs	No. of stock-outs	No. of items	% of stock-outs	No. of stock-outs	No. of items	% of stock-outs
By criticality	12	11	5.3	43	43	5.7	18	15	8.1

Source: Reprinted from *Hospital Materiel Management Quarterly,* vol. 3, no. 4, May 1982, published by Aspen Systems Corporation, © 1982.

using zero to reflect unfamiliarity, the scores were biased downward. Therefore, it is important to select reviewers who are familiar with the items they are asked to categorize.

The lasting benefit of the system is a comprehensive information operation that provides administration with an improved inventory control methodology, thus enhancing patient care and providing criteria for evaluating the performance of material management. With increasing emphasis on reducing the costs of health care, there is concern that quality of care may be sacrificed. The fact that the ABC criticality system can address both quality and cost issues makes it an extremely beneficial management tool.

NOTES

1. G.L. Calhoun and F.R. Wheeler, "ABC Analysis and Stockout Reports Reflecting Considerations of Criticality for Patient Care," *Hospital Materiel Management Quarterly* 3, no. 4 (1982): 45.

2. Ibid., 46.

3. H. Berman and L. Weeks, *The Financial Management of Hospitals* (Ann Arbor, Mich.: Health Administration Press, 1976): 286.

4. W.T. Steven, "ABC Inventory Control: An Analysis." *Hospital Purchasing Management* 5, no. 12 (1980): 10.

19. Supply Distribution Options— A New Perspective*

JAMIE C. KOWALSKI

The health care facility's distribution system is a complex network of storage (source) and user (destination) points.

Much of what has been written in the last few years has touted the benefits and advantages of exchange cart systems as a method of supply distribution in hospitals. Health care facilities may be surprised when they evaluate their systems for cost effectiveness and may find that other distribution methods may be even more efficient.

When conducting this analysis, hospitals should remember to take a broad systems approach. A study of the entire distribution network and requirements could reveal opportunities for streamlining it and reducing total costs. Such elements as food, drugs, supplies, linen (both soiled and clean), trash, mail, equipment, and paper movement can attest that the material flow in a hospital can be voluminous and complicated.

The goal of any effective distribution system should be to provide the right item to the right place at the right time for the least total cost. Studies have shown that for every dollar spent to purchase an item, another dollar is spent storing and moving it.[1]

A distribution system is an integral part of a material management program and can significantly affect its performance. Hospitals should keep in mind that there is no one best system for all situations.

KEY RELATIONSHIPS

Inventory Management

As a key component of a material management program, the supply distribution system affects many other operations and functions. The first relationship is that of supply distribution to inventory management. This is a direct linkup in that an effective system can directly support or impede the hospital's inventory management. The system can directly affect the amount of inventory maintained in a general storeroom and in user departments.

Numerous studies have estimated that there may be a one-to-three ratio for what is stored in the storeroom to what is in the user areas; that is, for every $1 of inventory in the storeroom there may be $3 in the user areas.[2]

The frequency with which the supply distribution system replenishes stock in user areas directly affects inventory levels. The more frequently inventories are replenished, the smaller the inventories needed at user points at any time.

Warehousing and Service Levels

The space available, the storeroom layout, and the location of items in it affect the order-picking methods employed in supply distribution. Lack of parking space in the warehouse/storeroom can virtually eliminate using an exchange cart system. Such systems need space to park all those carts.

The location system for items in the storeroom can have a positive effect on order-picking productivity. If items are stored in numerical sequence (by product number) or by product classification, storeroom requisitions can be printed in that sequence, thus reducing the time required to locate and pick orders, whether they be for an exchange cart, par level, or standard requisition system.

*This is an update of an article originally published by Aspen Systems Corporation, © 1980, reprinted with permission.

The service levels provided to user areas can be greatly enhanced by a proper distribution system. One that is proactive (replenishes inventories in the user areas automatically on a cycle basis) will require less user (patient care) personnel time.

Patient care personnel no longer need complete orders or put away supplies once orders have been filled and delivered. This can make more time available for patient care and can be done at no extra cost to the hospital. It is merely a reallocation and better use of personnel time—supply persons managing the system and care persons with patients.

The management of patient supply charges can be enhanced by coordination with the distribution system. As the frequency of replenishment increases, the timeliness of the reconciliation for charges and the opportunity for control and management of losses are improved. This not only can bring about reduced losses, it also may directly increase hospital revenue.

BASIC OPTIONS

Requisition System

The requisition system is basically controlled by the user area. Each department functions as a material manager and keeps track of its own inventories. At a given time or when inventory levels get low, it prepares a requisition and presents it to the central storage point. The requisition is filled, supplies are delivered to the user area, and users put the items in their appropriate place.

Advantages

Little capital investment is required. It is traditional, somewhat more easily accepted. Some employees feel a sense of importance or power by being able to control their inventories, even though few have had formal training or experience in this area.

Disadvantages

User department labor, usually highly skilled, educated, and paid, is used to a greater degree for the material control function instead of for patient care. More user department space may be used for storage instead of for patient care. This is brought on by general lack of control or management of the inventory because the departments may have so little expertise in managing inventories.

Hoarding also is a characteristic of this system. If a department ever experiences a stockout or back order from the storeroom, it may vow never to let it happen again and may maintain inordinate amounts of inventory in the user area. This ordering and maintaining of needlessly high inventory can create artificial stock-outs in the hospital storeroom.

A department may order an unusually large number of an item, totally depleting what is in the storeroom (even the most well-conceived reorder points and safety stock levels cannot anticipate unusual or irrational ordering patterns). Other departments ordering this item then find it unavailable from the storeroom even though it actually is available in the hospital but in a user area and "unavailable" to other requesters. This forces the storeroom to replenish its stock on an emergency basis and has the net effect of increasing the total inventory investment in the hospital (the storeroom plus the "hoarding" department) without improving availability.

One easy method of improving the requisition system is by maintaining a catalog of what is required in each of the user areas and establishing a schedule of order intervals for all departments. The frequency of these intervals may encourage the users to maintain lower inventories, and the catalog at least will identify what is generally maintained in those areas in case another department needs to "borrow" from them.

Par Level System

A par level system is one in which each user department stores supplies in an assigned location in its own area. Physical stock levels in that user area are predetermined, based on a usage rate and the frequency of the replenishment process. At periodic intervals (e.g., every 24 hours, twice a week, or weekly), supply personnel conduct a physical inventory of what is available, then order and obtain supplies to return the on-hand levels to the predetermined or par level.

Advantages

This type of system is easily implemented and requires little capital investment in terms of remodeling costs or purchase of material-handling equipment. It also improves hospitalwide inventory management by establishing a standard level in all user areas and, based on the frequency of replenishment, can reduce total levels. Lower inventory levels in the user areas will need less space, possibly creating more area for patient care.

Furthermore, this system, managed and implemented by supply personnel, places the management responsibility for the inventory control and supply distribution functions where they best belong—with supply personnel. It eliminates the need for patient care personnel to spend their time on this function. Again, this provides the hospital with the potential of improving patient care by providing more time for that function with no increase in cost.

The management of supply charges also is enhanced because this system is operated on preset intervals providing continuity and timeliness in the supply charge requisition process. This can reduce hospital costs and increase net revenue.

Disadvantages

A par level system is more labor intensive than others. It requires several trips to and from the user areas to conduct the physical inventory, return to the storage point to obtain supplies, then go back to the user area to deliver those supplies and put them away. This trip time is unproductive and, because it is unsupervised, can result in wasted time.

Another serious disadvantage is that the inventory status in a user department usually is dynamic—it changes continuously. In the par level system there is a gap between the time

inventory level is reviewed and the supplies are obtained and returned to the user area. During that time there may be a significant change in the status of the inventory. As a result, when the supplies are returned to the user area, they no longer may be adequate to bring the levels up to the predetermined par.

There also is considerable traffic with such a system. It may require several trips to and from the user areas. When the inventory status changes between the time of the review and the time of the replenishment, return trips may be necessary, making it even more labor intensive and even less cost effective.

Exchange Cart System

The exchange cart system has been the most popular of all systems implemented by hospitals in recent years. It is basically the same as a par level system in that there are predetermined levels and predetermined intervals for replenishing inventory to those levels. In the exchange cart system, however, the cart is used for storage and distribution. A duplicate of each cart in the user area is maintained in the storage area so that at the predetermined time the full cart can be taken to the user and exchanged for the depleted one. The cycle repeats itself at given intervals.

Advantages

An exchange cart system provides better utilization of labor. Less time is spent traveling, and order-picking time can be more productive if done in an area that can be supervised under conditions similar to those on a production line. If carts are set up in accordance with the item location in the storeroom and item locations on each cart are similar, order-picking time can be minimized. Given that supply personnel oversee the carts in the stocking area, management responsibility for and control over this function is optimized.

Standardizing the items on the carts—giving proximal locations to similar items—has advantages beyond order picking. User personnel who are required to float to different user areas can locate items more easily under this system. (This also can be true for par level systems.)

This system supports inventory management in that levels are controlled by the frequencies of exchange; however, it may require almost twice as much inventory as that of a par level system because of the duplicate carts.

The selection of the interval between cart exchanges will help in managing and controlling supply charges. Service levels to user areas improve because of the instantaneous restocking to 100 percent of the predetermined levels. There is no lag between the time the inventory is taken and the time the supplies are delivered; the full cart is delivered, the depleted one removed.

Disadvantages

There may be a substantial capital investment required to purchase carts as well as to remodel storage areas in the general storeroom and the user areas to accommodate them. The parking space required for these carts can be significant.

If this system is selected, care should be taken when specifying and selecting the cart equipment. There are many sources, styles, and materials available from cart manufacturers. The hospital needs to select the material that will provide the longest life and the design that will best meet the demands of the user areas

Given the cost of different materials (e.g., stainless steel, chrome, or zinc), care should be taken to carefully evaluate their expected life, the aesthetics they provide, and their relative costs. Whether or not the cart will be cleaned manually or in an automatic cart washer also must be considered.

The interchangeability of parts and the ease with which carts are assembled and changed are key considerations. A hospital may require many carts to implement the system so the time spent assembling and adjusting them as needs change may be considerable. Such a hospital is better off looking at carts that can be assembled by hand with no special tools and can be changed easily and quickly.

The type of caster also is important and must be based on intended use. They come in different surfaces and configurations, each with a unique application and associated cost. Again, careful evaluation is needed to bring the best selection.

Overviews

A capsulized evaluation of these three options is shown in Table 19–1. It should be obvious that there are advantages in each system and that it is up to a hospital to place a value on the factors involved.

Table 19–1 Summary of Comparisons of Options

Distribution System	Total hospital inventory reduction potential	Labor utilization	Capital expense	Space utilization	Management control
Par level	High (as high as 50% over requisition system)	Fair	Low	Good	Very good
Exchange cart	High (as high as 50% over requisition system)	Excellent	High	Good	Excellent
Requisition	Low	Poor	Low	Poor	Poor

Source: Reprinted from *Hospital Materiel Management Quarterly*, vol. 2, no. 2, November 1980, published by Aspen Systems Corporation, © 1980.

Possibly an even clearer picture of the differences and advantages is shown in Figure 19–1, the flow diagram. Clearly, the system that requires the fewest steps is the exchange cart system.

OTHER CONSIDERATIONS

Centralization and Delivery

Centralization of related distribution functions can lead to improved efficiencies. The receiving function, the distribution of nonstock merchandise, and the centralization of storage facilities can complement the supply distribution system and allow it to produce optimum benefits.

Scheduling these activities can further improve efficiency by making the workload even, which leads to better handling of peak demands and true emergencies. Assigning each department a given order day will help distribution personnel plan their workload and respond better to emergencies. Preprinting requisition forms for each department will encourage staff members to complete the forms correctly and on time.

Figure 19–1 Flow Diagram: Alternative Distribution Systems

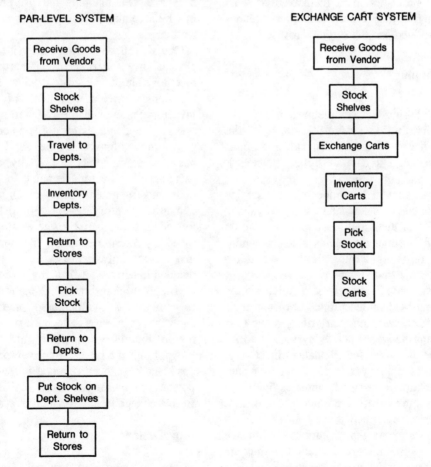

Delivering merchandise on a scheduled basis eliminates excess trips and traffic. The best delivery route is one that avoids retracing steps and minimizes the total distance to be traveled. Hospitals also should look at delivering nonstock items along with routine storeroom items. This obviously depends on the frequencies with which departments order and receive goods from the storeroom in relation to the frequency with which they receive nonstock items.

In addition, it may be feasible and cost effective to combine all physical distribution (supplies, linen, food, etc.) into a central function. This way, personnel can be more productive, schedules adhered to (lesser elevator congestion), and service levels maintained.

Centralization of related functions should allow standardization in the methods used. This should improve the accuracy of the clerical functions performed and the service provided.

Recordkeeping

Recordkeeping is a key element in any successful distribution system. Records of the activities that show usage, demand, and trends are invaluable. The data are utilized to review par levels and adjust them accordingly.

Hospitals should determine in-stock service levels to obtain data that can be used to evaluate the success of their routine supply distribution system. A hospital complains when a vendor provides only eight out of every ten items ordered on the first shipment. So hospital user departments should expect the hospital supply system to provide at least nine out of ten items ordered. Maintaining statistics on what is ordered and delivered allows system performance to be measured and evaluated objectively.

The maintaining of statistics for routine supply distribution is essential; statistics that show random requirements are equally important. Whenever a department places an emergency order, or a nonemergency order that is outside the routine system, extra time and handling are required and total costs increase. Table 19–2 shows how costly this can be.

Reviewing the frequencies of these requests, their sources, and the items sought can reduce or eliminate these needs. Frequently requested items can be placed in the department's normal inventory, or levels for those items can be increased. Abusers can be counseled as to how to work with the system and service as they are intended to be provided without creating extra difficulties and increasing operating costs.

ASSESSING THE CURRENT SYSTEM

Physical and Cost Factors

Evaluating a hospital's existing system as it relates to the options available is not difficult but does take some planning and effort to complete in a reliable manner that provides usable information.

One of the first steps to be taken is to conduct a physical inventory of the user departments. This inventory should be costed out at the current replacement price of each item to find the total inventory value available as a starting point.

Next, the demands for a given period should be determined for each of the user departments, based on set intervals (e.g., daily, weekly, or twice a week). The total demands should include both random and emergency requirements. The demand inventory levels should be costed, totaled, and compared to the existing physical inventory determined in the first step. This will give a picture of what to expect by establishing demand inventory levels and a given frequency of supply replenishment. Comparing the two inventory levels and their associated values will show the net increase or decrease that a change in the distribution system will bring.

Applying the hospital's inventory carrying cost factor to the difference will identify the potential savings in such expense that may result from a change in the distribution system.

Flow Design

The next step is to document, in detail, the steps required in the existing distribution sys-

Table 19–2 Supply Issue Frequencies from Central Supply Room (CSR)

Date	Unit	1E	2C	DR	3C	3E	2E	4C	4S	4W	3W	KU	ER	Total
12/02/78	Calls	12	9	1	6	2	8	13	11	15	0	5		83
	lines/A.M.	21	8	5	31	12	14	10	7	13	2	15		138
	lines/P.M.	8	8	6	13	3	17	11	6	14	7	15		108
12/01/78	Calls	5	8	0	7	2	7	18	15	18	1	3		84
	lines/A.M.	21	6	4	22	12	18	14	18	24	7	16		162
	lines/P.M.	11	6	3	5	1	4	4	3	5	1	4		47
11/30/78	Calls	16	5	0	20	7	9	16	9	9	1	5		97
	lines/A.M.	7	2	5	18	1	12	12	12	17	3	12	6	95
	lines/P.M.	7	3	2	4	0	15	4	4	5	0	4	6	54
11/29/78	Calls	7	4	1	9	1	4	16	25	14	5	6		91
	lines/A.M.	29	17	11	22	12	21	11	10	25	9	18		185
	lines/P.M.	5	3	0	4	2	11	7	4	2	2	11		51
11/28/78	Calls	2	7	0	7	0	6	17	14	21	1	2		77
	lines/A.M.	—	4	9	25	9	22	8	18	25	5	17		141
	lines/P.M.	—	3	1	5	2	5	8	5	11	3	13		56
11/27/78	Calls	5	5	0	13	4	6	17	16	16	1	4		87
	lines/A.M.	14	5	5	26	3	13	19	12	24	16	34		158
	lines/P.M.	6	2	4	11	0	7	10	9	14	6	18		87
11/26/78	Calls	0	0	0	2	0	1	10	10	11	0	0		34
	lines/A.M.	8	12	5	16	4	12	13	15	26	17	26	4	158
	lines/P.M.	7	3	3	11	0	20	3	3	7	0	6	16	79
Totals	Calls	47	37	2	64	16	41	107	100	104	9	25	0	552
	lines/A.M.	100	54	42	160	53	112	87	92	154	59	136	10	1050
	lines/P.M.	44	27	19	53	8	79	43	34	58	19	61	22	482
Daily averages	Calls	6.7	5.3	.3	9.1	2.3	5.8	15.2	14.2	14.8	1.3	3.6	0	78.8
	lines/A.M.	14.2	7.7	6.0	22.8	7.5	16.0	12.4	13.1	22.0	8.4	19.4	1.4	150.0
	lines/P.M.	6.2	3.8	2.7	7.5	1.1	11.2	6.1	4.8	8.3	2.7	8.7	3.1	68.8

Analysis
Lines
A.M. 150
P.M. 68.8
Total 218.8 avg. lines/day ÷ 12 departments = 18.2 lines/dept./day
Calls 78.8 avg. calls/day ÷ 12 departments = 6.5 calls/dept./day
Labor
Hours 78.8 avg. calls/day × 10 minutes/call ÷ 60 minutes/hour = 13 hours/day ÷ 8 hours/shift = 1.625 shifts/day

Note: 1. A line equals an item delivered, no matter what quantity.
2. Assumes an average of 10 minutes per call based on observation and previous experience.

Source: Reprinted from *Hospital Materiel Management Quarterly*, vol. 2, no. 2, November 1980, published by Aspen Systems Corporation, © 1980.

tem. A flow chart can help. Then a hospital can compare it to the processes involved in the other systems available. Figure 19–2 shows how a flow diagram can visually simplify the identification and evaluation of each process.

After the flow diagram has been completed, a detailed step-by-step procedure should be documented for each system. Applying standard times required for each step or function in the various systems provides a means by which each

Figure 19–2 Supply Distribution to Nursing Floor: Comparative Flow Diagrams

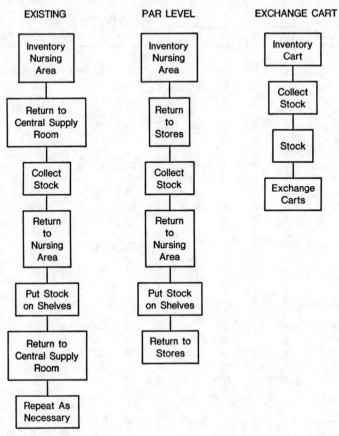

Source: Reprinted from *Hospital Materiel Management Quarterly,* vol. 2, no. 2, November 1980, published by Aspen Systems Corporation, © 1980.

can be costed for labor expense (Table 19–3). Standard times can be obtained from industrial engineering manuals or the hospital may conduct its own time studies to establish standards for each function. After those functions have been identified and the standard times applied, current labor rates should be used to cost out each step within each system and to arrive at a total labor cost.

It is important to document all other costs of the existing and optional systems and record them for comparison. Such things as the paper work, supplies, capital expenses, data collection, and physical rearranging of storage areas should be documented, costed, and compared. Table 19–4 shows the bottom-line breakdown of the three major factors: inventory carrying costs, labor costs, and other expenses. These are part of any distribution system and should be annualized for comparison.

Environmental Factors

Before any final decisions are made, environmental factors should be considered. These are the factors over and above dollars and cents that will help hospitals decide which is the best system for them. These include:

- the ability to supervise employees who are providing the service and performing the distribution function

Table 19–3 Operating Cost Comparison of Distribution Systems

| | | Daily Labor Requirements (in Minutes) | | | |
| | | CSR[1] | | Stores | |
Function	Present system	Par level	Exchange cart	Par level	Exchange cart
CSR inventories and orders from storeroom	20	20	20		
Fill CSR order, deliver it, and put away	40	80	80		
Pharmacy orders IVs from storeroom	20				
Fill, deliver, and put away pharmacy order	40				
Pharmacy inventories, floor par levels and restocks	60				
CSR inventories med./surg. levels and restocks	120				
CSR restocks dressing	50				
CSR distributes utensils	50				
Stores, fills, and delivers bulk med./surg. to floors	70				
Stores, fills, and delivers paper/plastic goods to floors	60				
Travel to all floors and return to storage area		20		30	
Inventory par levels		105		105	
Obtain stock		105		105	
Load truck, travel, unload truck, and put stock away		95		120	
Return to stock				5	
Exchange carts			42		72
Inventory carts			105		105
Pull stock and restock carts			105		105
Total Minutes	520	425	352	365	282
Total Labor Costs	$17,240	$14,090	$11,670	$12,101	$9,349
FTEs[2]	1.52	1.24	1.02	1.06	.82

1. CSR = central supply room.
2. FTEs = full-time equivalents (personnel).

Source: Reprinted from *Hospital Materiel Management Quarterly*, vol. 2, no. 2, November 1980, published by Aspen Systems Corporation, © 1980.

- the assignment of management responsibility and authority for the inventory management and supply distribution function

- the traffic required in the routes that must be followed

- the space for storage, working, and parking.

Some of these environmental factors could cause a hospital to select one alternative over another, especially when the direct costs are extremely close.

Life Cycle Costs

A careful look at the total life cycle costs of the options should be made. Table 19–5 com-

Table 19–4 Annual Cost Comparison of Distribution Systems

| | | CSR[1] | | Stores | |
	Existing system	Par level	Exchange cart	Par level	Exchange cart
Inventory costs					
Floors-med/surg.	$ 31,000	$ 8,000	$ 16,000	$ 8,000	$ 16,000
Floors-IV	2,500				
Total	33,500				
CSR	38,000	38,000	38,000	8,000	8,000
Stores	120,000	120,000	120,000	120,000	120,000
ER	9,500	3,100	6,200	3,100	6,200
Total	193,000	169,100	180,200	139,100	150,200
Inventory carrying cost	48,250	42,275	45,050	34,775	37,550
Labor costs					
Scheduled deliveries	17,240	13,924	11,670	12,101	9,349
Random deliveries	16,410	8,205	8,205	8,205	8,205
Total	33,650	22,129	19,875	20,306	17,554
Capital costs		100	1,700	100	2,100
Total costs	81,900	64,504	66,625	55,181	57,204

1. CSR = central supply room.

Source: Reprinted from *Hospital Materiel Management Quarterly,* vol. 2, no. 2, November 1980, published by Aspen Systems Corporation, © 1980.

Table 19–5 Ten-Year Cost Comparison of Distribution Systems

Exchange cart system					Year					
	1	2	3	4	5	6	7	8	9	10
Capital cost	2,100	2,100	2,100	2,100	2,100	2,100	2,100	2,100	2,100	2,100
Labor cost	9,349	10,284	11,312	12,443	13,687	15,055	18,560	18,216	10,037	22,040
Inventory carrying cost	37,550	37,550	37,550	37,550	37,550	37,550	37,550	37,550	37,550	37,550
Total	48,999	49,934	50,962	52,104	53,337	54,705	56,210	57,866	59,687	61,690

Total expenditures for 10 years = $544,944

Par level system										
Capital cost	100	100	100	100	100	100	100	100	100	100
Labor cost	12,101	13,311	14,642	16,106	17,716	19,487	21,435	23,578	25,935	28,528
Subtotal	12,201	13,411	14,742	16,206	17,816	19,587	21,535	23,678	26,035	28,628
Inventory carrying cost	34,775	34,775	34,775	34,775	34,775	34,775	34,775	34,775	34,775	34,775
Total	46,976	48,186	49,517	50,981	52,981	54,310	56,310*	58,453*	60,810*	63,403*

Total expenditures for 10 years = $541,979

Note: 1. Assumes a 10 percent increase in labor rates per year.
    2. Assumes carts are fully depreciated after ten years. Actual expected life is significantly more than ten years.

*At seventh year, par level costs exceed exchange cart costs and continue to increase each year thereafter because of increasing labor rate and constant capital and inventory carrying cost.

Source: Reprinted from *Hospital Materiel Management Quarterly,* vol. 2, no. 2, November 1980, published by Aspen Systems Corporation, © 1980.

pares the costs of par level and exchange cart systems for a sample hospital over a ten-year period. At the outset, in the case shown, the par level system is economically superior. However, over ten years, and assuming that labor costs will increase at 10 percent per year, by the seventh year the cost of an exchange cart system becomes less than that of a par level system. The total 10-year cost, though, is still less for par level.

This factor cannot be overlooked. Considering return on investment (ROI) and the continuing costs associated with a given decision, this type of analysis becomes absolutely essential. Looking beyond the first year can make a substantial difference in the final decision.

Implementation Planning

No matter what system is selected, proper planning will significantly enhance the probability of a successful conversion or change as well as achievement of the goals identified in the feasibility analysis. Because a requisition system is not recommended as a routine means of providing supply service to medium-to-large consumer departments, the following discussion refers primarily to the implementation planning required for exchange cart or par level restocking systems. Given the similarity of the two systems, this implementation plan also can be utilized for either.

Planning Team

Implementation planning should include various members of the hospital's management team in order to facilitate the input and communication process at various levels in the organization. Such entities as administration, finance, nursing, and medical staff should be involved at various stages. Certainly, the person to whom material management reports (has line administrative responsibilities) should be involved or at least informed throughout the entire process.

All departments immediately affected by any change in the distribution system should be involved in the implementation planning. This would include not only the department heads/managers but certain staff members as well. It certainly is no secret that staff members in a department frequently know more about what actually is happening and what the real needs are than the department manager. This involvement also gives staff members a sense of participation and can help develop support for the system since it becomes "theirs." This is important, given that some changes in systems can run into problems during the debugging phases and staff support will be essential to help resolve them.

These resources can be brought together in a task force or committee type of configuration that provides for a formal process. This also facilitates the documentation of progress and results. This is essential for effective communication of the planning, progress made, and ultimate results. This group also should be charged with the responsibility for making sure that the identified goals are in fact achieved by the conversion to whatever system is selected.

This means that some time after implementation, the situation must be reassessed to identify the savings and/or service improvements. If goals have not been achieved, changes or modifications should be made.

Planning Model

The program the planners develop should:

- Determine on-hand inventory levels in each affected department. This will be used as the basis for identifying current inventory level for appropriateness and costs as well as providing the foundation for establishing target inventory levels as well as turn rates.
- Identify supply demand/usage for each user department for a 24-hour period. The needs/demand can be established by sampling actual consumption for a period of time—31 days usually are adequate. High, low, and average daily demand figures for that sample should be noted. Numerical averages create a smoothing effect so the peak demands should be planned for. Finally, input should be obtained from the

users by having them evaluate the data gathered. Frequently they can identify where a peak is unrepresentative of routine activity and can help establish more appropriate levels of inventory.

- Draft a list of all products to be used for each department. This should include such information as: (1) item number, (2) source, (3) description, (4) unit of issue, (5) unit cost, (6) optimum inventory level, (7) charge vs. noncharge status. This can be prepared before taking physical counts and can serve as a master catalog/work sheet.
- Determine frequency of supply replacement. This depends upon the type of system selected as well as the targets for on-hand inventory levels and turns rates.
- Identify the functional requirements and specifications required for all exchange carts if that system is used. Different size carts may be required for different areas, depending on the volume of products being maintained on the cart as well as the frequency of restocking.
- Determine appropriate location for supplies at the user area. This should include a configuration for those supplies so that reordering and restocking as well as on-demand item location can be facilitated. It is important to include user department input in this vital process. Standardized layouts should be established as much as possible in order to enhance the productivity in the ordering, restocking, and retrieval-for-use processes.
- Determine the timing for inventory review, ordering, and restocking. Essential variables for making this decision include times of peak supply demand, corridor and elevator congestion, and staff availability.
- Identify and determine the preferred methodology, individual order processing, and batch or zone processing.
- Establish the appropriate paper work/recordkeeping systems. This includes designing forms, setting up automated data systems communications, and so on.

- Adjust layout, configuration, and inventory levels at the supply source in order to accommodate the new system.
- Conduct inservice education programs for all personnel involved and affected by the system.
- Establish a mechanism for tracking non-routine/random demand for supplies that occur outside the basic system to determine the continuing effectiveness of the system and the appropriateness of the product mix and inventory levels.
- Establish a policy and procedure for making changes as appropriate. It is essential to ensure that inventory levels will be adjusted routinely to match changing demand.
- Begin implementation on either a pilot project basis, batch or zone basis, or hospital-wide. These can be equally successful, depending on the degree of complexity and sophistication of the system selected and the extent of the impact of the change.
- Schedule meetings for reviewing progress and making any necessary modifications.

The importance of, and the benefits that can be derived from, adequate implementation planning cannot be overstressed. Without it, the system can be doomed to failure. Credibility established early in a program is essential.

SURGICAL CASE CART SYSTEM

One final consideration in evaluating the distribution system in the hospital is the possibility of including surgical case carts. If a broad-scope approach to a distribution system is utilized, surgical case carts should be considered an integral part of that system.

Bulk-Replacement

As with supply distribution systems, the most basic supply option for surgery is a bulk-replacement system. In this system, the surgery manager acts as a material manager and orders stock from several sources: general stores, central supply, and outside vendors. This may be done on a scheduled or nonscheduled basis.

The surgery department also may do its own sterile processing of instruments, basins, utensils, and linens. It basically is a self-sufficient operation.

Advantages

The inherent advantages of such a system are that it requires little interdepartmental coordination and, therefore, little conflict to deal with. Surgery controls its own destiny; it has virtually full authority.

Disadvantages

This system requires expensive, highly trained staff members to spend a significant portion of their time counting, ordering, and putting away supplies. Since they generally are neither trained nor primarily interested in inventory management or space management, they are likely to develop a significant overstock of supplies in the department. Empirical studies have shown that the extent of this oversupply can be so great that inventories turn only one to two times per year.

At the same time, space in surgery is expensive. If it is filled with an oversupply of products, and cannot be used for other purposes, it is a costly situation. In a rebuilding project, this "need" for more supply space adds costs to a department in which expenditures per square foot can exceed $250.

Product standardization for the hospital as a whole also is more difficult since surgery maintains basically full control of all of the products it uses. Again, studies have indicated that lack of standardization contributes to proliferation and duplication of products and overstocks of inventories.[3]

Finally, the control of supply charges in an environment where there are no checks and balances can lead to significantly higher numbers of lost items.

A surgery that does its own reprocessing of sterile products faces the same issues. Highly trained, expensive staff members do repetitive tasks that do not require their level of expertise. In addition, expensive space is used for staging, decontamination, and production. Sterilization equipment also is duplicated, which may lead to questions about whether or not appropriate quality control measures and procedures are being followed routinely by the persons responsible for this function on a part-time, fill-in basis.

Par Level System

As in the basic hospitalwide supply distribution system, a par level system can be used to meet the demands/needs of surgery.

Advantages

This system has the same advantages as those in the hospitalwide distribution system. In addition, it may require less instrument inventory. Also, as mentioned in the bulk-replacement system, less coordination is required so there is less interdepartmental conflict.

Disadvantages

Again, these are generally the same as those stated previously. Probably most importantly, the persons who will continue to have responsibility and authority for these functions will be doing these on a fill-in, part-time basis. It should be quite evident that surgery is an asset-intensive department where inventory and production management require full-time attention of experienced and educated personnel.

Case Cart System

The case cart system can be defined as one that provides all items (instruments, linens, and supplies) for a surgical procedure on a mobile cart. The cart is prepared in a storage area and delivered to the operating room scheduled for that procedure before the procedure is to begin. Items on the cart are used during the procedure. The top of the cart may be used as a back or gown table. At the end of the procedure, the items to be disposed of and/or reprocessed are collected, placed on the cart, and returned to the reprocessing area.

Advantages

The advantages of such a system are reduced inventory required in surgery because most or all articles required for a given procedure can be on the cart. Reduced inventory should mean a reduced space requirement. Given the area required for equipment and personnel functions, any extra space can be better utilized. It may even be possible to open another operating room, which can earn additional revenue (profit) for the hospital.

Labor utilization is improved because professional patient care personnel are not involved in obtaining supplies. This is similar to the discussion on par level and exchange cart systems. With less time spent on the routine supply function, more time can be spent on patient care. This makes possible improvement in the quality of that care without extra cost.

Finally, the management accountability for inventories is centralized and in the hands of the personnel trained in that function.

Disadvantages

Disadvantages of the case cart system are similar to those of an exchange cart system. It requires a significant expenditure for the purchase of carts. Parking space also is required.

The successful implementation of a case cart system requires an assessment of the reprocessing functions and may require centralization of instrument reprocessing. It also may require an additional investment in instrument inventory. This is directly related to the turnaround time associated with centralized instrument reprocessing.

Increased interdepartmental friction between the surgery and supply departments also can result, brought on by the human errors that inevitably occur. Under this system, the departments may and can blame each other. While this possibility is real, a firm commitment to the program and proper mechanisms for communication and problem solving can help keep those problems under control.

Requirements

To establish and implement a successful case cart system, it is necessary to have a schedule showing the time and room for each procedure. Also required is an ordering method that is easy to follow and provides a permanent record of what was ordered, delivered, and used, such as the requisition form shown in Exhibit 19–1. A preference card is needed to allow the surgeon to note items that are required because of personal choice or unusual conditions of a procedure.

An instrument-processing program that allows for standardization of sets, highly productive reprocessing, and adequate instrument inventory is vital. Equally essential is a trained staff that can effectively and efficiently assemble instrument sets and surgical case carts. The level of accuracy with which this is done can make or break a system.

There must be adequate planning and accounting for backup items that will be required. It is impossible to anticipate all items that may be required for a surgical procedure. There should be a method for obtaining the "emergency" items that are required and a place where they are located. This may be in the surgery or storage area. Wherever it is, it should be well organized, and use of these items should be well documented. Repeated requests for these backup items may signify a need to add them to the standard case cart requisition. Backup items should include supplies, instruments, and linens.

Timing is crucial as it relates to obtaining a completed and approved surgery schedule; ordering, filling, and delivering of carts; and returning used items to the reprocessing area and entering them into the reprocessing cycle.

Requisitions, random or emergency calls, or unusual requirements beyond what is ordered through the regular system must be documented.

Another key factor in selecting a case cart is the cleaning method. Hospitals with centralized processing areas frequently install automatic cart washing machines. A solid stainless steel cart that is not designed to be processed in an automatic cart washing machine will create tremen-

Exhibit 19–1 Sample of Case Cart Requisition Form

PROCEDURE	REQUESTED BY	DATE RECEIVED
SURGEON	DATE	FILLING TIME
PATIENT	TIME	FILLED BY
O.R. #		TRANSPORT TIME

REQ.	REC'D	USED		DISP. LINEN	REQ.	REC'D	USED	STERILE WRAPPED SUPPLIES
___	___	___	72-48741	100 Minor Pack	___	___	___	ABD Pads
___	___	___	72-65514	131 Lap Pack	___	___	___	Basin Set
___	___	___	72-76583	410 Lg. Gown	___	___	___	Lap Packs
___	___	___	72-76656	440 Xlg. Gown	___	___	___	Light Handles
___	___	___	72-36212	8376 Table Cover	___	___	___	Medicine Glass
___	___	___	72-32926	8355 Sm. Sheet	___	___	___	Prep Pack
___	___	___	72-32837	8346 Lg. Sheet	___	___	___	Retractor Covers
					___	___	___	Towels
				SURGEON GLOVES				
								INSTRUMENTS
___	___	___	68-08212	Triflex Size 6				
___	___	___	68-08263	Triflex Size 6½	___	___	___	Major Set
___	___	___	68-08417	Triflex Size 7	___	___	___	Minor Set
___	___	___	68-08549	Triflex Size 7½	___	___	___	Gall Bladder Set
___	___	___	68-08689	Triflex Size 8	___	___	___	Intestinal Set
___	___	___						
					___	___	___	Curved Hemostats
				SUPPLIES	___	___	___	Deaver Retractors
					___	___	___	Harrington Retractors
___	___	___	76-45155	Bulb Syringe	___	___	___	Haneys
___	___	___	84-12111	Bovie Cord	___	___	___	Kochers
___	___	___	84-54027	Bovie Plate, Disp	___	___	___	Long Rt. Angle Clamps
___	___	___	71-07382	Foam Head Rest	___	___	___	Long Needle Holder
___	___	___	72-70429	Incise Drape -3M	___	___	___	Ribbon Retractor
___	___	___	84-54043	K-Dissectors	___	___	___	Spring Retractors
___	___	___	66-61971	Sponge, X-Ray 4 × 4	___	___	___	Towel Clips
___	___	___	66-23573	Sponge, Dressing 4 × 4	___	___	___	Vanderbilts
___	___	___	84-39621	Suction Canister				
___	___	___	78-05799	Tube, Cond. Sterile				**SOLUTIONS**
___	___	___	84-00229	Urine Meter				
___	___	___		VI-Drape 7″	___	___	___	61-00104 1500 N/S
___	___	___		VI-Drape 9″	___	___	___	61-00066 1500 Sterile W
___	___	___	84-99748	VI Drape, Surgical Film	___	___	___	
								OTHER

Source: Reprinted from *Hospital Materiel Management Quarterly,* vol. 2, no. 2, November 1980, published by Aspen Systems Corporation, © 1980.

dous difficulties as the hospital attempts to clean it thoroughly and dry it quickly.

The materials used in the manufacture of that cart also are critical to its success. If carts are to be washed frequently (in a case cart system they should be washed after each use), parts should be able to withstand high temperatures and constant washing without unusual maintenance or frequent breakdown. Stainless steel generally meets these criteria. For infrequent washings, such as for backup carts, chrome or zinc may be acceptable, long-lasting, and economical. Casters must be selected carefully.

LASTING BENEFITS

Once the hospital has gone through the evaluation process and compared its existing system to others, a method should be established for evaluating the results once they have been implemented. This should include an analysis of all of the factors that the distribution system affects and is affected by. As mentioned, these include inventory management, warehousing, labor utilization, service levels, and return on investment (ROI).

As hospital material managers examine their distribution systems and consider options objectively, they may be surprised to find that there are many cost-effective ways to distribute supplies. They also may have overlooked good alternatives because they seemed too simplistic.

Although the evaluation process may be time consuming, the hospital that does not take the time to do it runs the risk of forgoing all the benefits of an efficient supply distribution system. This evaluation, conducted on a periodic basis, may bring different results each time as situations and conditions change. There is no one best way.

NOTES

1. Dean S. Ammer, *Hospital Materials Management Neglect and Inefficiency Promote High Costs of Care* (Boston: Northeastern University, Bureau of Business and Economic Research, 1974).

2. Charles E. Housley, *Hospital Materiel Management* (Rockville, Md.: Aspen Systems Corporation, 1978).

3. Studies conducted by the author in 60-, 405- and 500-bed hospitals.

20. Centralized Patient Transportation

PETER C. MIKE

Centralizing the patient transportation function under the control of the material management department can lead to improvements in overall transport time and increases in productivity through a more effective utilization of labor. The specific areas where better utilization can occur are:

- Labor available during low periods of demand can be utilized for activities such as supply picking, data batching, mail sorting, distribution, and printing.
- Labor available on the empty side of a patient trip can be utilized to distribute other items.

Why, then, in the hospital environment where cost containment has been publicized so frequently in the last decade is this system implemented so infrequently?

This chapter reviews some common pitfalls in centralizing the patient transportation function. A case study describes steps in centralizing and improving this operation and key elements necessary to centralization are identified.

The problems in centralizing the patient transport function fall into two broad areas: (1) administrative support and (2) departmental territorialism. Administrative support is critical to the success of the centralization process. The following factors do not encourage administrative support.

REVENUE MAXIMIZATION

The retrospective reimbursement system supports revenue maximization. The power to influence administrators is greater in areas that produce high revenue. Radiology and physical therapy departments generate 70 to 80 percent of the need for patient transportation. These generally are controlled by physicians and usually produce high revenue. Radiology operating hours tend to be closely integrated with physicians' office hours—in fact, office hours frequently provide the base for developing radiology scheduling.

The centralization process may create the perception that the revenue of these departments may be interrupted and fears that physician office schedules may be interrupted. These fears may cause doctors to resist centralization. Because physicians are critical to the overall success of the organization, administrators may be hesitant to press this issue unless the material manager can both allay the fears and demonstrate the value of the program.

Historically, patient transportation has been an ideal area in which to utilize volunteers. The ability to sell the concept of the cost effectiveness of a centralized patient transport system is severely restricted if a loosely organized volunteer system is used. From an economic perspective, what can be more cost effective than unpaid labor?

There is little documentation available from outside sources. Internally, data accumulation may be sketchy because of the inherent problems with a decentralized system. The process of accumulating data requires centralization of formats, terminology, and documentation.

The following factors do not encourage departmental support; taken together, they produce an umbrella of territorialism.

DEPARTMENTAL EMPIRES

The average department head seems versed in basic supervisory skills. Such techniques emphasize control on the departmental level.

235

Department heads are rewarded for control at that level. Instead of utilizing available resources, the department heads would prefer to control them, especially if they feel they are controlling the revenue generated from their areas.

Efficiencies are common when analyzing a function based only on the needs of the decentralized entity. In other words, if managers' only objective is increasing the number of procedures in their own departments, then they are not really concerned with the cost effectiveness of transporting patients. Managers who want it done probably can do it faster themselves, especially if they are appraising efficiencies instead of monitoring the effectiveness of the system of patient transportation and care.

Understanding an organization as a group of subsystems linked together is often as difficult to grasp as computer programming. This is even more pronounced in department supervisors who are striving to accomplish their own subsystem objectives and may be accustomed only to decentralized control.

A transport system will not operate effectively unless there are good support subsystems, including preadmission and discharge planning, patient scheduling, and department scheduling. The centralization process will reach a point in time where concentration on only staffing efficiencies will have provided its maximum impact. Establishing effective subsystems will smooth demand and eliminate excessive wait time, which will further improve the transport system.

These problems have been cited not to discourage the process but to identify appropriate target areas for a concerted plan of implementation and an educational program that should be undertaken before beginning the centralization process.

CASE STUDY

This case study tracks the centralization process in an investor-owned hospital. It follows the transition of a patient transportation system from a decentralized to a centralized structure. The key points in this case are:

1. increased transport efficiency of 47 percent (17 minutes to 9 minutes)
2. the influence of effective subsystems: (a) central patient scheduling and (b) predischarge system.

Hospital History and Environment

The hospital is located in West-Central Florida in a small community with a population under 38,000. One of the area's main businesses is tourism. Many retired persons live there, and the immediate surrounding area is residential, with families of above-average income.

The hospital is an investor-owned acute care institution. It began with 150 beds in 1973, within three years opened an additional 148 beds, and in 1980–1981, expanded all ancillary areas to meet the needs of the additional beds. The average annual occupancy is 81 percent, with peak periods November through April, which is the tourist season.

Patient Transportation History and Environment

During the hospital's first six months, transportation was decentralized, with all departments moving their own patients. The management philosophy was not participative; areas operated autonomously. After this period, which saw an increase in average census, the volunteer department took over responsibility for patient transportation. As the hospital expanded and census continued to grow, the all-volunteer staff found it increasingly difficult to meet the needs of the patients.

In 1976, transportation was placed under control of material management, with a paid staff, supplemented by volunteers. Until 1978, the transportation area had collected little statistical data regarding effectiveness and the management philosophy was by exception—that is, if nothing was heard, everything was all right. If there were complaints, the transport supervisor would spend time emotionally defending the department.

Continual complaints from radiology, billing, and other ancillary areas that patients had to wait too long to be transported stimulated action that resulted in the collection of statistical data. The year 1979 became the base. The survey and data collection were conducted by a management consultant. He identified a mean average time of 17 minutes to move a patient, using as the formula total trips divided by total time.

In the next year, the following improvements were made:

- dedication of a dispatcher
- relocation of office, resulting in reduced lost time trips
- concentration on part-time staff to create flexibility in adjusting staffing to erratic work flow
- creation of a direct call system.

These should have minimized the complaints. Instead, people continued to complain that the transportation section could not move patients fast enough. In 1980, data again were collected and analyzed, disclosing the following details:

- In 1979, the transportation aide waited on the floor for ten or more minutes for nursing to get the patient 38 percent of the time; by 1980, this wait had risen to 55 percent.
- In 1979, the mean average time for a patient transport was 17 minutes; in 1980, it was 14 minutes.
- In 1979, the discharge patient took 14 minutes to transport; in 1980, it took 67 percent longer—23.5 minutes.

In addition, these facts were identified:

- Nursing was operating with four separate patient transport schedules: (1) one for discharges written on a calendar, (2) one for surgery on a separate piece of paper, (3) one for radiology on a separate piece of paper, and (4) one for physical therapy on a separate piece of paper.

- Discharges all were occurring in small segments of time.
- Multiple transports were required for the same patient for varied procedures.

It was apparent that improvement only in the transport area would not be enough to improve overall efficiency. Something else needed to be done. A plan was established to make the transport patient a higher priority for nursing by:

- developing one central patient schedule to be used as a standard tool
- having the transport supervisor spend time each day with the nursing supervisors regarding transports
- encouraging the development of a participative environment involving representatives from all areas impacted by patient transportation
- implementing a predischarge system to eliminate excessive wait times at discharge.

In early 1981, data were collected again and compared with those of 1979 and 1980. The mean average time per transport trip had improved from 14 minutes to 11.6 minutes. In the last month of 1980, a survey was conducted at 14 hospitals in the state, varying in size from 175 to 625 utilized beds, and varying in organization from centralized to decentralized patient transportation services. The survey indicated that the transport area being described in this case study had the highest number of trips per employee, the fastest mean average time per trip, and the lowest nonsalary budget of the 14 hospitals.

In mid-1981, a central patient scheduling system was implemented. The goal was to improve care by coordinating and integrating the scheduling of patients in the ancillary departments. Specifically:

1. To provide advance information on patient appointments, thus enabling the nurses to plan care delivery more effectively on a continuous basis.

2. To inform patients about daily schedules in the morning and be confident that the information would prove reliable.
3. To minimize delays in patient transportation since they cause problems for departments involved in the care.
4. To make more efficient use of personnel in the following ways:

   • by reducing the number of trips a patient must make between the floor and departments
   • by relieving departments of clerical aspects of scheduling, thus freeing up trained personnel to perform in a more technical capacity
   • by placing the responsibility of resolving conflicts with the central patient scheduling office, thus requiring less effort on the part of nursing or other departments
   • by providing a means of collecting data to be used in planning for the delivery of patient services.

In early 1982, transport data were accumulated again. The mean average time to transport a patient had fallen to 10 minutes per trip. Also, in 1982 the predischarge system was to be implemented with these objectives:

1. To prepare the patient:

   • Arrange transportation
   • Arrange for home medical needs
   • Arrange for payment

2. To prepare the nurse:

   • Arrange for giving assistance with the patient's needs
   • Arrange for staggered discharges to eliminate bottlenecks at transportation, housekeeping, or billing.

3. To prepare ancillary departments so that staffing could be adjusted to handle the volume of activity.

After a short time, projected data indicated that the mean average transport time would improve to nine minutes.

This case highlights the importance of both the centralization of patient transport and the need to develop effective support subsystems. The key steps in achieving this are to:

1. Develop a reliable data base and performance tracking. This will identify where the transport areas are in level of performance—that is, time per trip or trips per operator hour.
2. Apply systems analysis, determining influence on indicators. This will target areas where performance is influenced either directly by transport systems and personnel or indirectly by nontransport systems and personnel.
3. Conduct an intensive education program, both one on one and group oriented. This should provide an objective review of performance levels and all influences on performance levels and allow all operating areas an opportunity to participate in improving the performance.
4. Improve performance. Identification of and communication as to performance increases on a regular basis will itself generally support the system.

IMPROVEMENT AND REWARD

With the changing methods of reimbursement and resulting emphasis on minimizing cost, hospitals will be rewarded for developing less costly and more effective systems. The environment is established for all hospitals to move toward a cost-effective patient transport system.

The dramatic improvement in patient transportation performance described in the case (47 percent) supports the centralized concept. Centralizing the function in the material management area, and merging the patient and distribution scheduling systems, will allow maximum utilization of labor for other tasks that can be scheduled with no increase in costs.

21. Offsite Distribution Centers

BRUCE G. HAYWOOD

Since the late 1970s, dramatic changes have taken place in health care institutions. One such change will reshape forever the long-range future of those institutions' basic distribution systems. This will place increasing demands not only on the material managers in the facilities but also on the ultimate users of various products and even their suppliers. As this change accelerates, lines of communication will be strained and sometimes broken; historic and long-time relationships among suppliers, material managers, and users will be altered drastically; procedures, policies, the industry's very way of doing business—all must be carefully reviewed and adapted.

What is this "new wave," this phenomenon of such magnitude that the health care industry must quickly adapt or be lost? It is the institutional offsite distribution center, often referred to incorrectly as the offsite hospital warehouse.

THE ROLE OF OFFSITE CENTERS

More and more institutions are turning to the alternative of offsite distribution centers, a trend that is examined here from the following perspectives:

1. What has caused this move from the traditional onsite to offsite warehousing?
2. What must be considered in the development, selection, and implementation of this type of facility?
3. Are there alternatives to offsite warehousing?
4. What are the staffing considerations for an offsite facility?
5. What are the design and layout considerations?
6. How may such facilities be financed?
7. What impact can suppliers of health care materials have on these centers?

DEFINITION AND REASONS FOR CHANGE

In defining warehousing versus distribution systems, as found in the health care field, it may be said that a warehouse is simply a structure or room for the storage of merchandise and/or commodities. It is basically a depository only. Distribution systems are sophisticated mechanisms by which materials are distributed. Thus, institutional distribution centers no longer are simply warehouses or storerooms but are major points of distribution within the institutional framework. These centers may handle everything from elaborate cart exchange systems to major shipping and receiving operations, to microfilming, printing, transportation, food preparation for shared service programs, and so on.

The transportation systems may run the gamut from a simple van or pickup truck to tractor/trailers running 24 hours a day, seven days a week. The facility itself may be as small as a few thousand square feet to as large as 40,000 to 50,000 square feet. The size, systems, and degree of sophistication are driven by the needs of the institution, not by the distribution center itself.

What has caused this move from traditional onsite warehousing to the offsite facility? The traditional concept of institutional warehousing is epitomized by the old "storeroom" tucked away in probably the most undesirable location on the institution's campus or building. The area often has been largely forgotten by hospital administrators until they are pressed to expand other medical, income-generating, or more glamorous services. Then the space squeeze begins and storeroom areas erode, or the storeroom may even be relocated from an existing area to one even less desirable.

Administrators are acutely aware of the space problems but tend not to fully realize the far-reaching effects of the material support areas in their institutions. However, new and growing medical services and limited on-campus or in-building space, limited capital resources, and politically charged decisions on space allocation all contribute to the erosion of the storeroom area. Options in dealing with the space needs in the institution may include:

- establishment of a space "czar" or administrator
- annual review of conditions in all hospital departments
- yearly submissions of space requirements by all department heads
- careful review of space requests by administration
- establishment of short- and long-range space needs and identification of problems
- determination of alternatives for space allocations and/or relocations.

Serious problems can arise from the reduction of in-house space allocated to the storeroom operation. Should a decision be made to relocate this department into an undesirable location, it can create an inefficient operation. Because of the critical nature of storeroom supplies, any decision about location or relocation must be made with great care. Some of the disadvantages of a poorly planned move are:

- Productivity generally drops.
- Inefficient physical arrangements cause increased errors and higher distribution costs.
- Various user departments become prime areas for storing and distributing supplies.
- Ordering costs increase dramatically.
- Efficiencies of bulk purchases decrease.

As can be imagined, productivity drops drastically with longer distances to travel between stores and user areas, often through a labyrinth of halls, corridors, elevators, etc. The central stores is, again, moved to an even more undesirable area—and thus an inefficient physical arrangement—increased errors, reduced efficiency, increased cost. The new space oncampus or in the building may have lower ceiling heights, reducing the advantages of cube storage; support columns in the most inconvenient locations; service and utility lines in the way of efficient order filling, etc. The costs associated with this breakdown of the supply/distribution cycle can be in excess of $100,000 a year.

A hospital may choose to establish an offsite center to deal with space problems alone or it may use the center to support additional hospitals or health care facilities. These may have a corporate affiliation or may be independent facilities that can buy support services from the hospital operating the offsite center. In either case, operating costs can be spread over a larger base. The potential revenue may also be attractive.

DEVELOPMENT, SELECTION, IMPLEMENTATION

No matter what the reason for deciding to go offsite, it is vital when considering the development, selection, and implementation of an offsite facility, that considerable planning go into avoiding the many problems and pitfalls associated with such a facility in order to ensure its overall success. In considering offsite facilities, one overriding factor is the cost per square foot both oncampus and offsite. Codes and regulations governing hospital building put the cost of warehouse space at a minimum of $110 to $130 per square foot, while the same facility in an industrial environment offsite would cost $25 to $30 a square foot. The rental cost of an offsite facility may range from only $1.50 to $2 a square foot, which is quite inexpensive.

Once the decision has been made to move to an offsite facility, the hospital must recognize that it is doing something very different from just opening another internal department. It now has a unique opportunity to develop a center that will be an effective and integral part of its overall material management program.

Advantages and Other Factors

Advantages of an offsite distribution center include the following:

- Space, being offsite, generally is protected from encroachment by other departments.
- Sufficient room can be planned for expansion.
- Productivity generally increases by smoothing out the workflow.
- Purchasing may experience fewer emergencies, as a result of an overall improvement in inventory control practices.
- Storage will be sufficient for cart filling, storage, repair, etc.
- Availability and capacity for shared services programs are increased.
- The cost of space is much lower than onsite ($30 per square foot vs. $130 in construction costs).
- The site can take advantage of the cube storage or high-rise storage concept.
- Trucking needs and location near major truck routes can be met more easily.

Major additional points to consider when determining the feasibility of an offsite facility include such factors as:

- Operating cost will increase by $50,000 to $100,000 a year.
- A good, sound trucking system, with additional employees to staff it, must be established.
- Ready access to elevators, and vertical and horizontal material flow patterns, are needed in each user institution.
- Square footage of 20 to 25 square feet per bed will be required.
- Stores, processing, and distribution (SPD) concepts should be considered.

- The general cost of space per square foot within the institution should be evaluated.
- Storage space must still be available in the hospital, even with the offsite facility.
- Emergency requests often are difficult to handle efficiently.
- Response time becomes critical.
- A good computer system is essential.
- The various disciplines of organization must be taught and learned.

Working Plan and Space Needs

The institution should have a working plan to solve both the immediate space needs and to identify and resolve future requirements. The long-range space needs of the various departments and support functions are most important in relation to the overall effectivenss in determining the facility's ability to deliver needed services to its clients. The modern, efficient institution must recognize the real needs of its storage and distribution functions and their value to its overall success.

There are a few basic considerations during the planning process that will ensure that adequate space has been allocated to the distribution function. Most institutions, ideally, need 20 to 25 square feet of space per bed for the overall distribution function, i.e., shipping and receiving, general warehousing, supply cart exchange, and so on. Some manage with less but they generally are in larger metropolitan areas with frequent immediate delivery systems from reliable, close-by vendors.

STAFFING CONSIDERATIONS

The idea of establishing an administrative position totally responsible for space needs and/or allocation of space is revolutionary in health care institutions and must be evaluated carefully from a cost/benefit perspective. The generally accepted practice has been the ''oil-the-squeaky-wheel'' approach, assigning space based on revenue generation, political pressure within the organization, and so on.

The advantages noted all fall under the general heading of sound, long-range, strategic planning of space. However, whether or not a formal, continuing review procedure is in place, no consideration should be given to offsite distribution until space needs within the institution, based on both short-term and long-term needs, have been clearly assessed.

These changes in traditional distribution systems have created new challenges to health care material managers who have been able to adjust to the fast-changing scene. New demands and careers have opened up for farsighted managers in the areas of (1) traffic management, i.e., transportation; and (2) distribution management (PDM—physical distribution manager).

New Role for Managers

No longer is the head of the distribution center referred to as the storeroom supervisor. Many managers have become physical distribution managers responsible for transportation systems, traffic control, and total material management support services groups. These individuals have developed into important members of the institutional management team, responsible for a considerable percentage of its resources.

Distribution managers in health care for the first time are joining such organizations as the Society of Traffic and Transportation and the International Materials Management Society. These same people are entering the field with higher educations and improved backgrounds and experience, thus demanding higher salaries.

With today's multitude of changes in the health care industry, and in particular its distribution systems, the traditional narrow focus of the storekeeper no longer is applicable. Rising energy costs, inflation, information systems changes and advances, plus the acceptance of the physical distribution management concept, all have helped open new opportunities and new career paths.

The distribution manager of the future must possess a wide variety of skills to deal with the many changes in distribution systems. What will be demanded of the distribution manager of the future? More attention to basic management skills, a clear understanding of nondistribution elements in health care, a concise view of the distribution system's place in the overall health care environment.

Individuals now assuming positions of leadership in health care institutions have more advanced educational backgrounds and a broad range of experience that encompasses not only the traditional warehousing aspects of distribution but also logistics, warehouse layout, location, and organization, and a broad picture of the total institution.

Functional Decentralization

The general trend in offsite distribution centers is to decentralize functional processes, placing each under the leadership of qualified supervision. Thus, once offsite, a centralized shipping and receiving department may be appropriate. This will allow for a concentration of expertise on Department of Transportation regulations, familiarity with shipping papers, claims filing, and so on in one area under one manager without spreading this program through the facility. In addition, such elements as cart exchange systems and material filing and distribution can and should be centralized and considered as individual programs, each demanding its own expertise.

The typical organizational structure will include a director of distribution systems (who could be titled director of material services, distribution manager, etc.) and, depending on the facility's size and other factors, an assistant director, with an array of supervisors for each operational program, i.e., shipping and receiving, material filing and distribution, cart exchange, printing services, microfilming services, and transportation services.

It is important to note that the size, scope, and staffing of the offsite distribution system will depend on the size, location, and number of institutions this facility is required to support. Similarly, the extent of the services offered by the center, i.e., printing, microfilming, food factory, will depend on the needs and corporate direction of the various institutions. However, it is important to be innovative in staffing considerations, keeping in mind that the main factor is the support of the various institutions in an effective, efficient, and cost-conscious manner.

DESIGN AND LAYOUT

The design and layout of the offsite distribution center will vary, depending on a number of factors such as the types of programs involved, i.e., cart exchange, shipping and receiving, printing, used equipment storage, etc., and the budget. However, there are some general guidelines that can prove helpful.

The general tendency in offsite warehousing, whether it be an institutional or commercial operation, is to view storage in terms of cubic feet, not square feet. By effectively utilizing cube storage techniques, overall square footage can be reduced. This is desirable for a number of sound reasons: (1) construction and lease costs are based on square feet, (2) heating and air conditioning costs can be reduced with a smaller roof square feet area, (3) lighting expenditures can be lowered by reducing the number of square feet.

A number of operations consider anything from 30-foot high usable ceiling heights on up as ideal. The narrow aisle concept, used for many years in industry, is beginning to take hold in offsite health care distribution facilities. This approach has been enhanced by the usage of electronic material handing equipment that can operate on an FM beam buried in the floor down the center of narrow aisles.

In general, consideration must be given to the separation of shipping and receiving from other operations with their own dock doors adequate in size and number to handle both small van-type vehicles and larger semitrailers. Space also must be adequate for incoming goods not yet received, goods received but not yet placed in the proper bin or shelf location, and goods to be returned to vendors. There must be similar space, with appropriate dock doors, for shipping goods out to various locations.

Bins or shelving should be arranged so that the flow of materials for the receiving areas in and filled orders out do not require unnecessary travel time or going around shelving or aisles. It goes without saying that in utilizing the cube concept, fast-moving items should be stored in lower areas near the front of the facility and generally in one central location, while slow-moving or overstock can be stored further back, on high shelving. Stock locations should be determined by the particular picking list format utilized so as not to cause backtracking or lost motion.

The secret to any warehouse design or layout is quite simple: (1) keep it simple, (2) keep it compact, (3) reduce travel time, (4) increase efficiency and productivity, (5) keep it flexible. That final point is vital since changes in both health care and distribution systems may necessitate alterations at any time.

Assistance in warehouse design and layout can be obtained from many sources, such as architects or designers hired by the hospital, dealers and manufacturers of shelving, industrial warehouse operations, and various health care suppliers. The efficiency of the operation will depend to a large extent upon the attention given to this design and layout. This is an element where expense is secondary to the quality of the design.

Hospitals of various sizes have achieved real success with their offsite facilities when carefully planned, developed, and implemented with the full support of administration. Such centers become even more valuable when they also can provide services to satellite hospitals within a local or even regional system. The ideal offsite operations can provide a group of local medical facilities with centralized purchasing, shipping and receiving, distribution, supply cart exchange systems, a standardized inventory, and even shared services programs to nonaffiliated institutions.

If, during the planning process, it is determined that the long-range objectives of the material management distribution center will be met most successfully if it is located offsite, consideration may be given to purchasing rather than renting or leasing a facility. Financing options thus need to be considered carefully.

FINANCING

There are a number of financing alternatives, including:

- lease/purchase
- construction out of operating capital
- straight bank mortgage
- reallocation of current capitalized priorities
- inclusion in general funding for other major capitalized projects
- establishment of a separate corporation, letting the project be self-funded.

The lease on a 30,000-square-foot warehouse facility could range from $48,000 to $54,000 a year while a constructed and owned facility may be paid off in as little as 10 to 12 years. However, it is important to note that when an institution is planning to purchase and/or build its own facility, the planning and development stage becomes even more critical so as to ensure that it will not be locked into undesirable facilities.

COORDINATING THE MOVE

Once the decision has been made to go offsite, the move must be well coordinated so as to cause the least amount of disruption to the overall organization. Careful attention to detail will ensure a smooth transition.

The first step is to announce, well (perhaps months) in advance of the move date, when the old facility will be closed and the new one will open. The announcement should include not only the health care departments and institutions involved but also all of the suppliers, local and regional trucking operations, and anyone that interfaces in any way with the current and future distribution system.

Generally, it is inadvisable to try to continue to operate the old facility while moving into the new one. The distribution operation thus could

be closed for one to three days, depending on the items and programs to be moved, the distance to the new location, and the number of persons available to assist in the move.

New programs, procedures, and processes must be implemented to ensure that acceptable service is given to the customer institutions once the offsite facility becomes operational. The real key to success is the transportation system. This can be as simple as a van or bob truck or as large and complex as a fleet of tractor-trailers. The size and extent of the system will be dictated by the needs of the customer institutions.

A well-defined order/requisition system must be developed even before the facility is offsite so it can be implemented on Day 1 and the operation can land running. This can be handled via an automated data processing order entry system between users and the offsite facility or manually by simply designating specific departure times for the appropriate paper work. Deliveries of goods from the new site must be established on a regular, routine basis so users can rely on a specific schedule.

However, users must be informed that they no longer can simply "go down to the storeroom" or call for immediate delivery of goods. They also must organize their own operations to cope with the offsite location. The keys to success are: (1) a well-organized transportation system based on a regular published routine (not to be altered) schedule, (2) assistance to the users in organizing their supply order process to compensate for the offsite location, and (3) a plan to handle emergency needs that regrettably will always arise.

Once the system of handling the facilities' needs is established, the users' education is complete, and the move is announced, the process of the move itself is ready for implementation. It is suggested that outside help in the form of temporary labor be obtained, regardless of the size of the operation. Too often, distribution facilities try to rely entirely on their own personnel and find that they do not have the resources, the cost of their own labor is higher than outside help, and their personnel are too worn out to meet the opening deadline. Outside help can be obtained from church groups or students willing to work on an as-needed basis for a flat rate. Once the work group has been established, the institutions' personnel provide supervision. Work groups should be established in both the old and new facilities to ensure a steady movement of material during the move.

Several large facilities that have moved offsite have found that the use of one or two tractors and several trailers is the most efficient way to transfer the goods to the new facilities. Thus, one or several trailers can be loaded at the old site and others unloaded at the new location, with the tractors moving trailers as needed between the sites. Drivers and vehicles generally can be obtained from a local trucking operation or truck rental facility. Even in rather small, nearby moves, the tractor-trailer concept has proved very efficient.

Moves can be implemented best over a weekend or holiday when institutional activity is light and outside help easy to obtain. For example, the institution can announce that an operation will cease operations at the old location after business Friday and reopen with the start of business Monday.

RELATIONSHIPS WITH SUPPLIERS

What impact can the suppliers of health care materials have on an institution's offsite distribution facility? If they understand the rationale of such warehousing, they can more clearly appreciate the problems associated with oncampus hospital space needs and requirements. They should understand that the level of expertise in health care material management has risen markedly in recent years. They must recognize that with the ever-increasing outside pressure to contain costs, administration has come to realize the importance of an efficient material management department as the real key in a truly effective cost-containment program. The suppliers' experience can be of invaluable assistance in evaluating and formalizing the development of the offsite facility.

There may be room for brainstorming or innovative ideas in joint venturing of offsite facilities. This may include:

- vendor/customer sharing of a facility, which can achieve economies of scale, i.e., shared personnel, overhead, rental
- joint venture transportation, i.e., having vendor vehicles drop off supplies at the distribution center, then carry supplies to the institutions
- an extensive transportation system that can pick up supplies at vendor locations, drop them off at the distribution center, and carry other supplies to the institution.
- facilities inspection team sharing to ensure compliance with Department of Transportation and National Fire Protection Association regulations, if the vendor has such a group
- material handling specialist, architect, draftsperson sharing if the vendor has such persons on staff.

The suppliers should recognize that their impartial, objective, and often expert input may be a valuable contribution to the development of the offsite center.

Offsite distribution centers are being opened with increasing frequency. Effective material managers must be prepared to evaluate this option for their institutions.

22. Quality Control for In-Hospital Sterilization

Daniel E. Mayworm

Ensuring the quality of hospital sterilized products that will be used for the care of patients is an important responsibility. Material managers often have administrative responsibility for central sterile processing (CSP) departments, but may not be trained in this technical specialty.

If they do not understand quality control of a production process they may take a casual approach to sterilization in hospitals. The CSP supervisor, reporting to the material manager, may rely upon traditional methods—"we've always done it that way"—and occasional and/or uneducated use of mechanical, chemical, and biological monitors. It is important to understand that the sterilizer chart is measuring conditions at the drain and that chemical and biological indicators measure conditions only at their specific locations. It must be understood that a process cannot be controlled simply by measuring selective endpoints.

Inservice training is conducted most frequently by supervisors who were taught by their supervisors, who were taught by their supervisors. . . . This tends to reinforce by tradition what may never have been validated scientifically. It also makes innovation and change difficult. To make matters worse, outside educational programs most often are led by former hospital employees, who were taught by their supervisors, who were taught by their supervisors . . . and so on.

Little of what is standard practice in medical device manufacturing plants has found its way into hospitals. Because there are no formal educational programs conducted by practitioners steeped in scientific knowledge and practical experience, the sterilization process in most hospitals is out of control. Those who do not understand process control shrug off efforts to put the process into control as "too expensive." However, being out of control is always costly as well as ineffective.

Hospitals never seem to have the time or money to do it right but always find the time and money to do it over. The mere existence of outdates and expiration dating, and the way they are managed, is support enough for this harsh condemnation of the sterilization process as practiced in most hospitals.

This chapter constructs a plan of control, listing the elements involved, in the hope that their integration into the hospital's operation will result in making the process manageable. This plan relies heavily on manufacturing production control concepts and the use of the Joint Commission on Accreditation of Hospitals (JCAH) infection control standards, which are reasonable and attainable criteria every hospital should be expected to meet.

STERILIZATION PROCESS

The first step is to define "sterilization process." The process does not begin when the user shuts the sterilizer door and pushes the button, nor does it end when the person opens the door and removes the product. It starts when the item is used and ends when the sterilized item is presented for use again (Figure 22–1).

In the medical device industry, the probability of success (i.e., the probability that the item is sterile) is 10^{-6} or, said another way, only one item out of a million probably is not sterile. This high probability of success is achieved by taking each element of the process, writing a procedure, sampling statistically to ensure that the procedure is followed, and assigning responsibility (accountability) to ensure that it is done.

Figure 22–1 The 8 Steps in the Sterilization Process

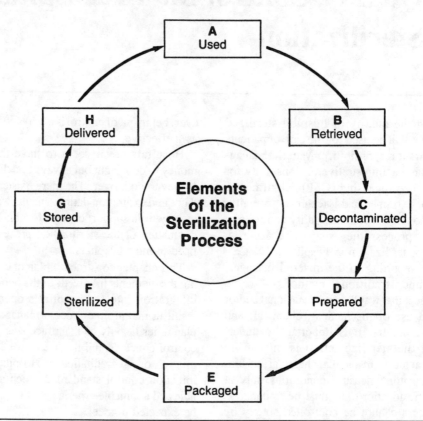

Hospitals generally have written procedures but neglect statistically sampling them to ensure that they are followed. Furthermore, hospitals rarely assign responsibility. Who is held accountable for seeing that each element is performed satisfactorily? Who is fired if it is not done properly?

To make matters worse, since the process overlaps departmental boundaries, control of the process often is lost because of divided responsibility—no one is in charge and everyone is in charge. How often have users seen packaging and sterilization procedures that differ in the operating room (OR) from those for floor items or used in respiratory care, obstetrics (OB), or the emergency room (ER).

It is beyond the scope of this chapter to attempt to assign a number representing the expected probability of success for in-hospital sterilization. All that can be hoped to do is to put that number (whatever it may be) into control. That

is, the process can be kept relatively constant from item to item, from day to day, from month to month. The only way this can be achieved is by breaking the process down into manageable segments, then controlling each segment. The probability of success (P_x) is the sum of the probabilities of success of each element (Exhibit 22–1).

Exhibit 22–1 Formula for Probability of Success

$$A_n + B_n + C_n + D_n + \ldots \mathbb{Z}_n = 10^{-6}$$

Probability of success, medical device industry

$$A_x + B_x + C_x + D_x + \ldots H_x = P_x$$

Probability of success, in-hospital sterilization

Where A_x = probability of success of element A,
B_x = probability of success of element B, ...

The most important elements of procedure writing are to define how, when, and by whom each step is to be monitored and who is to be held responsible. Unless there is accountability (with corresponding authority), written procedures are worthless.

Achieving control of the sterilization process depends upon these elements: administrative control, process control, and biological control.

ADMINISTRATIVE CONTROL

People

A process cannot be in control unless someone is in charge. There must be one person in charge of the entire process. Someone in the hospital must be given the final authority on all matters concerning the sterilization process, regardless of where it is done. This person should be the central sterile supply supervisor. The importance of the people element in the plan of control is emphasized by the infection control standards of the JCAH:*

> The director of central services shall be responsible to the chief executive officer either directly or through a designated department head. The director should be qualified for the position by education, training and experience.

---

*All JCAH extracts were taken from the JCAH *Manual* from the Central Services section under the general heading Infection Control.

The Joint Commission considers this position very important; otherwise, why would it make a point of reporting to the chief executive officer? (A relevant section of a typical organizational chart is shown in Figure 22–2.) The JCAH also does not define what qualifications are necessary. This means someone in the hospital must decide what they are and write a job description spelling out minimum qualifications of education, training, and experience.

This individual will be responsible for all sterilization and related functions in the facility. The hospital should not hire anyone who cannot write, teach, monitor, and enforce procedures related to the retrieval, decontamination, prep and pack, sterilization, storing, and delivery of sterilized products. All job positions in central supply should have written job descriptions. The JCAH states:

> New employees shall receive initial orientation and on-the-job training, and all employees shall participate in a continuing inservice education program, all of which shall be documented. Educational efforts, though directed primarily at sterile supply processing and handling techniques, should also include management concepts, safety, personal hygiene, health requirements and work attire.

The most important element of control is qualified people, well trained, performing well-documented and effective procedures. An important ingredient is continuing education. In-

Figure 22–2 Organizational Chart

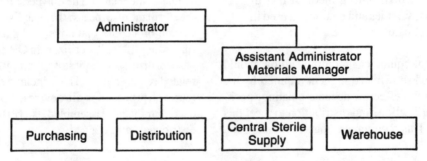

service programs should be given with a planned curriculum established in advance for every job title/function. They should not be casual training sessions given whenever time and/or subject matter presents itself.

Questions to be considered for each job function should include the following:

- When will general, hospital-related subjects (safety, health, management) be given?
- What are the important work-related subjects that must be taught?
- At what stage of the employee's development should these inservice programs be given?
- Are written tests given after each inservice course and what is a passing grade?

The last people-related considerations are appraisals and performance reviews. These should be given after the probationary period and reviewed at least annually. It is at this time that inservice scores, absenteeism, tardiness, and an understanding of hospital's personnel policies are reviewed with employees. These reviews also provide an ideal time to review career path opportunities.

Equipment

The JCAH has several strictures concerning sterile equipment:

> Equipment of adequate design, size and type should be provided for effectively decontaminating, disinfecting, cleaning, packaging, sterilizing, storing and distributing medical instruments, supplies and equipment used in patient care.

A capital equipment requirement/log should be prepared showing equipment required by the hospital to do effective decontaminating, packaging, sterilization, and distribution to meet this standard. This requirement/log should include a record of actual equipment in service, the date all equipment was acquired, its location, and all other necessary information such as make, model, and vendor code. It also should include information on written preventive maintenance procedures and maintenance records.

The JCAH standard on preventive maintenance logs says:

> There shall be written procedures for the preventive maintenance of all central supply service equipment, including performance verification record and reports.

Preventive maintenance procedures should be written for all equipment in central supply, including but not limited to sterilizers, sonic cleaners, and heat sealers. They should include a description of the procedure, qualifications for personnel involved, and calibration standards for all measuring instruments (such as those on sterilizers). These instruments should be labeled as to when calibrated, by whom, and the date it will be needed next.

PROCESS CONTROL

Written Procedures

The JCAH standard states:

> There shall be written policies and procedures for the decontamination and sterilization activities performed in central services and elsewhere in the hospital, and for related requirements.

Just as there should be one person in charge of the sterilization process, there also should be one written procedure that covers all such activities (including "flash" sterilizers in OR and tabletop gas sterilizers in respiratory therapy) as well as related requirements. These include defining the retrieval process for all devices, how they are decontaminated, assembled, sterilized, stored, distributed, and opened.

Monitoring

As to monitoring, the JCAH standard puts it this way:

> There shall be written procedures for the use of sterilization process monitors, including temperature and pressure recordings, and the use and frequency of appropriate chemical indicator and bacteriological spore tests for all sterilizers.

The Joint Commission thus requires that the sterilization process be monitored. Each element of the written procedure must provide direction on how the monitoring is to be done, its frequency, acceptable tolerance limits, and assigned responsibility. Statistics should be maintained documenting the degree of success achieved and steps to be taken when these limits reach unacceptable levels.

The standard does not limit what should be monitored. Hospitals therefore should not limit their interpretation of "sterilization process monitors" to temperature and pressure recordings and chemical and biological indicators. All elements of the process must be monitored. Neglecting any one element negates the effect of monitoring any of them. For example, if the environment in the prep and pack area is not monitored, it is very nearly useless to use chemical indicators. Bioburden has a decided effect on the probability of attaining sterility. Chemical indicators have no way of compensating for unusually high microbial counts.

However, those in the process should look at mechanical, chemical, and biological monitoring of the sterilization cycle.

Mechanical

Figure 22–3 shows what a perfect cycle should look like for a pulsing prevacuum cycle, a gravity displacement cycle, and an ethylene oxide (EtO) gas cycle for specific machines. Proper reading of these charts is imperative in any quality control program. It is not sufficient to record just time-at-temperature. The slope of the descending and/or ascending line is as important as its peaks and valleys.

All employees charged with the responsibility of interpreting these charts should be given a thorough inservice course by someone who understands what each blip and curve means. This could be the service representative from the sterilizer manufacturer. This individual should be asked hard questions; if the answers are not sufficient, another inservice source should be found. It is imperative to insist on understanding how the machines and charts work, why they work, and what every line means. Users should write this information into their procedure manual and inservice curriculum.

The solid state microcomputerized sterilizers, equipped with tape printouts of sterilization parameters, are far superior to the eyeball method of reading clock charts. Institutions

Figure 22–3 Perfect Cycles for Specific Machines

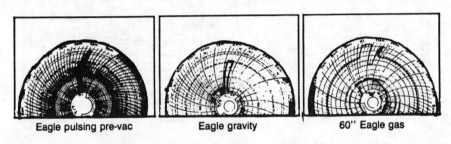

Eagle pulsing pre-vac   Eagle gravity   60" Eagle gas

Source: Reprinted with permission of American Sterilizer Company, Richmond, Va.

should convert to this equipment as soon as they can.

Chemical

The JCAH standard offers options:

Chemical indicators should be used with each package sterilized as required. The use of other sterilization monitors should be defined.

A strict interpretation of the JCAH standard will hold that a facility can either use chemical indicators or not—it all depends upon what is written in the procedure manual. The standard clearly says to use them *as required* by the hospital's policy. Indiscriminate use in "the center of every pack" is wasteful as well as potentially misleading and harmful.[1,2] Overreliance on these indicators can lead to sloppy procedures' being overlooked or disregarded.

To determine what constitutes "proper use," the hospital must test the variety of most commonly used packages (instrument sets, basin sets, linen packs, kits) to determine where proper placement of a highly specific type of chemical indicator would be useful. Figure 22–4 illustrates proper locations of chemical indicators within packs.

Proper placement of indicators is fairly simple to achieve and must be done in order to justify their use. Chemical indicators are designed to alert hospital personnel to a problem in the sterilization process—sterilizer malfunction, packaging, or placement that causes the entrapment of air or another problem that inhibits contact by the steam at the proper temperature for the proper time.

Testing for potential areas where air can be trapped in hospital's packs involves liberally distributing the chemical indicators normally used (or indicators being evaluated) throughout the package. The indicators should be marked carefully to aid in determining where they were placed in the package. A bad cycle then is purposely run—one in which it is known that some residual air was left in the chamber or the product was packaged or placed on the cart improperly.

The package then is opened and examined for the internal indicator that did not change properly. Where was it placed? That placement should be documented and the test repeated (with a new package). Is the test reproducible? Does it always indicate when there is a failure? That is to say, do the indicators always show where there was insufficient steam contact? If they do not, the user should ask: "Why am I using them?"

Statistically and strategically placing indicators of high specificity is a more professional approach to the problem of chemical monitoring and is more useful, because it will identify what users need to know, than the indiscriminate use

Figure 22–4 Placement of Chemical Indicators

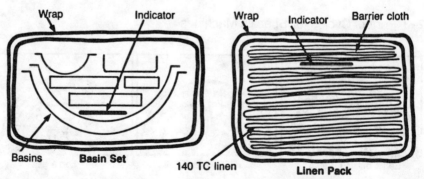

Source: Reprinted with permission from *Journal of Hospital Supply, Processing and Distribution*, vol. 2, no. 2, March/April 1984, © 1984, 42.

in "the center of every pack."[3] It is imperative to know why chemical indicators are being used and what they are showing.

The Bowie-Dick type test, which tests for sterilizer malfunction, should be run whenever a prevacuum type sterilizer is shut down for any reason.[4,5] The test pack should be made of new, unpatched, unworn cotton (linen) fabric of a sufficient size to contain the test sheet and show when there is entrapped air. The wrap should be loose—only tight enough to hold the pack together—and it need be only a single layer.

The test should be run for 3½ minutes (no more, no less) in an otherwise empty chamber. The fabric should be preconditioned between uses by partially breaking down the pack and air drying in a room of at least 35 percent relative humidity (rh) for a minimum of four hours or for whatever time it takes to reach equilibrium with the environment. Once a month, or more often as indicated, the entire pack should be laundered by itself (not as part of ordinary laundry) and rinsed thoroughly. The same fabric, put up exactly the same way, should be used again until it is determined that results are becoming unreliable.

This will become apparent to trained operators as they become experienced with the procedure. When in doubt, they should switch to a new test pack. (Since ink will offset onto the towels and could cause confusion in reading subsequent tests, it is a good idea to cover the Bowie-Dick test sheet with a disposable paper towel, which is discarded after each test procedure.) The important criterion for the Bowie-Dick test pack, as for any test pack, is to keep as many variables constant as possible. This means using the same pack, put up exactly the same way, as often as it continues to give reliable results.

Biological

The JCAH standard on biological monitoring of the sterilization cycle is as follows:

> Steam and hot air sterilizers shall be tested with live bacterial spores at least weekly. In loads undergoing gas sterilization a live spore control should be used at least weekly and is recommended for incorporation into each sterilizing cycle. When implantable or intravascular material undergoes gas sterilization, live spore controls should be used with each load. When feasible, the results of the spore test should be ascertained prior to use of gas sterilized items.

Thus, according to the JCAH, the hospital must test all of its sterilizers with live spores at least weekly. Most experts would recommend daily spore testing in the steam sterilizers and each load in the gas sterilizers. Common sense should prevail. If problems are suspected, the frequency of spore testing should be increased. This also is true when installing new equipment or when existing equipment is shut down for maintenance. If things are running smoothly and all other monitors are showing good results, surveillance can be cut back—but it must never drop to less than once a week.

The problem of spore testing the sterilization efficacy of implants has been addressed not only by the JCAH but also by the Centers for Disease Control (CDC) and the Association of Operating Room Nurses (AORN).[6] Hospital personnel are strongly urged to become familiar with the rationale behind this important issue and adjust their facility's policies accordingly. The ideal situation is to have available sufficient numbers of implant products and instruments and to be able to sterilize them far enough in advance of surgery so that spore test results can be ascertained, showing that the implants are safe to use.

Implants should never be "flash" sterilized unless there are absolutely no other alternatives.[7] Flash sterilization is gravity, as opposed to prevacuum, sterilization without the benefits of drying and packaging. Implants should have the highest probability of being sterile. Flash sterilization is an emergency procedure intended only for the occasional product that is dropped or otherwise soiled and there is no handy replacement. This is one area where close supply/distribution cooperation with vendors is critical.

A standard challenge test pack is required whenever a new sterilizer is placed in service or existing machines have been down for maintenance.[8] At all other times live spores should be tested in a pack that is the most difficult one to sterilize in that load. It is inappropriate to design and construct a test pack that is a far greater challenge than anything that will be experienced in actual production (and contains items difficult to procure), unless, of course, it is designed to build in this additional safety factor.

It also is inappropriate to simply drop the spore test into a paper/plastic pouch and toss it indiscriminately within the load. This is an insufficient challenge.

Spore tests should not be used as part of the Bowie-Dick test because its pack is designed to test sterilizer vacuum malfunction and the biological test pack is designed to test normal production. These are two different problems. The Bowie-Dick test pack is always run alone in an otherwise empty chamber; the biological test pack should be part of a full load.

Proper biological monitoring requires placement of the spores in the package that is most difficult to sterilize; the pack then is placed in the coldest spot in the sterilizer. This placement can be determined by running tests using maximum reading thermometers—these go up to the maximum point achieved and stay there.

Time of day and day of week should be randomized to provide a true overall picture of the safety of the sterilization production. If the test is always run at 9 a.m. on Mondays, all that can safely be said is that production is safe at 9 a.m. on Mondays.

Proper monitoring requires statistical testing at all times a piece of equipment is expected to be running, not only at one particular time. Steam quality and quantity vary as demands on the hospital's boiler vary. It is important to know whether this varying supply has any adverse effect on the sterilization process.

Lot Control/Recordkeeping

The JCAH also requires recordkeeping, particularly as part of lot control:

When possible, load control numbers should be used to designate the hospital sterilization equipment used for each item, including the sterilization date and cycle.

Load control numbers in hospitals are of dubious value. Most products are used before the results of biological monitoring are determined. Ideally, there should be enough inventory so that the products can be quarantined until the spore test results are determined. This probably is not possible for all items but it should be standard at least for critical articles such as implants and intravascular products.[9]

Lot numbers should be used only when they serve a specific function that warrants their expense. If lot numbering is to be done, it should be accomplished in a manner that provides patient traceability. The lot number should follow the product through the hospital to individual patients so that in the event of a potential problem, the patients involved can be monitored more closely.

Lot numbers need not be specific to the sterilizer, day, and cycle. In other words, they do not have to say "sterilizer number 2, 128th day of the year, and 4th cycle." Sequential numbers (or any set of numbers that are easy to use and may have some unique other meaning for the hospital) can be used as long as they can be traced back to a specific cycle.

Sequential numbers, for example, can have other benefits in that they provide exact counts of numbers of products sterilized per day, per week, per year; it thus is easy to locate the oldest package and, since they can be discrete numbers, it is helpful in patient traceability. All that is needed to set up a sequential numbering system is to have a space on the sterilizer log record for showing the sequence of numbers used each cycle (Figure 22–5).

All records (lab tests, Bowie-Dick tests, clock charts) used to monitor the sterilization process should be kept in one place, under one person's responsibility. This person should routinely sample the monitoring procedures to make sure that they are accomplished and that the results are satisfactory.

Figure 22–5 Sterilizer Log Using Sequential Numbers

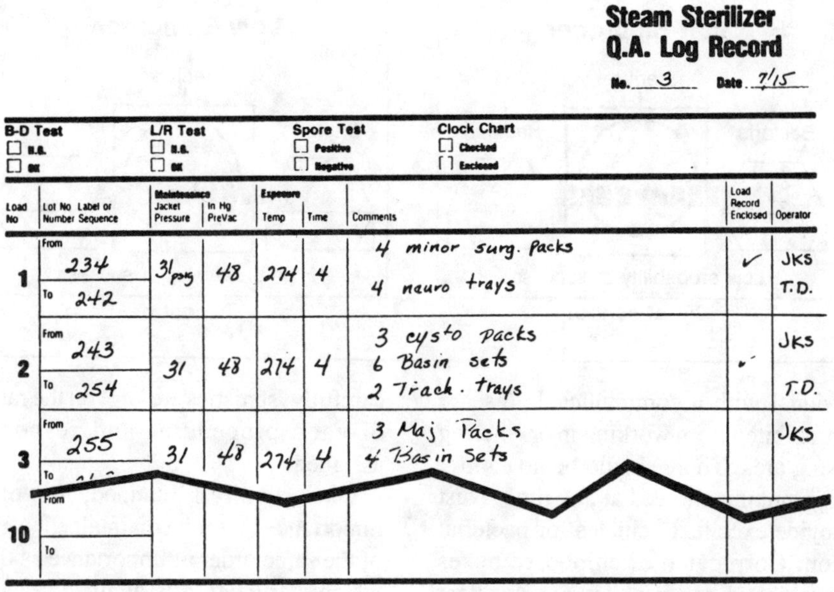

**Steam Sterilizer
Q.A. Log Record**

No. _3_ Date _7/15_

B-D Test	L/R Test	Spore Test	Clock Chart
☐ B.S.	☐ B.S.	☐ Positive	☐ Checked
☐ OK	☐ OK	☐ Negative	☐ Enclosed

Load No	Lot No. Label or Number Sequence	Maintenance Jacket Pressure	In Hg PreVac	Exposure Temp	Time	Comments	Load Record Enclosed	Operator
1	From 234 / To 242	31 psig	48	274	4	4 minor surg. packs 4 neuro trays	✓	JKS T.D.
2	From 243 / To 254	31	48	274	4	3 cysto packs 6 Basin sets 2 Track. trays	✓	JKS T.D.
3	From 255 / To __	31	48	274	4	3 Maj Packs 4 Basin Sets		JKS
10	From / To							

Source: Pharmaseal Company.

BIOLOGICAL CONTROL

Besides the routine biological monitoring in process control, it is extremely important to know the biological status of the environment, the products, and the personnel.[10]

Routine biological monitoring of the environment in the processing area is a must. There is no way to validate the sterilization process unless the user or tester first knows what the environment is and what needs to be killed.[11,12,13] Secondly, the user must know that it never gets any worse. This can be done simply and inexpensively with the use of auger plates or any of the several particle counters on the market.

The CDC, Association for the Practitioners of Infection Control (APIC), and others interested in epidemiological surveillance in hospitals do not recommend routine biological monitoring as being cost effective because nosocomial infection has not been related to levels of general microbial contamination of air or environmental surfaces and no meaningful standards for permissible levels have ever been established—and those experts are correct.

However, this should not be confused with monitoring the prep and pack area for total count. It must be remembered that the aim is to put a process in control. Unless the environment is in control (unless the maximum count that will ever need to be killed is known) the sterilization process will not be in control and cannot be validated.[14] Figure 22–6 illustrates the importance of bioburden control in the environment and on the product for sterilization validation.

Decontamination procedures should be such that the products being sterilized have the lowest possible bioburden before being introduced into the processing area. A physical barrier should exist between decontamination and the processing area, with negative air pressure in decontamination and positive air pressure in the processing area.

There should be a strict dress code in the processing area, one that protects the environment from the workers. Hairnets, lint-free smocks, and shoe covers are a minimum. No one should be allowed in the processing area except those who work there. The occasional visitor must dress the same as the area's employees.

Figure 22–6 Bioburden Control—2 Extremes

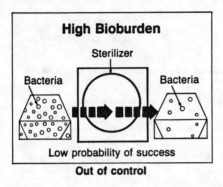
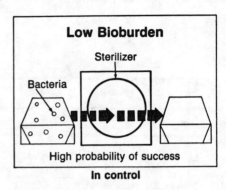

An individual with a communicable disease should be prohibited from working in or entering the processing area. There should be no eating, drinking, or smoking allowed at any time. Dust and lint provide excellent vehicles for bacterial transmission. Corrugated or chipboard boxes should be prohibited because they are excellent breeding grounds for bacteria, they cannot be cleaned, and they release tiny particles of chaff into the environment. Linen should be carefully delinted before being brought into this area.

All these precautions are necessary for assurance of biological purity and safety. Sterilization cycles can be validated only when the bioburden has been controlled at the minimum level achievable at the hospital.

Once bioburden is in control, users can back off on cycle times while continuing to lower the microbial count. This has the effect of lowering costs and extending the life of instruments and fabrics. This obviously is more professional and effective than current practice, which allows unknown bioburden to be present (sloppy control) and compensates by increasing cycle times (overkill).

These procedures will put the sterilization process into control only if they are monitored

carefully, statistics are kept on the rate of success of each procedure, and responsibility is assigned.

Once sterility is attained, it is of paramount importance that it be maintained. "Packaging is of the same order of importance as the means by which sterilization is attained."[15] It does little good to attain sterility unless steps are taken to ensure that it is maintained. Everything sterilized in hospitals should be packaged so that it stays sterile until it is used. The use of expiration dates and the reprocessing of outdates is an archaic, outmoded practice that should be eliminated as standard hospital procedure.

The distribution system for all sterile supplies, whether sterilized commercially or in-house, should be under one person's responsibility and authority. There should be no more inventory on the floors or in user departments than is needed for one day's normal use. Exceptions should be tolerated only under the most extreme circumstances.

These guidelines will ensure that the hospital has attained sterility and has maintained and delivered it to the patient, with the highest degree of probability and the lowest possible cost. Nothing less is acceptable.

NOTES

1. "Recommended Practices," *AORN Journal* 32, no. 2 (August 1980).

2. AAMI Recommended Practice, Good Hospital Practice, Steam Sterilization and Sterility Assurance (January 1980), (7.4.2.2).

3. David Birnbaum and Robert Smith, *Journal of Hospital Supply and Distribution* (March/April 1984): 36–41.

4. Daniel Mayworm, "The Bowie-Dick Test," *Journal of Hospital Supply, Processing and Distribution* (March/April 1984): 31–34.

5. AAMI, (7.8.1).

6. "New CDC Guidelines," *AORN Journal* 34, no. 6 (December 1981): 1010–15.

7. U.S. Public Health Service, "Nosocomial Infections," *Guidelines for the Prevention and Control of Nosocomial Infections*, U.S. Department of Health and Human Services, Centers for Disease Control (Washington, D.C.: U.S. Government Printing Office, 19), 1–6.

8. AAMI (7.6).

9. New CDC Guidelines.

10. Robert F. Morrissey, in *A Rational Approach in Sterilization of Medical Products*, vol. 2, ed. Eugene R.L. Gaughram and Robert F. Morrissey (Montreal: Multiscience Publications Ltd., 1981), 13.

11. U.S. Food and Drug Administration, "Sterilization of Medical Devices," *FDA Compliance Program Guidance Manual* (Rockville, Md.: August 1982).

12. AAMI Process Control Guidelines for Radiation Sterilization of Medical Devices, AAMI Recommended Practice (Arlington, Va.: Association for the Advancement of Medical Instrumentation, 1982).

13. Herbert N. Prince and Joseph R. Rubino, "Bioburden Dynamics: The Viability of Microorganisms on Devices Before and After Sterilization," MMDI (July 1984): 47–53.

14. John R. Gillis, in *Sterilization Validation in Sterilization of Medical Products*, vol. 2, ed. Eugene R.L. Gaughram and Robert F. Morrissey (Montreal: Multiscience Publications, Ltd., 1981), 5.

15. G. Briggs Phillips and William S. Miller, *Industrial Sterilization*, International Symposium, Amsterdam, 1972 (Durham, N.C.: Duke University Press, 1972), 99.

16. U.S. Public Health Service, "Microbiologic Surveillance," *Guidelines for the Prevention and Control of Nosocomial Infections*, U.S. Department of Health and Human Services, Centers for Disease Control (Washington, D.C.: U.S. Government Printing Office, October 1981), 1–2.

23. Designing a Safety Program For EtO

RANDALL L. CORN

The safe use of ethylene oxide (EtO) as a sterilant has been of great concern to hospitals since 1978. When the Environmental Protection Agency (EPA) issued the Rebuttable Presumption Against the Registration of Ethylene Oxide (RPAR) on January 27, 1978, EtO became a hot topic in central service.[1]

Several subsequent studies link EtO exposure to mutagenic and carcinogenic activity in laboratory animals.[2,3,4] None of the studies have shown conclusive evidence of carcinogenic activity, but mutagenic activity has been demonstrated in humans exposed to high concentrations.[5] The Occupational Safety and Health Agency (OSHA) has decided that even though the evidence of carcinogenic activity is inconclusive, EtO is to be treated as a carcinogen for regulatory purposes.[6] This section does not debate the exposure levels issue; instead, it focuses on problem areas and how to set up a department so exposures can be minimized.

BACKGROUND

EtO has had an interesting history as a sterilant. It was developed as an alternative sterilization method for heat– and pressure–sensitive materials. Today it is used regularly for hospital sterilization since many new materials developed for medical care are heat sensitive. In fact, 5 percent to 25 percent of the items sterilized in hospitals, and many of the presterilized disposable items, have been sterilized by EtO.[7]

Actually, little of the EtO produced in the United States is used for medical product sterilization. Its uses are diverse. Seventy percent is used to make ethylene glycol, or antifreeze. It is used in the manufacture of detergents, cosmetics, inks, plasticizers, lubricants, and many other products. It also is used as a sterilant or fumigant for spices, nuts, books, furniture, textiles, empty equipment bins, empty cargo holds, cosmetics, and dairy packaging.[8]

That leaves less than half of 1 percent of the EtO production for medical products. However, worker exposures in hospitals are much more numerous and at higher concentrations than those routinely recorded in other areas.[9] This is the reason for the great concern for hospital personnel.

The following is a summary of actions taken to regulate exposure to EtO:

1968	The American Conference of Governmental Industrial Hygienists (ACGIH) recommended a threshold limit value (TLV) of 50 parts per million (ppm).
1972	The Occupational Safety and Health Agency (OSHA) adopted the 50 ppm TLV as its personal exposure limit (PEL).
1977	The National Institute for Occupational Safety and Health (NIOSH) recommended a 75 ppm short-term exposure limit (STEL) for a 15-minute sampling period average.
Jan. 27, 1978	The EPA issued the RPAR for EtO. This showed that the benefits of EtO use were greater than the risks.
June 1979	ACGIH proposed a change to a 10 ppm TLV. (This group allows two years before putting a proposed change into effect to give time for further study.)
Jan. 1981	The Bushy Run study (at Carnegie-Mellon Institute) was completed. This study was funded by EtO manufacturers to investigate the effects of daily exposure for two years at 10, 33, and 100 ppm for eight hours each day.
May 22, 1981	NIOSH issued a "Current Intelligence Bulletin" to inform employees and employers about the potential carcinogenic hazard of EtO exposure.
June 1981	ACGIH adopted the 10 ppm TLV and proposed a change to a 5 ppm TLV.

Aug. 1981	The Public Citizen Health Research Group petitioned OSHA to issue an emergency temporary standard (ETS) for a 1 ppm PEL.
Sept. 1981	OSHA denied the petition on the ground that an emergency situation did not exist.
Sept. 1981	Public Citizen brought suit against OSHA to require the ETS by court order.
Jan. 26, 1982	OSHA published an Advance Notice of Proposed Rulemaking (ANPR) for EtO.
June 10, 1982	ACGIH proposed a change to a 1 ppm TLV to be effective in 1984.
Jan. 5, 1983	The U.S. District Court, District of Columbia, ruled that OSHA had erred in judgment by not issuing an ETS and ordered it to do so within 20 days.
Jan. 1983	OSHA obtained a temporary stay pending review of the District Court order.
March 15, 1983	The U.S. Court of Appeals in the District of Columbia ruled that the District Court was incorrect in ordering an ETS. However, the Appeals Court ordered OSHA to expedite its development of a proposed rule on EtO and to publish its proposal within 30 days and its final rule one year later.
April 19, 1983	OSHA published the Notice of Proposed Rulemaking (NPR) to cover EtO exposures resulting from sterilant or fumigant use.
July 19–30, 1983	OSHA held public hearings on the NPR.
April 18, 1984	EPA published interim regulations for continued EtO use in hospitals and health care centers. These regulations control workplace design and practices.
June 22, 1984	OSHA published its final rules on EtO control, effective August 21, 1984. One year from that date was given for compliance on engineering controls and 180 days (February 17, 1985) for compliance with all other provisions.
June 22, 1984	EPA withdrew its published interim regulations, claiming possible confusion or conflict with the OSHA regulations.

Research conducted since the RPAR was published has shown that routine hospital exposures were 1,000 ppm and greater.[10] Modifications to existing sterilization equipment, newly developed equipment, and changes in procedures have been shown to have a substantial effect on lowering those exposures.[11,12,13] (These are discussed later in this chapter.) With this information, a sterilization area can be designed that will virtually eliminate EtO exposure for the sterilizer operator and maintenance personnel.

The new OSHA standard set the personal exposure limit (PEL) for EtO at 1 ppm and the action level at 0.5 ppm.[14] Employers must keep EtO levels below the PEL or provide protective equipment if they exceed that limit for short periods. If the levels are below the action level, the employer does not have to comply with many of the provisions of the standard.

EtO CONTROL CONSIDERATIONS

Equipment Purchase

Ethylene oxide sterilization equipment comes in varied forms and sizes. Small tabletop sterilizers that use 100 percent EtO cartridges are available with same-size aeration cabinets. Large, built-in sterilizers using an 88/12 gas mixture (88 percent Freon/12 percent EtO) are made by several manufacturers. These also have matching aeration cabinets. New EtO sterilizers include automatic purge cycles so that most of the residual gas is removed from the chamber before the door is opened.[15] This modification can be added to many of the older sterilizers.

Some manufacturers have modified their equipment to add sterilizers that also aerate within the same chamber.[16] When another load is ready to be run, the aerating load may be removed and placed in an aeration cabinet if aeration is incomplete.

Equipment Installation

The methods for properly installing EtO sterilization and aeration equipment have changed in recent years because of new information on EtO characteristics and routes of exposure. There are two major concerns in deciding the location of this equipment:

1. The chosen area must not be in a general traffic path but instead should be several feet away from work areas.

2. The ventilation in the chosen area must be adequate to remove the gas that gets into the environment and not allow any buildup.

Research studies have shown that significant exposures occur when either of these recommendations is not followed. When equipment is in a general traffic area, all personnel who pass near it may be exposed to constant leak situations of up to 100 ppm.[17] This is compounded when the area is not well ventilated and allows leaking EtO to build up. If workers are routinely stationed next to the sterilizer, the exposure problem can be serious. When they are moved at least 10 feet away and the equipment area is well ventilated (10 + air changes per hour), exposure levels have been shown to be almost eliminated.[18]

Ethylene oxide sterilization equipment must be installed so that its location does not contribute to exposure to the gas. The sterilizer door should be 10 to 15 feet from any work station. If the sterilizer has a drain, it should be in an access room and not out in the workroom.[19]

The gas cylinders for large sterilizers should be out of the work area but still be easy to reach quickly whenever a problem occurs. This may mean a dedicated room with good ventilation for these tanks.[20] Hand valves should be added to the end of the gas supply lines nearest the gas cylinders to provide a positive shut-off.[21] It is best to have depressurization lines coming off the gas supply lines between the hand valves and the sterilizer shut-off valve. This will allow emptying of the supply line when filter changes and/ or maintenance are necessary.[22]

Storage of gas cartridges should be in a well-ventilated area, not in the same room as the sterilizer and workers. Only the cartridges necessary for one day's processing should be in the work area.[23]

Aeration cabinets should be located as close to the sterilizer as possible so that transfer times are minimized. The chamber exhaust should be connected to the exhaust system and not be allowed to vent into the room.[24]

All potential problem leak areas should be ventilated. The front of the sterilizer should have a local exhaust hood as close as possible above the door.[25] Baffles may be needed in the hood to help direct the air flow and not allow gas to escape when the door is opened. The exhaust drain should have an exhaust vent (capture box) nearby so any gas escaping from the exhaust water will be captured.[26] The safety valve should vent directly into an exhaust line so any overpressurization of the sterilizer will not result in a high exposure to EtO.[27]

All of the exhaust vents should be connected to a dedicated system that vents to the outside. None of the air should be recirculated. As an alternative, the exhaust vents could be connected to the room exhaust as long as this system is not recirculated. A sensor must be connected to the exhaust fan so that an alarm sounds in the sterilizer area whenever the exhaust fan is not running.[28]

Room Ventilation

Ventilation is a vital part of ethylene oxide control. The sterile prep area must have good air circulation and at least 10 air changes per hour.[29] Good circulation keeps any small gas leaks from pooling into a high concentration. The sterilizer access room also should have good ventilation. It should be at negative pressure in relation to the sterilization area so that any gas in the access room does not travel into the work areas.[30]

The EPA guidelines indicated that it was permissible for all of the exhaust lines to empty into the access room provided that the room's exhaust ventilation is not recirculated and is exhausted outside.[31]

OPERATING PROCEDURES

Exposure to ethylene oxide occurs frequently during the transfer of the sterilized materials from the sterilizer to the aerator.[32] To avoid as much exposure as possible, the following procedures must be followed by personnel involved. They must:

1. Containerize the sterilization loads. Put the packages and packs

into baskets and on carts so they can be transferred to the aerator without touching the sterilized materials. Use carts and baskets made of bare metal so they do not absorb any of the gas and can be handled without gloves.

2. Move the load directly to the aerator at the end of the sterilization cycle. Do not rummage through the load for any reason. Prepare biological monitor included in the load so that it can be retrieved easily.

3. Pull the cart to the aerator, if the load is on a cart, so the gas coming off the freshly sterilized goods stays behind the operator. Place the basket (if the load is in a basket) on a cart to move it to the aerator.

4. Always place freshly sterilized materials into an aeration cabinet. Place them onto a shelf in a well-ventilated area isolated from the workers if they must be shelf aerated.

5. Aerate all items for at least two hours before they are handled; this allows the removal of the gas from the package even if the sterile items do not absorb any gas (e.g., glass or metal items). Do not open the aerator door during the first two hours of the aeration cycle so the majority of the gas will be removed.[33]

EtO MONITORING

Purpose

Monitoring of ethylene oxide levels is mandated by OSHA's 1984 regulations.[34] Routine EtO monitoring determines employee exposure levels. It should be done in the worker's breathing zone. The monitor must meet the following minimum requirements: (1) at the 1.0 ppm TWA (time weighted average) level, the accuracy must be ±25% and (2) at the 0.5 ppm level the accuracy must be ±35%.[35] Several monitoring devices are verified as meeting these accuracy requirements, so when considering an EtO monitor, manufacturers' literature should be checked as to whether it meets these requirements.

Monitoring must be done to verify the exposure levels for every employee who may be exposed to levels above the action level at least 30 days each year. Classes of employees who have similar exposures may meet this requirement by the hospital's monitoring a representative employee for an eight-hour TWA.[36]

Monitoring initially seeks to verify the current level.[37] If this is below 0.5 ppm (the action level), routine monitoring is not necessary.[38] However, any time the sterilization equipment breaks down and is repaired or the sterilization routine is changed, monitoring must be done to show the levels still remain below the action level.[39]

If the EtO level is 0.5 to 1.0 ppm, the monitoring must be repeated every six months.[40] If the figure later is found to be below the action level, monitoring must be repeated at least seven days later. If this level verifies the first reading, the rules for the new level can be followed.[41]

If the initial reading indicates an EtO level above 1.0 ppm, monitoring must be repeated every three months.[42] If lower levels are found in subsequent tests, the rules for the new level may be followed after the repeat procedure is performed.

Protocol

A monitoring protocol should be custom fitted to the institution. This example is from the author's personal experience.

At the outset, a thorough area monitoring should be performed, including leak testing. This is best done with a real-time monitor such as an infrared gas analyzer. All areas where leaks may occur should be tested; this includes all gas supply lines and valves, sterilizer doors and drains, and nearby areas.

Personnel breathing zones should be checked, using dosimeter badge monitors. Personnel testing should be repeated according to the routine schedule above based on the EtO levels found. Personnel testing and leak checking also should be repeated after major repairs and after major changes in the sterilization routine.

EMERGENCY PROCEDURES

EtO exposure at very high concentrations can be the result of a spill or leak from a 100 percent cartridge or an 88/12 cylinder.[43] Precise rules must be followed in such an emergency to avoid high exposures. It also is necessary to know the symptoms of exposure so that proper treatment can be performed quickly after such an incident.

A respirator must be kept in the sterilization area.[44] It should be fitted properly to individuals who may have to enter a high-exposure area to shut off a gas supply valve or to rescue a worker who has been overcome. This respirator is to be used for only a few minutes because the filter may be quickly saturated by the gas.

Cartridge Leaks

A cartridge of 100 percent EtO may leak around the gasket at the top or may be punctured inadequately in the sterilizer so that, when dislodged from its holder, it begins to empty. If a cartridge is leaking:

1. Immediately place the cartridge into an aeration cabinet and aerate for a minimum of 2 hours to remove the gas.

2. If the leaking cartridge is already inside a sterilizer, close the door and run the sterilizer through a cycle.

3. If neither a sterilizer nor an aerator is available, confine the cartridge in a well-ventilated area where no people are working or take it outside.[45]

Cylinder Leaks

A gas cylinder containing an 88/12 mixture may leak because of overpressurization or faulty valves.[46] A major cylinder leak can be very serious and must be handled properly:

1. Leave the storage or access room immediately. If the exposed person loses consciousness, don the respirator and remove [the individual] from the exposure area. This must be done quickly because EtO gas will concentrate on the floor.

2. Evacuate the area. Only personnel who are protected from exposure should be allowed into the area.

3. Contain the EtO vapors. Close the doors and turn off the air supply, but leave the exhaust fans running. This will keep the gas from spreading easily and will help to remove the gas.

4. Notify safety personnel, particularly the local fire department toxic chemical division. Clean-up personnel should wear full acid suits with self-contained air packs.

5. Turn off ethylene oxide cylinders or otherwise stop leakage, if possible. Remove the problem cylinders from the hospital once the leakage is stopped.

6. Place sparkless fans in the area to increase the airflow toward the exhaust vents. Be sure to keep the air contained within the room.

7. Reenter the area only after the level is below 10 ppm.[47]

Exposure Symptoms

Exposure to EtO vapors may result in eye irritation, nasal and throat irritation, dizziness, weakness and mental fatigue, confusion, chest pain, nausea, and vomiting. Each person may exhibit some or all of these symptoms in varying degrees. Often, the symptoms appear as a delayed response.[48]

Exposure to liquid EtO usually occurs on the skin. The exposed area should be scrubbed thoroughly with a brush. If this is done quickly, a painful chemical burn will be avoided.[49]

Exposure Treatment

Whenever a worker is exposed to high concentrations of EtO, these specific procedures must be followed:

1. Take victim away from the exposure area to an area with plenty of fresh air. Be ready to assist breathing with oxygen. It may be necessary to resuscitate the victim.

2. Remove clothing that was splashed with EtO liquid and aerate thoroughly in an aeration cabinet.

3. Discard leather shoes if contaminated with liquid EtO. It is very difficult to remove EtO from leather. A chemical burn may result on the wearer's feet after a long exposure from wearing the shoes.

4. Wash contaminated skin thoroughly using a scrub brush for a minimum of 10 minutes to remove the EtO from within skin pores.

5. Keep the victim under medical observation so any further reactions can be dealt with immediately.[50]

REGULATION: HERE TO STAY

EtO regulation is here to stay. It took many years of battling to arrive at this situation. Caution has been taken to try to ensure that workers in EtO sterilization areas will not discover later that they were protected inadequately.

If correct procedures are followed after the sterilization equipment is properly installed and maintained, exposure levels should remain below the action level of 0.5 ppm. It is the employers' responsibility to keep the EtO exposure levels as low as possible and thus ensure the safety of their employees.

NOTES

1. *Federal Register,* "Ethylene Oxide Rebuttable Presumption Against Registration: Maximum Residue Limits and Daily Levels of Exposure," Department of Health, Education, and Welfare, Food and Drug Administration 43 (January 27, 1978): 3800.

2. J.W. Embree and C.H. Hine, "Mutagenicity of Ethylene Oxide," *Toxicology and Applied Pharmacology* 33 (1977): 172–73.

3. R.H. Garman and W.M. Snellings, "Final Report—Ethylene Oxide Two-Year Inhalation Study on Rats" (Bushy Run Research Center, June 7, 1983).

4. National Institute for Occupational Safety and Health, "Ethylene Oxide (EtO): Evidence of Carcinogenicity," *NIOSH Current Intelligence Bulletin* No. 35 (Cincinnati: DTS, NIOSH, May 22, 1981).

5. V.F. Garry et al., "Ethylene Oxide: Evidence of Human Chromosomal Effects," *Environmental Mutagenesis* 1 (1979): 375–82.

6. *Federal Register,* "Occupational Exposure to Ethylene Oxide; Final Standard," Occupational Safety and Health Administration 49 (June 22, 1984): 25743–44.

7. Thomas M. Samuels, "Controlling Passive Exposure to Ethylene Oxide," *Purchasing Administration* 2 (June 1978): 18.

8. *Federal Register,* "Final Standard," 25734–35.

9. _____, "Occupational Exposure to Ethylene Oxide; Advance Notice of Proposed Rulemaking," Occupational Safety and Health Administration 47 (January 26, 1982): 3567.

10. Thomas M. Samuels, "Personnel Exposures to Ethylene Oxide," *Hospital Topics* 56 (May/June 1978): 32.

11. Thomas M. Samuels and Randall Corn, "Modification of Large Built-in Ethylene Oxide Sterilizers to Reduce Operator Exposure to Ethylene Oxide," *Hospital Topics* 57 (November/December 1979): 55.

12. _____, "Evaluation of a New Generation Ethylene Oxide Sterilizer Relative to Reduction in Operator Exposure to EtO," *Hospital Topics* 58 (January-February 1980): 35.

13. Theodore R. Weidrich, *Guide for the Safe Usage of Ethylene Oxide in the Hospital* (Rochester, N.Y.: Sybron Corp., Medical Products Division), 2.

14. *Federal Register,* "Final Standard," 25796.

15. Samuels and Corn, "Evaluation," 32.

16. 3M Co., *Operators Manual, Model 400C Gas Sterilizer* (St. Paul, Minn.: Author, 1981).

17. Samuels, "Controlling Passive Exposure," 18.

18. Thomas M. Samuels and Mary Eastin, "EtO Exposure Can be Reduced by Air Systems," *Hospitals* 54 (July 1980): 66.

19. *Federal Register,* "Final Standard," 25801.

20. Ibid.

21. Ibid.

22. Ibid., 25802.

23. American Society for Hospital Central Service Personnel, *Ethylene Oxide Use in Hospitals: A Manual for Health Care Personnel* (Chicago: American Hospital Association, 1982), 19.

24. *Federal Register,* "Final Standard," 25801.

25. Ibid.

26. Ibid.

27. Ibid.

28. Ibid., 25802.

29. American Society, *Ethylene Oxide,* 19.

30. Weidrich, *Guide for the Safe Usage,* 2.

31. *Federal Register,* "Final Standard," 25802.

32. Samuels, "Personnel Exposures," 31–32.

33. _____, *Controlling and Monitoring Hospital Personnel Exposure to Ethylene Oxide* (Tucson, Ariz.: Health Information Development Association), 44.

34. *Federal Register,* "Final Standard," 25796–97.

35. Ibid., 25797.

36. Ibid., 25796.

37. Ibid.

38. Ibid., 25796–97.

39. Ibid., 25797.

40. Ibid., 25796.

41. Ibid.

42. Ibid.

43. Samuels, *Controlling and Monitoring,* 96.

44. *Federal Register,* "Final Standard," 25797.

45. Randall L. Corn, *Ethylene Oxide Report* (Chicago: American Society for Hospital Central Service Personnel, 1982), 18.

46. Ibid., 15.

47. Ibid., 18-19.

48. Zorach R. Glaser, *Special Occupational Hazard Review with Control Recommendations: Use of Ethylene Oxide as a Sterilant in Medical Facilities* (Rockville, Md.: Department of Health, Education, and Welfare, July 1977), 21.

49. Ibid., 22.

50. American Society, *Ethylene Oxide,* 24.

24. Maximizing Instrument Inventory Investment

Bernard R. Teitz and Lois Suhrie

Environmental factors are forcing hospital administrators to be more cost conscious and mandating that purchasing and inventory investments be monitored closely. Inventory control principles and terminology that have been common in industry are finding their way into the hospital environment. The broad concept of material management, which consolidates purchasing, inventory control, processing, and distribution, is becoming the standard throughout the hospital industry. The theories of inventory control can be applied to the operating room (OR) and central processing (CS) environment and particularly to instrumentation investment and management.

As a rule, OR nurse managers, CS managers, and purchasing agents receive no formal training on how to buy instruments, and only by on-the-job training and experience do they learn how to care for them. As a result, instruments are purchased in a nonsystematic way and, at times, are not handled in a way that will extend their life to the fullest. This chapter presents principles of instrument purchasing, inventory control, and care and handling to assist managers in obtaining the maximum cost benefit from their investment.

WHY A HOSPITAL BUYS INSTRUMENTS

Instruments are purchased by a hospital for a variety of reasons: (1) new hospital construction that adds ORs, (2) enlargement of existing OR suites, (3) addition of new specialties, (4) increases in an OR schedule, (5) introduction of new technology to a hospital, (6) conversion to a case cart system, (7) changing physician preferences, and (8) wear and tear, theft, or loss.

Since no historical data exist, the purchase of instruments for a new hospital, new specialty, or new technology is difficult to predetermine. The amount bought at the opening of a hospital is based largely on guesswork, with some idea of the type of specialties that will be performed. The decision to add a new surgical specialty or to purchase a piece of advanced technological equipment is often administrative, with the purchase of supportive instruments based solely on anticipated usage.

However, enlargement of OR suites and conversion to a case cart system will lead to additions of instruments that can be predetermined. There will always be some instruments out for repair that must be replaced to keep the OR running smoothly. Some instruments also will be lost through the linen and trash disposal systems and theft.

WHO MAKES THE PURCHASING DECISION

Any discussion of the replacement of a surgical instrument must take into consideration who is making the purchasing decision. Those involved are the material manager and CS manager, who assume the role of buyer, and the surgeon and OR manager, who assume the role of user.

One of the buyer's main concerns is price. The buyer may be aware of quality differences and may take into consideration the fact that a high-quality instrument will need fewer repairs and will last longer. However, to the material manager, who does not use the instrument, the quality factors may be of secondary importance. The user (surgeon) is concerned primarily about the feel and function of the instrument, with cost a secondary issue. This situation, where the buyer and user differ, creates a mediating role for the OR nurse manager. This person must stay within the OR budget yet purchase an instrument that will require minimum repair and meet the surgeon's requirements.

HOW TO PLAN THE INVENTORY SYSTEM

Human nature creates a dilemma for the material manager in that, by nature, people do not wish to be judged poorly yet a stock-out is perceived as a poor reflection on the management capabilities of the person responsible. As a result, managers tend to overcompensate for stock-outs by building inventory levels to a point where they feel secure. However, by applying basic inventory concepts, the manager is able to maintain levels that will provide optimal investment and service levels while minimizing the risk of stock-outs.

Key factors in the development of a successful instrumentation management system are:

1. standardization of instrument sets
2. communication
3. elimination of all informal instrument storage locations
4. documentation of current inventory
5. establishment of necessary instrument levels
6. determination of replacement quantities.

Standardization of Instrument Sets

Instrument standardization, strictly defined, would require all surgeons in each specialty to use the exact same instruments for specific procedures, eliminating all preferences they might have acquired over the years. Such standardization obviously would simplify inventory management. But since this is unrealistic and could even lead to unsafe patient care, standardization is best utilized in basic instrument sets, with individual preferences added.

The OR then must decide the number of basic sets to purchase and the number of additional individual instruments. This will depend on the cost of the preferred instrument and the number of procedures the surgeon performs in one day. For instance, a general surgeon may prefer three pairs of metzenbaum scissors for a gall bladder procedure, while the basic setup has only two. This surgeon also prefers an expensive special retractor that no one else uses.

The OR manager decides that the budget can afford extra packs of individually wrapped sterile metzenbaum scissors, thus making the addition of a pair to the surgeon's setup as easy as opening a sterile pack. The OR manager may decide, at the same time, that the purchase of more than one of the special retractors is an expense the budget cannot support, thus making it necessary to flash-sterilize this piece of equipment if more than one procedure is performed in one day. Through decisions such as these, standardization is possible, ensuring that the available instrumentation will meet the requirements of the OR schedule and budget.

Communication

One key to the success of instrument management is communication. A weekly meeting of representatives of the areas involved in instrument purchasing, processing, and usage is necessary to initiate a formal instrument management system. This group should delegate the steps in planning the system, share the information gathered, and develop effective policies and procedures for purchasing, usage, and care. Once the system is in place, this group will meet less frequently, and then primarily to discuss coping with new surgical procedures, new surgeons, and changing preferences.

Elimination of Informal Inventories

Since instruments are distributed throughout many patient areas, it is important to systematize stockkeeping records and locations. Inventories should be stored in central locations, i.e., sterile supply, clean holding, and equipment storage.

Sources of phantom (nondocumented) inventory, such as file cabinets, desks, or lockers, must be eliminated.

Documentation of Inventory

It is not possible to make accurate purchasing decisions without first determining existing inventory levels. Therefore, all instruments must be counted and recorded and the quantities listed on some type of perpetual inventory list. A perpetual inventory requires keeping a continuous record of additions to or reductions of instrumentation levels on a day-to-day basis.

As a procedure is scheduled, a requisition should be generated indicating the type and number of instrument sets required. The requisition is sent to the central storage area, the instruments are removed, the stock records are adjusted, and the instruments are sent to the OR. When the procedure is completed, the instruments are processed and returned to central storage. In the following transaction flow, those involved should:

1. Schedule surgical procedure.
2. Create a requisition for instrumentation.
3. Supply instruments based on the requisition.
4. Adjust stock downward in CS.
5. Reprocess and inspect instrumentation.
6. Count and document instrumentation shrinks.
7. Rectify quantity variances.
8. Return instrumentation to storage.
9. Adjust stockkeeping levels upward.

Since the volume and variety of instrumentation in a hospital is high, a computer system can greatly enhance the effectiveness of a perpetual inventory system. If a computer system is not available, a manual inventory is necessary. Either system performs the same function. However, an automated computer system can significantly increase productivity and allow an institution to review supply levels from one location regardless of where an item is stored.

To guarantee the integrity of the instrument inventories, an annual physical inventory is recommended. This will serve to correct any variances between stockkeeping records and actual quantities on hand. In the following basic steps in taking a physical inventory, those involved should:

1. Count the instruments and record the quantities on either a ticket left on the shelf or on a posting sheet.
2. Verify the count either by recounting all instruments, taking sample counts, or through cross-references to an inventory listing.
3. Adjust inventory records for differences in record and physical quantities.
4. Conduct recounts before adjusting inventory records if there are large discrepancies.

In situations where an annual physical inventory is not feasible, cycle counts may be taken. Cycle counting involves taking a physical inventory of specific instruments on a regular basis throughout the year, thereby verifying stockkeeping records on a more frequent basis rather than yearly. The cycle counts allow the institution to continue operations while the actual counting is being done.

Establishment of Instrument Levels

Since an instrument is a reusable resource, inventory levels should be based on the number of procedures in which it is used, the reprocessing time required to return it to use, and its expectable life, which includes wear and tear as well as loss.

For example, an OR has two major orthopedic sets and performs a maximum of three major orthopedic procedures in a seven-hour schedule. The CS department or processing area is planning on a four-hour average turnaround time for the sets. To meet the needs 100 percent of the time, this OR will require three major orthopedic sets, an increase of one.

Certain instruments, such as scissors, need more frequent repair so a hospital may choose to carry a buffer stock of these items in order to fully utilize its sets and avoid down time.

Determination of Replacement Quantities

How Much to Order

The economic order quantity (EOQ) (see Chapter 17) is defined as the order size that will achieve the minimal total annual costs of a purchased item. As an equation, the EOQ is defined as:

$$EOQ = \sqrt{\frac{2\,AP}{IC}}$$

Where A = Annual units used; P = cost per purchase order; I = inventory carrying percentage; C = cost per unit.

For example, an institution has determined that its cost per purchase order (P) is $1 and that its inventory carrying cost (I) is equal to 28 percent on the dollar. It also has determined by calculating the turn on instruments through loss, wear, and tear that it replaces 75 Adson tissue forceps annually at a cost of $15.50 apiece. The economic order quantity is:

$$EOQ = \sqrt{\frac{2 \times (75 \times 1)}{28\% \times 15.50}}$$

$$EOQ = \sqrt{\frac{150}{4.34}}$$

$$EOQ = \quad 5.9 \text{ (or 6 units)}$$

When to Order

The reorder point (ROP) is defined as the on-hand balance of units at which an item is reordered. As an equation, ROP is defined as:

$$ROP = (D \times LT) + SS$$

Where D = monthly demand, LT = lead time, and SS = minimum inventory.

For example, the minimum total number of Adson tissue forceps required to perform surgical procedures is 150 units. Instruments are lost or damaged at a rate of 6 per month (75 annual units/12 = 6.25). Lead time from the supplier is equal to one month.

$$ROP = (6 \text{ units} \times 1 \text{ month}) + 150 \text{ minimum units}$$

$$ROP = 156 \text{ units}$$

Theoretically, the ROP assumes that there is a preset demand pattern during the lead time prior to replenishment.

Maximum inventory level of Adson tissue forceps is equal to:

$$EOQ \ (6) + ROP \ (156)$$

$$\text{Maximum Inventory} = 162 \text{ instruments}$$

While not all institutions provide a computerized inventory and replenishment system, the standardizing of instrumentation and storage areas, taking of a physical inventory, and establishing of EOQ and ROP levels will contribute to reducing a hospital's stock levels and replenishment expenses.

HOW TO CARE FOR INSTRUMENTS

Once an instrument has been purchased, proper care and handling are necessary to obtain its maximum useful life, further reducing replacement costs. Most damage to an instrument is caused by abuse, misuse, or improper cleaning and sterilizing. The following four steps should be initiated to prevent instruments from being damaged:

1. An instrument should be used only for the purpose for which it was designed.
2. New instruments should be inspected carefully before being put into service. This includes looking for cracks in the box locks and being sure opposing jaws of instruments mesh properly and do not wobble in the shanks or spring open when lightly tapped against a solid object. Scis-

sors and other sharp instruments such as chisels, osteotomes, and gouges should be checked for burrs, nicks, chips, and loose fulcrum screws. When multipart instruments are disassembled for processing, their same parts should be reassembled and not mixed.

3. Instruments should be routinely checked after each procedure before the processing cycle. The criteria for inspecting new instruments should be used to check all instruments each time they are reprocessed.

4. The correct steps in reprocessing should be followed:

- All dirty instruments should be cleaned manually, using a mild detergent and soft brush, or put through a washer sterilizer. Initial manual rinsing of gross debris is best even when using an automated washer sterilizer.

- All box locks should be open, cutting edges protected, assembled instruments disassembled, and delicate instruments processed separately.

- Ultrasonic cleaning should be used to remove tiny particles of debris from cracks and corners.

- Lubrication is needed to maintain maximum efficiency and useful life. A nontoxic, nonsilicone water-soluble lubricant solution is best; it can be used for many sets of instruments.

- The instruments should be thoroughly dried to prevent corrosion and spotting in locks, hinges, and crevices before storing or sterilization.

If these steps are followed, the life of an instrument will be lengthened, with the resultant cost benefits.

The fundamental concepts covered in this chapter will allow an institution to achieve the maximum cost benefit from its instrumentation investment. Hospitals that have adopted these principles should be able to document cost savings in numbers of instruments and in time spent reordering.

In this age of cost containment, the benefits gained from developing these management systems should far outweigh the effort put into initiating them.

25. Developing a Training Program for Central Service

MARIMARGARET REICHERT

A training program that is complemented by clearly defined procedures will help the central service department be more cost effective. A training program can decrease reprocessing due to errors, decrease "ask somebody else" time because employees know where to locate the information necessary to do their job, decrease repair bills, and, most important, increase planning time because supervisors are not constantly needed to put out fires. A staff that is knowledgeable and efficient will be a cost benefit.

DEFINING PURPOSES AND NEEDS

The first step in developing a program is to define the purpose of the department. At Robinson Memorial Hospital in Ravenna, Ohio, the central sterile reprocessing (CSR) department is responsible for all reusable medical devices, including instruments and utensils used in labor and delivery (L&D), the operating room (OR), cardiac cath lab, radiology, respiratory therapy, intensive care (ICU), cardiac care (CCU), emergency room (ER), clinic, and patient care areas.

CSR also is responsible for portable and central line vaccum suctions, K-pads, hypo/hyperthermia equipment, Emerson pumps, transducer cables, and resuscitation equipment. CSR develops standardization of preparation and packaging of supplies.

The second step is to identify the department's needs. This can be done by the manager's asking questions such as the following:

- What is the difference between what is being done and what is supposed to be done?
- What specific events caused me to think things aren't right?
- What would happen if I left the situation alone?
- Do I have an objective way to evaluate an employee's performance?
- Is there a way I can do this job better?
- How much of my time is spent putting out fires?
- How many supplies processed by my department are opened but never used because the package is labeled incorrectly or the instrument tray is incomplete or improperly packaged or damaged?
- How much time do I spend repeating instructions to my employees?
- How often are multiples of the same item inconsistent in final package size and labeling?
- Am I just supervising the daily activities and never seeming to get beyond that?

Once needs have been identified, they should be prioritized, beginning with the greatest need. The most time should be spent in the top three to five items. A step-by-step implementation plan to meet these needs should be outlined.

ESTABLISHING THE PROGRAM

The third step is to set up the program. The department should be broken down into basic work stations or functions, such as floor supply preparation, OR set preparation, sterilization, and decontamination. Each area is further broken down into work operations. For example, the person assigned to sterilization prepares supplies for terminal processing, selects appropriate cycle and time, maintains all records, prepares all test packs, and reviews all monitoring controls.

The general knowledge the employee needs to work efficiently at this area should be established. For example, the person assigned to sterilization must be familiar with the procedures in the manual, possess a knowledge of sterilization process controls, understand the recordkeeping system, and know the sterilizer function.

Specific technical information the employee needs to know should be listed. The person assigned to sterilization needs to know about the hazards of ethylene oxide (EtO) (see Chapter 23) and the sources of environmental residual EtO. The individual needs to know how EtO sterilizes not only to place supplies properly on the cart but also to be aware that improper loading may subject them to excessive degassing of EtO during transfer from sterilizer to aerator. The employee should be aware of and understand EtO monitoring and/or alarm systems established in the department.

The employee should begin at the station that requires the least amount of technical knowledge and progress by steps to the most difficult. At Robinson Memorial, the rotation begins with floor supply preparation, learning wrapping procedures and techniques and basic care and handling of instruments, sharps, and needles. Once these basic skills have been mastered, the employees continue to learn all other tasks and procedures at that station. They then rotate to OR set preparation, sterilization, and finally decontamination.

The use of procedure manuals is beneficial. Standardized procedures eliminate the problems associated with giving, interpreting, and recalling oral directions; make it possible for employees to correctly disassemble, reassemble, package, and sterilize supplies; decrease the time spent repeating directions; and increase productivity and self-confidence.

The information is written and placed in an area where it is readily available to employees at all times. The use of a well-developed procedure manual throughout training provides continuity and enables new employees to perform their job at the high level of efficiency expected of them.

THE LESSON SERIES

Next is development of a series of lessons for each station. The lesson format should organize information, assist in planning, list demonstration materials, and define the evaluation process. (See Exhibits 25–1 and 25–2.)

Proper employee preparation is essential and enhances the learning process. Was the assignment explained at the beginning of the week? Were the objectives stated clearly? Did the employees complete these objectives? Too often the daily changes in routine interfere with the planned program and it is assumed new employees have mastered the assigned skills. The use of the Employee Objectives Form (Exhibit 25–3) eliminates many of these problems and makes it possible to document their progress in the program. Because new employees share the responsibility of the training program (i.e., they must communicate to the managers that the goals were not met), they must know what is expected of them for a particular time frame.

Robinson Memorial chose weekly breakdowns for documentation. On Monday new employees receive the objectives for the week and on Friday afternoon review them and sign off that they were fulfilled. If they were not, the employees remain at that phase until they are. This also has eliminated employees' completing the program without mastering the skills necessary to staff a station.

Teaching should be supplemented with testing and documentation of results to assess the new employees' ability to research. They are given the pretest on Monday, which is to be worked on throughout the week (see Exhibit 25–4). The primary purpose of the training program is not for the employees to retain massive amounts of information but to know where to find it. The procedure manual contains most of the answers to the pretest.

The training program should include a method for assessing the employee's performance and level of knowledge. A skill checklist is used to evaluate the employees' ability to perform the task and their ability to follow sequential steps while performing it (Exhibit 25–5). The use of a

Exhibit 25–1 Central Sterile Reprocessing Orientation Program

Station: _____Week: _____of 4 weeks. Date: _____

I. A. What do I expect the employee to learn?   I. B. Why do I expect the employee to learn these things?

II. How am I going to teach this?
    [ ] Demonstration
    [ ] Lecture
    [ ] Individual work—selected readings
    [ ] Audiovisuals
    [ ] Quiz or test

III. What materials am I going to use? (books, visuals, paper, etc.)

IV. How am I going to evaluate this?

V. What is tomorrow's assignment? Purpose? Did I explain it?

Source: Reprinted with permission from *Journal of Hospital Supply, Processing and Distribution,* vol. 1, no. 1, p. 24.

written test documents the employees' level of knowledge or understanding of the "why" of what they are doing. (See Exhibit 25–6.) These two evaluation tools may be used separately or together.

THE LEARNING ENVIRONMENT

The next primary concern is to provide an environment in which the employees can learn. This environment should allow them to relax—stress and tension are two deterrents to learning. Employees given too much information too quickly will be overwhelmed; relaxed persons retain more information.

It should be remembered when preparing the program that they will retain little of what they hear, more of what they hear and see demonstrated, but most of what they hear, see demonstrated, and actually do themselves. It is essential to be realistic in expectations and

Exhibit 25–2 Central Sterile Reprocessing Orientation Program

(Completion of First Week)

Station: _____Sterilization_____   Week: _____1_____ of 4 weeks. Date: _____

I. A. What do I expect the employee to learn?

Concepts of the steam sterilization process.

Protocol established for cart loading.

Knowledge of load numbering system.

Accurate recording in load record book.

I. B. Why do I expect the employee to learn these things?

To be aware of factors or situations that could impede this process.

To be able to process supplies.

To be able to recall any supply due to malfunction or inadequate processing cycle.

To realize the importance of accurate recording.

II. How am I going to teach this?

[x] Demonstration
[ ] Lecture
[x] Individual work—selected readings
[ ] Audiovisuals
[x] Quiz or test

III. What materials am I going to use? (books, visuals, paper, etc.)

Association Advancement Medical Instrumentation, "Good Hospital Practice: Steam Sterilization and Sterility Assurance."
Perkins
Berry & Kohn, "Introduction to OR Techniques," pp 25–35; answer questions, pp 35–36.

Procedure Manual   Supplies
Load record book   Sterilizer
Label gun   Loading cart

IV. How am I going to evaluate this?

Return Demonstration
Quiz

V. What is tomorrow's assignment? Purpose? Did I explain it?

Dust Cover Station

Exhibit 25–3 Employee Objectives Form

WEEK ONE—STERILIZATION

1. Will demonstrate accurate recording in load record book.
2. Will demonstrate acceptable procedure in loading supplies to be steam sterilized.
3. Will possess an awareness of dedicated loads.
4. Will possess knowledge of labeling procedure.
5. Will demonstrate accurate use of labeling gun.
6. Will demonstrate awareness of the steam sterilizer, particularly all dials and gauges on front panel and their purpose.

Monday

Reviewed with employee _____

                                                              Date

by _____.

Friday

These objectives were fulfilled _____

                                                       Date

_____.

                                      Employee's signature

---

always remember that feedback is essential. Trainers must listen to what the employees tell them. This input should be used as one part of a continuing evaluation process to identify the effectiveness of the program.

A system to evaluate the effectiveness of the program in tangible terms must be implemented. Controls must be established. Does the training program address the defined needs? Does it do so in a cost-effective manner? Development of objective measuring tools such as audits and quality assurance checks is necessary to obtain answers to these questions. These tools permit checking the end product rather than relying on users' feedback.

Training programs cannot solve all problems. Total needs must be considered. In addition to a training program, needs include a comprehensive procedure manual, a method of continuing assessment, and a quality assurance program.

OVERALL VALUES

In reviewing the benefits of a procedure-based training program, it must be remembered that once it has been developed, it is not stored on a shelf until needed to train new employees. Developing this program should create awareness of existing problems in the department. The concepts are modified to be useful every day.

Skill checklists are developed for any new procedure such as preparation of the intubation tray or blue alert suction. These checklists are used when a procedure is implemented—and employees are reviewed every six months. This review also provides objective documentation for employees' appraisal, makes managers aware of supplies that may have changed or how implementation of another procedure affected this one, and reassures the workers. They should look forward to these reviews with their super-

Exhibit 25–4 Sterilization Pretest I

Name:

Date:

1. Explain why we list all supplies in the load record book.

2. List the following items in the load record book.

    4—Suture sets, 2—CSR small basins, 3—skin hooks, 1—CSR cutdown tray

Load Contents Identification			Reviewed by:
Test Pack			
1 month: _____	_____	_____	
_____	_____	_____	
6 month items:	_____	_____	
_____	_____	_____	
_____	_____	_____	
_____	_____	_____	
_____	_____	_____	

3. Explain what each number on the date sticker means.

Load No.	
173	108
EXPIRES	
Jul 15 83	

Exhibit 25–4 continued

4. Explain where the date sticker is placed on pouch packaging.

5. Identify where the date sticker is placed on wrapped supplies.

6. Explain how Julian dating differs from monthly dating.

7. Discuss whether the supplies are guaranteed sterile if a correct sterilizing cycle is completed.

8. Name the different types of steam sterilizers in the department.

9. Identify the mechanical controls on the sterilizer that ensure the processing cycle was achieved.

10. Explain the purpose of a dedicated load.

11. Explain how steam kills bacteria.

12. Name supplies that are kept in the sterilization station.

    Explain why.

13. List the normal time, temperature, and dry time for both the HiVac and Gravity Pull Sterilizers.

Exhibit 25–5 Central Sterile Reprocessing Skill Checklist

Name:

Date:

Ethylene Oxide Sterilization

	Ratings	
	Yes	No

Preparing Supplies for Processing

A. Prepare biological test pack according to established procedure

B. Prepare chemical processing indicators according to established procedure

C. Review items to be sterilized

D. Place control sticker on each supply according to established procedure

E. Record in load record book

F. Follow established procedure for placement of pouches—in metal bin

G. Follow established procedure for placement of bin on cart

H. Place biological and chemical process controls on cart, according to established procedures

I. Check sterilizer for correct time/temperature settings

J. Check gauge for adequate EtO for cycle

K. Turn on environgard system

L. Open door, place load in sterilizer

M. Close door, secure, initiate cycle

N. Precondition aerator

O. Open aerator door at completion of processing (IF NO ALARM IS ACTIVATED)

P. Open sterilizer door, place carriage in racks, remove cart from sterilizer using metal hook

Q. Release carriage and pull load to aerator

R. Place load in aerator, close door

S. Set timer according to established procedure

T. Record "TIME OUT" on chart and initial

U. Check sterilizer graph, ascertain accuracy, and initial

Exhibit 25–6 Sterilization Posttest I

Name:

Date:

1. What do you check before you can transfer a load to sterile storage?

2. How could you recall the items on a load that was unacceptable but had been put away?

3. If the HiVac cycle was 2 minutes @ 270°, is this an acceptable processing cycle? Why or why not?

4. How are ER suture sets placed on an autoclave cart? Illustrate and briefly explain why.

5. Which of these items would you sterilize first? Why?

       L&D cart   Containers (including vascular set)
       30 prep sets

6. What is the purpose of the gauges on the front of the sterilizers?

7. Why should pan sets be placed at an angle with the taped edge up on the autoclave cart?

8. What should you do if you are pulling an autoclave cart out of the sterilizer and you notice one of the packages does not have a date sticker?

9. What should be the first package put on an autoclave cart?

10. If at the end of a day you have the following items, can they be placed on a sterilizer load together?

      6—preps, 2—ER suture sets, 1—pan set, 1—basin, 1—containerized OR instrument set

11. If you had one containerized OR set on a load by itself, what time, temperature, and dry cycle settings would you use?

visor. Because this is a one-on-one process, it gives them an opportunity to ask questions or explain their difficulties.

All employees experience problems when under stress. New hires have difficulty remembering and mastering the skills—but experienced employees also have these same difficulties. Quality assurance audits developed to support the value of a training program also identify times of stress in the department. The work volume/error ratio increases.

The implementation of clearly defined procedures can reduce the total departmental budget. Standardized procedures will decrease reprocessing necessitated by errors in preparation, packaging, and labeling. Developing employees' researching skills decreases "ask somebody else" time because they know where to locate the information. Repair bills drop because employees know how to properly disassemble, clean, reassemble, package, sterilize, and store products.

The development and implementation of a procedure-based training program provides a system to evaluate the performance of the department objectively. The CS manager should be planning for the long term, not putting out short-term fires.

PART IV
SPECIALTY DEPARTMENTS

More material managers are being given direct operating responsibility for specialty departments such as linen service, printing service, and pharmacy. The material manager rarely comes to the job with specific training in these areas. While much has been written about these functions in the literature specific to their areas, little mention has been made in texts devoted to health care material management.

This Part, Chapters 26–28, provides material managers with a good deal of specific detail about the operation of these functions.

26. Laundry and Linen Service

DAVID M. GIANCOLA

The laundry and the linen service system cannot be considered as separate and distinct entities. The laundry must be designed to become an integral part of a total linen service system that monitors and controls the articles from the areas of use to the laundry and back to the areas of use. In addition, the laundry must be designed with enough flexibility to accommodate different linen system concepts.

THE SYSTEM DESCRIBED

Quality service is the provision of an adequate supply of clean, good-looking linen, in good repair, properly folded, and properly presented for use by nursing to serve predetermined functions in accordance with established use policies and procedures in sufficient quantity to meet normal fluctuations in demand. The system should have continuous, constructive input from nursing. It should include all aspects of service, from the linen mix itself to the manner in which each item should be used.

The linen service department should always have data available to determine whether the user areas are following their own policies and procedures. In addition, every effort should be made to pinpoint linen misuse and loss.

For many years the efficiency of the laundry has been measured on a cost-per-pound basis. This has led some laundry managers to allow unnecessary increases in poundage because it reduces the cost per pound, making the operation "more efficient." If a hospital has 100,000 patient days, the cost for processing laundry is 28 cents per pound; if it uses 18 pounds of linen per patient day, the cost per patient day will be $5.04. The laundry manager in this hospital will be reluctant to reduce consumption to 12 pounds per patient day (which is closer to where it should be) because the cost per pound would increase.

If the cost per pound increased to 33 cents as a result of this reduction in poundage, the cost per patient day will be $3.96—a $108,000 annual savings. Clearly, the laundry manager's reluctance to reduce consumption would not be in the best interest of the institution. Cost per patient day is the only accurate way to measure the efficiency and effectiveness of a linen service because it requires a balance between the cost per pound and the level of consumption.

A hospital linen service system consists of two interrelated functions: (1) the laundry and (2) the linen service. Over the years, hospitals have concentrated a majority of their management efforts in the laundry, with limited attention to the linen service. This has resulted in an inordinate concern for laundry productivity and for the cost of producing a pound of clean linen.

When a hospital is confronted with a linen service problem, it usually blames the laundry. The laundry manager, in turn, points the finger at the inability to produce clean linen fast enough. This usually results in the purchase of new and more automated equipment. Hospitals have spent thousands of dollars on new equipment, only to find that their linen service problems remained.

In recent years the linen problems in the nation's hospitals have grown increasingly complex. Some hospitals have endeavored to resolve these problems by joining with other institutions to build central laundries, others have opted for commercial service, and many continue to operate in-house laundries. The following sections give the material manager and/or administrator an overview of the laundry/linen service system to provide direction for problem solving and to make it possible to avoid the pitfalls encountered by so many others.

PHYSICAL PLANT PARAMETERS

For hospitals that operate in-house laundries, the laundry itself is an important part of a total linen service system. The material manager and/ or administrator in charge of the linen service function should have a basic understanding of the physical plant parameters involved.

Equipment Layout and Workflow

The workflow in a hospital laundry can follow several configurations. The most common are the straight line, the U-shaped, and the L-shaped. The flow should progress from the soil sorting and/or counting area to the washers (or washer/extractors), to the extractors (if extraction is separate from the washers), to the dryers, to the ironers, to the tumble dry fold area, and to the delivery preparation area.

Throughout the flow pattern there should be space to store work in process. The laundry should be well lighted and well ventilated. Surfaces should be clean and finished so that they can be cleaned easily. Walls, ceiling, and equipment should be free of lint. The space should be sprinklered. The floor should be smooth, free of standing water, and slip-proof.

With reference to the workflow, some of the generally accepted physical plant concepts are unfounded. First, the Joint Commission on Accreditation of Hospitals (JCAH) does not require that there be a wall between the soil room and the rest of the laundry; instead, it requires a "functional separation." The soil area must be maintained under a negative air pressure to prevent the movement of contaminated air to clean areas. Some states require a wall; if that is the case, the JCAH will accept the tougher standard.

Second, pass-through equipment is not required by any licensing or accreditation body. Many of the washers or washer/extractors that cause the work to pass through a wall from soil to clean are more costly, more difficult to load and

unload, and more labor intensive. As a result, they will not survive an objective cost/benefit analysis.

Finally, the construction of an air-conditioned separate linen room at the end of the process is superfluous. There is no need for a separate room. The delivery preparation can be accomplished at the end of the process with "shelves on wheels" or fixed shelving. This makes this process easier to supervise and the laundry less costly to construct and operate.

The workflow in a laundry can be evaluated by looking for the following problems:

1. build-ups of work in specific areas throughout the day
2. areas where the clean and soiled linen move in close proximity to each other
3. hallways full of soiled or clean linen
4. a laundry so crowded with work in process that straight-line travel from point to point is impossible.

Equipment Selection

Many types of equipment can be used to process hospital work. These fall into three groups. First, there are conventional washers and separate extractors. Some of these washers "dump" to make unloading easier. Others turn straight up to load and straight down to unload, making both loading and unloading easier. A hospital can select squeeze extractors, which rely on pressure to remove excess water, or centrifugal extractors, which use centrifugal force to do the same job. Conventional washers and separate extractors lend themselves to the use of overhead monorail systems to load and unload the equipment and to transport the work among the washers, extractors, and dryers.

The second major type is the washer-extractor. This washes and extracts in the same machine. Because of the high RPMs involved, these machines must be more substantial than a conventional washer and require vibration isolation mounts or a solid cement foundation. A washer-extractor can cause structural problems if it is located above the ground floor and/or is located near an area that cannot stand vibration (such as the laboratory).

There are two types of washer-extractors: end loading and side loading. An end-loading machine loads through the end of the cylinder. Because the centrifugal force is not against the doors, this type of machine can withstand higher RPMs in the extract mode. However, it is more difficult to load. Side-loading machines load through the side of the cylinder, the centrifugal force is against the door, and they will not withstand extremely high extraction speeds as well as an end loader. However, they are easier to load and unload.

Washer-extractors are not as conducive to material handling equipment options as conventional washers and separate extractors. In recent years, however, manufacturers have developed unloading washer-extractors that tilt to facilitate loading and unloading, along with various methods to automate those processes. These improvements make the washer-extractor much more efficient from a labor standpoint.

The final equipment concept is the tunnel washer, which washes, extracts, and dries the linen in the same machine using a tunnel process. In recent years, batch-type machines, which process work in separate batches, have gained popularity over the continuous-type machine, which handles linen in a continuous rope-type manner. Batch-type machines move discrete batches through the wash, extract, and dry processes. Many such machines control the processing of each batch with a microcomputer.

The rest of the production process is the same (except for tunnel washers, which include the dryers). Some work processed in centrifugal extractors or in washer-extractors can be flat-ironed without removing more water in a dryer (called conditioning). In any laundry, some of the work must be fully dried before folding.

There are three types of dryers: gas fired, oil fired, and steam heated. Gas generally is considered the most efficient, followed by oil, then steam. The choice of dryer usually is dictated by the fuel available, and its price. Most dryers can have gas/oil burners for situations where only an interruptible gas rate is available. Steam dryers impose a heavy demand on the steam-generating equipment.

For many years all ironers were steam heated; today, ironers heated by both gas and oil are available. These alternate fuel ironers can be of real value in a situation where steam-generating capacity is a problem or when a new laundry is being planned to operate without such equipment. There is a continuing debate concerning the efficiency of oil vs. steam:

1. A hospital that has marginal steam-generating capacity may find oil-heated equipment preferable.
2. A hospital may be able to operate on low-pressure steam if it does not use steam-heated ironers. In some areas of the country this means that the boiler does not require around-the-clock supervision.
3. Superheated oil can be too hot, will melt polyester, and can generally disrupt ironer performance.
4. An oil-heated ironer is costlier if steam is available because the oil heater must be purchased in addition to the ironer.

As to folding equipment, many folding and feeding concepts have been proved. Folders and folder/cross-folders can be used with work that has been ironed. Stackers automatically stack the folded work. Automatic feeders can be used to feed the work into the ironers with a minimum of labor. Quality grading devices will reject stains and tears at the folder when they are spotted at the feed end.

Before purchasing a complex folder or feeder, a hospital should evaluate the capabilities of its maintenance department. This equipment is complex both mechanically and electronically and requires daily preventive maintenance. Every manufacturer has maintenance schools that can be helpful to those responsible for keeping this complex equipment functional.

As to folding work that has been fully dried, there are several considerations. Reliable automatic folders can fold towels, patient gowns, blankets, and spreads automatically. Any laundry that processes more than 1,000 pounds an hour should have one of these. In addition, some type of lift aide should be installed to minimize the bending generally associated with folding small pieces from a cart.

Purchasing Considerations

When selecting equipment for a laundry, a material manager or administrator should keep the following concepts in mind:

1. Equipment purchases should never be based solely on the performance or capacity claims of the manufacturer or distributor. The prospective purchaser should visit other installations and endeavor to collect performance data.
2. The problems that confront most hospital laundries can be divided between linen systems (such as inventory levels and delivery systems) and equipment. The purchase and installation of new equipment will not resolve the system problems.
3. Hospitals are prone to gravitate toward romantic equipment concepts. This has given rise to complex automation. Before opting for some of the more complex concepts, the material manager and/or administrator must consider reliability, the long-term effectiveness of the equipment, and the capabilities of the hospital maintenance staff.
4. Hospitals considering the more expensive equipment concepts should ascertain whether or not the projected operating cost savings (labor, utilities, and supplies) will exceed the increase in debt service (or opportunity cost) and depreciation.

When selecting equipment, the material manager and/or administrator should remember the purpose and definition of the laundry and quality linen service described at the start of this chapter. If there are no scrub pants in surgery, surgeons are not going to be impressed by the fact that the hospital has a highly automated laundry.

Energy Efficiency

In recent years there have been many advances in energy efficiency in the laundry. The hospital should make every effort to gather reliable data from an operating laundry on energy-efficient machines for every processing area. As noted, manufacturers' claims can be misleading because they are based on optimum operating conditions, which may not be applicable in a particular laundry.

Several proved energy management concepts deserve mention. First, there is the "open" hot water system. This system saves energy because it levels out the energy required to heat water. It stores hot water in an insulated tank and recirculates it to the washers, at constant pressure, via a series of pumps. This system does not rely on the pressure in the street to provide water to the washers.

The second is the waste water heat reclaimer. It can be installed in conjunction with an open hot water system. This utilizes the residual heat in the waste water to preheat the incoming cold water before sending it to the hot water storage tank. Depending on the cost of the fuel required to heat water and the amount of water used, such a reclaimer can pay for itself in less than three years. Third, dryer manufacturers have developed devices that recirculate any heated air that is not laden with lint. This optional extra can reduce the fuel cost for dryers by 20 to 30 percent.

In addition to these energy-saving options, there are many other devices on the market: boiler stack economizers, superefficient gas water heaters, dryer air heat reclaimers, and water reclamation systems, among others. Each of these has pros and cons and must be evaluated carefully. There is no all-inclusive answer.

Finally, energy efficiency can be greatly improved through intelligent management:

- All of the steam pipes and hot water pipes should be properly insulated.
- All steam leaks should be fixed.
- The water level switches in each washer should be operative.

- The wash chemistry should be properly conceived.
- All makeup air heaters should be set to recirculate the heated air during the off hours.
- The hot water temperature should not exceed 165°F.
- The ironer traps should be properly installed and maintained.
- The dryer duct work and lint collectors should be cleaned regularly.
- Steam should not be used to heat the water in the washers unless absolutely necessary.
- The steam-generating equipment should be shut off during off hours if possible.

Another common management problem that reduces energy efficiency is the laundry that operates over extended hours on a daily basis. If the operating hours can be condensed, significant energy savings will result.

This section has addressed workflow, equipment layout, equipment selection, and energy efficiency. In each of these areas the capital expenditures are high and the risks are great. The construction of a new laundry never has solved all linen service problems. If this has been portrayed differently, hospitals should proceed with caution. A hospital laundry should not be the place for an equipment manufacturer to field test the latest equipment concept. The workflow and equipment selection process is wrought with pitfalls.

To be effective the laundry must be a part of a total linen service system. In most cases, decisions on linen service are more important than those on the equipment. In a nutshell, a material manager or administrator who builds a reliable and reasonably efficient laundry with enough capacity to meet the needs of the system easily will have created a successful laundry.

LAUNDRY MANAGEMENT

Most persons in hospital administration are familiar with the primary parameters of performance for laundries. The next section addresses some of the gray areas.

Productivity

The literature is full of examples of laundries that produce 100 pounds per productive labor hour. The key phrase is "productive labor hour" and there is considerable disagreement as to who constitute "productive workers." Some laundry managers omit those who do lead work, delivery preparation, and soil sort, as well as everyone related to management. Other laundry managers include one or more of these classifications in the calculation of pounds per labor hour.

A better way to calculate productivity is to include all laundry employees. This includes everyone on the laundry and linen service payroll—the manager, supervisors, lead workers, maintenance personnel, soil sort, delivery preparation, and even the truck drivers (in the case of an offsite laundry). All of the mending, marking, and inspection functions also should be included.

In an in-hospital laundry, maintenance and housekeeping personnel usually are assigned to their respective departments, much of the clerical work is accomplished in accounting, and there are no truck drivers. A highly productive in-hospital laundry will produce 40 to 50 clean pounds per paid labor hour. This calculation includes everyone on the laundry payroll. Larger in-hospital laundries process more than 1,000 pounds of linen an hour and may reach productivity levels greater than 50 pounds per paid labor hour.

Most off-site laundries are larger and the economies of scale enable them to be more efficient. They should produce 50 to 70 pounds per paid labor hour, even if maintenance, housekeeping, and office personnel are included. Some large off-site laundries will exceed even that rate.

The pound per paid labor hour calculation is only a general indicator of productivity. As noted, this figure can be misleading. The correct way to determine staffing requirements is to subject each processing department to a detailed analysis based on production standards related to pounds per operator hour or pieces per operator hour. These standards will determine the exact hours required to staff each position. The proper use of partial full-time equivalents (FTEs) to a large extent will determine overall efficiency. Once a departmental productivity level has been determined, the actual productivity should be monitored on a regular basis so that problems can be discovered and corrected in a timely manner.

Employee Morale

Employee morale is another laundry area that is not easy to measure. Here again some rules of thumb can be useful. An annual employee turnover rate of more than 25 percent usually means problems, so does average daily absenteeism of more than 5 percent of the total work force. Unusual absenteeism on paydays, on Fridays and Mondays, and on days immediately preceding or following holidays means trouble.

Every hospital or free-standing laundry should have a formal grievance procedure. An unusual number of grievances can indicate problems, whether the complaints are real or imagined. Good first-line managers should be able to resolve most problems before they reach the written grievance stage.

Managers can learn a good deal about workers' morale from their general appearance and demeanor. If the workers are bright, clean, and happy, their morale usually is good. If they appear dull, listless, grumpy, and somewhat disheveled, there is a good chance that labor problems will appear.

It goes without saying that constant union problems indicate workers suffer morale problems. Indicators of problems are clear: (1) if the workers are nonunion and there is regular union activity and (2) if they are unionized and there are constant union difficulties. Unions do not like constant unrest any more than does management.

Preventive Maintenance

This area often is overlooked. Many smaller in-house laundries do not have full-time maintenance personnel and do little (if any) preventive servicing. Even larger in-house laundries and central laundries tend to overlook preventive maintenance—and they have full-time persons assigned.

Every hospital laundry, regardless of size, should have a preventive maintenance program for the processing equipment. The program should consist of lubrication, adjustment, and calibration at recommended intervals—daily, weekly, monthly, semiannually and annually. A program should be created and implemented for every piece of equipment. The program should be in writing, and a system of paper work should be created to allow management to continuously check on the status of the maintenance.

As for staffing, maintenance personnel should be designated and trained to work in the laundry. Every laundry equipment manufacturer conducts periodic maintenance seminars, which should be attended by all such personnel.

To ensure success, maintenance personnel should be assigned to the laundry so that the regular preventive servicing can be performed on a routine basis. If this takes one worker four hours, its staffing basis should be one person, four hours a day. Additional time or staffing should be based on experience. Regular preventive maintenance should reduce the number of equipment problems but additional help will be needed from time to time. When the routine preventive work approaches eight hours a day, a full-time maintenance person should be assigned.

Another area often overlooked is creation and maintenance of an adequate stock of replacement parts. To support laundry maintenance, the parts most likely to wear out or fail on each piece of equipment should be stocked. The manufacturer or distributor can assist in determining which parts to keep on hand. Usually, a wire cage in the maintenance shop will suffice for parts storage; of course, all parts and tools should be kept under lock and key.

Many hospitals feel they cannot afford to assign maintenance personnel to the laundry on a full-time basis. A quick check of the in-house maintenance cost (plus the cost of outside repairs and parts) should shed some light on this issue. A properly conceived (full-time or part-time) effort will eliminate a majority of the current outside repair costs as well as the overtime resulting from equipment that is out of service because of breakdowns.

Quality of the Work

The quality of the finished work can be assessed visually. If there is a problem, one thing will stand out: the loss of whiteness of polyester-cotton sheets. Many hospital laundries accept sheets and pillowcases that are a dull blue-gray as one of the drawbacks of such sheets. This does not have to be the case. Properly conceived wash formulas will maintain a satisfactory degree of whiteness in polyester-cotton goods.

The need for mending and/or rewash should be determined as items are processed. Carts should be positioned throughout the laundry to accumulate linen that must be rewashed or mended. The ironer(s) should be outfitted with quality grading devices to help spot repairs and stains before the merchandise is folded mechanically.

On quality of work, standards of acceptance should be set so that laundry personnel know when a particular item should be repaired, rewashed, or discarded. Detailed records should be kept on such items and should reflect both the number of pounds and the number of pieces involved. These data should be expressed as a percentage of the total being processed.

Lint can be an enormous problem in a hospital, especially in surgery and delivery. Lint is a normal part of laundry operation. Too much lint, however, may indicate that the linen is disintegrating prematurely. This may mean a problem with water levels or with the wash chemistry. Lint can be a fire hazard. To prevent fire, and to keep the linen as free of lint as possible, the entire laundry should be cleaned daily. Some laundries feel daily cleaning is too expensive but cleanliness is one of the most important aspects of sound hospital laundry management. While it is not necessary to clean the laundry's upper extremities daily (this can be done weekly or even monthly), the equipment and the floor must be cleaned daily without fail.

A lint problem is not always caused by the laundry process. Some hospital products are made from short-staple yarn products that create lint as they are being used. If this is the case, the fabric should be changed. This problem is particularly acute with absorbent towels used in surgery and delivery. All hospital linen should be soft and as absorbent as possible. Problems result in an abnormally high number of linen-related rashes, bed sores, and general patient discomfort. These problems usually can be corrected by modifying the wash chemistry.

To help ensure good quality hospital linen, every laundry should presort the soiled linen. This removes all foreign matter, separates the linen by color and type of soil, segregates the wash categories so that each can be washed with the proper formula, and prepares the linen for proper flow through the finish departments.

Protection Against Contamination

All hospitals are concerned with the proper handling of isolation linen. This linen should be double-bagged in the patient room, marked properly, and transported to the laundry unopened. In the laundry this linen should be washed and extracted before being returned to the soil room for proper sorting. This can be done easily using a water-soluble isolation bag. If a water-soluble bag is not used, the laundry personnel will be exposed to contaminated linen.

Employees who work in the soil room should wear a protective gown to minimize contact with their personal clothing, wash their hands and face, and remove the protective gown before leaving the area. Under no circumstances should soil room employees be allowed to work in a clean area without washing and without removing the protective gown.

Recent studies indicate that the major cross-contamination problem in a laundry is not airborne bacteria but actual touching. For this reason every precaution should be taken to make sure that the soil room personnel do not contaminate themselves, other employees, or the clean linen by carrying bacteria on their persons into the clean areas.

40-Hour Work Week

Even though a hospital operates seven days a week, that is not a valid reason for operating the laundry more than 40 hours a week. Some laundries work six or seven days a week because of linen inventory shortages or inadequate equipment capacity. Sometimes, however, the six-day operation—and considerable overtime—results from improper production scheduling.

To determine whether a particular laundry can operate on a 40-hour basis, the annual workload requirement (soiled weight) should be divided by 1,950 hours (7.5 productive hours a day, 5 days a week, 52 weeks a year). This will determine the average hourly workload requirement. If the laundry is capable of producing this much work, plus 20 percent (to allow for peak loads), there is enough equipment capacity to operate on a 40-hour week. If adding another dryer will make it possible to cut the work week from six days to five, it will be paid for quickly.

On the other hand, if the laundry is short of processing capacity in more than one area, or if space is limited, it may be necessary to operate more than 40 hours a week. This can be determined by completing a simple cost/benefit analysis.

Production scheduling is more difficult to evaluate. There should be a smooth and even flow of work, in-process work should be stored in front of the major processing departments, different categories of work should be processed each hour in proportion to that type's relationship to the total requirement, and no equipment should be allowed to sit idle waiting for work.

The biggest single problem facing hospital laundries today is inventory shortages. Many laundries operate six days a week, or incur heavy overtime cost, because there is not enough linen in circulation. This shortage does not have to occur throughout the linen mix. If several key items are in short supply, the problems will be acute, and overtime or extra-day operation will result.

Regular Inventories and Piece Counts

There is no way to operate an efficient and effective hospital laundry without either: (1) conducting regular total system inventories or (2) counting the soiled linen and returning it to the use areas on an even-exchange basis. Every laundry should maintain perpetual records on the linen sent to every use area. This should be accomplished on the basis of pieces, not poundage. Different sizes of the same item should be treated as completely different articles. This kind of perpetual recordkeeping system will make it easy to determine the average daily consumption for every item processed in the last 30, 60, or 90 days. The consumption level is based on a seven-day week.

Many hospital managers feel it is too expensive to maintain perpetual piece counts, but this is not as costly as it appears. The person who makes the deliveries has to count the linen in order to complete the delivery; if the amount sent to each use area each day is recorded, the piece count can be maintained easily.

To evaluate the adequacy of the amount of linen in circulation in the absence of a soil count, periodic total system inventories must be conducted. This requires the cooperation of many persons, including nursing. A cutoff time and date should be established for the collection of soil; all of the clean linen in use should be counted immediately after the cutoff; and the rest should be counted as it comes out of the laundry. When the inventory is complete, the number of every item in use should be compared with the average daily consumption for that item over the previous 30 days. For an in-house laundry operating five days a week, the inventory level for each item should be five to six times the average daily consumption. An eight- to ten-day supply of the lesser used items may be required. This applies to many of the specialty items used in surgery.

The amount of linen required is determined by making the following calculation when the laundry ceases operation on Friday afternoon, when the following must be in use:

1 day on the use areas
½ day clean in process
½ day soil in process
1 day for Saturday
1 day for Sunday
<u>1</u> day for Monday
5 days total

If the hospital is being served by an off-site laundry that operates five days a week, there should be seven times the average daily consumption of each item in use. In this instance, a 10- to 12-day supply of lesser used items will be required. If the in-house or off-site laundry operates more than five days a week, the inventory levels suggested here can be reduced by one day for every additional day the laundry operates.

This type of inventory versus piece-count analysis is essential. It determines accurately how much new linen should be put into use and determines a rate of issue for every item. This enables management to put new linen in use, based on this rate of issue, between inventories. In addition, the rate of issue can be translated easily into new linen requirements for the purchasing department.

Linen replacement cost typically is measured on a cost-per-pound basis. As mentioned, the greater the poundage, the better the linen replacement cost looks. A better measure is the replacement cost per patient day. A hospital that uses 12 pounds a patient day, with 6 cents a pound in replacement expense, will incur a cost of 72 cents a patient day. This is based on linen that wears out normally, plus what disappears. A laundry with normal wearout in excess of 25 cents per pound, or a hospital with misuse in excess of 50 cents per patient day, has a definite linen replacement problem.

For a laundry to operate effectively, an adequate linen inventory level is critical. If there is a replacement problem, inventories should be taken quarterly; where replacement cost is more reasonable, semiannual inventories will suffice. Based on the inventory piece-count analysis, new linen should be fed into the system weekly, based on the replacement budget. In the purchasing department, this rate of issue can be used to arrange annual contracts with textile vendors. If these contracts call for periodic drop shipments of linen, based again on the rate of issue, the new linen inventory level can be reduced drastically.

Numerous linen service systems effectively eliminate the need for troublesome inventories. These systems are based on a soil count and delayed even-exchange to the use areas. They require that new linen be added to the inventory level at each use area to correct shortages. The laundry, of course, replaces normal wearout. These systems also allow for use-area credits, based on the return of surplus linen to the laundry.

Cold-Water Washing and No-Iron Linen

In view of the national concern for energy conservation, many hospital laundries are turning to cold-water washing and/or no-iron linen. Cold-water washing uses chemicals rather than water temperature for proper bacteria kill. This, of course, saves the energy required to heat water.

No-iron linen ordinarily would be finished in a flat iron but to eliminate the need for ironing, it has been treated with resins to "set" the finish. However, the resins are destroyed if the temperature of the wash water rises above 140°F. Once the resins have been destroyed, the linen loses its no-iron properties and looks soiled and wrinkled when in use.

No-iron linen saves energy because it lowers wash temperatures and eliminates the need for a flat iron. Because this linen can be processed in a simple wash-extract-dry-fold process, it is popular in hotels and motels. The flat iron is expensive to purchase and operate and requires substantial floor space.

With regard to the acceptability of no-iron linen and cold-water washing in a health care facility, controversy surrounds the requirement that hospital laundries wash in 180°F water. The Department of Health and Human Services (HHS) requires that hospital laundries have 180°F water available as needed. This standard may be lowered to 160°F. Many state health departments require wash temperatures to reach or exceed 160°F.

The basis for the present standard is the fact that most authorities feel that proper bacteria kill can be accomplished only through a combination of high wash-water temperatures, time, and wash chemicals. Of course, those who support cold-water washing and no-iron linen are doing a considerable amount of bacteriological testing in an effort to have the standards modified. Laundry managers should follow this debate closely, as it will have significant impact on future cost-containment efforts.

Cost Per Pound

The overriding concern for cost per pound can cause interesting discrepancies in the number of pounds processed. Most laundries maintain all production records based on soil weight. Some load the washers without weighing the linen and base the weight on the rated capacity of the machine. This invariably results in inflated workload numbers because of the amount of lightweight fabrics now in use and equipment manufacturers' tendency to rate the capacity of their washers based on fully loading the machine with 100 percent cotton goods.

The subject of linen consumption is controversial in hospitals. Those that consume 20 or more pounds of linen per patient day invariably point to their teaching programs, large surgical load, and large outpatient load to justify this rate. The fact remains that there are large and complex acute care hospitals that use only 12 pounds per patient day—and they have large outpatient and surgical loads. The difference between 12 pounds per patient day in one hospital and 20 pounds in a comparable institution is the realization that the cost of linen service should be measured by cost per patient day, not by a super-low cost per pound. This has led to increased efforts to measure consumption and control excess consumption and waste.

Analysis by cost per patient day also has caused hospitals to realize that linen service is more than an efficient laundry and that the cost-

containment efforts often are more effective if management concentrates on the nonlaundry aspects of the system.

LINEN SERVICE MANAGEMENT

This final section includes an analysis of management factors that pertain almost entirely to the operational elements of the linen service system. This area has been somewhat neglected in the concern for productivity and efficiency. These comments pertain to hospitals served by central and commercial laundries as well as those that continue to operate in-house laundries.

The Linen Mix

In most hospitals, the laundry management team has little or no input into the decisions concerning the mix of linens and garments it must process. In some hospitals, each department decides which items it uses, and these articles are purchased and sent to the laundry for processing; in other hospitals, purchasing makes these decisions.

In the nation's hospitals it is not unusual to find 100 to 200 different linen and garment items in a single institution. Some operating suites alone use more than 50 different articles. In those hospitals, the various departments exert tremendous influence, resulting in several different items that serve the same function from department to department. A good example is the frequent use of green scrub wear in the surgical suite and white scrub wear in delivery.

In addition to duplication, many hospitals continue to use items constructed of fabrics that are heavy and difficult to process. Soil bags of 100 percent cotton weigh considerably more than polyester/cotton bags of the same size, are difficult to process, and do not wear as well. Although many hospitals no longer use explosive anesthetics, and in spite of the fact that polyester-cotton blends have been proved to meet conductivity standards, some continue to use 100 percent cotton scrub wear and scrub gowns even though these traditional fabrics shrink, fade, cause lint, and require ironing.

To prevent such problems and to deal with the available alternatives, each hospital should create and maintain a linen service committee. The committee should consist of members from nursing, surgery, delivery, purchasing, the laundry, and administration. One of its purposes should be to streamline and maintain the linen mix. Members should agree on a single item to accommodate every linen function; whenever possible, different functions should be combined to be served by a single item.

When reviewing the linen mix, the laundry's capacity and any processing limitations should be considered. If there is an ironer capacity problem, for instance, every effort should be made to select items that can be tumble dried and folded; if there is a dryer capacity problem, lightweight, easy-to-dry fabrics should be used. Few hospitals are complex enough to warrant a linen mix containing more than 100 items, including those for surgery, so every effort should be made to keep the number below 100.

Once the linen mix has been streamlined and the final purchase specifications written, all problems should be funneled through the linen service committee, which should strive to maintain the integrity of the mix—one item for every function. As new products are introduced, the committee should conduct the evaluations and determinations for inclusion in the mix.

The Use of Disposables

When viewing the total linen mix with regard to disposables, there appear to be two major reasons for converting to such products: (1) reduced cost and (2) enhanced aseptic technique. Although these areas tend to run together at times, one of these reasons generally is used to justify a conversion from a reusable to a disposable product. The following sections look at each area separately.

Cost is probably the biggest problem area because the expense of the reusable usually is divided between laundry and one or two other hospital departments. This is further compli-

cated by the fact that laundry cost may not be broken down by the piece. If the cost of processing a pound of linen is 27 cents, that figure pertains to many items. Some of these are heavy and easy to process, such as a laundry bag; others are light and difficult to process, such as a face mask or laparotomy sponge. To pinpoint the cost of processing a reusable linen item, that figure must be estimated accurately. This, of course, must include the cost of replacing each item periodically.

The cost argument over reusables and disposables will go on forever. In most cases, studies will justify whatever course of action appears to be appropriate at the time. However, cost should not be the only factor considered.

Some items, such as masks, shoe covers, and scrub hats, are more trouble to process than they are worth. They disappear quickly, get lost in the production process, and tangle easily. These items should be disposables in any laundry.

Another disposable factor involves products that improve aseptic technique. The best example is disposable surgical drapes. It has been demonstrated that a draping technique that prevents strikethrough is superior to one that allows this to occur. All of the disposable draping material on the market is more impervious to strikethrough than the traditional muslin drapes. However, tight weave mercerized cotton drape now on the market also prevents strikethrough, although it is more expensive than muslin.

In reviewing the feasibility of disposable drape programs, the hospital sometimes overlooks the benefits to the laundry:

1. elimination of difficult handling problem
2. increased wash capacity for other work
3. reduced wash chemical costs
4. increased dryer capacity for other work
5. increased ironer capacity for other work
6. elimination of enormous inspection and repair problems
7. great reduction in linen replacement cost
8. elimination of user complaints about lint.

Whether or not these benefits are offset by the cost of the disposables is debatable. One fact is irrefutable, however: processing surgery and delivery drapes in a laundry is difficult, time consuming, and costly. Any laundry will be much better able to serve the hospital if a disposable drape program is adopted as part of the standard linen mix.

Disposable vs. Reusable: Cost Analysis

On the surface the expense of disposable drapes appears prohibitive, in part because the cost of the program is hidden in so many areas. To complete an objective cost analysis, the expense of the present program must be determined accurately. Since disposables cause a significant cash outlay, the cost of reusables should include only cash expenditures.

To determine the cost of a reusable drape program the following elements should be included:

1. The cost of purchasing and warehousing the reusable components.
2. The cost of manufacturing or altering some of these components in the sewing department.
3. The cost of processing these components in the laundry. The fact that it costs at least 50 percent more to process surgery or delivery linen, compared with patient room linen, must be considered. Slower wash formulas, greater wash chemical expense, increased rewash, longer drying time, slower ironing speeds, more complex folding, and more careful inspection all contribute to this added cost. The full cost of operating the laundry also must be considered, including maintenance, utility, housekeeping, and administrative allocations.
4. The cost of light table inspection, delinting, and pinhole repair.
5. The cost of folding, assembly, and wrapping.
6. The cost of disposable wrappers, plastic wrap, autoclave tape, and sterilization indicators.
7. The cost of autoclaving the packs.
8. The cost of warehousing the finished product.

9. The cost of resterilizing the packs that become outdated without being used.

If these costs are determined accurately, the differential between reusable and disposable drape programs will narrow considerably.

One last thought: If disposable gowns are included in the drape packs, the cost of the disposable program will be prohibitive. If the hospital utilizes a modern nonpermeable front surgeon's gown, there is no benefit to be gained from using a nonwoven gown. To make the program feasible from a cost viewpoint, the laundry should continue to process surgeons' gowns, absorbent towels, and instrument wrappers.

Pounds or Pieces

To provide the maximum potential for cost containment, every hospital should record the number of pieces sent to each linen use area each day. This should cover every item in the linen mix, including different sizes of the same item. If exchange cart or quota systems are used, the recordkeeping should make allowances for the unused items that remain on the cart or in the linen room before the level is restored to the quota.

To make the use-area delivery data meaningful, the number of each piece consumed should be divided by some measure of workload for each area. In patient areas the number of items used per patient day is meaningful; in the surgical suite, the consumption per patient visit; in the emergency room, the consumption per patient visit; and so on.

In hospitals with computer support, a computer analysis of the number of pieces used per measure of workload in every department can be a useful cost-containment tool. This is pursued further in the following sections.

Linen Use Policies and Procedures

Every hospital interested in cost containment in linen service should create, maintain, and enforce a set of use policies and procedures for all departments. The linen service committee should be responsible for the establishment of these policies and procedures. A good rule is that no linen item can be added until a policy and procedure has been adopted pertaining to its use.

Linen policies and procedures should pertain initially to the major use items. Should all the linen in the room be changed each day? Should the top sheet be moved to the bottom and the bottom sheet changed? Should the thermal spread blanket be changed daily, when it is dirty, or on discharge? How many towels should be placed in the bathroom? Should unused linen be stored in patient rooms? Should surgery personnel change scrub clothes when they leave and return to the surgical suite or should they wear a cover coat? Should surgical personnel use the same cover coat all day or take a clean one each time they leave the suite? These are the kinds of questions that must be answered in preparing linen policies and procedures.

Few hospitals create, maintain, and enforce such policies and procedures. In a majority, linen has always been regarded as a free commodity; more has always been better, and more linen has always meant better patient care.

To enforce the policies and procedures described, the number of pieces consumed by unit of workload by use area must be analyzed. If the policy states that the thermal spread blanket should be changed when it is soiled or upon discharge, and a particular nursing unit consumes 1.5 such blankets per patient day, it is obvious that this use area is not following the hospital policies. Nursing administration can be alerted to this fact and appropriate measures taken to correct the problem. The end result: cost containment.

Hospitals that have implemented policies, procedures, and systems to monitor consumption levels have realized significant savings. Many economies result from the fact that these measures have made nursing personnel aware of the cost of linen service.

Control of Linen Misuse

Many hospitals in every area of the nation suffer from rapidly accelerating linen replacement costs. As noted earlier, any hospital with a linen misuse cost that exceeds 50 cents per patient day has a replacement cost problem.

In some hospitals, linen theft is not a crime, it is a fringe benefit. If linen theft goes undetected, it will grow quickly. An employee who has stolen linen successfully once will steal more, and other employees will begin stealing. The high cost of domestic linen, combined with the greater acceptability at home of institutional linen, has caused this problem to snowball in recent years.

To curtail this kind of problem a hospital must take definite and unusually strong steps. Everyone must be made aware of the theft problem. This includes the patients. The hospital should communicate the fact that linen theft is a crime, not a fringe benefit, and that persons caught stealing will be prosecuted. All employees, especially physicians, should be made aware of the fact that garments should not be taken home for processing and convenience. Polyester-cotton scrub wear is a big problem because it has become popular as a fashion garment.

To back up the hospital's effort to stop linen misuse, the security program can be directed more toward curtailing theft. Closed-circuit TV has proved successful; all employee parcels leaving the hospital should be searched; suspicious off-hour activity in the parking lots should be investigated; and all exits should be checked regularly during off hours. Although it seems unlikely, there is a good market for stolen linen. Theft is not always limited to a couple of items here and there; wholesale hospital linen theft operations are becoming commonplace.

Some hospitals have difficulty justifying the cost of a closed-circuit TV system and are worried about the labor relations problems that can result from searching all employee packages. These measures must withstand an objective cost/benefit analysis. If a hospital has 100,000 patient days per year and the cost of linen misuse is $1.50 per patient day, the potential savings approach $100,000 a year. This usually warrants the added cost of closed-circuit TV and the labor relations risk.

All of these security efforts are universal in nature and should be a continuing part of any hospital's program. If linen theft problems persist, however, the area or areas where it is occurring must be pinpointed. It does no good to shotgun an entire hospital with security measures if it has 40 or 50 areas that use linen and as many exits and entrances. In such situations, the culprits must be confronted with the fact that the security program has zeroed in on their particular area of activity.

The biggest problem is that it is difficult, if not impossible, to tell where the linen is being stolen. To complicate matters, most linen service systems replace stolen items each day. The only way to pinpoint theft is to count the soiled linen, return it to the use areas on an even-exchange basis, and record new issues to determine which areas require the most new items.

Those are the areas with the major security problems and where security efforts should be centered. Hospitals that have adopted this type of system have found that three or four use areas out of 25 or 30 account for 75 percent or more of the linen replacement costs. Beefed-up security in these trouble areas can pay tremendous dividends.

Mention should be made once again of policies and procedures. Unused linen should never be stored in patient rooms. This is an invitation to patient theft. Few people steal soiled linen. All unused items in a use area should be stored in the linen closet, which should be locked if at all possible. If unlocked, the closet should be under visual supervision from the nurses' station.

Linen Service Systems

There are three types of linen service systems in common use in hospitals today: the nurse requisition, the quota, and the exchange cart. The nurse requisition approach, the oldest, is basically a demand system. At the beginning of each day, the head nurse estimates the needs for that day and requisitions that much linen. This system has little relationship to actual consumption. The problems inherent in a system based on guessing at each day's requirements led to the development of the quota system.

This operates by sending enough linen daily to each use area to meet peak demands. This ensures that a predetermined quantity of linen is present on each area at the beginning of each day. These quotas should be adjusted periodically based on actual experience.

The exchange cart system is basically a quota system. The only difference is the manner in which the use-area inventories are brought up to the quotas. The quota system requires that linen service personnel visit each use area to replace articles on the spot. The exchange cart system requires that the service deliver a full cart and return the partly empty cart to the linen room where it is refilled to the quota for the following day. Because the unused items are returned each day, the exchange cart system requires more linen in use to function effectively.

The quota and the exchange cart systems are superior to nurse requisition because they have some relationship to actual consumption. They replace linen removed from the cart or from the linen closet. "Removed from the cart or from the linen closet" are the key words. If the linen is removed and stored elsewhere, it must be replaced; if it is stolen, it must be replaced. Depending upon the degree of hoarding, misuse, and theft, each of these systems requires the laundry to process and deliver more clean linen each day than it receives soiled, so it must continually place new articles into use.

This is one of the biggest problems facing hospital laundries; it is a particular concern to central laundries and to commercial laundries serving hospitals.

Soiled Linen Counting

There is one system that does not require that the laundry deliver more linen than it receives. This is based on a count of the soiled linen returned to the laundry from each use area. To operate this system, the laundry creates an inventory on each area large enough to handle peak loads. As this linen is soiled, it is placed in soil bags that have been tagged to identify the use area in question.

When this soiled linen arrives in the laundry it is counted and the same amount of linen is returned to that use area the following day. If an area runs out of linen, additional items are requisitioned and placed into its inventory. Using this type of system, a seven-day supply of linen can be counted and returned to each use area in five days. The soiled count can be used to analyze consumption by area and to compare it to the established policies and procedures. The records on new linen added to the system can be analyzed to pinpoint misuse and/or theft problems.

A soiled count delayed system of even exchange such as this closes the circle between linen deliveries and actual consumption. It can be an effective cost-containment tool because it analyzes and pinpoints consumption and replacement problems. It allows the hospital to budget replacement cost by use area and to compare actual experience to that figure.

The single biggest problem with such a program is that most laundry managers feel that it costs too much to count the soil and administrators feel that there is a significant health threat to the people who do the counting. Laundries that have implemented soil count programs have effectively refuted both of these arguments. If a hospital is sorting the soiled linen, the employees are not exposed to the soil to a greater extent if they also count the soil. Although it costs more to count than simply to sort linen, the saving realized as a result of the management information created by the count has significantly exceeded the extra expense. With regard to possible contamination of the soil count personnel, all isolation linen must be decontaminated by washing it before it is returned to the soil room for counting.

There are many other aspects of linen service systems that are beyond the scope of this writing. Each system has some benefits and some problems that have not been mentioned. Depending on the size and complexity of the hospital, one of these systems, or a combination, can work effectively.

COMPUTER APPLICATIONS

The foregoing sections discuss the benefits of dealing with pieces instead of pounds. To monitor linen use policies and procedures, the number of pieces consumed by a particular use area should be recorded, summarized, then divided by some measure of workload for that area. To control linen replacement cost, hospitals, central laundries, and proprietary laundries increasingly are counting soiled linen. To conduct an effective cost-containment effort, this type of data analysis is essential.

The biggest problem is the enormous amount of data that must be handled. It is time consuming to do it manually, and accuracy is always a problem. Smaller hospitals (fewer than 200 beds) may be able to handle such data manually. All other hospitals will require some kind of data processing assistance.

To make use of data processing equipment, the deliveries or the soil count must be entered and accumulated for a period of time. Most hospitals can readily accumulate use-area data on a monthly basis. At the end of each month the number of pieces delivered to each area can be used to charge that area for linen service for the period. In addition, the number of each item each area used can be divided by the area's workload during the period to reveal consumption per unit of workload. These data then can be used to monitor linen use policies and procedures.

A hospital that spends $3 to $5 per patient day or more for linen service can easily afford some sort of data processing assistance. The data can be accumulated off-line and processed on the hospital computer once a month. These reports can be produced during the off hours. If the hospital is large enough, an onsite microcomputer or minicomputer can be justified. Advances in technology have reduced the cost of computers to the point where a special purpose departmental installation is entirely affordable. It costs no more than some of the laundry equipment and the payback will be quicker.

A discussion of computer applications is not complete without mention of the software required. The software described here is simple and easy to program. The computer merely adds, subtracts, and divides periodically—nothing complex or sophisticated.

When developing software for this type of system there are two problems: (1) the system itself must be conceptually sound and (2) the software and hardware must allow for the enormous amount of data that will be handled. Many computer programmers, after viewing this type of system, assume that it is simple and begin programming without a good understanding of the data accumulation and analysis required. The laundry manager must provide this insight.

LINEN SERVICE DIRECTOR OR LAUNDRY MANAGER

For many years, laundry managers have been talking about their limited role with regard to linen service. Many hospitals split the responsibility by sending clean articles to a linen room administered by another department for distribution to the floors. As a result, some laundry managers never leave the laundry. They are not aware of the problems in the hospital and do not realize how the linen they process is used. Under such circumstances, it is not surprising to find that only a limited number of laundry managers can talk intelligently about control of replacements and reductions in consumption.

To administer a laundry and linen service system, hospitals should be employing linen service directors, not laundry managers. The linen service director should be given the responsibility and authority to operate all facets of the system described here. As to buying new linen, control of that function should remain with the purchasing department. However, the linen service director should help develop the purchasing specifications and participate in establishing new linen inventory requirements and minimum order quantities.

Any hospital with linen service problems that has split responsibilities between the laundry and any other department, or that has a manager who never leaves the laundry, can improve by becoming concerned with the total system. If the laundry manager cannot handle this broadened scope, a linen service director should be employed and placed over the manager. Such a director should have a good understanding of hospital systems and an ability to communicate with all levels of personnel.

Because laundry and linen service cost represents only a small percentage of total hospital expenditures, it is an area often neglected. Certainly it is near the bottom of the totem pole with regard to the rest of the institution. When there is a choice between satisfying the linen service director and most other department heads, that director usually loses. When the money for new construction runs short, the laundry often is the first place to be cut. When a single department is left behind when the rest of the hospital relocates to a new building, it usually is the laundry.

In the past, administration became involved in laundry matters only when there were problems, usually complaints from other departments. Unfortunately, many linen service directors quickly realize that the best way to avoid complaints is to spend money. Any director who can get the linen inventory in circulation up to seven or eight times the average daily usage should not have any service complaints.

The situation regarding laundry and linen service is beginning to change. In many hospitals, this cost is accelerating more rapidly than others. In some hospitals, the cost of replacement has gotten totally out of proportion to that of processing. Hospitals that have contracted for service with a central or commercial laundry are becoming increasingly disenchanted with the cost, the service, or both. These problems have caused more and more administrative involvement in this important but neglected area of hospital operation.

If hospital administration becomes involved with laundry and linen to improve the service and lower the cost, those involved must take the time to understand the problem thoroughly. It looks simple on the surface but it can get complex very quickly. If the ideas presented in this chapter are to be implemented successfully, strong administrative support and understanding are essential.

Appendix 26–A

Alternatives for Linen Service

There are three basic alternatives for service: the in-house laundry, commercial service, or participation in a central laundry. Each has advantages and disadvantages.

IN-HOUSE LAUNDRY

The most popular type of service is the in-house laundry. For many years off-site alternatives did not exist and many older hospitals still operate in-house laundries.

In-house laundries offer a customized service. The linen mix is tailored to the needs of the hospital, many items are custom made, and articles are placed into use for particular departments. In addition, the laundry manager usually is on a first-name basis with most of the key people. This leads to a level of service tailored to the needs of each department.

In many hospitals it is difficult to determine the cost of service from an in-house laundry. The absence of separate utility meters, inaccurate weight records, inappropriate overhead allocations, and incomplete maintenance records all contribute to this problem. In some hospitals, linen distribution and collection is assigned to material management or housekeeping and that factor is not included in operating cost. In other hospitals, some of the linen replacement cost is assigned to the departments and that expense is excluded.

When an in-house laundry manager discusses the cost of operation, it is usually on the basis of cost per pound and includes only the direct costs (labor, fringe benefits, wash chemicals, and linen replacement). The expenses that are not included easily double the direct costs.

If a hospital is interested in calculating the true cost of service of an in-house laundry, the following elements must be considered:

- laundry wages and fringes
- distribution wages and fringes
- seamstress wages and fringes
- wash chemicals
- productive supplies
- in-house maintenance labor
- outside maintenance costs
- maintenance parts and supplies
- utility costs
- linen replacement, normal wearout
- linen replacement, misuse
- administrative overhead (administration, accounting, personnel)
- support overhead (purchasing, housekeeping, maintenance)
- equipment depreciation
- building depreciation.

If possible, the utility costs should be based on separate meters. If this is not possible, they should be based on engineering estimates.

The in-house laundry is a capital-intensive, nonrevenue-producing area. In many hospitals, it occupies valuable floor space next to the elevators on the ground level. It also places major demands on the utility systems. These considerations have caused some hospitals to be constructed without laundries and others to discontinue their in-house operation. A shortage of capital for nonrevenue-producing functions has led hospitals in this direction despite the fact that the off-site alternatives offer less in the way of custom and personalized service.

COMMERCIAL SERVICE

There are two levels of commercial service: wash job and linen supply. Any hospital interested in exploring a commercial service should understand the difference. These commercial laundries usually service two or more hospitals in an area.

The wash job is the most basic level of service. Any laundry that can wash, dry, and iron a sheet can provide service at this level. To implement such a service, the hospital merely contracts to have its linen washed. Sometimes this does not even include mending. Because the level of service is so simple, the laundry does not have to gain an understanding of hospital operation.

Many hospitals prefer wash job service because it allows them to maintain title to the inventory. The biggest disadvantage is that it leaves such a large portion of the total cost in the hospital. To complete the service provided by the laundry, the hospital must:

1. purchase the linen
2. warehouse the linen
3. mark the linen
4. mend the linen
5. prepare the linen for distribution to the floors
6. distribute the clean linen
7. collect the soiled linen
8. manage the service.

In most hospitals, this adds 70 to 100 percent to the cost of the wash job service.

On the other hand, it is important to note that a wash job level of service can be delivered effectively. To accomplish this both the hospital and the laundry must have a clear understanding of the pitfalls:

1. This level of service should never be delivered without mending. The laundry is the only point in the system where the need for mending can be both spotted and accomplished.
2. The hospital must assume responsibility for the level of inventory in use. This must be accomplished by maintaining a perpetual piece count and by conducting total system inventories. The laundry should

assist with these inventories. If the laundry operates five days a week, the hospital should maintain seven times the average daily consumption of high-use items. This level should be increased to 12 for lesser used items.
3. If the laundry that provides the wash job service is astute, it can encourage the hospital to use standard linen. This will allow it to process the linen effectively.
4. The laundry should endeavor to finish each item in a standard manner. These efforts are in the best interests of the hospitals being served and should not be resisted.

If a hospital elects to pursue this level of service, material management and housekeeping officials should be wary of low bids. Some commercial laundries do not have significant experience serving hospitals and underestimate costs. Because a large portion of cost remains in the hospital, the lowest processing level does not always result in the lowest total service expense.

Over the long term, one of the most troublesome aspects of this level of service is that so many laundries can submit proposals to do the work. As hospitals become increasingly concerned with the cost of operation, low-priced proposals look very tempting. This can lead to a series of ineffective contractors and to a steady decrease in the quality of service. Because most public hospitals are required by law to bid service contracts periodically, unqualified, inexperienced low bidders can become a particular problem.

The linen supply level of service requires that the laundry "supply" the linen. In other words, the hospital rents the linen from the laundry. The rental is covered in a charge levied each time a piece of linen is delivered. The charge varies with each piece and is not a simple function of weight.

In most instances, the laundry is able to earn more revenue on a linen supply basis than on a wash job basis. For instance, a laundry may be willing to wash a hospital's linen and provide the mending for 25 cents per pound. That same laundry, if it were to provide the linen, might earn as much as 38 cents per pound for linen supply service. This will not be easy for the hospital to determine, however. To convert a linen supply proposal into a cost-per-pound analysis, the hospital must know the unit weight of each piece and the number of pieces it will consume.

Since the linen supply service makes use of standard linen that is owned by the laundry, some mechanism must be created to determine the daily deliveries to the hospitals being served. Some laundries wash the standard linen on a "keep separate" basis and return only what is soiled. In such a system, the laundry usually can tell how much new linen is added to benefit each hospital.

Other laundries help with the creation of a logical in-hospital distribution system, usually exchange cart or quota. The hospital, using forms provided by the laundry, records the amount of linen required to bring each use area up to the quota. These data then are summarized on a linen requisition that is sent to the laundry. On this basis the linen delivered to the hospital replaces what was used to refill to the quotas. To operate effectively, this system requires a rather substantial linen room inventory. It also has no sound basis to charge for replacements, and the replacement cost is averaged over all of the hospitals being served.

Finally, some of the more progressive commercial laundries have begun programs to count the soiled linen returned from each use area in each hospital. This soil count, in turn, becomes the basis for preparing carts or bundles for distribution directly to the use areas upon delivery to the hospital. These systems create an inventory on each use area that rotates through the laundry on an even-exchange basis. To implement such a system, the laundry includes the processing cost (plus normal linen wearout) in the charge per piece. To convert this into a cost per pound, the hospital again must know the unit weight of each piece and the number of pieces it will use.

One important aspect of a system based on soil count is that the hospital can be given the prerogative of adding linen and incurring this cost on a prospective basis. This is accomplished by placing a "reserve" of linen in the hospital (under lock and key) that still belongs to the laundry. This linen, in turn, is issued to particular use areas to supplement their inventory in use. Upon receipt of the documentation pertaining to this issue, the laundry charges the hospital and the use area for new linen and returns an equal amount to the "reserve" as part of the next delivery.

This type of system also allows for credits when surplus linen is returned from the use areas. The system allows the areas to adjust to peaks and valleys without stockpiling linen and without causing unnecessarily high issues of additional items.

This system is relatively complex but no more so than the problem. This complexity cannot be managed effectively without the introduction of computer technology. If a laundry has detailed records of consumption and replacement by use area, it can provide a detailed analysis of the cost of service for each hospital being served. This analysis can be beneficial to each hospital when conducting cost-containment programs in linen service.

The linen supply level of service eliminates one of the in-hospital costs inherent in the wash job service: that of purchasing, warehousing and marking the linen. Laundries that deliver this level of service usually have a better grasp of hospital linen service problems and can be helpful in reducing the other in-hospital costs. When reviewing linen supply proposals, a hospital should remember that if the laundry does not charge separately for replacements, their cost (for all hospitals served) is included in the cost per piece. This can be expensive for a hospital that has good control of linen in use.

If a laundry has successfully implemented a use-area delivery system based on soil count, a hospital should keep two factors in mind. First, this type of system drastically reduces the remaining in-hospital cost. Some hospitals have operated such systems with .5 FTEs per 100 beds, compared with one to two FTEs per 100 beds for a more typical system. Second, the hospital should remember that linen misuse will be charged for on an experience basis (via the issues from the reserve). This will reward hospitals with tight controls.

CENTRAL LAUNDRIES

The central laundry concept in the United States and Canada dates to 1960. Originally, hospitals banded together to build central laundries to take advantage of the operating efficiencies inherent in larger entities. Under increasing governmental and public pressure to share services, the central laundry concept gained in popularity during the 1970s. Today there are about 50 central laundries in the two countries.

Most central laundries are organized in the same manner. The participating hospitals become members of a separate nonprofit corporation formed to own and operate the central laundry. As members, the hospitals appoint the board of directors of the new corporation. The laundry corporation, in turn, signs long-term service contracts with the member hospitals that require them to pay "whatever it costs" for linen service during the time required to repay the loan needed for start-up. The service contracts are assigned to the lender as collateral. On some projects, the hospitals also become joint and severally liable for borrowed money. Some laundries are financed with tax-free bonds, and others on a participation basis (at conventional rates) by local lenders.

Central laundries deliver the same levels of service as commercial laundries. In recent years, they have been turning toward systems that use soil counting. This is to allocate the linen replacement cost accurately among the hospitals being served.

Some central laundries have been successful and some have become an embarrassment to the member hospitals. Some have been marked by a consistent operational and management philosophy, others have wandered in search of satisfactory answers. Many central laundries were constructed to allow the participating hospitals to avoid less than optimum commercial laundry service contracts and to allow the hospitals to "control" the laundry. However, many hospitals have found that running a central laundry is far from easy, and in several instances were pleased to sell the entire operation to a commercial laundry to escape the problems inherent in ownership and control.

The history of central laundries' success has been spotty. If they were well conceived and administered, they have become models of efficiency and effectiveness; if they were poorly conceived and/or poorly administered, they have become troublesome burdens to the hospitals they serve.

It is increasingly difficult to put a central laundry project together. The varied success of other such projects, combined with high construction costs and interest rates, makes their feasibility questionable. These problems are compounded by the fact that many community hospitals are competing in earnest for patients and most administrators are so preoccupied with more critical problems that they do not have time to sit down to discuss shared service projects of any kind.

Even though the popularity of central laundries may be waning among individual hospitals, multihospital systems and proprietary hospital chains are constructing them at an increasing pace. For hospitals planning central laundries, the cost effectiveness of the venture is more important than ever, and some words of caution are in order.

- Someone who has had meaningful central laundry experience should guide the project. This can be an administrator, a material manager, a laundry manager, or a consultant. Meaningful experience means material involvement in all phases of planning, construction, and operation.

- Hospitals should beware of inflated workload projections. A majority of the central laundries were overdesigned by 20 to 30 percent. In this regard, more is not better.

- Hospitals should beware of the performance claims by equipment manufacturers and dealers. Some modern equipment is so expensive that (in order to justify the high capital outlay) it must operate with half of the personnel, water, utility consumption, and supply costs of more typical equipment. All equipment comparisons should be based on actual operating experience.

- The laundry must be designed as an integral part of a predetermined linen service system. Some consultants, and most equipment suppliers, will divert planners' attention away from the total system and toward the laundry itself. Many laundries have been constructed that purported to be "state of the art" and "finest in the world,"

only to become dismal failures because of a lack of attention to the systems concerns.

If a laundry is constructed without enough space to count the soiled linen, to load use-area delivery carts, or a new linen storeroom, it is almost impossible to implement the more comprehensive levels of service. There is much more to building a successful central laundry than constructing a fine physical plant. If the related linen service decisions are made correctly, a less-than-optimum laundry can be the nucleus of a successful linen service system.

27. Printing Services

MARTY WHITACRE

Whether printing services are performed in-house or purchased from outside, they will always be needed—and provided. The cost of printed material is considerable and often is overlooked as an area of potential reduction in expenses.

The material manager will rarely be trained in this specialty. Therefore, it is important to have at least a general grasp of the principles of effecting printing services management; this chapter presents an overview.

IS IN-HOUSE PRINTING NEEDED?

If there is no in-house operation, the question becomes more basic: Should one be started?

The justification of an in-house printing service must (1) take into consideration the hospital's long-term goals, (2) prevent duplication of services, and (3) lead to increased cost effectiveness.

In-house printing can cost 20 percent to 30 percent less, according to many in-plant publications. A commercial printer must make profits. In an in-house situation, the profits are put back into the parent institution. Commercial printers also must pay for some services that in-house operations receive automatically from the hospital. These include sales, marketing, bad debts, and support services needed to purchase supplies, issue bills, and pay employees. The benefit of being able to utilize complete, hospital-provided accounting and purchasing departments, yet in most cases not be charged back for their time, is lower costs for the printing department.

The first step in evaluating the need for an in-house operation is to talk to the hospital purchasing agent. This person is responsible for buying printing and knows what types are needed. Samples and prices of all printing being purchased should be obtained. Department managers should be asked about their printing needs, present and future. At this point, vendors can be asked to look at the samples to give an idea of the processes required to do such printing.

Managers should contact local trade associations such as, the In-plant Printing Management Association (IPMA), Printing Industries of America (PIA), and the National Association of Printers and Lithographers (NAPL). (See Appendix 27–1 for trade resources.) These groups can provide contacts with hospitals that have in-house printing services and their managers. They can assist in determining whether an institution's needs lend themselves to an in-house situation. They also are good contacts in the search for a qualified manager.

The goals for the type of printing that may be done in-house must be outlined. For example, these might be to concentrate on one-color business forms on standard papers, letterheads, envelopes, and some two-color advertising that does not require extensive bindery work. Goals might be to buy all four-color work outside or to include some bindery operations, such as collating, stapling, and plastic binding, then buy outside services for perfect binding, folding, and numbering. As noted earlier, each in-plant shop will have its special needs. Each function must be justified on its own merits.

FEASIBILITY STUDY

The feasibility study should cover increased security of confidential information such as financial reports, feasibility studies, employee relation documents, and public relations material. The study should review delivery time: How long does it take to get something printed?

Does rush work require a premium price? An in-house shop often has better control over scheduling.

The study should acknowledge that an in-house shop cannot and should not try to do all of the facility's printing. A hospital never could have or afford all the machines necessary to do all printing processes—and even if it could, they often would sit idle. The goal should be to establish the best mix of in-house printing and outside buying.

To whom should the printing services manager report? Will this service stand alone as a separate department or report to the head of purchasing, material managing, public relations, or even finance? This will depend on the size of the operation and the nature of the hospital. In many cases, it will fit most logically into the material management division.

As the printing service grows, it almost will certainly have to stand on its own. It will require a separate budget to permit proper planning. A separate cost center is particularly helpful in a chargeback system. The ability to control expense and revenue (chargebacks) and to develop realistic budgets is an important requirement for the manager.

If the feasibility study leads to a decision to go forward, the next step is to select a manager, who will coordinate the actual setup of the operation. The size of the operation dictates the complexity of the job description for that position. Once the description has been established, the hospital begins looking for a qualified manager within the printing industry, particularly one with in-plant experience. The first place to look is the IPMA; other possibilities are advertising in trade magazines, local newspapers, and through local trade organizations. Vendors also are good sources of leads.

SETTING UP SHOP

After a qualified manager is hired, the actual makeup of personnel, space, equipment, and systems must be decided upon.

The selection of personnel can be the manager's hardest and most subjective task. So much of a manager's time must be spent increasing productivity, tending to employee morale, and training that it may keep the individual from concentrating on systems design and other areas of material management. As a general rule, it is wise to hire experienced people to operate technical equipment rather than trying to train on the job.

Experienced personnel can be found through advertising and trade associations. Again, the IPMA is a good source of leads. Other sources are trade schools or technical colleges. However, printing students will have varying degrees of experience. Cooperative programs are worthwhile because they provide students with work experience that complements their classroom training.

Location

The location of the in-house printing department often does not get sufficient attention although it is important in enhancing effective management. In-plant shops often have been located in basements, with little or no regard for atmospheric conditions or effective use of space.

Paper and graphic arts supplies are greatly affected by temperature and humidity. More in-plant shops now are being designed to accommodate temperature and humidity controls and space planning requirements. This must be considered when planning any new facility, as must both short-term and long-range goals to allow for future expansion. Long-range goals may include going to in-house graphics, or adding a complete bindery operation or a complete darkroom for making negatives.

An in-plant printing department should be located near or have reasonable access to a receiving dock for delivery of paper and supplies. Its stockroom should have adequate space for storing paper and supplies, with the same atmospheric conditions as are found in the print shop itself. Paper characteristics are such that performance is improved when it is stored at or allowed to adjust to pressroom conditions. The size of the storage area will depend on the availability of supplies and the anticipated turnover rate of stock.

The print shop should be accessible for users of the service, deliveries, and mail. If the location is less than adequate and cannot be changed, then the layout and the ability to renovate become extremely important.

Layout

The layout of equipment and work stations often is subject to uncontrollable constraints. Work should flow from one station to the next in a straight line but the space allocated often does not permit such a linear flow. A good layout will reduce the need to move materials over great distances, unnecessary rehandling, backtracking, and crowded work spaces and will minimize the risk of lost work in progress.

The in-plant layout generally involves process grouping (printing in one area, bindery in one area, typesetting in another, etc.), which means that the work must be moved from one area to the next work station. Process grouping involves arranging machines of like character into work stations, unlike product grouping where each function is aligned consecutively and work flows in a straight line. An assembly line is an example of product grouping.

In-plant printing is so constituted that a single job may go from camera department to the copier, then to the bindery. Another job may skip the camera work, go to the press, then bindery, and back for additional imprinting. An assembly type layout would not lend itself to this jumping around from one function to the next.

Designing a layout for an existing structure involves drawing plans that include all windows, doors, columns, utilities, stairwells, and heat and air conditioning ducts, and then using templates or cutouts that represent equipment, tables, shelves, storage places, and so on. First, the templates are placed on the plans to determine good material handling requirements; then, a natural flow from one job function to the next will begin to take shape.

Space should be provided for future equipment, and such plans should be preserved for later evaluation of layouts. A good floor plan provides adequate space at each work station to reduce pileups of work in progress, which can lead to lost print jobs and time wasted moving materials unnecessarily.

The floor plan must include space for blank paper. The amount kept on hand will depend on several factors: its availability from local merchants, turnover targets, and the amount of space available.

EQUIPMENT SELECTION

The hospital's printing needs will determine the type of equipment selected. For example, it might be found that 75 percent of the printing being bought outside is forms work on regular $8\frac{1}{2}'' \times 11''$ and $8\frac{1}{2}'' \times 14''$ paper, and two-, three-, and four-part carbonless forms, and one- and two-color letterheads and envelopes. These forms generally are not revised often.

This overview makes it clear that the hospital does not need a 25″, four-color press. Rather, it needs a basic one-color duplicator press, and perhaps a camera platemaking system to make inexpensive paper plates (negatives and metal plates can cost five times more than paper plates). Forms work does not require the excellent quality that metal plates provide. Forms usually are not viewed by the public, so money can be saved with paper plates and they still will give a good-looking result. For letterheads and envelopes, it may be preferable to have metal plates prepared outside.

What about the other 25 percent of the printing? It will be found that 10 percent is multicolor brochures and special label papers, another 10 percent is snap-out and continuous forms, and five percent is specialty envelopes. Of this 25 percent, the brochures and labels may be printed on the same presses used for forms work. A second color head may be the answer for multicolor work.

If the mix of printing changes to 75 percent, $11'' \times 17''$ multicolor brochures and only 10 percent forms, the shop probably would need an $11'' \times 17''$ press with a two-color head. Depending on the quality required, the facility might choose to have metal platemaking capability. In both cases, snap-out and continuous forms should be bought outside because of the small quantities and the complexity of the printing.

It should be noted that most material managers do not have the technical expertise to make these decisions on their own. It is imperative to select an experienced and competent printing manager who can be relied on to make appropriate equipment recommendations. Final decisions also can be enhanced through the use of supplemental information from competing vendors and from the professional associations such as the IPMA.

When all is said and done, however, good decisions will be the result of having a clear picture of current demand, a good forecast of future requirements, and sound judgment on the part of both the printing services manager and the material manager.

Sources of Equipment

Buying dependable used equipment is a good way to offset the start-up costs of an in-plant operation. Larger equipment manufacturers sell used and reconditioned equipment at up to half the cost of new machinery. Remanufactured equipment usually comes with a limited warranty and is eligible for preventive maintenance contracts.

In larger metropolitan areas there are graphic arts dealers that specialize in used equipment. They have service personnel with a wide range of experience. Used equipment is available through other in-plant and commercial printers as well. A hospital should expect to pay an additional 10 percent when buying from private sources for parts that may need to be replaced. An experienced service person should examine the equipment and provide advice as to the availability of service and parts.

Selecting New Equipment

Anyone can buy equipment but it is the careful and thorough print shop manager who purchases machinery that will prove profitable. This manager knows best what type of personnel will be operating the equipment and what type of work will be produced. With this in mind the manager

needs to observe the prospective equipment recommended by vendors.

It is important to wade through the sales pitch about equipment. Visits to printers operating the proposed equipment are helpful. Vendors can supply names to contact. The visit should be to the owner, without sales people looking over one's shoulder. The owner should be asked whether the equipment met expectations and if not, why not. Service is a vital consideration. Machine wear and breakdown are common. Does the print shop use a service contract; if not, was one available?

The equipment should be justified by the same methods as in any other operation. What will be the return on investment? What is the life expectancy? Will technology change before the return on investment is realized? Each piece of equipment should be evaluated by the answers to these questions and by feature and price. The right choices can be made with confidence with this information.

Replacement Schedules

An equipment replacement schedule is a valuable tool. It helps pave the way for future purchases and in planning long-term needs. The schedule consists of a complete list of equipment, dates purchased, purchase prices, expected lives, remaining book values, and anticipated replacement dates and costs.

Another important document is the maintenance log. This helps in determining the point at which a piece of equipment no longer is cost effective because of excessive and unpreventable downtime or the availability of new technology that can enhance productivity. Decisions about preventive maintenance contracts or new purchases always are justified more easily when based on complete and accurate records.

FORMS NUMBERING SYSTEM

Establishing a forms numbering system can be a relatively simple process if approached logically. One approach is to start with form number

A–1 and proceed to A–100, then B–1 to B–100, and so on. If the print shop will process more than 2,600 new forms in a five-year period, the numbers could go up to 200, 300, or even 400 for each letter.

Some shops try to make form numbers represent specific departments or functions, such as P for Payroll. However, P could stand for Personnel as well, so ambiguity should be avoided.

Straightforward form numbers make it easier to file job jackets and to stock preprinted forms. A form number should be put on everything possible, including letterheads and envelopes. Form numbers on advertising is an acceptable practice; they then can be put on a master list and cross-matched with the title of the form.

Before the new form number is filed, a cross-reference card is filled out and filed under the title of the form. The card also should have a brief description of the characteristics of the job. The cross-reference can be used for locating numbers for like forms. When a form is updated, all forms with similar titles should be checked to determine whether they can be incorporated into one form or if the new one can be used to replace one or more others.

Forms Control Committee

A hospital can set up a forms control committee consisting of two or more persons designated to review all new or revised forms. This committee can use the cross-reference file to avoid duplications and to recommend development of combination forms whenever possible. The committee can help in reviewing slow-moving forms and recommending deletions when necessary. It also can serve as a screen to make sure that forms decisions are made appropriately and that the printing services system is not misused.

The forms control committee should include, at a minimum, the printing services manager, the purchasing agent, and the director of medical records or that person's designate. The relationship between the forms control and medical records committees must be close and supportive. It is helpful to include a product specialist

from the company from which business forms are bought if these are not produced in-house.

All requests for new forms must be accompanied by—appropriately enough—a form that answers these questions:

1. Why is the form needed?
2. What other departments are involved in the use of the form?
3. Have these departments been consulted about this request?
4. Can this form replace all or part of any other existing form?
5. What is the estimated yearly usage?

The printing services manager should receive the request and present it to the committee, which decides whether to request more information or to approve or deny the proposal.

Other Controls

Another control is a running sample file of all forms. This serves as a quick reference when answering questions about existing forms.

Job requests should be dated upon receipt and processed on a first-come-first-served basis. Priorities should be agreed upon in advance as to what types and sources of work will receive first call. With prior authorization, the print shop has justification in hand if someone's work has been delayed.

In most cases, proper planning can allow rush jobs to be processed with relatively little effect on scheduling. However, rush orders should be discouraged and customers should be educated as to their side effects. The person most knowledgeable about the schedule should be the only one authorized to promise rush orders. In other words, the material manager should not intervene to make promises; the printing services manager should have sole authority to schedule.

PRODUCTIVITY

High productivity is the key to any successful operation, and the printing services manager must continually explore new methods that will increase productivity in a cost-effective way. It is important to measure the existing performance accurately before an attempt can be made to improve it. This can be done in two ways. The manager can:

1. Break each job down into separate functions and measure these to determine standard times for each.
2. Divide each job into sections, such as press runs for 1,000 sheets, to determine standard times per unit, such as thousands.

Considering the variability among jobs, standards are the handiest method for allocating costs.

Once standards have been developed, performance can be compared with industry levels. These can be obtained by contacting professional organizations.

Cross-training employees to perform multiple functions within the shop is an excellent way to provide flexibility in staffing patterns as well as an interesting work environment for them. When done properly, this has the effect of developing employees who can perform more work in less time at higher quality levels.

How can a manager tell whether an operation is performing in a productive manner? The best way is to use the standards set up previously in conjunction with historical performance data for the department—in other words, to calculate how much output is obtained per unit of input from year to year.

Goals should be set for a growth rate that can be compared with production figures once the plant is in operation. Good recordkeeping is essential from the start. Records serve as the basis for identifying realistic standards and are used as a measure for increasing performance.

A frequently used measure of output is impressions produced. Many shops use impression counters to log all impressions produced each year. This method has a number of variables and does not always reflect other functions performed in the department.

If the shop is going to count impressions, it must count them the same way year after year.

For example, does printing a four-part form on carbonless paper count as four impressions or one? How about four forms up on one sheet? It is vital to establish a standard measurement and stick to it. Once standards have been devised, a log should be implemented for recording daily output, whether it be impressions, negatives, plates, sheets collated, or whatever. Another productivity indicator is the financial statement; this can be used only in conjunction with a budget and chargeback system.

Once the manager has begun to collect output data in a standardized way, it is possible to make meaningful comparisons with industry standards and manufacturers' recommendations.

CHARGEBACK SYSTEMS

An in-plant printing shop is one of the few support services that can completely justify itself by charging back its costs to users. The degree of success of this effort is directly related to the abilities of the printing manager and the degree of support received from the material manager and the administrator.

Chargebacks can be calculated in either of two ways: (1) by charging all costs for each job, including labor, materials, and overhead or (2) by calculating what percentage of the annual output is used by each department, then allocating that percentage of total expense. The more businesslike, as well as the most accurate, is the first method.

There are a number of advantages to charging back costs:

- It forces both the printing services manager and the user to be aware of what the costs are.
- It prevents the customer department from misusing the printing service by ordering excessive and unnecessary "free" material.
- It makes proper budgeting easier because accurate data always are available.

The disadvantages are that it is relatively cumbersome to develop a workable system and many persons, including some administrators, view this as just moving around money on paper and not worth the cost of the exercise. This viewpoint must be discouraged because the chargeback system is the single best method for controlling demands on the printing department and ensuring that its services are used appropriately.

QUALITY CONTROL

Quality control needs to be stressed for every job every day. The quality standards will be determined by the customer's specifications, the capabilities of the equipment, and above all by the expectations of the printing services manager. Employees must know what quality is expected of them. There is no reason why 95 percent of forms work and a majority of special work cannot be operator-approved if the operator has all of the facts about the job and knows what is expected. To validate the quality level, the manager should perform periodic doublechecks and should check back with customers to confirm that they are satisfied with the printing and overall service. All of these findings should be documented for future reference.

Another quality control mechanism is the job information sheet. Every job should have a sheet listing all details of the work along with a brief explanation of the expectations or special requirements. The manager should make sure that each employee forms a habit of not relying on word of mouth and memory but of working directly from the requisition and information sheets.

OTHER CONSIDERATIONS

Copier Services

Where do copier and quick print services fit into the total picture? Ten managers can be asked the following questions and they will provide ten different answers:

- Who should be responsible for decentralized copiers?

- Should the hospital lease or buy?
- What should be the maximum number of copies available from centralized and decentralized copiers?
- How much control over decentralized copying is desired?
- What are the comparative labor costs between the two systems?

These questions are answered using the same process that was followed in setting up the printing service. It may be helpful to call on the services of the hospital's management engineer, if one is available, or on the copier companies' product engineers or systems analysts.

The question of control should be answered for either system. In designated areas where a few persons have access to the copier, it probably will be necessary to resort to operator control cards or machines operated by code number. If the copier is used by several departments, or if unauthorized use is a concern, controlled copiers are a must. An added benefit is the ability to track copier usage by department for workflow planning and budget purposes.

The trend is to have a mix of small decentralized units, with large volume, high-speed copiers located in the printing department. The printing services manager should have responsibility for all copier units.

It is important to establish and enforce guidelines for maximum numbers of copies to be run on decentralized units. Manufacturers often have special discounts for meeting volume billing targets. On the other hand, overuse of small copiers can cause parts to wear out prematurely and can lead to excessive downtime because of overheating.

Obsolescence stemming from accelerating changes in technology is a real concern when making lease-or-buy decisions. Determining the most cost-effective way to provide maintenance also is a factor. Cash flow must be considered. The lease-or-buy decision is best made by a team consisting of the material manager, the finance manager, and the management engineer.

Customer Relations

The in-plant manager also must be a salesperson. In some instances, all requests for printing are routed through that individual, who can determine whether the job should be printed outside or inside. This is ideal. However, in many cases, the manager must compete against outside printers and must prove time and again that the customer can get better prices, quality, and service in-house. Therefore, the manager must be prepared to visit user departments, provide price estimates, and answer questions about production capabilities.

Estimating Prices

This is an important function often overlooked by in-plant managers. When comparing the hospital's shop with that of a commercial printer, it is vital to provide accurate estimates of cost or price. Quotes should allow the customer to clearly see the cost savings available by using the in-plant service. This is the best advertising.

The manager should be able to use predetermined productivity standards and historical cost figures to determine a labor cost. This factor plus the expense of materials provide a direct cost figure. It is advisable to add a standard factor for departmental overhead. When these items are taken together, the manager should be able to compete with commercial printers on price. If the operation is run effectively, the manager certainly should be able to surpass the commercial printer on service.

Cost estimating is subjective but can be made as accurate as possible by using current figures for labor, materials, and time standards. Methods for calculating costs are available from professional organizations and some trade journals.

An effectively managed in-plant printing operation can be a source of timely, high-quality printing service for a hospital as well as providing cost savings. The key is to identify the proper mix of inside/outside printing for the particular institution. The material manager must be able to select the right printing manager and guide the planning and management processes. The printing services manager must be responsible for selecting equipment, training employees, maintaining quality, fostering positive interdepartmental relationships, and ensuring that the print shop effectively meets the hospital's goals. When all of this is done successfully, everyone benefits.

Appendix 27–A

Trade Resources

Graphic Arts Technical Foundation
4615 Forbes Avenue
Pittsburgh, Pa. 15213

The Printing Industries of America
1730 North Lynn Street
Arlington, Va. 22209

National Association of Printers and
Lithographers
780 Palisade Avenue
Teaneck, N.J. 07666

In-plant Printing Management Association
(IPMA)
2475 Canal Street, Suite 300
New Orleans, La. 70119

Porte Publishing Company
952 East 21st S.
Salt Lake City, Utah 84106

In-plant Printing Magazine
Innes Publishing Company
425 Huehl Road, Building 11B
Northbrook, Ill. 60062

In-plant Reproductions
North American Publishing Company
401 North Broad Street
Philadelphia, Pa. 19104

Graphic Arts Monthly
Technical Publishing
875 Third Avenue
New York, N.Y. 10022

28. Material Management for Hospital Pharmacy

RICHARD L. SEIM

The pharmacy department is unique among hospital departments in its mix of product-management services and product-based informational services. Departments responsible for product management typically incorporate into their services either comprehensive information about a relatively small spectrum of products (respiratory therapy) or basic, fundamental information about a very broad spectrum of products (central supply).

The pharmacy department, in contrast, must be capable of providing comprehensive and detailed information about a large spectrum of products. The pharmacy, therefore, is torn at times between the pressures associated with cost-effective management of pharmaceuticals and the knowledge-based informational responsibilities involving them. The regulatory and legal controls with which the pharmacy must comply consider its distributive aspects almost exclusively.

However, the less tangible—yet "professional" and aesthetic—calling, from the perspective of the pharmacist, is embodied in the compilation and dissemination of information about its products. The pharmacy's internal organization often reflects this dual responsibility with separate components for distributive and clinical/drug information functions.

BALANCING RESPONSIBILITIES

Material management must consider pharmacy's balance of responsibilities toward these dual interests. The pharmacy also must recognize that, while material management is focused more on product handling, it also must consider its distributive and informative roles and that the two elements can and must mutually coexist.

Material management has been defined as "management and control of goods, services, and equipment from acquisition to disposition."[1] This definition translates into "management and control of drugs, pharmaceutical services, and pharmacy-related equipment from purchase to patient administration or use." This broadened definition encompasses a simplified description of hospital pharmacy services. The supplies or material expense of the typical pharmacy is nearly three times that of its personnel expense.[2] Consequently, it is imperative that the management and control of pharmacy materials be based not on intuition but on the scientific principles of material management.

The considerations relating to control of materials (drugs), although perhaps not formally called "material management," are not new to pharmacy. The nature of the profession has always required pharmacy to manage a broad range of products and a correspondingly large inventory. Pharmacy has always been acutely aware of potential lost opportunity costs when drugs are out of stock. The evolution of modern hospital drug distribution systems has focused on the need to optimize accuracy and control while minimizing waste. Sterile admixture services incorporate standardization and centralization. Pharmacists have been performing material management functions since before the concept was defined.[3]

It is unlikely that pharmacy's material management responsibilities will be absorbed or assigned elsewhere. The practice of pharmacy is regulated or strongly influenced by legislative, regulative, accreditive, and professional bodies through standards, laws, regulations, and guidelines. The Joint Commission on Accreditation of Hospitals (JCAH) states that "drug storage and preparation areas within the Pharmacy and throughout the hospital must be under the supervision of the director of the pharmaceutical department/service or his pharmacist-designee."[4] The JCAH adds that maintenance of an adequate drug supply[5] and intrahospital drug distribution systems[6] are pharmacy responsibilities. The American Society of Hospital Pharmacists (ASHP) has adopted formal guidelines for selection of pharmaceutical manufacturers and distributors.[7] It states that "pharmacy is responsible for the procurement, distribution, and control of all drugs used within the institution."[8] This statement is identical to the one in the ASHP's Minimum Standard for Pharmacies in Institutions.[9]

Regardless of pressures to centralize material management functions, the unique selection, control, and recordkeeping requirements for pharmaceuticals make it difficult and even redundant to transfer from pharmacy more than the purely clerical aspects of the procurement, distribution, and disposition of drugs.

However, the pharmacy does touch many other hospital departments in its performance of material management functions:

- Purchasing and accounting provide major assistance to the pharmacy in the management of materials.
- Purchasing should handle all requisitions for direct-from-manufacturer purchases. This maintains consistency in the purchasing-receiving-accounts payable cycle.
- Purchasing serves as a valuable resource on procedures and concepts and provides an efficient clerical source for purchase order generation that need not be duplicated in the pharmacy.
- Accounts payable should be involved in a coordinated relationship to ensure that accurate, timely payments are processed for pharmacy purchases.
- Accounting has established fine-tuned budgeting and financial reporting systems that are vital in monitoring and evaluating the performance of pharmacy's material management.

Nursing and the medical staff must be included among interdepartmental relationships. Pharmacy cannot handle product addition, deletion, standardization, and substitution effectively without the agreement and cooperation of the groups ultimately responsible for prescribing and administering the products. Therapeutic efficacy and cost effectiveness are essential considerations in product selection discussions with the medical staff. Pharmacy must be sensitive to storage requirements, product stability, final preparation, and ease of administration as vital nursing considerations.

The interaction with nursing and the medical staff on product management requires pharmacy to consider both its business and clinical interests. For example, it may not be cost effective to use an expensive antibiotic when a less expensive one should provide adequate coverage. However, the more expensive one may provide coverage against a broader spectrum of bacterial infections—a valuable asset when identification of the bacteria is uncertain. In many cases when dealing with therapeutic effectiveness of medications, it may be difficult to serve both economic and clinical interests impartially, although both will be present.

There has been much debate about the proper organizational positioning of the pharmacy department as a result of the economic interests associated with material management and the clinical interests of product effectiveness. Those who believe that pharmacy belongs under the material management umbrella consider the large inventory and the cost of its optimal management; those who would position it with professional services argue that pharmacy's status is built on its knowledge base of drug information and would be diluted by being in a group identified primarily by products rather than informational services.

Pharmacy provides multifaceted services. Ultimately, its performance must be judged on the quality and effectiveness of both types of activities. Its performance will suffer if either one is emphasized at the expense of the other. Consequently, pharmacy's positioning is not as important as the organization's sensitivity to its balance of services. Strong interdepartmental relationships, respect, and rapport can be developed and maintained within any organizational structure.

DRUG PROCUREMENT

Pharmacy frequently has several source-of-supply alternatives, depending upon the product. The same product, or equivalents, may be available directly from a number of manufacturers or labelers. (In some instances, a drug is manufactured by one firm but marketed, labeled, and distributed by several firms or labelers). Products also may be available from distributors or wholesalers. It is not unusual for several wholesalers to be competing in the same service area, handling identical products. Some manufacturers or labelers permit only direct purchasing, others distribute exclusively through wholesalers.

Direct Purchasing

Pharmacies traditionally have purchased most of their pharmaceuticals directly from the manufacturer, although this trend is changing. Direct purchasing often affords the best price because the middleman is eliminated. It also enhances the buyer's opportunity to take fuller advantage of special or promotional pricing.

For example, if the buyer normally plans to purchase seven items but the manufacturer is offering "one free with the purchase of eight," the hospital would be advised to purchase the eight, assuming that storage requirements and projected usage would warrant taking advantage of the sale. Direct purchasing also affords the opportunity to take advantage of promotional payment plans, such as delayed payment for specified periods if the order is placed before a designated date.

However, direct purchasing may be a costly process. There are not-so-obvious expenses in both materials and personnel time for purchasing, receiving, and accounts payable departments associated with purchase order process-

ing. Organized recordkeeping is required to keep track of orders in direct purchases from numerous manufacturers. Significant delivery delays may be inherent. Time spent generating orders and time in delivery can require inflated safety stock, resulting in increased inventories. Increased inventory results in lost opportunities to put the cash to other, more productive uses for the hospital. Any apparent lower prices in direct purchasing must be weighed against other system-related expenses.

Wholesale Purchasing

The primary alternative to direct purchasing is buying from drug wholesalers. They charge a fee for warehousing and distribution services. This expense typically is built into the price or is identified as an added fee, often stated as percentage of purchases. Wholesale purchasing reduces or eliminates generating orders by providing for telephoned or electronic orders and making payments on the basis of invoices. The availability of increased frequency for ordering and reduced delivery lead times combine to shift a portion of the pharmacy inventory (and the expenses of maintaining it) to the wholesaler. The wholesaler often provides tangential services to the pharmacy that further contribute to inventory control, including:

- shelf labels for individual product identification
- product stickers for individual pricing information
- inventory movement reports
- notification of price increases and emergency deliveries
- physical inventory capabilities.

On the other hand, any benefits of buying from a wholesaler may be reduced by inconsistent availability of products and inaccuracies in filling orders. Hospital inventories of critical products cannot be reduced if confidence in product availability and timely delivery are low. However, high order-filling rates are in the best interests of both the pharmacy and the whole-saler. When order-filling rates are poor, the wholesaler forgoes the immediate opportunities to sell out-of-stock items and also risks loss of business. It is not unusual for wholesaler con-tracts to commit to 90 to 100 percent levels of order-fill rates. It is important to monitor per-formance to ensure that the commitment is ful-filled.

Prime Vendor Agreements

Recognition of the advantages of purchasing from wholesalers is reflected in the progression to prime vendors. In this relationship, the phar-macy commits itself to make all possible pur-chases through a single wholesaler in exchange for reduced service fees and lower prices. This potentially benefits both sides. The pharmacy should expect not only the economic advantages of a reduced fee but also a strengthened commit-ment from the wholesaler to provide all possible drug inventory management services. The prime vendor concept enhances the value of many wholesaler services. For example, inventory usage reports vastly increase utility when all, rather than a fraction, of drug purchases are represented.

The prime vendor concept increased its desir-ability for both wholesalers and pharmacies with the evolution of the chargeback system. In spite of the many advantages associated with the prime vendor concept, the manufacturer's direct purchase prices to the pharmacy frequently were lower than to the wholesaler. This situation can arise either as a result of the terms of group purchasing contracts or as a result of special prices that the manufacturer is willing to provide to get patients started on a product while in the hospital, but which the manufacturer does not want to make available to all of the wholesaler's customers. In many of these cases, it was eco-nomically unreasonable to purchase such items from the wholesaler. However, many manufac-turers find that it often is more economical for them to ship to one wholesaler rather than indi-vidually to the large number of hospitals the wholesaler can service. Consequently, the

chargeback payment has evolved into an indus-trywide practice.

The chargeback system allows the manufac-turer to reimburse the wholesaler for the dif-ference in prices if the manufacturer has agreed to sell its product to the hospital at a price below what the wholesaler must pay for the product. The prime vendor concept, refined by the chargeback system, enables pharmacies to nego-tiate directly with manufacturers to minimize purchase prices while buying these products through wholesalers to maximize inventory con-trol.

Competitive Bidding

Many pharmaceuticals are available gener-ically from more than one labeler or manufac-turer. This encourages the pharmacies to have numerous suppliers bid for such products. Com-petitive bidding produces three primary benefits:

1. It identifies the most advantageous pur-chase price for the pharmacy.
2. It locks in that price for the specified con-tract period, providing immunity to gen-eral price increases.
3. It ensures the manufacturer of exclusive sales for that product, to the extent that the pharmacy can control drug selection.

However, the clerical and administrative effort required to identify multisource products and suppliers, project product usage, solicit and compare bids, and award contracts can be con-siderable. Therefore, it may be prudent to limit the bid process to multisource products that have the most budgetary impact.

Buying Groups

Two predominant factors that manufacturers consider in submitting bid prices are the phar-macy's potential purchase volume and its com-mitment to honor a contract. Pharmacy can increase its potential purchase volume leverage by bidding collectively with other pharmacies. Recognition of this leverage, along with the clerical expenses of competitive bidding, has led to the proliferation of organized buying groups. These may focus exclusively on drug purchasing or may be part of a larger group program purchasing many categories of supplies. Buying groups typically charge a membership fee as a fixed dollar amount, a percentage of purchases, or a combination to cover its expenses. As the group increases in size and purchasing leverage, a dichotomy frequently occurs. Group consensus and resulting commitment to honor group contracts become increasingly difficult to achieve. The sustained success of a growing buying group depends a great deal upon how well the individual members can maintain the integrity of the contract awards.

Inevitably, the buying group will be second-guessed. Prices are compared from one group to another. While some groups certainly enjoy greater success than others in obtaining low prices, several factors must be considered. Groups may award contracts based on aggregate product line prices rather than on low bid for individual items.

For example, a product available in multiple strengths may receive the award for all strengths to maintain consistency for that product, even though the bid for a particular strength of it may not have been low. Depending upon the cycle of the contract year, prices achieved by buying groups may leap-frog ahead of one another. Finally, although the expectations of larger groups to hold down prices may be greater, in reality the bid prices they receive can set the new prices in the market. As a result, larger groups may be driving the price for purchases outside the group as well as within the group.

Lending and Borrowing

A final, but limited, source of supply is the potential for a ''loaned'' supply from another pharmacy. Despite a large inventory, the pharmacy may need additional supplies when normal channels are not open, such as on weekends and nights. To ensure that the interpharmacy relationship affords the opportunity to borrow when necessary, the pharmacy also must be willing to

lend. Of course, thorough documentation of loans and borrowings, and timely repayments, are essential to minimize abuses.

The typical hospital will find it necessary to utilize each of these drug procurement systems and concepts. Total procurement expenses for each should be analyzed to determine the preferred system, which may vary from one institution to another. Even with identification of the preferred system, factors such as size of drug lot, cost, delivery time, etc., frequently dictate the type of procurement used.

INVENTORY CONTROL

Inventory control, although directly related to procurement, encompasses the broader objectives of identifying the following:

- appropriate purchase quantity
- appropriate purchase interval
- appropriate minimum and maximum stock levels.

The goal is to ensure product availability when needed at minimal expense. The discussions of inventory analyses elsewhere in this book have direct application to pharmacy. However, a few concepts deserve additional emphasis here.

Two categories of drugs can be identified from the large spectrum of pharmaceuticals making up the pharmacy inventory that merit close attention in inventory management. One category is composed of drugs that are used infrequently, are relatively expensive, and are absolutely critical to have on hand. This category requires that adequate inventory levels be maintained at all times. As a result, these drugs generally require higher onhand inventory than their historical usage would appear to justify.

The second inventory category is composed of drugs that, when ranked by their unit cost times frequency of use, account for the largest portion of pharmacy expenditures. These drugs are readily identifiable by ABC analysis, one of the most useful inventory control concepts. An ABC analysis of the pharmacy inventory provides a foundation upon which all other control functions can be built. Because of the significant time required to monitor all medications, and the limited resources, ABC analysis provides opportunities to control the inventory by focusing on the A items alone.

Identification of the reorder point and corresponding reorder quantities are the two most fundamental aspects of inventory control. The determination of these points can range from simply filling spaces on shelves when they become empty to calculating the economic order quantity (EOQ) (see Chapter 17). For low use items, the reorder point can be as simple as keeping one order unit in stock. High usage items justify a more sophisticated calculation of reorder points and quantities that considers the costs of holding the inventory in stock and of placing purchase orders.

Regardless of the methodology, it is useful to label each product location with the reorder point and quantity. Shelf labels often are included in the services of prime vendors or wholesalers. Wholesaler shelf labels typically list minimum quantities, maximum quantities, and product identification numbers. The minimum and maximum quantities provide the same basic information as the reorder point and reorder quantity.

Economic Order Quantity (EOQ)

The economic order quantity is a sophisticated analysis of the most cost-effective quantity to purchase for each product and a correspondingly cost-effective purchase frequency. Although this concept promises great theoretical benefits, they are somewhat reduced in direct purchasing. In pharmaceutical purchasing, multiple products often are bought from a single manufacturer. Therefore, orders to such manufacturers are initiated on a predetermined periodic basis (e.g., monthly or biweekly), typically determined from the aggregate purchase volume of the maker's products. Direct purchasing, therefore, is not driven so much by calculated economic order quantities as by frequency of order placement.

The EOQ applies to a greater extent when the majority of purchasing is through a wholesaler.

This minimizes the expense for placement per order, so quantities need not be influenced as greatly by predetermined order frequencies. In fact, the expenses per order are reduced so significantly in a prime vendor arrangement that the EOQ formula becomes preoccupied with inventory holding costs. The EOQ formula, therefore, encourages buying the smallest quantity possible in order to minimize inventory. This quantity can be provided by the wholesaler on shelf labels for individual products, designating quantities that reflect targeted inventory turnover rates calculated from the wholesaler's purchasing history information.

Purchasing strategies designed to minimize inventory also can maximize inventory turns. Many prime vendor arrangements incorporate one major wholesale order per week. Under such a scenario, the pharmacy could plan to maintain an average two-week stock on hand and order a one-week supply each week, producing 26 turns a year. The turnover rate is typically far below 26 turns a year even in pharmacies with well-managed inventories. However, by targeting the A inventory items for 26 turns a year, many pharmacies can substantially improve the overall rate and realize a larger proportion of the savings suggested by EOQ models.

Computerization

Inventory control and analysis of pharmaceuticals seem the ideal candidates for computerization. Software programs are available for a variety of automated systems. The computerized inventory can be linked to the drug distribution systems to automatically relieve the inventory of dispensed amounts. Automated systems can facilitate keeping track of pricing on an updated basis. They can generate reorder notices and even purchase orders.

However, despite the benefits, the value of computerized inventory is widely debated. For the automated inventory system to be timely, accurate, and valuable, great time and effort are required to enter change information. Order receipts, vendor changes, product changes, shorted items, returned items, and destroyed items all must be entered into the computer.

While such information requires some form of documentation in the absence of a computer, a computerized system may require duplication of such documentation to some degree. The pharmacy must weigh the benefits of computerizing against the data entry requirements. In some instances, it may be more prudent to computerize only a portion of the inventory, such as the A items.

A distinction should be made between inventory control functions that require a pharmacist's judgment and those that do not. Inventory control aspects related to product selection should be under the direct review of a pharmacist. Product selection decisions must consider such factors as bioavailability, formulation, labeling, dosage form consistency, manufacturer reputation, and therapeutic efficacy—all of which call for the skills of a pharmacist. No other clerical and mechanical functions of inventory control should be performed by a pharmacist.

DRUG DISTRIBUTION SYSTEMS

Drug distribution within a hospital should aim for maintaining optimal control and accountability without compromising availability of critical medication to patients. These goals typically require that the pharmacy make drugs available throughout the hospital using several different distribution systems.

Floor Stock

The most basic of the drug distribution methods is the floor stock system. This offers optimal availability for patient administration with the least control and accountability. Floor stock medications are not labeled or specified for any particular patient but are stocked in the area because of high probability of use and the need to have them readily available for immediate administration. Medications designated to be floor stocked in particular areas should have assigned par stock levels to provide what little control is available with this system. Floor-stocked medication can be replaced either by

requisition from the stocking area to pharmacy or by automatic replacement upon receipt in the pharmacy of a patient charge for the item.

Accurate patient medication charging is a problem because it relies on nursing's initiation of drug charges. This is not likely to be a nursing priority because of the multitude of other patient care pressures on nurses. Automatic charge replacement combined with designated par stock levels for each medication offers the ability to monitor the rate of charge capture for the floor-stocked medication.

Qualitatively, floor stock distribution systems sacrifice the benefits of pharmacy's double check in the dispensing process. Floor-stocked medications are a necessity in limited circumstances; however, the spectrum of drugs that are floor stocked should be minimized and such distribution discouraged because of the inherently minimal control and accountability.

Individual Patient Supply

The evolution of drug distribution systems progressed from floor stock to individual multi-day patient supply. Individual patient supply distribution closely parallels traditional prescription dispensing in retail pharmacies. It offers enhanced drug control and accountability since each medication supply is individually labeled and charged to a specific patient. The individual labeling adds the qualitative benefit of a double check on the proper medication for the patient. This double check is enhanced further if pharmacy dispenses the individual patient medication supply from a direct copy of the physician's original order rather than from a drug requisition transcribed from the order.

The major disadvantages to this distribution system arise from the multiple-day or multiple-dose supply. The multiple-day supply requires the maintenance of a large inventory of drugs on the nursing units. This system also necessitates a cumbersome crediting process for returned and unused drugs if an equitable patient charging system is desired. The disposition of these returned and credited medications also creates a dilemma: Can these drugs be determined to be uncontaminated and subsequently redispensed?

If they are determined to be redispensable, how will they be temporarily returned to stock? How will they retain identification by manufacturer's lot number in the event of a drug recall?

This system may be preferred on rehabilitation units where patient self-administration is an objective. Although individual multiple-day patient supply is considered preferable to floor stock distribution, because of such concerns it is not generally the preferred system for frequently used, routinely administered medications.

Unit Dose

The unit dose drug distribution system is preferred for medications that are ordered and administered routinely. This system addresses some of the shortcomings of floor stock and individual multiple-day supply systems while retaining many of their advantages. Unit dose drug distribution involves the dispensing of not more than a 24-hour individual patient supply of individually packaged and labeled medication in as ready-to-administer a form as possible. This system minimizes the drug inventory on nursing units and reduces the volume of medication crediting. The individually packaged and labeled medication ensures against contamination and safely allows for redispensing. The label also provides a source of manufacturer lot number identification. The labeled unit dose medication also maintains the double check in the dispensing-administration process and ensures the ability to track the medication up to the patient.

While a pharmacy patient medication profile may be maintained with floor stock and individual multiple-day supply systems, profiles are a necessity in providing daily dispensing information with the unit dose system. Patient medication profiles enable pharmacy to monitor total drug therapy to minimize duplications and drug interactions. This system also provides a more efficient system for nursing by significantly reducing dose preparation time.

Adaptations of the unit dose drug system have assigned pharmacists to the nursing units to review original physician orders and dispense initial doses for new orders. This often is referred to as a decentralized system. The decentralized pharmacist offers improved communication with physicians, nursing personnel, and patients. This system also expedites the availability of first doses and enhances pharmacy's monitoring of their administration.

A comparison of operational expenses for the floor stock, individual supply, and unit dose systems, looking only at pharmacy and ignoring revenue capture, would rank floor stock as the least costly. However, in a comparison of global, life cycle costs of the systems—which includes consideration of nursing time savings—the unit dose system has been shown to be the most economical.[10]

Intravenous Solutions

There are two specialized distribution systems that involve: (1) intravenous solution/sterile admixture services and (2) drugs defined by the federal Drug Enforcement Administration as "controlled substances." Sterile admixture services encompass preparation of sterile solutions, most typically parenteral (for intravenous administration), and their profiling, distribution, and charge initiation.

Parenteral solutions, because of their size, preparation time, and frequent refrigeration requirements, present unique distribution problems. Their efficient preparation encourages that they be batch-prepared by type of solution additive. These solutions must be delivered directly to the nursing units and some must be stored under refrigeration until administered. This delivery often necessitates using heavily loaded transportation carts several times a day. These factors combine to require that many solutions be prepared hours in advance.

This preparation schedule creates problems when there are discontinued or changed solution orders. The parenteral mixtures frequently have very short dating, with customized doses for specific patients, reducing the opportunities for redispensing them to other patients. Consequently, the potential exists for a significant percentage of waste in a product category that is relatively expensive. Solution preparation and delivery should be developed around schedules that minimize preparation for dosages ultimately not administered to patients.

Many hospital pharmacies limit individual patient labeling and distribution of IV solutions to those that require admixture preparation, while distributing nonadmixture solutions by the floor stock system. This limitation frequently results from a shortage of solution storage space or personnel resources. Although individually labeled solutions do require more personnel time both in labeling and in distribution, all labels provide the same qualitative benefits over floor stock as are offered with unit dose distribution, including the reduction of lost solution charges. In fact, individual labeling of IV solutions approaches the purest form of unit dose distribution.

Furthermore, accurate scheduling and preparation of solutions with additives requires that profiling also include solutions without additives. The sterile admixture service should include the labeling and distribution of all intravenous solutions.

Another key element is the IV therapy team. The primary function of these teams is starting all intravenous solutions, including blood products, and frequently the maintenance of intravenous therapy. The teams concentrate this form of nursing care into one group that services for the entire hospital. The alternative is to incorporate IV therapy teams' responsibilities into the duties of individual nursing unit staffs.

There has been debate whether IV therapy teams should report to pharmacy or to nursing. These teams are an extension of the pharmacy admixture service as well as a specialty of nursing care. Regardless of the organizational reporting structure, it is imperative that pharmacy maintain close coordination with the team because—when it exists—it can significantly assist pharmacy's scheduling and control of IV solution distribution.

Controlled Substances

The distribution of drugs categorized as controlled substances by the Drug Enforcement Administration (DEA) requires exceptions to normal distribution by the pharmacy because of strict federal regulations. The Controlled Substances Act of 1970 regulates the manufacture, distribution, dispensing, and delivery of certain drugs or substances that have a high potential for abuse or dependence. The DEA, an arm of the Department of Justice, is the federal agency responsible for enforcing drug laws.

Controlled drugs are categorized into five schedules. Schedule I drugs are those that have a high abuse potential with no generally accepted medical use in the United States.[11] Schedule II includes drugs having currently accepted medical use, high abuse potential, and severe psychological or physical dependence liability.[12] Schedules III, IV, and V include drugs with decreasing potential for abuse.[13] Many of the drugs in these five schedules were referred to as narcotics before 1970, categorized into Class A, B, X, or M, and regulated jointly by the U.S. Treasury Department and the Internal Revenue Service under the amended Harrison Narcotic Act of 1914.

The hospital must register with DEA as a dispenser of controlled substances and keep the following records of such drugs:

- initial and subsequent biannual inventory
- receipt
- dispensing
- disposal.[14]

These records must include the following information:

- name of controlled drug
- dosage form
- strength
- amount.[15]

Dispensing records must include:

- number or volume of drug dispensed
- name and address of the person to whom the drug is dispensed

- date of dispensation
- name or initials of dispensing pharmacist.[16]

Purchasing and receiving records of Schedule II drugs must use the official order form for Schedule II Controlled Substances (DEA-222c). Commercial invoices will suffice for Schedule III, IV, and V drugs but these should be clearly flagged on the invoice to make them readily identifiable.

Drug records in hospitals may differ from those in outpatient pharmacies. The latter must fully document the dispensation of controlled drugs individually on prescriptions. Prescriptions for Schedule II drugs must bear the original signature of the prescribing physician, cannot be refilled, and must be filed separately or readily identifiable from those for Schedules III, IV, and V.

In hospitals, the frequency of orders and quantity of doses would make it unduly burdensome for the pharmacy to maintain records for each individual dispensation. Hospital pharmacies also frequently dispense medications, including controlled substances, that for legitimate reasons ultimately are not administered to patients. The required prescribing and administration records also are available in patient charts or medical records.

For these reasons, it has become common practice to consolidate such prescription, dispensation, and administration information onto proof-of-use records for each drug dispensed as floor stock to each nursing unit; these records document the nurse responsible for the administration of each such dose. This document provides not only a concise record of controlled drug disposition throughout the hospital, it also is more easily reconcilable against pharmacy's records of dispensation to each nursing unit. However, the additional effort required to maintain proof-of-use documentation has resulted in its generally being limited to Schedule II drugs. Schedule III, IV, and V drugs typically are dispensed via the unit dose system, which represents adequate control for those in the categories with lower abuse potential.

Outpatient Medications

Outpatient prescription services represent the final major distribution system in a hospital pharmacy. Outpatient drug distribution essentially consists of dispensing multiday supplies of individual medication pursuant to a physician's prescribing document and the pharmacy's dispensing record. Prescriptions must be dated, initialed by the dispensing pharmacist, and numbered serially.[17] The prescription must be filed as stipulated by DEA regulations in a manner that allows for the ready retrieval of those for Schedules II, III, IV, and V drugs. The prescription label must contain at least the following to comply with federal requirements:

- name and address of dispensing pharmacy
- serial number of the prescription
- date of prescription filling or refilling
- name of prescribing physician
- name of patient
- directions for medication use.[18]

Significant factors in the provision of outpatient prescription services are the ramifications to hospitals of the Robinson-Patman Act. This law essentially held that hospitals that receive preferential, institutional discounts from drug manufacturers cannot use such preferred pricing to compete unfairly with retail community pharmacies.[19] The hospital's uses of such drugs must be limited to dispensation for inpatients, hospital clinics, discharge patients (for limited discharge prescription supplies), and for employees.

These limitations, under the Robinson-Patman Act, do not apply to drugs purchased at the retail pharmacy market price. The hospital pharmacy therefore may choose to maintain separate drug inventories: one for dispensing to qualifying hospital-related patients and the other for nonhospital-related patients. Pharmacy space for duplicate drug inventories as well as the hospital's desire to compete for the retail pharmacy market with its associated for-profit considerations will determine the scope of the outpatient prescription services.

Patient Package Inserts

Patient package inserts (PPIs) are related to a limited degree to the distribution of drugs. In 1977, the Food and Drug Administration (FDA) required that patient informational inserts be provided for every issuance of a prescription of estrogenic and progestational drug products.[20] The PPI must be presented to hospital inpatients at initial dose administration and at least every 30 days of continued therapy thereafter. The PPI requirement was designed to ensure that the patient was alerted to the hazards associated with taking the medication.

Documentation that the PPI was provided may be entered in the patient's medication record or on the prescription by the pharmacy. Despite considerable efforts by consumers and legislators to expand the PPI approach, however, the only results have been voluntary patient educational programs.

DRUG UTILIZATION

The hospital pharmacy's operational budget is material intensive—that is, drug expenses account for the largest percentage. Pharmacy cannot directly control this important portion of its budget, it can only influence it. However, the dollars involved, the training and character of the pharmacy profession, and the essential purpose of the pharmacy department have a considerable impact on drug usage in the hospital.

Two concepts of drug equivalency assist the pharmacy in controlling the cost of utilization: (1) generic equivalency and (2) therapeutic equivalency.

Generic Equivalency

Drug products may be referred to by a chemical name. This often is long and unwieldy and frequently is altered to a simpler generic term. The generic name may be used by any manufacturer of identical drugs. New drug products frequently are marketed by the manufacturer under an additional trade or brand name to increase public awareness of that particular item. The trade name is protected legally and cannot be used by other manufacturers without authorization. The marketing of new drugs is protected by a patent period. When the patent expires, other manufacturers may submit applications to market the generic drug either under their own trade name or the generic name.

Some companies elect to market the drug as a generic, perhaps assuming that greater value lies with identification of the proved product rather than a new trade name or its generally lower cost. Regardless of whether or not a trade name is used, all drug products with the same generic name in the same dosage form (e.g., tablet, capsule, suspension) and in the same strength or concentration are generically equivalent.

Therapeutic Equivalency

A more subjective concept is therapeutic equivalency. Therapeutically equivalent (or therapeutic alternate) drugs are not necessarily generically equivalent but elicit a similar response when administered. One of the best and least controversial examples of drugs treated as therapeutic equivalents are combination vitamin products. Similar vitamin products may not be identical in chemical composition but still produce essentially the same results.

As noted, however, therapeutic equivalency may be somewhat subjective. Variations in formulation of even generically equivalent products may produce differences in bioavailability (available drug at its site of action) that result in therapeutic inequivalence.

Formulary Systems

Generic and therapeutic equivalencies are of significance in the drug selection process. It would be virtually impossible, as well as an extraordinary waste of resources, to stock every major product brand of pharmaceutical in the pharmacy. Consequently, a drug formulary concept must be established to limit stocked medications to nonduplicative generically and therapeutically equivalent drugs.

A drug formulary is an institution's system for the selection and stocking of medications, particularly a continuously updated list of items that have been determined to be acceptable for stocking in the pharmacy department. The appropriate decision-making body on drug formulary decisions is the pharmacy and therapeutics committee of the medical staff.

Drug formularies are definable by a number of terms, such as open, closed, and restricted. These terms may be defined differently from institution to institution. Closed formularies are those that strictly limit the drug choices. A physician cannot prescribe a nonformulary medication in such a situation because such medications are simply not stocked. A closed formulary represents the strictest type, and drugs are added only after surviving a rigorous review by the pharmacy and therapeutics committee.

In an open formulary, drugs are added with only a cursory review or simply upon the request of a physician. Obviously, an open formulary, while offering physicians the greatest prescribing freedom, poses the greatest problems of inventory control.

A restricted formulary is generally a compromise between the open and closed systems. In a restricted formulary, some drugs may be available only after predetermined conditions are satisfied. One of the more common and lenient forms of restriction is that all nonformulary drug orders be clarified by the pharmacist with the physician. This type at a minimum requires the pharmacist to suggest formulary alternatives to the physicians. The generally accepted practice is to permit physicians to confirm their desire to have the original order dispensed if they so choose after this consultation.

A second restriction makes nonformulary orders valid only if countersigned by specified physician levels. For example, a nonformulary antibiotic may require countersignature by a physician member of the infectious disease department or a nonformulary preanesthetic drug may need countersignature by the director of anesthesia.

A third example is to place time limits on nonformulary medications. A nonformulary antibiotic may be permitted for administration only until culture and sensitivity results pinpoint the appropriate formulary selection.

There also are numerous additional types of drug formulary restrictions. The important point is that the administration of formulary decisions carries significant financial impact. Generic substitutions should be used when available from reputable manufacturers and therapeutic substitution should be sought at least for selected drug categories. The drug formulary must be more than a mere stock list of drugs available from the pharmacy.

Drug Information

One of the most important and potentially cost-effective responsibilities of the pharmacy department is to provide drug informational services to physicians. Closed formularies and restrictions are insufficient without timely provision of information to support drug decisions. Communication between pharmacists and physicians is imperative, whether in face-to-face discussion, written communication, telephone conversation, or newsletter.

The formulary must be readily available to physicians; a current copy should be displayed prominently in each patient care area. The provision of drug information, therefore, while normally considered a professional service, is directly related to effective product management in the pharmacy.

Treatment Protocols and Standardization

Medical staff committees, such as pharmacy and therapeutics, in addition to drug formulary review can assist with drug product control in other ways. The committee(s) can endorse and approve drug therapy protocols and standardized formulations. Protocols are preestablished order sets that may be initiated if strict patient criteria are satisfied.

An example is standardized medication orders for routine postpartum patients after a delivery. Such drug therapy protocols reduce the potential for inadvertent orders of nonformulary medications. These protocols also contribute to more consistent usage estimates for drug purchasing.

Standardized formulations can be particularly beneficial in maximizing the efficient preparation of medications that have to be compounded. Standardized formulations may be prepared in larger quantities to allow multiple dispensing from a single batch. Two common examples of preparations that, if standardized, can yield savings are oral liquid analgesic preparations for cancer patients and basic hyperalimentation solutions.

Standardized hyperalimentation solutions not only reduce dosage calculations associated with the admixture time but also increase the potential to use the expensive solutions for another order if the initial one is discontinued before the solution is used.

Drug Utilization Review

The effectiveness of drug utilization systems and controls should not be taken for granted. Strong formulary policies supported by effective purchasing and distribution procedures will realize only limited success in minimizing drug expenses if physicians prescribe costly medication while more cost-effective alternatives are ignored. Drug utilization reviews are an effective means of monitoring the appropriateness of prescribing. Drug utilization review can be accomplished by three methods: retrospective, concurrent, and prospective.

Retrospective review requires defining appropriate conditions or criteria for the use of a particular drug or treatment protocol. Such criteria must be carefully selected, founded on professional literature and accepted standards of practice, and agreed upon by audit committee members of the medical staff. A review of medical records of patients who have received the drug then are audited against the criteria.

Concurrent drug utilization review is similar but it is conducted during a current course of therapy on the audited item. Concurrent review is a specialized form of patient medication profile monitoring conducted by pharmacists in the routine performance of profile maintenance.

Concurrent review offers several advantages over retrospective reviews. Retrospective reviews rely upon completed medical record documentation and only promise future corrective action where indicated. Concurrent review allows for completion of missing patient information as well as for the opportunity to have a positive influence on drug therapy in progress.

Prospective reviews are conducted between the time that a drug has been ordered and administration of the first dose.[21] The criteria for prospective reviews are slightly different from those for retrospective and concurrent reviews in that they are not as closely correlated to current changes in the patient's condition. Prospective evaluations provide opportunities to influence drug therapy before it is initiated; however, the time frame in which to accomplish this obviously is limited.

Each of the drug utilization review methods has the potential for producing both qualitative and economic advantages. Retrospective reviews are generally the least difficult to perform, prospective reviews the most difficult. The time and effort needed to perform any utilization reviews require that the process be limited to a relatively small number of drugs. Therefore, the ones to be reviewed must be selected judiciously.

The drug utilization review process will be incomplete if it ends at the initial statistical stage. There must be a feedback mechanism to the medical staff that identifies utilization deficiencies. Ideally, the deficiencies will be reevaluated later to determine the effect of corrective measures that may result from the review.

Clinical Pharmacy

The many pharmacy interests, concepts, and strategies that affect optimal drug utilization have come to be known collectively as clinical pharmacy. Clinical pharmacy is an ideology that has existed with varying emphasis as long as the profession itself. Despite this, it continues to defy precise definition. Clinical pharmacy may be embodied in many activities, including:

- medication profile review
- patient medication history
- dosing calculations
- participation in cardiopulmonary resuscitation (CPR) efforts
- rounding with physicians
- patient education.

Clinical pharmacy does not embrace the full scope of material management in that it largely does not include the acquisition and distribution of drugs. However, it does fully cover drug disposition. Clinical pharmacy derives its purpose from the relationship of drug and patient. It is mentioned in this material management text because it has become a dominant force in the growth of the profession and because it speaks directly to the need for and use of pharmacy's product.

CONTROLLING MATERIAL EXPENSES

The path of drug products through pharmacy's material management involves many of the same decision points that exist in other material departments:

- Purchase ready-packaged or repackage?
- Buy disposables or reusables?
- Elect packaging consistency or lower price?
- Select quality or lower price?
- Risk equipment failure or obtain service contract?
- Emphasize material savings or labor savings?
- Minimize short-term or long-term expenses?
- Elect departmental savings or institutional savings?

While many of these decisions may offer acceptable alternatives either way, in some instances they may be mutually exclusive. Many

of these are addressed in depth elsewhere in this book but several are discussed here because of their specific pharmacy applications.

The purchase of unit dose packaged medications versus bulk medications and repackaging into unit doses is one example of acceptable alternatives. Bulk packaging (e.g., bottles of 1,000 tablets, pint bottles of liquids) is nearly always far less costly per dose than are unit dose packaged medications. Even after adding the cost of packaging material and labor, the per dose expense of repackaging from bulk to unit frequently is less expensive. The decision as to which to purchase varies among hospitals and among individual medications. Reasons for purchasing commercially packaged unit doses, even when more expensive, include the following:

- The manufacturer's package integrity is maintained, ensuring longer package stability.
- The potential for mislabeling is reduced.
- Labor expenses for repackaging are avoided.
- The manufacturer's packaging material, seal, and label generally are of higher quality.
- The drug product is available more quickly for dispensation.
- The total expense per dose frequently is not significantly greater.

Decisions on purchasing disposables or reusables must be considered in many hospital departments. Nearly all such decisions in the pharmacy are related to the use of disposables. The choice between disposables and reusables can involve sterile filters, refilling syringes, ointment slab/papers, stock containers, protective gowns, and even towels or linens. The selection of disposables in such situations generally is preferred. Labor savings and convenience usually more than compensate for their additional expense.

Packaging consistency is an important component for sterile admixtures. Many medications for intravenous piggyback administration may be added to a piggyback minibottle or minibag or may be purchased from the drug manufacturer in an original container suitable for the addition of the solution. The dispensing of medications in the intravenous solution supplier's minibottle or minibag offers a consistency in packaging and labeling that may be valuable in pharmacy's preparation and nursing's administration.

However, the less consistent packaging in manufacturers' piggyback containers may be less expensive. The selection of these alternatives will include consideration of overall system efficiencies, storage, and delivery requirements as well as costs. The goal as always is to optimize the balance between quality of care and cost of care.

The increasing availability of generic drugs and the concept of therapeutic substitution are expanding opportunities to select drugs on the basis of lower cost. Lower cost does not necessarily mean compromising quality; however, quality must always be considered when comparing drug products. Two products may be chemically or therapeutically equivalent but their bioavailabilities (e.g., abilities to be absorbed into the blood stream) may differ because of differences in formulations. Despite increasing pressures to control expenses, cost should continue to rank below efficacy (which certainly includes quality) and toxicity in drug product comparisons.

In many instances, the least costly alternative to the pharmacy may not be the least costly to the institution. The growth and development of hospital pharmacy services, along with increases in operating expense, have been justified on the basis of improved economy, efficiency, and quality of overall patient care.

These justifications have been present throughout pharmacy's drug purchasing, packaging, and distribution systems. The constantly changing health care delivery environment requires that pharmacy remain vigilant in analyzing systems and services and their responsiveness to the total needs of the institution. The costs of new drugs, new packaging, and methods of drug distribution and administration must continue to be analyzed with a view toward minimizing the total expense to the institution and ultimately to the patient. A more expensive drug or drug package, which adds to pharmacy's expenses, in some instances may have to be accepted to achieve potentially greater savings to the institution.

The pharmacy department provides services with a unique orientation toward both material (drug) distribution and information distribution. Either of these elements may be examined independently. However, the ideal combination will elevate the overall quality of pharmacy services.

The principles of material management have definite and positive application in the provision of institutional pharmacy services. The successful management of the pharmacy will be judged increasingly by the degree of proper drug usage and control throughout the hospital.

NOTES

1. Housley, C.E., *Hospital Material Management* (Rockville, Md.: Aspen Systems Corporation, 1978), 2.

2. Carl H. Deiner, ed., *Lilly Hospital Pharmacy Survey '84* (Indianapolis: Eli Lilly and Company, 1984), 17–22.

3. Ammer, D.S., "Materials Management and the Pharmacist," *Hospital Purchasing Management* 3 (1978): 10.

4. *Accreditation Manual for Hospitals 84* (Chicago: Joint Commission on Accreditation of Hospitals, 1983), 134.

5. Ibid., 136.

6. Ibid., 138.

7. *Statements and Guidelines of the American Society of Hospital Pharmacists* (Bethesda, Md.: American Society of Hospital Pharmacists, 1982), 22.

8. Ibid., 24–30.

9. Ibid., 50–52.

10. U.S. General Accounting Office, "Unit Dose: Life-Cycle Cost Analysis and Application to Recently Constructed Health Care Facility," in *Unit Dose Drug Distribution Systems* (Washington, D.C.: American Society of Hospital Pharmacists, 1972), 225.

11. Joseph L. Fink, III, ed., *Pharmacy Law Digest 1984* (Media, Pa.: Harwal Publishing Company, 1984), CS–4–CS–6.

12. Ibid.

13. Ibid.

14. Ibid., CS–15.

15. Ibid.

16. Ibid.

17. Ibid., DC–9–DC–16.

18. Ibid.

19. DeMarco, Carl T., ed., *Pharmacy and the Law* (Rockville, Md.: Aspen Systems Corporation, 1975), 208.

20. Fink, *Pharmacy Law*, CL–77.

21. Stolar, Michael H., "The Case for Prospective and Concurrent Drug Utilization Review," *QRB Quality Review Bulletin*, special ed., 1984): 5–6.

PART V
GENERAL CONSIDERATIONS

A number of topics that did not fit into the framework of the preceding sections but that are important to the successful operation of a material management department are included in this Part, Chapters 29–35. Many of these are forward thinking in nature and are intended to provide guideposts for leading the program into the future.

One of the most critical skills for any manager involves organizing, conducting, and following up effective meetings. One of life's great frustrations is to waste time in ineffective meetings. Managers, to be truly successful, must master this skill. The following chapter on cost-containment committees provides a perfect place to apply the material discussed in the chapter on meetings.

As the average age of the population increases and the focus of health care shifts to older patients, the industry is presented with a great opportunity. It must be prepared to meet the challenge of effectively managing material in long-term care facilities.

The pace of technological change in the field of computer applications is continuing to accelerate. Nearly every hospital has some degree of computer support. The possibilities of creatively manipulating data to support decision making are exciting. It is imperative that every material manager develop the ability to conceptualize, obtain, and utilize computer support capabilities.

This Part provides a detailed plan for developing an improved capital assets managment program, an area that deserves increased attention in many organizations.

One of the current buzzwords in the health care industry is marketing. Unfortunately, many managers do not really understand the concept. This Part provides a detailed guide to developing a marketing plan for material management.

The concluding chapter provides additional guideposts. A manager who successfully applies the concepts in all of the preceding chapters certainly will have a strong present-oriented program and will deserve high praise. However, as the industry continues to change, it will become increasingly important to maintain an orientation for the future. This chapter is designed to help in preparing managers to take the next step.

29. Conducting Effective Meetings: A Critical Skill

DAVE LEWIS

Ever been to a meeting that lasted too long? Or one that shouldn't have been held in the first place?

Of course, everyone has if they have held a job in business or industry. The major concern here is, "What causes meetings to be so unproductive?"

Any group asked this question will produce fairly predictable answers: "Dull speaker," "poor material," "couldn't get anyone to agree," "some people talked too much," "too darned many distractions," and so forth.

The list of complaints is endless, or seemingly so. Everyone undoubtedly can add a few complaints of their own. Whatever list is developed, the grievances should be divided into two major categories: planning and controlling. Most meetings that fail do so because the leader did not adequately plan or control the session—nay, even lead the meeting. Or both! (The hallmark of an effective manager is leadership in all aspects of the job, including conducting meetings.)

What can a manager do to plan and control meetings more effectively? Here are a few tips that have been found to be helpful.

PLANNING THE MEETING

The manager's job as a meeting leader is to help people make decisions, coordinate thinking, impart information, solve problems, and generate new ideas. That's a big job, one that normally requires hours of planning and preparation.

Since the success or failure of a meeting often can hinge on the physical requirements, this is perhaps a logical place to start the planning cycle. It is essential to have a checklist of items to go over before virtually every meeting. Ignoring any one of these can spoil an otherwise well-conceived session.

- Is the meeting room appropriate—not too small, not too big? If it is too small, participants tend to get grumpy and rush proceedings. If it is too big, the speaker can be dwarfed and acoustics are not conducive to lively exchange between members.

- Is the lighting adequate? At a minimum, the leader must make sure participants can see, hear, and breathe easily.

- Can the lights be worked conveniently if need be by the conference leader? This is particularly important if the lights have to be dimmed to operate a projector or for any other reason.

- Is the seating arrangement appropriate for the meeting? For information-dissemination meetings, a classroom style generally is all right. Where conferees are expected to contribute opinions and exchange information, a U-shaped seating arrangement usually is best.

- Are the chairs comfortable? This is particularly important if the meeting lasts too long. Conversely, chairs that are too comfortable can invite a too-relaxed environment.

- Can seating be arranged so conferees can enter and exit from the rear of the room? It is distracting for people to enter and exit constantly from the front.

- Will conferees have tables or some other hard surface on which to write?

- Is the seating arrangement such that conferees will not be distracted by outside activities?

- Has someone checked to make certain no distracting activities will be taking place in adjacent rooms, if the meeting is outside company facilities? The leader might not be able to preclude conflicting interests but at least can prepare for them.

- Have arrangements been made for coffee breaks that will not disturb the meeting?

- Are ashtrays available? Is the ventilation adequate to permit smoking? Is the room divided into smoker and nonsmoker sections? Should there be a no-smoking rule?

- Are name plates, pencils, and writing paper available if needed?

- Are all props and visual aids in order? Are sufficient outlets available for planned visual aids?

- Is the room absolutely clean? Cleanliness is next to godliness—and getting a meeting over on schedule.

There is much more, of course, than simply having all props and visual aids in order. They must be carefully planned and coordinated with the program itself.

Visual aids such as a blackboard, charts, slides, handouts, and demonstrations can help inform, stimulate, and motivate participants. Individuals learn better and remember more when they both see and hear the information being communicated.

Handouts should be brief and to the point. They are most useful for listing points to be discussed or reproducing data that will be referred to throughout the meeting.

Perhaps the first thing to do when planning the meeting's content is to ask, "Is this meeting really necessary, or would a phone call or memo serve just as well?" If it is necessary, it is essential to decide precisely what is hoped to be accomplished. Writing the objective down can help crystallize the leader's thinking.

Next, what kind of meeting will best suit the manager's needs: one emphasizing information, policy, or problem solving? Most meetings actually are a combination of the three. The leader then decides whom to invite and what they are expected to get out of the meeting.

In most cases, the main issues of the meeting should be researched beforehand. The leader obviously must have a working knowledge of all phases of the issues that could affect the decisions made.

In preparing the manager's own presentation, the leader should at least write down notes. If thoroughly familiar with the material, a simple outline might suffice but in other situations it might be wiser to write out the entire presentation.

Planning for a policy meeting is much the same as for an information session but the purposes are different. In an information meeting the goal is to tell the conferees something; a policy meeting asks for their opinions and ideas. The recommended steps in preparing for a policy session are to (1) state the specific aims of the meeting, (2) prepare introductory remarks, (3) write an outline or make notes for the leader's own presentation, and (4) make notes for conducting the meeting.

CONTROLLING THE MEETING

Many consider controlling participants in a meeting, especially in policy or problem-solving sessions, the most difficult part of conference leadership—and for just cause.

After all, the manager selected a group of experts to attend the meeting because they were knowledgeable, articulate (in most cases), and presumably interested in finding solutions and making decisions. But rarely do such conferees agree on what the problem is, much less the solution to it. As a result, they tend to argue, pontificate, digress, and in general do things that obfuscate the real issues and prolong the meeting.

Therein lies the dilemma. If the conference leader overcontrols, participation might be discouraged; if the leader undercontrols, the session may get out of hand (another one of those unproductive, too-long meetings).

The partial answer lies in being able to ask questions confidently and tactfully. Properly phrased questions can determine the direction the meeting takes and ultimately how long it lasts.

Types and Purposes of Questions

In controlling discussion, meeting leaders generally use four types of questions: direct, overhead, reverse, and relay.

The direct question usually is aimed at a specific member of the group. The overhead question is "thrown out" to the group as a unit. There are obvious pros and cons to using either type.

The reverse and relay questions are used in responding to questions asked by conferees. For example, in using the reverse question, the leader simply turns the question tactfully back to the person who asked it. In the relay technique, the leader passes the question on to the group as a whole. But it is the way questions can be used that gives the meeting leader the most potent weapon for control. Here are some ways questions can be used to virtually dictate the direction the meeting will take.

To Open Discussion

"I appreciate your taking time from your busy schedule to attend this important meeting. The main issue I'd like to address today is, 'How can we improve on our quality control?' Jim, you've had some experience in this area. Have you got any ideas?"

This line of questioning presumes, of course, that Jim has been properly notified of the purpose of the meeting and has had time to come up with some cogent ideas. It is at points like this that planning and controlling go hand in glove.

To Change the Course of Discussion

"Okay, we've had good discussion about reducing sick time, and that's certainly an interesting peripheral issue. But remember, the real purpose of our meeting today is to work out a new policy on our vacation schedule. John,

you've been working on this problem for some time now. What are your views?"

The idea is not to thwart relevant contributions but to bring the discussion back into focus when it gets off track. Many feel the single biggest waste of time in meetings are the digressions that go unchecked by a lenient leader.

To Limit Discussion

"It seems to me we've covered this subject rather thoroughly. Unless someone has an idea we haven't discussed, why don't we move on to another subject? Our time is running a little short."

The leader will be pleasantly surprised at how rarely participants will have new ideas on a subject that has been kicked around at length.

To Reach Conclusions

"All right, we've kicked this subject around pretty thoroughly. The consensus, as I see it, is that we should adopt a system of positive discipline in all areas of our operation. The positive discipline process would entail, as we've discussed it here, three stages: (1) Employees would be given a verbal warning the first time around. This gives them the benefit of any doubt about not knowing the policy. (2) On the second offense, they would be put on probation, and a letter would be put in the personnel file to this effect. If everything works out all right, the letter would be removed after 90 days. (3) For the third offense, the employees would be put on a three-day leave of absence and either be terminated or be permitted to come back after the probation period, depending on their attitude.

Summing up is one of the most difficult things leaders have to do but usually is necessary to keep issues in perspective and move the meeting along.

To Stimulate Participation

"We've talked about a number of ways to improve communications in the organization. Let me make a suggestion. How would a formal suggestion program work out?"

It must be remembered that the leader's job is to prepare thoroughly and, in some cases, evolve a solution to the problem. Through effective questioning, the leader in some cases may lead participants to what the person feels is the best solution. The caveat is that the meeting leader not impose views on the group. In many policy or problem-solving meetings, the leader stands to lose objectivity and effectiveness by taking sides.

To Clarify a Contribution

"Tom, as I understand it, you're saying a manager can't motivate employees but can create an environment in which people motivate themselves. Is that correct?"

People do not always say what they think, and even when they do, the other party hears something else. Misinterpretations lead to confusion—and more too-long meetings. The successful meeting leader avoids such situations by summing up or clarifying contributions that are not clear or do not make sense. And sometimes they do not.

To Stress Points

"Sue has said that she feels that if a management by objectives program is to really work, the employees' objectives must be coauthored by both the boss and the subordinate. Can you see any clear-cut advantage to having the boss and the subordinate determine the employees' measures and standards?"

To Encourage Group Feeling

"What can we do to help the department solve the high accident rates we've been having?"

To Gain Information

"Lyn, how does Herzberg differentiate between 'maintenance' and 'motivation' needs?"

The danger in asking such a direct question is that Lyn may not know the answer, possibly embarrassing her and precluding her contributing to the meeting later on. Naturally, if the leader knew for certain that Lyn knew the answer, it might have been an effective way of getting her involved in discussion. When in doubt, it generally is best to ask an overhead question of the group.

Handling 'Problem People'

Another important aspect of controlling a meeting is to be able to cope with the "problem people" who can prolong it or, in some cases, disrupt it entirely. These so-called problem people can be put into four main categories: (1) Those who talk too much; (2) Those who talk too little; (3) Those who try to usurp the leader's power; and (4) Those who try to force the leader into making a decision.

Skilled meeting leaders will need to know how to recognize and be able to cope with all types. Otherwise, they can have a devastating effect on the best-planned meeting.

For example, that overly talkative member frequently is the biggest problem. It is important to remember that the leader invited this person to the session because the individual had something to contribute, so it is undesirable to discourage the contribution. The most effective way is to remind the person somewhere along the way— and in privacy—that all other members have been invited for the same purpose and they need equal time to present their viewpoints. If it is recognition the individual wants (and often it is), the leader should give plenty of that; frequently that will work. Only in extreme cases would this offender be dealt with directly and sternly.

Getting a "silent" member to contribute can be equally challenging. That person also was invited because of specialized skill and knowledge. If these people don't contribute—for whatever reason—their expertise is negated. Creating a warm, friendly atmosphere is important in such cases. Beyond that, the best methods are to ask a direct question that the leader knows this individual is fully capable of answering or, when the situation permits, go around the table and solicit a brief contribution from everyone.

Side discussions are perhaps more of an annoyance than a time-waster. The trick here is to break up the side discussions without making the participants feel like grade-schoolers. At the break the leader can diplomatically inform the sidetrackers of the problem they are causing or simply ask them if they have something to benefit the rest of the group. Of course, they can always be ignored, but not for too long.

Finally, what about the member who tries to force the leader into making a decision, or to take sides? Such a person must be dealt with tactfully, of course, since no one likes to be reprimanded in public. Experienced meeting leaders use a variety of tactics to cope with this problem, including explaining their leadership role carefully at the outset, using an overhead or reverse question to get the question back to the group (or the individual who asked it), and explaining that it is the group's job to make a decision, not the leader's. Finally, if the situation warrants, the leader should answer directly if information must be imparted that the group needs to make a decision.

ENSURING FOLLOW-UP

Another frustration for people who must attend meetings is to invest their time, then see the decisions reached fail to be followed up. The meeting leader who has the responsibility for implementing the decisions can control this process. However, in many cases, actions must

be taken by various participants. Controlling whether they, in fact, carry out their assignments is a more difficult task.

The most effective way of doing this is by distributing typed minutes as soon as possible after the meeting. It is helpful to:

1. Obtain a commitment from each participant to carry out assignments in a timely manner.
2. Take complete and accurate minutes. It often is helpful to assign a secretary to handle this work, freeing the leader's time for note-taking.
3. Assign clear accountability as to who will carry out specific assignments, by when, and how completion will be determined.
4. Distribute minutes as soon after the meeting as possible, as noted.
5. Make a notation if a member fails to complete an assignment, or if a standing committee fails to send a qualified representative. By the same token recognize members who are especially reliable in carrying out assignments.

The manager who plans the next meeting thoroughly, uses some of these techniques to control it, and ensures follow-up will begin to develop a reputation as an effective leader. People will want to attend that manager's meetings.

30. Developing Effective Cost-Containment Committees

DALE R. GUNNELL

Someone coined the phrase "a penny saved is a penny earned." Today, in the health care industry, "a dollar saved is $1.16 earned." This ratio is based on the financial statements of one major university teaching hospital. The hospital industry generally follows this ratio, given the commonality of third party payers. To generate a desired bottom financial line, more revenue must be generated from rate or volume increases or expenses must be reduced.

A rigorous, effective, continuous, and formal approach to cost containment is as much a part of the successful hospital as is patient care.

WHY FORMAL STRUCTURE IS ESSENTIAL

Cost-containment efforts can become disorganized and ineffective very quickly without coordination. An organized approach under the control of a responsive committee can fulfill the objectives of timing, quality, communication, and results as compared to a quick-fix, hit-and-run approach. A formal committee can and must have the support of the entire institution, including the physician staff, and carry sufficient weight to counter opposition, providing the objectives are sound. Formal structure is imperative to recognize and reward the personal efforts of those contributing to cost containment.

Most, if not all, hospitals have launched a cost-containment effort at least once. Those that have been most successful have established and pursued objectives over a long period. Less successful ones have picked off the easily accomplished savings and soon drifted back to customary operations. The urgency of placing continued emphasis on costs must be recognized because of the effort required to make changes

that will reduce expenses. It must be remembered that habits and systems may have developed over many years and are not easily changed.

It also may take months or even years for some cost-reduction ideas to jell. This is because of the reluctance of many individuals, some of whom are highly professional, to change, particularly in areas that have patient care ramifications.

Another danger arises when hospital administration is not supportive of the committee's efforts. Administrators may tend to supersede committee programs with thoughts of their own. Obviously, the committee cannot be allowed to control administration but the two groups can and must work together. Part of the committee's operational protocol must be an approval process, which includes administration support.

DEPARTMENT AND STAFF COHESIVENESS

Generally, any department can find ways to reduce expenses with little effort. Reluctance to implement the ideas stems from the belief that expense reduction will lead to service or quality cuts that may be perceived as inefficiency by peer departments or employees. This may lead to the "why haven't you done this all along" syndrome. To counter this reaction, the formal structure is necessary to communicate what is happening, and why, to all departments and employees.

The committee must be looked upon as a formalized method for supporting the desires of everyone in the organization. It should be considered "our" committee working to promote "our" efficiencies. If the committee is perceived to be anything else, it may fail. It must work through people and to do so requires total support of all employees.

OBJECTIVES

Many benefits can be derived from a cost-containment committee. However, the major impetus should be to reduce expenses within the framework of maintaining an acceptable service level. The governing board and the chief executive officer must be the driving force behind the decisions to operate more efficiently.

Quality Levels

It must be recognized that changes in third party reimbursement methodologies, consumer perceptions, competition in the health care industry, and other influences may reduce the quality of care to some degree. This fact must be recognized up front as the committee formalizes and pushes for cost containment.

Now that a significant percentage of reimbursement no longer is related to cost, and there is no incentive to increase cost to increase reimbursement, quality of care could become vulnerable. This potential makes it imperative that hospital resources be consumed in such a way as to maximize quality and minimize cost. For this purpose cost-containment committees will become the standard for most hospitals.

During the mid-1960s, before the era of massive capital outlay to support construction of provider facilities and before massive infusion of capital into research and development of health care technology, things were different. Morbidity and mortality for the nation's population were fairly stable and health care consumed 4 to 5 percent of the Gross National Product.[1] Since then, with the morbidity and mortality levels greatly reduced, health care consumes about 11.0 percent of GNP.[2] This has resulted from consumer demands, as well as from general inflation and the increased cost of technology. Now, consumers no longer are willing to pay the price of the current quality level of care, and the cost-containment committee must understand

that attitude. If this point is understood, then the rest of the hospital employees can be taught.

Improved Quality of Services

It is essential to understand that quality improvement relating to a given task may be extremely costly. The key is for the committee through value analysis techniques to find the least expensive way to arrive at the desired quality level. It is up to the committee to determine where in the efficiency/cost-saving spectrum any proposed modifications may fall.

It must be recognized that no matter how a hospital task is performed, it can be done better. Realizing this concept, the committee members should utilize all available resources to further increase productivity and in so doing reduce costs.

Fostering of Communication

A major task of the committee is to establish interdepartmental communication lines as policies are changed and innovations are implemented. Each member of the committee must be visible in that role to members of the hospital staff. This can be accomplished by presentations to staff and departmental groups, postings of information and success stories on bulletin boards, and, perhaps most important, informal discussions in corridors and other areas of the hospital.

Casually chatting with a custodian or laundry aide about how things are going, with a discreet intent to solicit input for task improvement, can work well. It should be understood, however, that due credit must be given whenever these informal discussions produce benefits. A violation of this principle will dampen future progress.

Generally, employees thrive on recognition of personal contributions to an organization. This motivating factor is basic to obtaining suggestions for cost savings. Many employees will perform their assigned tasks in a continually improving mode if they feel that their efforts are recognized. The committee should recognize what a valuable resource the combined thinking of hundreds of individual minds can be. Such recognition also may reduce employee turnover, which in itself is a major contribution to cost reduction.

It is easy to gain support for cost-saving efforts from the community served by the hospital since the expectation is that, as costs go down, everyone benefits. This is as true in the major university teaching hospitals as it is in the smaller community facilities.

One hospital was so successful in its cost-containment program that the state auditor's office became interested. The auditor then led a massive effort to introduce the concept to other state agencies. The press picked up on the activity and few agencies were untouched by cost-reduction programs patterned after the hospital's. Later, several counties developed committees utilizing the hospital principles.

The chairman of the cost-containment committee was much sought after to speak to other hospital groups, industry task forces, and educational groups.

COMMITTEE STRUCTURE

The committee chairman must possess the characteristics of leadership, including intelligence, aggressiveness, respect from peers and others, perseverance, and personality. The individual should be goal oriented and conduct the meetings in an organized and efficient manner. Each meeting must be productive and must instill within members the motivation that feeds upon itself when things happen.

Because most committee members will be busy with other assignments, one alternative might be to hold meetings during lunch hour on a weekly basis. This will accomplish two things: (1) Members who are truly interested in serving and in being effective will be willing to dedicate their own time, such as a lunch hour, to the project. (2) It generally is easier to get the committee together at that hour of the day since most other individual commitments do not generally compete with the lunch hour.

The chairman must be capable of directing the activities in a professional way. Otherwise, members will soon learn that the time wasted is their own and they will lose interest.

Because the material manager is responsible for providing effective management of supplies and related support staff, that person is the logical choice to chair the committee. However, the most important thing is to select an effective group leader, no matter what official position that person may hold.

Cross-Section of Institution

Membership on the committee, in addition to the chairman, should include a physician, a nurse, the budget officer, the purchasing agent, and a systems analyst. Obviously, those from other areas of the hospital may be included as appropriate. Ideally, the committee should number five to seven individuals in order to cover a broad spectrum of the hospital but not so large as to become unwieldy.

Documentation

All committee activities should be documented. This is essential because of the time span between the conception of an idea and its actual implementation.

Since many ideas will be rejected for valid reasons, properly recorded minutes also can be used to show that all ideas receive due consideration and to keep time from being spent on an idea that was rejected previously.

The committee soon will learn that many of the same ideas will be put forth over time from varying areas of the hospital. Properly recorded minutes with adequate distribution also will give credit to the individuals who developed the thoughts first, thus preserving the due-credit concept.

Members must be willing to serve on the committee for a reasonable time. Periods less than two years will not allow them sufficient time to see some cost-containment ideas prove their worth, as this may take a year or two. However, since it is advisable to have new members with fresh ideas join the committee, some members should not expect to serve longer than two years in order to create vacancies for new members. Some standing or permanent members may be helpful because of the overall group's need for continuity.

If a particular member is absent an excessive number of times, a replacement should be obtained; a qualified designate should be sent in the absence of any member. The chairman must be adamant in enforcing the principles of sound and effective operation of the committee.

Some cost-containment committees are geared to failure. This happens when the chairman is not committed, lacks time, or is not recognized for any accomplishments. The committee may be organized on a moment's notice to deal with a specific issue, over a short period, after which efforts drop off. It cannot be emphasized enough that a cost-containment program is a long-term, methodical, and formal process and that results usually are not instantaneous.

Employee suggestions to a cost-containment committee must be followed up and the final disposition—acceptance, continued study, or rejection—must be reported back to the originator.

As these suggestions are made, the employee must receive prompt acknowledgment that the idea is under consideration. There is no quicker way to diminish the submission of ideas than failure to acknowledge that proposals are being considered. Some ideas may seem absurd at first, and some will be absolutely nonsensical, but an employee who is sincere in the suggestion deserves a response.

MECHANICS

It goes without saying that formal minutes of the cost-containment committee must be maintained. One document that will ensure order and effectiveness is the Governing Body Communications Memo (Exhibit 30–1). This document is designed to record the input, give the committee a perspective as to when the idea was submit-

ted, and arbitrate situations where two or more employees developed the same proposal. This form should be completed on all suggestions that are accepted and each must be signed by the administrator or designee.

The form provides a brief description of the proposal. The potential annual operating costs and/or savings are identified in order to put the idea into financial perspective. Since some suggestions involve capital outlay, this form has a provision for identifying that component. Finally, the proposal, having been fully reviewed by the committee, must be approved by the administrator or chief operations officer before being implemented. In the event the hospital rewards the employee financially or otherwise, this form will be the basis for that, as well.

Exhibit 30–2, Project Status Report, is a continuing chronological listing of all cost-containment suggestions or projects. It identifies the project number, brief title or description, assignees to work out details of each project, and status. This report should be updated monthly.

Table 30–1, Cost-Saving Projects, Cumulative Saving, shows project description, potential cost saving, any added expenses, net saving, and required capital expenditures, if any. Grand totals of each component of cost saving or any additional revenue are totaled on a periodic basis.

INCENTIVE PROGRAM

Should employees be offered an additional reward, financial or other, beyond the regular established compensation level? The answer is yes, and no. Employees should be expected to work as efficiently as possible without added incentives; however, there are situations in any organization when added incentives will pay off. These arise when risk increases.

For example, the storeroom manager may run five inventory turns on an item. The manager can increase to six turns and run the risk of running out of that particular article during the year. The employee may feel that saving the hospital the cost of a higher inventory is not worth the per-

Exhibit 30–1 Governing Body Communications Memo

Date _____

TO: Governing Body

FROM: Cost Containment Committee

A. Project name and number

    Cost containment analysis assignees:

B. Description:

C. Estimated annual savings:

    1. Salaries, wages, benefits $ _____

    2. Supplies and expenses   _____

    3. Other _____   _____

         Gross saving $ _____

D. Less: Added expenses $ _____

    Net annual saving $ _____

E. Required capital expenditures $ _____

F. Approximate date of implementation   _____

G. Hospital administration approval

                                       Administrator's signature

                                       Date

---

sonal risk for the stock outage. However, an employee who can earn a few extra dollars may take the risk and pay more attention to the stock item and its availability.

During a three-year period, one major university medical center provided a suggestion box as a forum for employees to express concerns, seek responses, or communicate cost-containment suggestions to administration. Most input related to complaints, general comments, or nonsensical statements expressing irritation over some point.

Later, the hospital replaced the suggestion box with an employee incentive program geared to a financial reward to individuals whose suggestions were implemented. This approach resulted in 121 submitted suggestions, of which 67 (56 percent) were implemented, saving the hospital $697,000 annually and rewarding employees with about $13,000 in incentive pay.

This experience convinced management that employees can contribute to effective innovative solutions but that ideas should be recognized, publicized, and rewarded.

Exhibit 30–2 Project Status Report

No.	Description	Assigned to	Status
100	Purchase paging system		Analysis complete: Net annual saving, $20,000
101	Acquire minicomputer		Analysis complete: Net annual saving, $19,000
102	Provide benefit pay for unused sick leave		Delete from further consideration
103	Install automatic teller machines		Analysis complete: Net annual saving: $6,000; added revenue, $7,200.
104			
105			
106			

It should be remembered that most sales personnel in every industry usually are paid based upon volume or profitability of sales. It could be argued that sales people are only doing their job when they try to sell a product and they could be paid a salary without regard to production. It is well known that sales volume would drop. The same principle applies to employee rewards for cost-containment suggestions, e.g., without incentives, the ideas do not come forth.

An approach to financial remuneration might be to give any employee up to 10 percent of a bona fide year's savings to a maximum of $200 a year. Before this award is made, the cost-containment committee should review the proposal in sufficient detail to be assured that the saving will become a reality, including the impact on the institution as a whole.

For any cost-containment activity to be successful, employees at every level in the organization must be informed of its impact. If employees gain the impression that these efforts are self-serving to one individual or department, chances are that the program will fail. To avoid this, constant and continuous internal publicity through in-house communications programs is essential.

The goodwill that can result from a hospital's cost-reduction efforts can be valuable. As documented efforts are developed, they should be passed on to area hospital associations and the press and relayed through other forums of infor-

Table 30–1 Cost-Saving Projects, Cumulative Saving

Project description	Gross saving	Added expenses	Net saving	Required capital expenditures
Beginning balance 7/1/82	$294,024	$ 32,908	$261,116	$ 14,202
No. 100: Purchase paging system	20,000	0	20,000	0
No. 101: Acquire minicomputer for budget office	19,000	0	19,000	0
No. 102: Install automatic teller machines	6,000 7,200*	0 0	6,000 7,200	0 0
Subtotal	$ 52,200	0	$ 52,200	0
Grand total	$346,224	$ 32,908	$313,316	$ 14,202

*Additional nonoperating revenue.

Exhibit 30–3 Checklist for Organizing a Cost-Containment Committee

Yes	No		
☐	☐	1.	Has administration recognized the need and value of a formal committee?
☐	☐	2.	Does chairman have financial and operational background of the organization?
☐	☐	3.	Do members represent the following areas: administration, physicians, nursing, financial, purchasing, data processing?
☐	☐	4.	Have bylaws been developed?
☐	☐	5.	Does a mechanism exist to publicize results throughout the institution?
☐	☐	6.	Are forms used by the committee understandable?
☐	☐	7.	Is there a mechanism for communicating results to the governing board?
☐	☐	8.	Are financial rewards offered to employees for participating?
☐	☐	9.	Does a mechanism exist for communicating with employees who submit suggestions?
☐	☐	10.	Will committee meeting frequency be adequate to deal with an ever-changing environment?
☐	☐	11.	Does each member participate in group discussion and follow-up research?
☐	☐	12.	Have committee goals and objectives been set?
☐	☐	13.	Are committee members willing to share success with other area health providers?
☐	☐	14.	Are committee members willing to work together without personal biases?

mation. This will help the public and third parties responsible for paying patient charges to feel that they are optimizing their health care dollar.

EVALUATING RESULTS

If cost-containment efforts are to be successful, an effective monitoring and follow-up system must be followed. This can be done best by maintaining a chronological summary of the projects, showing the date of implementation and dollar savings (Table 30–1). As the list grows, enthusiasm will follow. It would be appropriate to assemble and distribute on an annual basis a summary of the preceding year's activity.

Areas of consideration for maximizing savings generally relate to reduction of employee numbers because of the labor-intensive nature of hospitals. For this reason, the committee should devote a significant time looking for savings in departments with the largest concentration of people. However, there are numerous other opportunities—energy and fuel, for example— to reduce costs that may not appear to be worthwhile because of the limited dollar reduction potential but every dollar saved counts toward the objective of quality care at a reasonable cost.

The checklist in Exhibit 30–3 may be of value for purposes of establishing an effective, continuing cost-containment committee.

NOTES

1. U.S. Department of Commerce, *Statistical Abstract of the United States, 1974*, Bureau of the Census (Washington, D.C.): Table 99.

2. Robert M. Gibson and Daniel R. Waldo, "National Health Expenditures, 1980," *Health Care Financial Review* 3 (September 1981): Table 5.

31. Material Management in the Long-Term Care Setting

JOAN DYER

The woman in the back of the crowded room seemed to be listening intently throughout the presentation. Because the audience was primarily chief executive officers (CEOs) or long-term care administrators, it was necessary to carefully outline the benefits of material management in the long-term care setting. The savings and increased efficiency of operation and controls were emphasized. She seemed interested and eager to learn.

A few questions were expected at the conclusion of the presentation and it was obvious that this woman had a few in mind. Eventually, she raised her hand and asked the one prime question that was inevitable and one that was on the minds of more than half the audience: "How can I justify paying the salary of a material manager? My nursing home is not as large nor as innovative as yours. My board would never agree."

How can this position be justified? How big must a home be? How advanced and progressive must the board members be?

The size is not the issue here, nor the complexity of the operation. Although a home with fewer than 20 to 35 beds would need to package the position quite differently, the job itself still can be justified.

SPENDING AND CONTROLS

Material management is a tool used in cost containment, probably one of the most important ones available. What motivates an organization to control spending? Numerous factors: profit, government regulations, public outcry, stockholder demands for accountability. In private industry, the need for larger profits led to cuts in unnecessary spending. In hospitals, the motivating factors have been the combination of public outcry, increased government regulations, and the implementation of prospective payment systems.

What wolf is at the door of the long-term care facility? What will be the consequences if spending is not controlled in this field? It must follow the pathway of hospitals.

What salary is paid to the assistant/associate administrator or director of nurses? Are they involved in:

- looking over the latest array of copy machines on the market, bringing one or two in for evaluation, then negotiating price with the supplier?
- talking with the medical supply representative about the latest latex catheter?
- doing a thorough evaluation of incontinent briefs and comparing prices quoted with those of neighboring facilities?
- implementing a new patient charging system because of time and money lost with an ineffective old-fashioned system?

If they are, they should consider creating a position of material manager.

If the administrators and managers in long-term care are interested in bringing spending in line, then the role of the material manager must be considered and understood, for separating cost containment from this valuable position in a facility is like separating salt from sea water.

The person for this position should be thought of as an efficiency expert, a buyer, an inventory clerk, a records manager, a forms controller, a mail and printing coordinator.

It has been estimated that for a 120-bed nursing home, costs which lend themselves to control by a material manager may be as high as

$340,000 per year. Reducing costs by only 5 percent, can cover the salary of a material manager and relieve administration of time-consuming demands.

GROUP PURCHASING

The American Association of Homes for the Aging (AAHA), headquartered in Washington, D.C., operates a national group purchasing program for its members. The program enables members to purchase hundreds of products at prices consistently below those being paid currently. To cover the expenses of operating the program, AAHA receives an administrative fee from the vendors, based on total volume of purchases made by its members.

For various reasons, many long-term care facilities have not joined purchasing groups. Managers owe it to their organization to seek out and join an effective group. First, it usually offers better prices than one facility can negotiate on its own because it draws on the combined clout of all other members. Second, it saves time because individual homes do not need to meet and negotiate with every vendor for every item. Finally, the group can provide such other services as analysis of the facility's purchasing system, and so on. Because a material manager in a long-term care facility has to wear so many different hats, any time saving is of great value. For these reasons, even though group purchasing shouldn't be viewed as the answer to all problems, it is an option that should be considered.

PURCHASING TECHNIQUES

It must be kept in mind that a long-term care facility differs from a hospital—a difference that affects the decisions of the person responsible for purchasing. Hospitals purchase primarily for the assurance of medical care, and to meet physicians' preferences. Patient comfort is important, but not paramount.

Nursing homes are just that—homes. When patients enter a nursing home for care, they stay for two to three years, and longer; the average is

seven to 12 years. So when a nursing home looks at a piece of furniture, a cubicle curtain, or a wheelchair, it automatically connects a person with the item. Mrs. B will be living with that piece of equipment for a long time. The following examples highlight the importance of careful product selection.

Committee members of one home's product selection committee were squeezing rolls of toilet tissue and the "Mr. Whipple" of the group was encouraging them to do so. Why? Because older people have sensitive skin; they also have been buying their own toilet paper for 50 or 60 years. The paper provided through the group purchasing program was fine for the hospitals involved; their patients usually were many years younger, with less sensitive skin, and would be returning home in a week or less.

The nursing home was supplying a coarse quality paper; at times, the perforations were not deep enough, causing a stroke victim or someone with severe arthritis intense frustration. Residents are encouraged to be as independent as they can manage, yet the facility complicated their lives by offering them a toilet paper too difficult for them to manipulate or too rough for them to stand.

Softness also comes into play with body lotion. A hospital admissions kit is geared to patients whose skin is firm and somewhat younger. The same product cannot be used for nursing home residents with thin, tender skin. Coffee cups can suddenly become problems in long-term care. The facility had purchased china cups for residents in the nursing section, with the intention of making their meals more pleasant and homelike. The incident report committee noted that some residents had been burned or scalded by spilling hot coffee or tea. The mystery was soon solved when it was discovered that patients with arthritic fingers could not put them through the handle of the china cups and instead were using light, unstable plastic cups that aides had given them without realizing that these cups (not purchased for residents) had a tendency to tip easily. The home then purchased thermal cups with a wide handle and base that are safer and easier to hold.

How many times has someone said, "A shiny floor is a clean floor." This thinking has led to the development of high-gloss nonskid floor wax. To most, it looks fine, but to older persons it looks like a skating rink. The anticipation of a fall (tightening the muscles) sometimes causes a fall.

The janitorial supplier should be asked for the lowest gloss floor wax available and to get the company working on an even lower gloss.

Excessive light produced by glare from sun and shiny floors, gleaming bath fixtures, even shiny magazine covers can be painful to the older eye. Glare can be controlled through window coverings, blinds and draperies, shades, non-reflective surfaces, space arrangement, placement of lighting fixtures, and indirect lighting. Fluorescent lighting is uncomfortable for many, particularly older adults. There is a product that can be placed over the light with tiny holes that defuse the glare while allowing the illumination to remain. This product can be purchased for about $16.

Solar film for windows also is helpful in reducing excessive and glaring light. Several types need to be evaluated and staff members, as well as residents, should examine the samples.

A few other suggestions:

- Purchase an exercise bicycle to be placed in the laundry rooms; it will encourage motion and allow residents to enjoy wash day.
- Purchase full-length mirrors and install them in resident rooms; they can encourage good grooming.
- Purchase chairs with older persons' needs in mind; they require less depth, optimum height, a level seat, and especially arms so placed that full weight can be put on both without fear of tipping. Seat height should be 18 to 19 inches.

NEW CONSTRUCTION

The advantage of working on a new project is that the mistakes of the past can be corrected. Rather than solar shields on windows, new win-

dows can be insulated and tinted. Window seats can be installed for enjoyment and added storage. The nurse call, telephone jack, TV antenna, and electrical outlets can be located on both sides of each room to permit maximum flexibility in furniture arrangement.

Rooms can be proportioned so that beds can be placed on any of four walls, giving residents the power to make decisions and the ability to change the environment when bored.

Wardrobes can be designed so that heights of shelves and poles for hanging clothing can be adjusted for those in wheelchairs.

Questionnaires should be sent out to both residents and staff before final specifications are written. Their ideas are crucial in designing a home in which the residents can live comfortably and a working environment that offers the staff the ultimate in care for patients.

RECEIVING PRACTICES

Undetected errors can be costly if they are not identified during the receiving process. Short shipments, overshipments, incorrect items, outdated items, and damaged merchandise can be expected if the home does not routinely inspect incoming material. If damaged goods are received that were shipped F.O.B. the facility, the claim goes to the vendor; if the home took ownership at the point of shipment, the claim goes to the carrier. Regardless of who processes the claim, it is important to keep the shipping carton, especially in claims of hidden damage.

The nursing home has a right to expect all materials to be received in perfect condition. When they are not:

1. The vendor must be notified of the discrepancy in shipment, or damaged goods, and authorization for return must be given to the home.
2. The facility should package the goods securely and select the means of transporting them back to the vendor or manufacturer.

3. A letter explaining the reasons for and conditions of returns must accompany all such goods.
4. The value must be determined so that the shipment can be insured for its total replacement value.

The Uniform Code states that any rejection for deficient materials be made within a "reasonable amount of time." This statement can be ambiguous, however. It is the facility's responsibility to inspect incoming shipments within a reasonable period of time, surely within 24 hours of receipt.

THE STOREROOM

Storage areas always are in demand yet architects somehow never allow enough space. If they do, by the time the final figures come in, and cutting must be done, it usually hits storage areas.

A rule of thumb in inventory control is that hospitals require about 3,000 square feet of space of storage per 100 beds (or 30 square feet per bed). Nursing homes do not have to allow space for items such as laboratory supplies, IV solutions, sponges, or sutures. Therefore, half that figure, or 15 square feet per bed, would suffice.

Every storeroom has physical limitations that extend beyond size to type of floors, walls, ceilings, and lighting. For individuals who use this area, these are as important as their available square footage:

- The floors in the storeroom should be sealed concrete. Terrazzo or vinyl tile floors look good but are impractical to maintain.
- Walls also should be concrete or concrete block and painted a bright, cheerful color. Nothing is more depressing than a storeroom with gray walls.
- Ceiling height should be at least eight to ten feet clear (floor to bottom of light fixture or sprinklers). Anything less will reduce the available cubic space.

- Lighting patterns should be adequate to prevent dark areas in aisles. Storeroom personnel cannot find what cannot be seen.
- The area should be locked, with only a very few persons being permitted entrance. Material should enter and leave the locked area only with an official document.

If a facility does not have a material manager, then by all means it should at least have a receiving clerk. This person will be responsible for receiving, guarding, and distributing inventory. Other possible tasks include:

- keeping the loading dock swept clean and tidy
- tagging all capital equipment when it arrives in the building
- conducting an annual inventory
- wrapping packages for residents for mailing (this is especially helpful during holidays)
- acting as an outside errand person
- doing some duplicating work, either on an offset press or copying machine.

Having one person (and a substitute) to handle all receiving and inventory makes good sense, especially when the responsibilities can go beyond that scope. That salary surely can be justified.

DISTRIBUTION AND CHARGING

Once items have been purchased, received, and put in the storeroom, there still is the challenge of how to make sure they are distributed to users in the right quantity and in an efficient manner. Requisition, exchange cart, and par level systems all have their place (as discussed in other chapters). These should be evaluated to determine which will work best for the facility.

Once supplies have reached patients, they must be charged to the clients' bill. One method involves sticky label systems in which a peel-off label imprinted with the charge number is placed on the item, removed at the time of use, then entered into the patient's charge file or bill. As easy as this system is to use, it still will result in lost charges if it is not monitored. The best control is to count how many chargeable items go to a nursing unit, how many charges return, and count the difference. These must be followed up with the person in charge of that unit. Discrepancies that cannot be resolved should be reported to the administrator on a monthly basis.

Long-term care facilities often are thought of as less important than hospitals in terms of their place in the health care system. As the average age of the nation's population increases, this situation is changing more and more rapidly. Long-term care facilities will not be able to take their rightful place in the industry, however,

unless they follow good business practices. If they do, they will be able to keep the quality of care up and the cost of care down.

The effective management of materials plays a major role in determining which facilities succeed and which fail. Hiring a knowledgeable material manager, who can implement and maintain effective systems for purchasing, receiving, storing, distributing, and charging for supplies and equipment, not only will pay for itself but will give the facility an edge in successfully meeting the challenges of the future.

Administrators and managers can analyze their system and their facility on purchasing, inventory, and distribution using the scoring test in Appendix 31-A.

Analyzing the Nursing Home System

Administrators and managers can analyze their nursing home with the following test. They can keep their scores to themselves, but must share the ideas with those who will assist in making a change—for the better.

			YES	NO
I.	a.	Does one department or official centrally manage and supervise purchasing, inventory control, and supply distribution?	____(3)	____
	b.	If yes, is that department or official responsible for awarding and evaluating the performance of contracted services (i.e., for heating and air conditioning, elevator, office supply equipment)?	____(3)	____
	c.	Is there a written policy statement:		
		1. to distinguish capital asset purchases from routine purchasing, outlining dollar value?	____(2)	____
		2. to cover a code or standard of conduct for persons doing the purchasing (i.e., Christmas gifts, free lunches, etc.)?	____(2)	____
	d.	Are there written instructions for either centralized or individual department purchasing procedures?	____(3)	____
	e.	Are purchase orders issued and used for all purchases over a specific amount?	____(3)	____
	f.	Are specific forms used for authorization of individual department requisitioning of nonstock items?	____(3)	____
	g.	Is there a system to control and/or monitor emergency purchases?	____(3)	____
	h.	Is there a system to forward receiving slips to accounting for invoice verification?	____(3)	____
II.		Are there written instructions for:		
	a.	Competitive/comparison shopping by purchasing official or department head on capital and noncapital items over specific dollar amounts?	____(3)	____
	b.	A system to be followed outlining specifics for evaluating bids and awarding contracts?	____(3)	____
III.		Do you participate in a group purchasing program?	____(3)	____
	a.	Are resultant savings routinely documented?	____(3)	____
	b.	Is the value of the program periodically reevaluated?	____(3)	____
IV.	a.	Is there a central storeroom from which departments requisition supplies?	____(3)	____
	b.	Are there written instructions/procedures for the organization and operation of this central stores area (including the instructions for requisitioning and distribution of stock items)?	____(3)	____
	c.	Is access to the supply area restricted to supply personnel?	____(2)	____
	d.	Is the inventory reviewed periodically to remove slow-moving or obsolete items?	____(2)	____
	e.	Is the stock properly rotated?	____(2)	____
	f.	Are there controls against pilferage?	____(2)	____
	g.	Are annual physical inventories reconciled with accounting department accounts?	____(3)	____
	h.	Is the physical inventory taken or supervised by a member of another department?	____(3)	____
	i.	Do the auditors examine results of this inventory and suggest improvement?	____(3)	____

V.   a. Are records maintained so that using department is charged for items received when medical supplies leave central stores? _____(3) _____

     b. Are charge slips reconciled with supplies used? _____(2) _____

     c. If so, are discrepancies investigated? _____(2) _____

     d. Is this reported to administration? _____(2) _____

     e. Is there a consistent mark-up procedure for patient chargeable items? _____(2) _____

     f. Is there a built-in system to indicate lost charges on patient charge items? _____(2) _____

VI.   a. Is a par level or other system used for distributing linen? _____(3) _____

     b. Are linens and textiles bought by a purchasing official? _____(3) _____

     c. Are periodic physical inventories taken of all linen in the facility? _____(3) _____

VII.   a. Is food buying done by a purchasing official? _____(3) _____

     b. Is dietary encouraged to purchase other than brand-name products? _____(3) _____

     c. Is a food management company used by the facility, and if so, does administration:

        1. Compare its costs and benefits with those of providing the service in-house? _____(3) _____

        2. Audit the contractor's billings and determine the reasonableness of the charges? _____(3) _____

        3. Compare the contractor's charges for food purchases with prices available under group purchasing? _____(3) _____

VIII. Have the home's purchasing procedures been reviewed in the last three to five years? _____(3) _____

IX. Does the home participate in a group purchasing program? _____(3) _____

Total Score: _____

90 to 100 = Excellent.
75 to 90 = Not bad.
55 to 75 = Glad you're reading this chapter.
under 55 = Read the chapter over, roll up your sleeves, and start to work!

Source: American Association of Homes for the Aging, Workshop, Joan Dyer, Westminster-Canterbury House, presenter, November 9–12, 1980.

32. Expanding Possibilities for Computer Support

ROBERT L. JANSON

In the old days, hospitals used filing cabinets and an adding machine to produce an inventory system. So it was called an inventory system. Today, they use a computer to produce an inventory system. So they call it a computer system. Why?

A 4-PHASE APPROACH

Years ago, a medium-sized hospital began a four-phase, 20-year program to establish a fully integrated computer system:

1. blending manual procedures with computer reports prepared on a service bureau machine
2. expanding computer involvement by purchasing a central mainframe
3. shifting to cathode ray tubes (CRTs) tied to the mainframe, using operator input with batch processing at night
4. establishing a distributed processing network linking the central mainframe to local use minicomputers in the various offices and storage locations.

Blending Manual and EDP Procedures

During the design of an EDP system, it is important to build in maximum flexibility to anticipate probable future advances in equipment and methods without regard to hardware limitations. This flexibility should be limited only by the imagination and ingenuity of those participating in the system's design. The flexibility applies to the basic concepts of the system, which in turn determine the logic for programming the computer.

If management is not careful, it is at this point that a computer programmer or system designer may impose inflexible thinking, which may be based on a desire to achieve simplified or conventional programming. The material manager should not accept as gospel the explanation that technical computer restrictions will prevent ideas and specific needs from being designed into the system.

As refinements are continually made in the hospital's EDP plan, however, it is inevitable that some portions must be dropped. This will be kept to a minimum if each department head has done a thorough job of preplanning before sending a representative to the planning meetings. It is possible to design and develop a system for any department but it must be tailored to the organization's needs and financial structure and the department's business objectives. While performing the change, a bit of computer public relations like placing the following footnote on a computer report always helps:

> This new inventory statement takes the place of your old Kardex. The world hates change but progress comes only through change. Please help make this work.

Choices Available

A widening range of hardware (the physical equipment used in data processing, e.g., the computer and its terminals) is now available. There are several different types of computer systems.

Batch

In a batch system, information is collected during the day and is keypunched, usually at night, in one group called a "batch" of information. Not only is the information keypunched at

357

one time, it also is put into the computer system in the same manner. Controls over the input are based on a batch number, using a summary total of selected data contained in each group.

On Line

On-line systems utilize a CRT terminal linked to the main computer. Using the typewriterlike keyboard that is part of the terminal, authorized personnel can call up a variety of information from the computer data bank. The information appears on the CRT, which is similar to a television screen. The data may have been batch-processed the previous night and therefore may be as current as 5 p.m. the preceding day. In other instances, information—receiving reports, for example—could be as current as one hour ago, although up-to-the-moment calculations of inventory levels are not available. Data also can be entered in the main computer through the terminals.

Real Time

A real-time computer program also uses a CRT terminal. The information is entered on line into the computer but is updated simultaneously. For example, open or incomplete orders will be updated based on the time the last receiving report was entered into the system, also through a CRT.

Special Terminals

Many special-purpose terminals are available. One model has an optical mark reader, a bar code printer, and an alphanumeric printer. It can be used for processing requisitions by reading optical marks and for translating marks into numbers and letters. It also can be used as a turn-around document terminal to validate the requisition or to supply additional data.

Computer-to-Computer 'Conversation'

A computer terminal in a department at one hospital's inventory department can "converse" directly with a computer at the vendor's order entry department.

Distributed Processing System

A more recent development is the use of distributed processing systems. In these systems, a major computer processing unit is linked with a smaller computer in another location, such as a warehouse. The local, smaller computer becomes an extension of the larger computer, which is called the host. This system often gives the user greater control of data entry and document preparation. It relieves the host computer of some functions and tends to reduce total operating costs. Sometimes planning functions are done at the host computer while certain operating functions are performed at the local computer.

COMPUTER OBJECTIVES AND CONTROL

Computer objectives include systems that:

- provide service that is cost justified and timely
- obtain user input on scheduled basis
- develop appropriate systems for the hospital
- Develop short- and long-range materials plan compatible with business and strategic plans.

Characteristics of good control include computer systems that:

- use a common data base to avoid duplication of files
- consist of accurate documentation of procedures, applications, and programs
- permit periodic review and update
- ensure control of input data, accuracy, and completeness of output
- safeguard against intruders, fraud, fire, etc.
- leave a system "audit trail."

PLANNING A COMPUTER SYSTEM

For any organization, the transition to a fully integrated computer system can be traumatic. As Figure 32–1 illustrates, several phases of confidence—emotion—frustration often occur when much work needs to be done.

Before moving to convert to or upgrade a computerized system, material management must clearly and completely define its objectives in taking the action. Once this is done, the basic steps in planning, justifying, and obtaining a computer system are those in the next list. However, these steps should be modified to suit the specific environment in which the institution is working. All the steps may not be necessary, especially in a small hospital or when a minor system change is being made.

Steps in the Planning

Before getting involved in the rather elaborate program described next, material managers should read some basic information on computers, visit trade exhibits, and have preliminary discussions with hardware and software sales representatives. Many also interview computer users to find out what good experiences and bad problems they have had with the various types of machines. Managers then should:

1. *Analyze the Existing System.* Critically evaluate the existing system to identify satisfactory procedures, forms, reports, etc., as well as those that are inadequate or missing. For all unsatisfactory items, recommendations should be made concerning improvements necessary.
2. *Define the Purpose of the System.* Determine the primary problems and the desired objectives of computerization. Be guided by the hospital objectives and policy, both overall and for material management.
3. *Develop a Project Team and a Steering Committee.* Establish a team or committee of material and systems personnel, perhaps assisted by others such as the biomedical specialist, that will work as a group, headed by the material manager. A steering committee, consisting of higher level hospital executives, should review the work of the project team, critique it, approve it, and authorize continuing efforts. Then a tentative work plan (Exhibit 32–1) should be developed that includes priorities, schedule, and work force.
4. *Obtain Information for Preliminary System Design.* Identify what kinds of information will be required, when it will be required, and what its unique characteristics are.
5. *Develop a Conceptual Design.* Set up a large flow chart of a generalized nature showing the inputs, reference documents, and outputs of the desired system.
6. *Prepare a Justification.* List both qualitative and quantitative benefits expected from the investment, including all the elements of the total system. Prepare an example of a cost-benefit analysis that could be used to initially summarize the expected cost and return on the proposed system. Costs often are distributed in

Figure 32–1 Computer Confidence vs. Work Phases

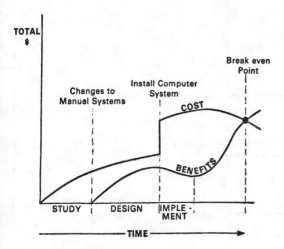

Exhibit 32–1 Tentative Work Plan

STEP	TASK NO.	DESCRIPTION	DOCUMENTS REQUIRED	SALARIES	EXPENSES	CAPITAL EQUIP.	TARGET DATE	RESPONSIBILITY
(CONTROL NO.)				ESTIMATED COSTS				

about three equal parts—programming, equipment, and operation.

7. *Present the Proposal.* Use the entire project team to present the proposal to management via the steering committee, stressing the advantages of the system, the time required, and the expected benefits. Sometimes it is desirable to use visual aids in making the presentation.

8. *Design the Necessary System.* Stipulate that the desired system design should expand on the conceptual flow chart developed in step 5. It should, of course, be cost justified, as described previously.

9. *Develop System Specifications.* Give the characteristics and explain the technical detail of the desired system. These specifications should be prepared using common sense. They should not be restricted to those in any particular package available, nor should they exclude desirable features because they might cost too much. Remember to include data base requirements.

10. *Establish an Estimated Price Breakdown for the Vendor Proposal.* Show detailed costs of the subcategories of computer equipment, such as hardware and peripheral equipment. Estimate the software required for the computer program. A computer department programmer also should make a cost estimate for an internal change method. Then the trade-off can be studied. Exhibit 32–2 is a cost-analysis work sheet that can be followed for information and contents.

11. *Send Requests for Quotations.* Send a well-prepared request for quotation to at least four hardware and/or software vendors, carefully describing the various items required in the system. Then discuss proposals separately with individual suppliers.

12. *Develop a Quotation Evaluation System.* Use formal documents or large spread sheets to list the information furnished by the hardware and software vendors to create a comparative matrix evaluation system. Study closely the software user system documentation (an outline is suggested in Exhibit 32–3).

13. *Select the Two Best Suppliers.* Look not only at the lowest-priced but also the least overall cost computer system and invite the two vendors with the best bids to separate meetings to discuss in depth the details of their quotations. In carrying out this step, keep in mind that the price on the request for quotation is not necessarily the vendor's final price.

14. *Select the Best Supplier.* Negotiate the final specifications, price, terms, and conditions.

15. *Set Up a Schedule.* Begin the implementation phase with a revised design and implementation schedule. Communicate broadly both the plan and the rationale for it. Conduct a series of training sessions to brief material personnel and others about the planned revisions.

16. *Work on Installing the System.* Pay particular attention to hardware equipment and the software programming instructions during installation. Perform necessary customizing or tailoring of the programs. Remember to document the procedures in standard operating procedure manuals.

17. *Test the Computer Output Report.* Debug as necessary until the programs are as accurate as possible. Have the material users sign off their agreement on the final format. Make certain the software suppliers continue their assistance. Do not accept the system until fully satisfied.

18. *Conduct Computer System Familiarization Seminars.* Do not rush these seminars, since many studies have shown training is essential for success. Keep the sessions interesting but explain all aspects.

19. *Perform a Postaudit.* Check the accuracy of the original cost-benefit justification for the new system. Do this at the end of the first full year of use and again at the end of three years.

Exhibit 32–2 Cost Benefit Analysis

Project description _____

Control number _____

Submitted by _____ Date _____

Approved by _____

	First year	Second year	Third year
Cost of project			
Development			
System design			
Consulting			
Programming			
Documentation			
Testing			
Training			
Implementation			
Subtotal			
Computer			
Software package			
Maintenance			
Hardware			
Subtotal			
Operating expense			
Other (specify)			
Subtotal			
Total project cost			
Benefits expected			
Cost savings/ cost avoidance			
Supplies reduction			
Payroll			
Other (specify)			
Total benefits expected			
Return on investment			

$$\text{Return on investment} = \frac{\text{Total benefits expected}}{\text{Total project cost}} = \underline{\hspace{1cm}} \times 100 = \underline{\hspace{1cm}}\%$$

Exhibit 32–3 User Documentation System Outline

PROCEDURES

Introduction - explaining the purpose of the "how to do it" regarding the system procedures.

Preconversion forms - those documents which help the user gathering correct data.

Conversion process - the steps and timing by which data is formally placed into the system.

TRANSACTION INFORMATION

Introduction - general information regarding the transactions of the system.

Transaction - specific description of each transaction, providing name, code, and brief description.

INPUT FORMAT

General - relating inputs with the procedures previously described.

Entries - describing the various forms which must be completed for the reports outputs to be developed.

REPORTS

Introduction - explanation of general report contents, either conversion, routine and on request type.

Report Description - description of each report's name, type, run frequency and contents.

SYSTEM OVERVIEW

Introduction - a general description of the objective of the computer system, features, and options.

Inputs - description of the method(s) of entering data into the system, mentioning the various transaction categories.

Reports - explanation of the various system outputs begining with transaction edits to identify input errors, then describing the routine, exception and special request reports.

GENERAL INFORMATION

User Responsibilities - expresses the duties of user's regarding input data.

Completing Input Forms - describes how information is translated into computer format.

Field Notation - explains the name of each section on an input form.

Entry Rules - concerning proper rules for input coding so data will be accepted by the system.

DOCUMENTATION LEVELS OF SYSTEM DESIGN

All of the work in establishing the new material system will be of little value until adequate documentation is prepared. These types—called levels—should be developed:

1. Conceptual Design: A well-thought-out plan prepared by the users and data processing system designers, then approved by management. Provides a top-level overview of the proposed system showing basic interrelationships and general procedural flow. The output of a conceptual design is: A written narrative accompanied by an overview style flow chart.
2. General Design: A highly interactive description developed by the user and system designer based on approval assumptions in the conceptual design. Provides a second level of detail for each individual system, further amplifying the processing from a generalized viewpoint to assist in obtaining additional understanding. The output is: A written description of each system's output reports.
3. Detailed Design: A more mechanical step by the system programmer consisting of tested and debugged programs for final user and management sign-off approval. Provides a third level of detail for each system that clarifies the individual component subsystems by highlighting the essential transaction processing and their required data files. The output is: A detailed list of transactions, master files, and operating procedures.

TYPES OF DATA BASE

A data base is a collection of information processed by the computer. Creation of a uniform data base requires standardization of a number of elements. For the requisitioning cycle, for example, there should be standard ordering specifications, nomenclature, ordering units, units of measure, and commodity codes of all repetitively purchased materials and stores items.

Standardization of commodity data is essential in the cycle because the information is perpetuated in mechanical form for subsequent processing in other functions. Four major types are identified in Table 32–1.

A terminal on every desk is the question facing material managers who wish to use a CRT.

Table 32–1 Types of Files

File type	Purpose	Examples
1. Master file	Relatively permanent records containing statistical, identificational, and historical information. Used as a source of reference and for retrieval.	Inventory file
2. Transaction file (also called detail file)	Collection of records describing transactions by the organization. Developed as a result of processing transactions and preparing transaction documents. Used to update a master file.	Purchase order file
3. Report file	Records extracted from data in master files in order to prepare a report.	Report file for delinquent customer accounts
4. Sort file	A working file of records to be sequenced. This may be the original or a copy of the master file, transaction file, or report file.	Transaction file

Three choices are available (Exhibit 32–4). Then there is the question, does this employee really need a dedicated CRT since these are the trade-offs:

Printed report	*vs.*	*CRT inquiry*
• Multiple references		• Few references
• More paper files		• Fewer paper files
• Lower cost		• Higher cost
• Some delay		• Instantaneous

Lastly, no matter which CRT is selected, three methods are available to use the terminal:

1. On-line inquiry, such as determining the purchase order status
2. On-line entry, when it is necessary to revise the order promise date
3. Real time, for obtaining the latest inventory status date.

As with any machine, carefully planned training is required to introduce a CRT to a new operation. Some of the points to be covered include:

- Menu
- Messages
- Security codes
- Create files
- Inquiring
- Input date/ Update files
- Display
- Print document
- Cursor

EVALUATION OF SOFTWARE PROGRAMS

Figure 32–2 shows five important steps necessary to make this most critical decision. At each step, certain less qualified software vendors are eliminated. At the first step, perhaps eight software houses might be in contention; at the third step, two or three, and in the fifth step, the best vendor is selected.

Step 2 is accomplished by providing the selection committee members lots of prestudy material, followed by a day-long discussion of the merits of the vendors not eliminated in step 1. At the end of the discussions, each person "votes" by ranking each of the remaining possible vendors, using three criteria groups. These groups consider various computer company experiences, the ability to meet the hospital's system specifications, and the hospital group's opinion of several important system elements:

I. Computer company experience

- Software name
- License fee
- Hardware required
- Number of terminals
- Query facility
- Report generator
- Number of installations

Exhibit 32–4 CRT Alternatives

Dumb Terminals	**Smart Terminals**	**Intelligent Terminals**
simply provide a two-way communication link between the user and a computer	have a limited microprocessor, a small memory, and generally are not user programmable	include a powerful microprocessor, a larger memory, and are user programmable in a high-level language
Computer dependent	Partially dependent	Stand-alone

Figure 32–2 Software Evaluation Process

Proposal Review Process	*Vendors*

1. • System requirements met
   • Conceptual design called adequate
   • Very high and very low proposals eliminated

2. • Evaluation criteria reviewed

3. • Better qualified vendors met

4. • Vendors meeting held
   • References followed up
   • Installed systems visited
   • Subjective factors considered

5. • Best vendor selected

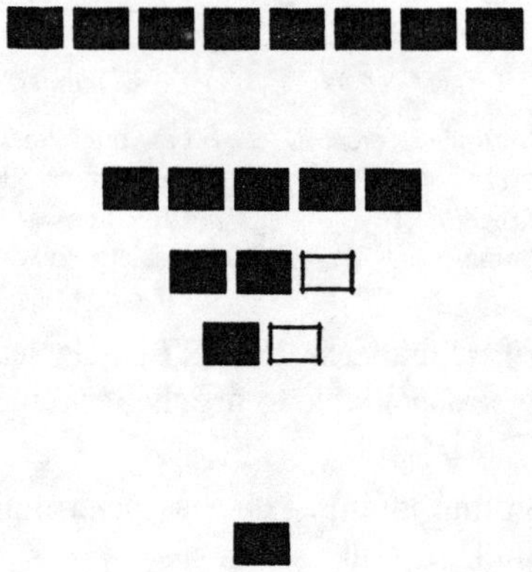

- Date of first installations
- Level of integration
- On-line and interactive.

II. System specifications

- Inventory item by class codes
- ABC analysis
- Inventory location
- Lead times
- Reorder points
- Safety stock
- EOQ analysis
- Inventory status and tracking inquiry
- Material availability projection
- Inventory valuation
- Inventory picking list
- Receiving notice
- Inventory multiple storerooms
- Inventory shortage report
- Physical inventory
- Cycle counting
- Inventory adjustments
- Summary of inventory activity
- Item costing
- Statistical measures.

III. System elements

- Simplicity
- Documentation
- User
- Programs
- Support
- Standard system
- Training
- Security
- Stability
- Vendor interest
- Performance
- Processing time.

IV. Overall evaluation

- Computer company experience
- System specifications
- System elements
- Total rating.

THE VALUE OF ALL THIS WORK

Hospitals that successfully install a computerized material management system find they achieve these 12 benefits:

1. a virtual elimination of filing
2. easier implementation of volume purchasing and large-scale contracts with resultant savings
3. a substantial reduction in overall clerical time and time for supervision
4. a sizable saving in inventory carrying costs
5. a great reduction in paper work
6. standardization of pertinent data and terminology, with everyone using same data base
7. ready accessibility of data to all authorized personnel, controlled with built-in security checks
8. reduction in time required for all forms of input, retrieval, computation, and response
9. adaptability and fast response to changes in priorities, prices, and other variables of material management
10. centralized management without loss of utility of personnel to any outlying departments
11. savings in equipment and floor space, principally through elimination of files
12. improved communications among all personnel in the hospital.

Lastly, some thoughts about the future for computerized materials management:

- Management Terminals: These are an integral part of the system, accumulating information in a chain-of-command control that begins with the inventory controller, progresses to the material manager, and ends with the hospital administrator.

- The Computer-Aided System: This still requires manual procedures, so the electronically prepared data should be integrated carefully with the pencil-created information.

- Menu and Files: These consist of a display of variables, called parameters, and options that can be selected to complete a task using data that are analogous to file drawer contents or a set of inventory cards.

- Completeness of System: A finished computer system rarely will provide more than 90 percent of what is desired. This is true whether the hospital purchases software or designs the system itself. The hospital thus should freeze what it has and add the other 10 percent later, but only after it has received considerable return on the time and money invested.

- Implementation: This is difficult because many people do not understand a computer system and fear touching the CRT buttons.

- Training Types: There are three: (1) conceptual, on how the new system will operate; (2) functional, the software impact on each department; and (3) operational, how to get there from here, including what to do when a mistake is made.

- Data Input: The day of the keypunch operator will soon be over; in the future, users will do their own data input.

- But Always Remember: If a hospital installs a computer system and does not change its way of doing business, thus becoming more productive, it will have wasted its time and money.

33. Developing a Capital Assets Management Program

WILLIAM L. SCHEYER

Most hospitals do not have an effectively integrated program for managing their capital assets. Despite the fact that they spend millions of dollars each year for these items, they tend to invest time and energy in controlling the acquisition process but fail to invest equal efforts in controlling and coordinating their management once they have entered the system.

Whether or not they are officially identified, hospitals experience losses every year as a result of the inadequate management of these assets. The losses are both tangible and intangible, and include:

- direct expense incurred in buying new items when acceptable surplus items exist within the organization
- direct expense in buying spare parts when these are salvageable from equipment to be scrapped
- increased expense as a result of not centrally storing and handling surplus material
- revenue lost as a result of failure to file legitimate insurance claims
- revenue lost as a result of failure to sell items no longer needed
- inaccurate accounting records, which pose both a legal liability and a problem in inaccurate cost accounting
- increased clutter and the aggravation of working in a system that is not under control.

To obtain the greatest total value for the dollars expended, hospitals must improve their systems for managing capital assets. As a step in this direction, the following "ideal" system is proposed. This can serve as a starting point in planning systems for individual facilities.

COMPUTER SUPPORT

The following system assumes computer support (see Chapter 32). It probably will be most feasible to run this on a microcomputer or personal computer. Interface with the hospital's mainframe would be helpful but not mandatory. Because computer support is so essential to this program, it will be necessary to obtain active participation by either inside or outside data processing specialists throughout the development phase of the project.

STEERING COMMITTEE AND ORGANIZATION

Ultimate management responsibility for the capital assets management program should rest with the material manager. However, a steering committee should be formed to assist in the design and development of the program. This group should continue to meet as an advisory board once the program is in operation. It can review any significant operating problems, review the results of the annual audit, and, with the material manager, approve the annual capital assets status report.

The material manager will receive an added benefit by adopting this approach. Because the members of the steering/advisory committee have a strong interest in the effective management of capital assets, and because they all have a good deal of authority invested in their positions in the organization, they can provide strong support in resolving operational problems that arise in areas not directly managed by the material manager.

The steering committee should include representatives from the following departments:

- purchasing
- supply, processing, and distribution (SPD)
- finance
- clinical engineering
- maintenance
- risk management
- internal auditing
- information management (computer support).

The role of the committee should include five elements. It should:

1. define the purpose and scope of the program
2. identify program objectives and the methods that will be used to measure their achievement
3. design the program
4. plan program implementation
5. monitor implementation and continuing results of program.

The material manager should fulfill two roles: (1) chairing the steering committee and (2) having final management responsibility for the program. The day-to-day operation of the program can be handled by a capital assets control clerk, who reports directly to the material manager. This person also can take minutes and assist the manager in coordinating the meetings of the steering committee.

If at all possible, this person should be selected early in the process so as to be directly involved throughout the development of the program. Once the program is in full operation, the volume of daily transactions and coordinating activities will determine the required staffing level. It is possible that this person might be a scheduled part-time employee.

THE CAPITAL ASSETS MANAGEMENT PROGRAM

The purpose of the program is to provide an integrated system for effectively keeping track of and managing all capital asset items throughout their existence in the organization, i.e., from the point of acquisition to final disposal. The program includes the following four elements:

1. entry to the system
2. management of active items
3. management of surplus items
4. continuing program evaluation.

Entry to the System

A capital asset number should be assigned to each item at the time the purchase decision has been approved. This number should be included in the purchase order and the receiving document. Needless to say, the purchasing agent should do everything possible to coordinate elements, such as estimated arrival date, provisions for installation, trade-in of equipment being replaced, temporary storage during installation, and so on. The purchasing agent also should provide the capital assets control clerk (CACC) with the capital asset number and all related information so that the CACC can begin setting up the file on the item.

Before the estimated arrival date, the CACC can check with all relevant departments, such as ordering, receiving, clinical engineering, maintenance, and construction, to make sure everything is ready for the receipt, inspection, and installation of the item. This would include the disposition of any item that is being replaced.

When the item arrives at the receiving department, the control clerk there should contact representatives from the appropriate departments to assist in inspecting it. Once the item is found to be acceptable for initial receipt, the clinical engineer should affix a tag, bearing the capital asset number, to its surface. It then can be delivered to the ordering department and installed.

Management of Active Items

The CACC should be the person responsible for obtaining all information necessary to operate the program. This will come from such sources as the purchasing, receiving, maintenance, clinical engineering, and original ordering departments. Systems should be in place for these departments to provide information routinely and easily. However, control of the system should rest with the CACC. This person should be held accountable for ensuring that all files are continually kept up to date. This is an information-based system, and the constant maintenance of files is vital.

Current status of the following information elements should be available for each item at the press of a button:

1. item description
2. serial number
3. location
   - department number
   - department cost center number
4. date of purchase
5. date of actual installation
6. vendor information
   - manufacturer name, address, and phone number
   - distributor name, address, and phone number
   - service company name, address, and phone number
7. purchase price
8. estimated life
9. depreciation schedule
10. current book value
11. warranty information
    - terms
    - expiration date (before expiration date, an automatic reminder should be printed out, asking if a service contract is to be instituted)
12. required service schedule (before scheduled dates, standard inspection/service documents should automatically print)
13. service history
    - preventive maintenance
    - routine internal inspections
    - special service
    - dollars expended
14. anticipated replacement date, for use in future capital budget planning (total planned capital replacements can be printed before the annual capital budgeting process)
15. update
    - transfer—new location name and cost center number
    - sold—date of sale and price received, and who approved sale
    - scrapped—date, and who approved transaction
    - surplus—storage location
    - stolen—if items are not active, sold, scrapped, or surplus, they should be listed as stolen or missing, and the filing of insurance claims should be coordinated with the risk manager.

Management of Surplus Items

Requests for used equipment should be directed to the purchasing department and handled as part of the normal acquisition process. The purchasing agents should work closely with the CACC in maintaining an active list of requests for used equipment. This can be routinely matched against the current list of surplus equipment available. As items are no longer needed by a department, they should be reported to the CACC, who will change their file status from active to surplus. The following three options then become available:

1. transfer immediately to a department that can use the item
2. hold in the original department awaiting future movement
3. move to surplus storage area.

The CACC should coordinate the transaction and enter the new location in the file.

Physical handling and storage of surplus material should be under the control of the stores, purchasing, and distribution (SPD) department. Space that is adequate in size and environment, as well as being able to be secured, must be made available. This is a critical element and one that often is supported inadequately. The manager of SPD must ensure that appropriate storage and control techniques are used in the area. As items enter, they must be logged in. Their length of stay should be monitored. When items have remained in storage more than six months, active efforts should be undertaken to find a department that needs them, locate a buyer, or try to use them for trade-in value on another purchase.

If all of these efforts fail, the items should be reviewed by the advisory committee and a decision made as to their final disposition. The goal should be to maintain a proper balance between efforts to obtain the last bit of value from an article and the cost of holding it in storage. If a decision is made to scrap the item, it must be removed from the inventory record of the surplus storage area and must be disposed of physically. The CACC then converts the file status from surplus to scrapped. A subfile may be maintained that provides information about the total value of items scrapped over a period of time.

Start-Up and Continuing Evaluation

Once the system has been designed and tested, it is time to begin building the files. This starts with capturing data on new acquisitions as they are made. It probably never will be possible to build adequate files for all existing capital items. A plan is developed, based on the 80-20 rule, in which files are built for items or groups of items that have the highest dollar impact. Existing capital asset and purchasing records can serve as the basis for this.

Building the initial data base will require investments of time and energy from representatives of the purchasing, finance, maintenance, and clinical engineering departments. This work initially will provide a full-time job for the CACC. Progress should be monitored by the steering committee every two weeks until an acceptable data base is in place. At that point, progress of the file-building effort can become a standard, but relatively minor, agenda item for the committee's regular meetings.

Once the program is in full swing, the CACC should be the person responsible for ensuring its proper daily operation. This person should be responsible for solving any routine problems, reporting unusual ones to the material manager, and submitting monthly program status reports.

The only effective way to document the accuracy of the data in the system is to conduct periodic physical inspections. One approach is to schedule full physical inventories of the capital assets on a periodic basis. The drawback is that it is extremely time consuming and therefore expensive. An alternative is to perform frequent random spot checks. This is similar to the cycle-counting alternative in inventory control. The internal auditor is best suited to assist in setting up this program. The CACC should coordinate this activity, using predetermined guidelines. Results should be documented and maintained for review by the material manager, the advisory committee, and internal and external auditors.

If desired, the internal auditor can conduct an annual audit of the capital assets management process. The advisory committee should meet two to four times a year to:

- review any significant operating problems
- review summary data
- review results of physical inventory inspections
- review results of annual audit
- approve annual program status report submitted by material manager.

The implementation of a capital assets management program requires an investment of time, energy, and money. Unless there is a strong commitment to make the program an integral part of the management of the hospital, it should not be undertaken. However, once the program is in place, the continuing operating costs are relatively small. The benefit, on the other hand, is large.

The program provides a way to tie together the purchasing, receiving, maintenance, clinical engineering, and accounting functions as they relate to the management of capital assets. These functions already are being performed but often have not been linked into a common information system.

As the demand for improved economic performance of health care institutions increases, it will become even more imperative that their capital assets be kept under control.

34. Marketing Material Management

WALTON A. JUSTICE, JR.

Marketing is still relatively new to hospitals. Hospital managers sometimes confuse marketing with sales. Marketing involves identifying potential customers (or markets) and their needs, and then developing products or services to meet those needs. The sales function should come after market identification and product development.

With the current emphasis on cost-savings programs, material managers often have a ready-made line of services to sell to customers such as smaller hospitals or nursing homes. These services may be sold as is or customized to meet needs. The material manager is best suited individually to serve as the technical support specialist for purchasing, distribution, laundry services, and so on and may also be involved in the sales effort. Whenever possible, however, it is wise to call upon the hospital's marketing specialists, if available, to assist in developing the marketing program. This chapter is intended to help a manager work more effectively with the marketing specialists, or, if need be, to develop the program alone.

With this trend in hospitals toward marketing services, the material manager is in an excellent position to generate nonpatient revenue by providing support services or consulting services to other facilities. Many of these services can be provided with little or no staff additions; in some cases, as inpatient activity declines, excess capacities to provide services may be used to avoid personnel layoffs.

Before the material manager decides to offer services to others, it is important to understand recent hospital marketing and the basic principles of marketing.

REASONS FOR MARKETING

There are a number of reasons a hospital should give detailed consideration to embarking on, or expanding, a marketing operation:

1. Sales decline. Although this is a "commercial" circumstance, hospital administrators can relate to declines in admissions or utilization of inpatient services. Sales decline is recognized as the most common cause of an interest in marketing activities.
2. Slow growth. This generates interest when companies (hospitals) reach the peak of growth in their respective industries and start to look for new markets. It now is common to find hospitals owning hotels, restaurants, home health agencies, printing companies, and ambulance services.
3. Changing buying patterns. Health care providers have felt the impact of consumer concerns for costs. As consumers have sought alternatives to costly hospital-based services—such as emergency medical centers—health care managers have moved quickly to offer such services. As industries look for ways to reduce employee health care expenditures, health maintenance organizations (HMOs) have increased in growth and businesses are beginning to seek out preferred provider arrangements (PPOs).
4. Increasing competition. With hospitals now being paid for services by the prospective method, there is an increasing competition for patients in most service areas. Advertising campaigns, once con-

sidered taboo, are prevalent today as hospitals use radio, television, and newspapers to sell their services.

5. Increasing advertising expenditures. Hospital administrators frequently see rising expenditures for advertising and must find ways to control them.

DEVELOPING A MARKETING PLAN

It is important that the material manager understand the basics of marketing in order to develop a plan.

The first step is to determine how the material management marketing plan will fit with the hospital's overall strategic plan. Will the service be offered at cost, must it make a profit, or will it be subsidized by the hospital? Will it be offered as a loss leader or will it be expected to stand on its own merits?

Next, the plan is drafted, using the following guidelines:

1. Target the consumer. Since all potential customers' needs cannot be met, pick one target area to serve. Examples would be all hospitals within a ten-mile radius, or all nursing homes within the city.
2. Determine what the consumer needs. This can be done by:

   - Performing a needs assessment. Ask the customer what is needed. Are deliveries of linen or drugs needed seven days a week, instead of five? Are individual unit deliveries desired, instead of bulk deliveries?
   - Conducting other market research. Are there commercially prepared research documents or government reports that will provide needed information? Have colleagues performed similar services?
   - Determining whether the needs are something material management can meet. Does the manager have the resources needed or can they be

obtained? Is there an urgency in the unmet needs? Does the requirement fit within the overall marketing strategy, e.g., is association with a nursing home consistent with the image it is desired to project? Finally, does the manager have the technical skill and management time to do it?

Next, the marketing mix is designed. This generally is known as "the four Ps," described as:

1. Product. The service should be designed to suit the customer's needs, not the department's.
2. Price. This is what the customer is willing to pay for the service, although this is not always stated in terms of dollars. This should have been discovered in the needs assessment.
3. Place. The customer should have the right product in the right place at the right time, which means that the material management department may have to deliver it at 3 a.m., or it may mean that the customer wants to pick up the printing order each Friday at noon.
4. Promotion. This is the communication that informs target customers that the department has what they want or need, as determined in the original needs assessment. The targets should also guide the promotion plan, which should address:

   - The audience. This is the target customer, i.e., nursing homes or hospitals under 50 beds. It also is critical to identify the key decision maker(s) in that audience so the message can be directed to the appropriate person(s).
   - The message. This should relate to the main need the service is filling for them. This should emphasize the major benefit of the service—be it cost, convenience, increased quality, etc.
   - The media. Depending on the target and message to be conveyed, material man-

agement can use flyers, letters, direct-mail brochures, or sales people to get the message to the potential consumer.

POTENTIAL MATERIAL MANAGEMENT SERVICES

The following is an analysis of the functional areas of material management—planning, procuring (purchasing), receiving and storing, manufacturing, and distributing—as a "menu" approach to assist in determining which services to market.

Planning

Both short-term and long-range plan development for material management departments can be performed by skilled material managers, as well as by members of the hospital's management engineering department.

Purchasing

A group purchasing program is probably the most commonly marketed material management service today, being sold by both material managers and other organizational sales people. With the emergence of "super" group purchasing programs, many other material managers now have an opportunity to market their program's contracts to other hospitals and health care organizations. However, it is important for the material manager to develop a marketing strategy for these contracts to ensure that these efforts are compatible with the organization's strategic plan.

Receiving, Storing, and Distributing

Facilities that subscribe to central warehousing programs are potential customers for the distribution of supplies via bulk delivery or cart exchange programs. Additional service possibilities include par stocking programs, particularly with the advent of bar coding devices to facilitate the transfer of orders, and the development of subcontracting arrangements with regional suppliers to provide distribution services to small hospitals and extended care facilities.

Manufacturing

Manufacturing functions of material management programs include central processing, printing, pharmacy, and laundry:

Processing

This has been one of the least marketed material management functions, but substantial interest now has developed in establishing regional processing facilities, similar to those operated by the government in England and Canada. One company, Medical Sterilization, Inc. (MSI), a Long Island, N.Y., venture, plans to become the country's first regional sterile processing facility for hospitals and to open regional centers in other metropolitan areas. The key selling point in this venture appears to be cost containment, as hospitals can avoid the cost of renovating facilities to meet new federal guidelines for handling ethylene oxide.

In addition, central service managers are looking at ways to reduce operating costs, particularly in light of the prospective reimbursement system. It also appears that manufacturers are seeking hospital partners to form joint ventures, which would give hospitals backward vertical integration—that is, a direct pipeline from manufacturing facility (partially owned by the hospital) to the hospital. For example, a hospital may enter a joint venture with a company that would provide disposable products to the institution.

Printing

The printing services manager has an excellent opportunity to expand the scope of service and bring in additional revenue through marketing of printing services, or the hospital administrator may elect to buy a commercial printing company to gain such revenue. A typical menu of in-house printing services would include:

- Consulting: This service may be offered to hospitals of all sizes.

- Printing: This service should provide almost any kind of material, including two-color; exceptions would involve high-volume, sophisticated design and carbon snap set forms.

- Typesetting: This service has the potential for a significant return on investment since the equipment is relatively inexpensive and there is an almost limitless need for all forms, booklets, brochures, and other material that must be typeset in preparation for negative/platemaking operations.

Pharmacy

In some instances, the pharmacy is not considered part of the material management team. Nev-

ertheless, this department has great potential for marketing services, which include, but are not limited to:

- Consulting and contract management: Small hospitals or nursing homes that do not employ a full-time material manager or that have operational problems would be potential targets for marketing efforts.

- Retail pharmacy operations: The growth of physician office buildings adjacent to hospitals or on the hospital campus creates physicians, their patients, and those recently discharged as potential customers for this service.

Exhibit 34–1 Marketing Plan, Material Management Division, Anytown Memorial Hospital

Anytown Memorial Hospital's Strategic Marketing Plan for 19xx:

1. To increase admissions through the construction of a four-story physicians' office building on the east campus.
2. To develop tertiary care programs needed to serve the needs of patients within a 50-mile radius of Anytown Memorial Hospital.
3. To enter into a joint venture with a durable medical equipment company to provide services to patients leaving the hospital.

The Material Management Division's Marketing Plan for 19xx:

1. To support all strategic marketing efforts of Anytown Memorial Hospital's staff by:

   - conducting a feasibility study for establishing a retail pharmacy in the professional office building
   - conducting an analysis of proposals received for DME joint ventures

2. To expand the scope of laundry services by marketing to all hospitals of 100 beds and under within a 50-mile radius of Anytown Memorial Hospital.
3. To expand the scope of distribution services by marketing to all hospitals of 100 beds and under within a 50-mile radius of Anytown Memorial Hospital.
4. To promote laundry and distribution services through:

   - visiting the administrators of all hospitals within the target area
   - arranging for tours for all interested hospital personnel to see the laundry and warehouse facilities
   - conducting cost comparisons of current laundry and distribution services

5. To communicate that the laundry and distribution of Anytown Memorial Hospital are:

   - of the highest quality
   - cost effective—Anytown's laundry costs per pound are lower than the national average
   - customer oriented.

Laundries

The possibility of developing a marketing program for a hospital-based laundry service depends primarily upon the number of hospitals or nursing homes in the service area that are purchasing such services or have deteriorating laundry equipment they do not want to replace.

One other area in which the material manager has an opportunity to establish a marketing program is that of durable medical equipment (DME), such as patient beds for home use by the discharged patient and/or patient nutrition programs. Whether the organization chooses to set up its own DME program or enter into a joint venture arrangement with a national or local DME company, patients will need equipment and/or parenteral or enteral nutrition products, and the material manager has the resources that can be used by the joint venture.

SAMPLE MARKETING PLAN

Now that the basics of marketing, how to develop a marketing plan, and possible services have been analyzed, the next step is to look at a sample marketing plan for the material management division of a hospital (see Exhibit 34–1).

The material manager who is interested in marketing should now have an understanding of its basic concepts, a menu of marketing ideas, a sample marketing plan for guidance, and an opportunity to develop a revenue-producing program.

35. Material Management: Past, Present, Future

WILLIAM L. SCHEYER, ROBERT L. JANSON, AND DONALD G. SOTH

MATERIAL MANAGEMENT: PAST

When Genghis Khan moved across the Gobi Desert in the 13th century, he carried all of his supplies, including food, in the form of dried products. His armies were spread out and communication methods had to be devised to coordinate the movement of men, equipment, and supplies. In the 19th century, Napoleon used similar, but more sophisticated, methods. He never would have achieved the success that he had if he had not been concerned with the logistics of obtaining and moving supplies. Thus was born the concept of "material." Modern armies still practice this logistics of material.

Industry before the 19th century was confined to the home. Each family was given or bought supplies from which it created desired products. Mechanization began in that century and gave rise to factories, with people leaving their homes to work in central locations. Textile mills of this era were to be the home of the first primitive computer. This was not successful, but the need had been identified.

There are those who say the United States would not have won World War II if the concept of material management had not been used in the aircraft industry, where virtually overnight the nation was able to develop and build warplanes by the thousands. There has always been this connection between the military and industrial sectors of society. The common thread is the single-source management of inventory, manufacturing, and distribution of supplies. Today, modern industries could not realize profits, and thus could not survive, if not for the use of sophisticated forms of material management, such as material requirements planning.

How does this apply to health care professionals? It now is commonly understood that health care provision must be viewed as an industry like any other. The products and underlying value systems are somewhat different but the basic managerial structures are alike. Techniques that improve performance in one industry must be evaluated for feasibility in others. Material management has been recognized as an effective tool in other industries for years. It is only a matter of time before its value is fully realized in health care.

Hospitals should be viewed not only as a group of coordinated activities in a structure but also as a series of neighborhoods, each concerned with the acquisition, processing, and distribution of materials, as well as with the provision of diagnostic and treatment services related to the care of patients. These neighborhoods, or departments, are relatively autonomous, yet live together as they would in a city. They all have the same underlying objective, which is to care for patients' medical needs. Their common goal must be to find the most efficient and effective way of achieving this basic objective.

It must be remembered that, at one time, hospital supplies were limited. Bed linen was changed infrequently. Food was brought to large patient wards in buckets. Patients had a plate and spoon apiece, recyclable dressings, and a few medications. To complicate matters, supplies that were used on patients had to be cleaned, packaged, and sterilized for reuse. The need for these manufacturing functions led to the development of laundries and small, decentralized processing areas. As technology grew, a myriad of tests and procedures developed as a result of advances in anesthesia, microbiology, and radiology. Each technological advance spawned a new stock of supplies necessary to support it.

The need for supplies and equipment unique to health care gave rise to a profusion of manufacturers anxious to meet these requirements. Their needs and objectives sometimes were at odds with those of health care providers. This, at times, led to high prices and unnecessarily large stocks of supplies. To cope with this situation, a new activity arose in health care institutions: the acquisition, storage, and distribution of materials. Unfortunately, these activities often were performed by people who were neither trained nor interested in doing them effectively.

However, in the 1970s the sheer volume and cost of these activities reached a point where some hospitals began to adopt material management concepts and practices. The single-source control system of inventory management, processing, and distribution of materials became the key to bringing order out of chaos.

A system can be defined as a logical sequence of concepts or components designed to accomplish a specific function efficiently. Material management, therefore, qualifies as a system. Systems have the following components: (1) inputs, (2) processes, (3) outputs, and (4) controls. These components may be seen within the four material management subsystems of procurement, inventory management (which includes acquisition), processing, and distribution.

As feedback on the performance of this system is monitored, and adjustments are made to its design and operation, a continuing cycle of logical and effective material-related behavior is established. This system of material management is one of the elements that ties the total organization together.

This, in essence, is what has been discussed in this book. The evidence is surely in on the fact that the concept of material management must be integrated into the total operating philosophy of a hospital if that facility is to be efficient.

MATERIAL MANAGEMENT: PRESENT

A few years ago, it was not uncommon to find hospitals that did not use centralized material management. As the economy tightened and regulatory and consumer constraints on the health care industry increased, more and more material management programs came into existence. However, the industry still is in the early stages of development in terms of being recognized as a specific and credible discipline.

It is true that increasing numbers of managers have undergraduate and graduate degrees and have studied the managerial and logistical techniques developed in other industries. However, the amount of time spent in specifically studying health care material management has been small.

It also is true that more and more material managers are reading books and journals devoted to this subject, attending seminars, joining professional associations, and taking certifying examinations. To be sure, much of the structure and foundation of this discipline is in place. However, all too often, material managers still can be heard speaking of themselves as order takers, not direction setters. Too often, these managers accept the idea that departments such as surgery, radiology, and laboratory are outside the realm of material management. Far too often, they are only on the implementation end of the hospital's long-range plan instead of being involved in its development.

Why is this the case? The answer is to be found in three areas. First, all of the information and techniques related to the management of materials in this specific industry has not been synthesized into a common body of knowledge that can be identified and taught in colleges and universities. To a large extent, as long as the body of knowledge does not exist, the discipline does not exist.

Next, the disparate professional organizations that represent the various aspects of health care material management have not been integrated into one unified political body. There must always be effective representation of the specific interests of the special areas such as central processing, laundry, purchasing, and so on. However, these simply are different aspects of a central entity called material management. If these managers are to obtain the broad recognition and deep support they require, they must be represented by a unified body.

Finally, material managers, in the aggregate, have not been successful in proving to administrators, physicians, and boards of directors that they are qualified, competent, and have earned the right to participate in the broad direction-setting process for their organizations. Many have proved that they can effectively manage routine daily operations. What they have not done is to prove that they have the vision, expertise, and skill necessary to be accountable for the material management of the total organization.

This is the challenge that faces these managers today. The longer it takes them to rise to this challenge, the longer it will be before their hospitals will be able to realize the full benefits of effective material management.

MATERIAL MANAGEMENT: FUTURE

The previous section was not intended to cast a negative light on the current state of material management in hospitals. In fact, great strides have been made since the mid-1970s. This field is at a normal and healthy point in its development. The levels of education and expertise of its practitioners are increasing, performance and practices are becoming somewhat more standardized from hospital to hospital, and it is gaining recognition. However, the challenges and opportunities of the coming years will be even greater. The measure of how fully managers realize the potential of their field will lie in how assertively and effectively they grasp these opportunities and make them reality.

To move with confidence into the future, they must have at least a general sense of what that future will be like. The authors of this book certainly do not have access to a crystal ball and cannot describe every aspect of material management in tomorrow's health care facility. However, some trends are apparent and can serve as starting points for managers as they design future material management programs for their facilities.

Administrative Support

Every effectively run facility will have a clear policy statement, issued by the chief executive officer and approved by the board of directors, that establishes firm support for, and a clear expectation that, material management practices will be carried out effectively. As this operating philosophy is handed down from the top of the organization, it will serve as the stimulus for all department heads to work with the material manager in finding ways to improve their operations. It also will serve as the basis of a statement to vendors outlining the ground rules for doing business with the health care facility. Finally, and perhaps most important, it will serve as part of the conceptual framework for the organization's long-range plan.

More organizations will establish corporate level positions, such as vice president, that will have total responsibility for the management of materials throughout the facility. This might involve direct control over 70 percent of the material resources and strong monitoring/consulting influence over the other 30 percent.

Health care facilities expend millions of dollars each year on training and education activities. In the past, a relatively small portion of this has been devoted to developing material management personnel. As administrators gain a fuller realization of the total dollar impact of these people's daily activity, more money will be devoted to training them to perform more effectively. There will be a greater need to develop both educators and training programs.

The selection of employees will receive greater attention. Staff level material management jobs often have been regarded as entry level positions, requiring little background. As a result, less than optimal selection procedures have sometimes been used. This has resulted in a high investment in basic job training, inadequate performance, and high turnover. To obtain an adequate return on the investment in training and development, hospitals must select employees with appropriate skills and characteristics who have high potential. This has been done in the clinical departments for years and must be done now in material management.

Finally, the environment within material management departments will become more motivational. The value of investing in effective physical layouts, equipment, and systems will be increasingly apparent. Employees will be trained to make better use of these resources. Perhaps most important, the material management employee's contribution to the patient care effort will be recognized more often. Patients, physicians, nurses, and others will come to realize that when the facility achieves such objectives as high fill rate, high turnover rate, and high-quality products at reasonable prices, patients will benefit just as they do when high-quality diagnostic tests are performed.

Organizational Design

As hospitals strive to replace declining inpatient revenues with income from alternate delivery systems and services, material managers will play increasingly valuable roles in improving the bottom lines of these services. Hospitals' ability to reduce operating costs while maintaining quality of service will be a vital factor in whether or not these alternate services succeed or fail.

The development of centralized material distribution centers to support a facility or group of facilities will accelerate. These centers will operate around the clock, will be staffed by well-trained specialists, and will be designed to fulfill the total supply management needs of the organization. A major emphasis will be to ensure that clinical people spend their time in direct patient care and that nonclinical support functions are performed by those best able to do so in a cost-effective way.

Performance targets for material management functions will be established for all operating areas of the organization. For example, inventory dollars to be invested in the surgery department, as well as turnover rates and rates of availability, will be determined jointly by the material manager and surgery manager, monitored, and adjusted as needed. The emphasis will be on how this investment contributes to the primary goal of patient care and to the organization's total bottom line.

Active standardization committees will play an even greater role in the hospital's daily operation. These groups will have strong administrative support and will be involved in the standardization of products, systems, and actual performance. For example, such a committee may routinely review inventory turnover by department and serve as added support to the material manager in correcting performance problems.

It often is forgotten that 20 percent of the average cost of materials is related to capital equipment that many times has been acquired without adequate involvement from the purchasing department. Administrators of effectively managed hospitals will demand that a triad approach, involving the requesting department, purchasing department, and biomedical engineering department, be used to manage all major capital acquisitions from start to finish.

Techniques

Computer support will be the order of the day, even in smaller hospitals. With the continuing expansion of the microcomputer and personal computer markets, many organizations will operate in an on-line, real-time environment. Material managers will have to stay abreast of changes in computer support if they hope to remain competitive in the health care industry of the future.

Forecasting models and other techniques, such as material requirements planning (MRP), which have been well established in other industries, will be modified for use in health care. Standardized material requirements will be established for each diagnosis and procedure at each hospital. As projected admissions and surgery cases are scheduled, the computer will generate lists of required materials. These will be compared to on-hand/on-order quantities and replenishment orders will be generated automatically.

Thus, the flow or consumption of materials will be tied directly to the actual workflow of the institution. The need to develop these standard material requirements will serve as the springboard for improved communication between material managers and clinical managers. This also will accelerate all parties' understanding of the interrelated nature of everyone's contribution to direct patient care.

As a corollary, every health care facility will adopt standard cost accounting practices. This will be critical in ensuring that patient care ("the product line") can be provided at an acceptable level of quality and at a profit. Unprofitable hospitals, even in the not-for-profit group, will simply disappear. The mark of the effective organizations will be their use of an interdisciplinary team approach to developing standards and managing costs. Team members will include representatives from finance, clinical departments, medical records, and material management.

There will be increasing use of direct computer-to-computer communication between health care facilities and major vendors. In addition, bar code and optical character recognition (OCR) devices will be used routinely in streamlining the handling of the materials. This will require an increasingly effective interface between manufacturers and users of medical products.

Along these same lines, there will be more demand on vendors to ship goods "just in time." This is based upon the Japanese inventory system and leads to significantly reduced inventory costs for health care providers. It will provide a great challenge to material managers to ensure that it does not result in increased stock-outs. It will be in the best interests of manufacturers, distributors, and users to work together to find effective systems that can satisfy everyone's profit needs while meeting patients' need for quality care at reasonable cost.

Another area in which health providers and vendors will work more closely is in the provision of value analysis programs. Value analysis involves analyzing a function or product in terms of its components, then attempting to identify the most effective method of achieving the functional objective and the most effective product for applying that method. The goal is to find the most efficient method or product. This concept has been talked about frequently in hospitals but rarely has been implemented on a broad scale. The material manager and the product standards

committee will serve as the brokers for seeing that this service is provided to the organization. However, vendors will play larger roles in its actual provision.

Monitoring

Administrators will demand that material management performance be monitored routinely and reported using standardized, statistically valid protocols. These will become somewhat more standardized throughout the industry so that administrators will be able to measure the performance of their organizations more easily both against themselves and against their competitors. As a result, managers will be held more accountable for the actual performance of their departments. As the industry becomes more competitive, this will be reflected in the annual salary review. Thus, the manager's personal bottom line will be tied directly to the organization's bottom line.

This should not be viewed as a negative situation. Effective managers, who can help improve their company's bottom line, will stand out in a quantifiable way and can receive significant rewards. Managers who are not able to do this will be replaced ultimately. This is how it should be in a healthy, economically viable environment.

The Future Is Bright

What can individual material managers do to see that the health care industry reaps the full benefits of effective material management? First, they can become involved in professional associations at the local, state, and, ultimately, national levels. Within this framework, they can strive to see that the groups achieve the following objectives:

- increased communication between the different disciplines of material management
- increased communication between material management entities and related organizations such as those for surgical nurses and infection control practitioners

- development of a unified political body to represent the interests of all material management specialties
- presentation of regular educational programs designed to meet the specific needs of the members
- sharing of performance statistics among members with the aim of increasing the average level of performance within the community
- increased recognition for individual members and the group for contributions to cost-effective health care in the community.

The next step is to establish a personal development plan. This can be enhanced by soliciting suggestions from a superior, the head of the human resource department of the health care facility, and key people in the professional organization. Managers should plan specific steps that will lead to measurable improvement in the following three areas:

1. knowledge and skill
   - college-level courses leading to higher degrees

- college-level courses designed to correct specific deficiencies
- seminars
- reading of professional journals

2. major performance objectives related to their current position

3. recognition of the value of their achievements and those of their staff as they relate to an improved bottom line for the organization.

The industry is filled with challenge and opportunity. Its future is bright. Material managers have learned and grown over the years. In addition, they are in the fortunate position of having expertise in an area that is becoming increasingly vital to the long-term success, and even survival, of the health care industry. Their star is rising and their success is bounded only by the breadth of their vision and the degree of assertiveness with which they grasp their opportunities.

Index

A

ABOUT THE EDITOR

William L. Scheyer approaches the field of health care material management with both a business and a clinical perspective. He holds a certificate (C.P.H.M.) from the Health Care Material Management Society as well as a certificate (C.R.T.T.) from the National Board for Respiratory Therapy. He is director of supply, processing, and distribution at Bethesda Hospital, Inc., in Cincinnati. He served previously as director of cardiopulmonary services at Bethesda.

Mr. Scheyer is past president of the Tri-State Central Service Association, which represents members from Southwestern Ohio, Southeastern Indiana, and Northern Kentucky. He is a charter member of the Cincinnati Tri-State Chapter of the Health Care Material Management Society and has participated as a speaker at both local and national meetings.

Mr. Scheyer has a strong interest in adult continuing education. He holds a degree in sociology from Northern Kentucky University and has done graduate work in business at Xavier University. He has taught numerous courses in allied health and cardiopulmonary technology at Cincinnati Technical College and currently teaches one in health care material management at the University of Cincinnati.

His primary interest is in developing systems that can assist people in increasing their productivity while at the same time increasing their enjoyment of their daily work.

ABOUT THE CONTRIBUTORS

Gary L. Calhoun is associate hospitals director, University of Michigan Hospitals, Ann Arbor, Mich. He is a graduate of Trinity University, San Antonio, Texas, in health care administration and the University of Iowa in business administration.

Karen A. Campbell is the assistant hospital director for ancillary services at the University of Michigan Hospitals, Ann Arbor, Mich. She has a master's degree in public health from the University of Oklahoma and is completing a Master of Business Administration from the University of Texas.

Edwin E. Carty, Jr., is the director of materials management for Republic Health Corporation in Dallas. He has held top-level materials management positions in large for-profit and not-for-profit multihospital management firms. He has served as a consultant to a number of health care facilities and has been a frequent speaker on materials management and group purchasing for hospitals.

Randall L. Corn is director, Stores, Processing, and Distribution, St. Joseph's Hospital, Tucson. He received his B.S. degree in biological sciences from the University of Arizona in 1974 and has been working in central service ever since. He has been active in ethylene oxide research since 1978. He has had several articles published and been a speaker at numerous seminars on EtO control. Mr. Corn has monitored EtO levels in hospitals throughout Arizona. He is a Distinguished Member of the American Society for Hospital Central Service Personnel and is on its board of directors.

Joseph A. Dattilo is vice president, support services for St. Francis-St. George Management Company, an affiliate of St. Francis-St. George Health Services, Inc. He formerly held positions in materials management at St. Francis-St. George Hospital and Bethesda Hospital, both in Cincinnati. Mr. Dattilo has been an instructor in the University of Cincinnati's Health Planning Program. He received his B.S. degree in administrative management from the University of Cincinnati and his M.B.A. degree from Xavier University, Cincinnati.

Joan Dyer, a native of Brooklyn, N.Y., received her liberal arts degree at Brooklyn College and is pursuing a degree in business administration. She is director of materials management at Westminster-Canterbury House, a continuing care facility in Richmond, Va. She is a member of the editorial advisory board of *Today's Nursing Home*. She serves as president of the Virginia Society of Hospital Purchasing Materials Managers, chairman of the Shared Services Committee of the Virginia Center for Health Affairs, and chairman of the Purchasing Utilization Committee of the American Association of Homes for the Aging.

David M. Giancola is a graduate of the University of Michigan School of Industrial Engineering, where he was one of the first persons in the nation to apply the industrial engineering discipline to health care management problems. Upon graduation, after a short stint with General Motors, Mr. Giancola joined with Michigan classmates to become a managing director with the Ann Arbor-based

Community Systems Foundation. In 1966 he founded Giancola Associates, Inc. In the ensuing 10 years half of his consulting activity related to laundry and linen service, the other half to more general hospital management and community planning projects. In 1976 he directed all of the Giancola Associates energies and resources toward laundry/linen service activity. Mr. Giancola is a member of the American Hospital Association, the Textile Rental Services Association, and the Hospital Management Systems Society.

Thomas J. Gruber, C.I.A., C.P.A., is a graduate of St. John's University, Collegeville, Minn., with a B.S. in accounting. His career includes both accounting and internal auditing practice. His auditing career has been marked by innovation. While a senior auditor with Arthur Andersen & Co., he developed a transaction flow auditing model that served as a prototype for that firm's utility clients. Later, at Super X Drugs, a wholly owned drugstore chain of the Kroger Company, he was responsible for developing a financial and administrative auditing function. Since 1980, Mr. Gruber has been employed by Bethesda Hospital, Inc., Cincinnati, where he established and manages the internal auditing and data control activities. He also developed and promoted the standard operational audit methodology.

Dale R. Gunnell, M.B.A., is associate administrator of finance at the University of Utah Medical Center in Salt Lake City. He formerly was budget director there. Mr. Gunnell is a graduate of the University of Utah and a member of the American Management Association.

Darlene Hardwick, R.N., is supply, processing, and distribution supervisor at the Shriners Hospital for Crippled Children, Cincinnati Burns Institute, Cincinnati. She is president of the Tri-State Central Service Association, which represents members in Southeast Indiana, Southwest Ohio, and Northern Kentucky. She is a member of the Education Committee of the Ohio Society for Central Service Personnel, as well as an active member of the Tri-State Cincinnati Chapter of the Health Care Material Management Society.

Bruce G. Haywood, C.P.H.M., vice president of the support services division of Methodist Hospitals of Memphis, is a business graduate of the University of Missouri, with additional work at Wichita State University, Memphis State University, and Rockhurst College. He has an extensive advanced educational background and has spent more than 25 years in the fields of purchasing, materials management, and management. Mr. Haywood frequently presents programs to professional groups, such as the International Materials Management Society, the American Society for Hospital Purchasing and Materials Management, the American Surgical Trade Association, the American Hospital Association, annual state Hospital Association meetings in Tennessee, Mississippi, Arkansas, Georgia, and Louisiana, and at various seminars. He is a consultant in materials management, was president of his own materials management consulting firm Health-Med Services Management Corporation, and has published articles in professional journals—*Hospitals, Hospital Materiel Management Quarterly,* and *Purchasing Administration.* He has a chapter in the book *Hospital Purchasing* by Charles Housely and is noted in *Materiel Management and Purchasing for the Health Care Facility* by John Holmgren and Walter Wentz. He teaches a senior level class on the principles of inventory management and material management at Memphis State University. He is an active member of a number of professional organizations.

Robert L. Janson began his career as a junior buyer for the Clevite, Bearing Division of Gould. All of his business experience has been in various aspects of materials management—as an inventory controller, production control manager, and plant manager for Otis

Elevator. For the past 15 years he has been a materials management consultant for Ernst & Whinney in their Cleveland office. Mr. Janson has written three books for Prentice-Hall: *Production Control Desk Book, Purchasing Agent's Desk Book,* and *Computerized Inventory Management.* His concept of productivity measurement, "Graphic Indicators of Operations," was published in the *Harvard Business Review.* A Purdue graduate, he is a member of NAPM, as well as APICS and ASHMM. He is one of the few persons who have been awarded the Certified Purchasing Manager (CPM), the Certified in Production and Inventory Management (CPIM) recognition, and ASHMM Fellow status. A designer of numerous hospital materials management systems, he has presented papers on this subject to the American Hospital Association, several state Hospital Associations, and for the HFMA Institute.

Walton A. Justice, Jr., is director of materials management for American Healthcare Systems in Chicago. He previously served as assistant vice president, materials management, at Bethesda Hospital, Inc., Cincinnati. He received a bachelor of science degree from East Tennessee State University and has completed the didactic portion of the Master of Hospital and Health Administration program at Xavier University, Cincinnati. Mr. Justice is a nominee of the American College of Hospital Administrators and is a Fellow of the National Association of Hospital Purchasing and Materials Management. He also served on the task force for the development of the Material Management Program, American Healthcare Systems, and as first vice president, board of trustees, Cincinnati Speech and Hearing Center.

Jamie C. Kowalski, M.B.A., C.P.H.M., is president of Kowalski-Dickow Associates, Inc., a Milwaukee-based management consulting firm that specializes in operations management applications to the health care industry. He has held line management and staff positions for hospitals and a supply manufacturer/distributor. He is a frequent seminar speaker and has published many articles on the subject of operations/materials management. Mr. Kowalski earned B.S. and M.B.A. degrees from Marquette University. He has been awarded Certification by the Health Care Materials Management Society and Fellowship status by the American Society for Hospital Materials Management.

Dave Lewis is an experienced seminar leader. He has presented a variety of management and developmental seminars to organizations such as the Management Center of Cambridge, National Management Association, City of Dallas, General Dynamics Corporation, Moore Business Systems, and many others. He is a graduate of Southern Methodist University, with a diversified background in sales, public relations, and management development. He is the author of six books, plus a number of full-length programs for the American Management Association.

Daniel E. Mayworm is a well-known consultant, author, and lecturer on the medical device industry and hospital packaging and sterilization. He is the publisher of the *Journal of Hospital Supply, Processing and Distribution* and president of Mayworm Associates, Inc. He is the former president of Tower Products, Inc., a manufacturer of packaging materials for the medical device industry. Mr. Mayworm was president of the Health Industries Association at the time it merged to form the Health Industry Manufacturers Association (HIMA). He served as treasurer, director, and member of the executive committee of HIMA from its inception until recently. Mr. Mayworm testified before both the House and Senate on the Medical Device Amendments to the Food, Drug and Cosmetic Act. He has served as cochairman of the Industrial Liaison Committee of the American Society for Hospital Central Service Personnel and as a member of the AORN and IAHCSM Exhibitors Advisory Committees. He is a member of AAMI, ASHCSP, IAHCSM, HCMMS and ASHMM. He is the author of numerous articles that have appeared in *Tower Topics, AORN Journal, Purchasing Administration* and of course his own *Journal of Hospital Supply, Processing and Distribution*. His "Dating Game" seminar for Materials Management, Central Supply, Operating Room and Infection Control has been given in every state and province in the United States and Canada. Mr. Mayworm is on the board of directors of the Arthur J. Schmitt Foundation, Chicago; the Self Help Center, Evanston, Ill., and Journey House, Pasadena, Calif.

Gil Meredith, M.S., R.T. (R), is radiology department manager at St. Francis-St. George Hospital, Inc., in Cincinnati. Earlier, he held posts as a radiologic technology educator, having received an M.S. from the School of Allied Medical Professions of the Ohio State University. Mr. Meredith has served as consultant to the American Hospital Association in the application to radiologic systems of the AHA's Technology Evaluation and Acquisition Methods for Hospitals program. He has published articles on his development of the system of generic functional specification in radiology equipment purchasing and on the impact of prospective rate setting on equipment purchase decisions.

Peter C. Mike, F.A.S.H.P.M.M., C.P.H.M.M., is assistant administrator, materials management, Tucson Medical Center, Tucson. He has written articles about materials management, most recently in *Hospital Purchasing*, 1983. Mr. Mike is a member of the American Society for Hospital Materials Management and the Health Care Section of the International Materials Management Society.

Robert Mosenkis joined ECRI in 1968 as a senior project engineer, has been editor of ECRI's journal, *Health Devices*, since its inception in 1971, and is presently also vice president for publications. He has conducted product evaluations and written numerous guidance articles and editorials for *Health Devices* and has participated in ECRI seminars on managing health care technology. Mr. Mosenkis has bachelor's and master's degrees in electrical engineering from City College of New York and the University of Pennsylvania, respectively. He is a Certified Clinical Engineer and a member of the Medical Devices Standards Board of the American National Standards Institute.

Joel J. Nobel, M.D., is president of ECRI, a nonprofit bioengineering and technology assessment institute. He bears overall responsibility for the development and operation of ECRI's publication, consulting, and field technical programs and its product testing and hazard investigation activities. He received his B.A. in English from Haverford College, his M.A. in international relations from the University of Pennsylvania, and his M.D. from Thomas Jefferson University, Philadelphia. He also served in the United States Navy submarine force. He has been a consultant to many hospitals, and governmental, and voluntary agencies. Dr. Nobel has been principal investigator for a number of federal, state, and foundation-funded research projects. He has published more than 150 scientific papers and book chapters related to emergency medical services, health care technology, medical device safety, risk management, biomedical engineering, and hospital design.

Jerry W. Rayburn is the director of materials management information systems for American Medical International, Beverly Hills, Calif. He has been with AMI since September 1982. He is a 1975 graduate of the University of Nebraska-Lincoln, where he received an M.B.A. degree with an emphasis in management. He has held hospital materials management positions, including assistant director of purchasing, inventory control manager, and materials manager in nonprofit hospitals and regional materials manager for AMI. In each, he has provided progressive exposure to alternative manual and automated systems for control of inventories. His current focus is in the development of a fully integrated materials management and payment system for all AMI hospitals and subsidiaries.

Marimargaret Reichert, R.N., B.S., is director of central sterile reprocessing at Robinson Memorial Hospital in Ravenna, Ohio. Her diverse background, particularly in vascular surgery and in staff orientation and education, was helpful in implementing a case-cart system for surgery and labor and delivery and in training central service employees in the new system. Mrs. Reichert was president of the Cleveland Chapter of the American Society of Hospital Central Service Personnel (ASHCSP) from 1979–81 and achieved advanced membership status in ASHCSP in 1983. She has served the Association for the Advancement of Medical Instrumentation (AAMI) in several positions—co-chair, Hospital EO Sterilizer Working Group; chair, Good Hospital Practices, Decontamination of Reusable Medical Devices Working Group; and member of the AAMI President's Council of Regional Advisers. She has published more than 20 articles on many aspects of central sterile reprocessing and product evaluation. Her paper, "An Appropriate Reuse of a Medical Device: A Case Study," received the 1984 International Association of Hospital Central Service Management Past Presidents Award for outstanding paper. She is currently pursuing a master's degree in technical education at the University of Akron.

Donald B. Rhoad is director of purchasing at 787-bed Bethesda Hospital, Inc., an organization that includes two hospitals, a retirement community, and four free-standing medical centers in the greater Cincinnati area. He is a member of the American Society for Hospital Materials Management and has participated as a speaker at both local and national seminars sponsored by various groups. Before joining Bethesda, Mr. Rhoad held positions of increasing responsibility in the purchasing department of the Procter & Gamble Company.

Rodger E. Rourke, M.B.A., C.P.M., C.P.H.M., is assistant vice president–materiel management at University Hospitals of Cleveland, Cleveland, Ohio. Prior to that he was director of materiel management at Mount Carmel Hospitals in Columbus, Ohio, for more than 11 years. He previously held management positions in industrial and military purchasing, inventory control, logistics, and data systems. He has conducted numerous seminars and published articles on hospital materiel management and has taught business and logistics management. Mr. Rourke is a national vice president and director of the National Association of Purchasing Management and a member of the editorial board of *Hospital Materiel Management Quarterly*.

Richard L. Seim is the director of pharmaceutical services for The Christ Hospital, Cincinnati. He has a B.S. degree in pharmacy and an M.S. in pharmacy administration, with a Certificate of Residency in hospital pharmacy. Mr. Seim has been employed in management positions in both the pharmaceutical and hospital industries. He has been active in professional organizations and is a past president of the Ohio Society of Hospital Pharmacists.

Larry E. Shear, Ph.D., is a health care consultant with specialized expertise in hospital operations and marketing. He has conducted materials management studies in more than 30 hospitals and hospital systems, has been a speaker at national forums on materials management issues, and has published more than a score of articles and texts on health care systems and perspectives. In addition to a doctorate in management systems, he holds M.H.A. and bachelor of science degrees in industrial (management) engineering.

Donald G. Soth, recently retired, was formerly director of creative programs, Education Division, AMSCO, Erie, Penn. He is a charter member of the board and executive committee of the Health Care Material Management Society and is also serving as vice-president of strategic planning and marketing. He currently is on the editorial board of the quarterly journal *Hospital Materiel Management Quarterly*. He has been a consultant in space and equipment planning with Louis Block Associates and with Anthony J.J. Rourke Associates. Mr. Soth has authored numerous articles relating to material and space management in health care institutions.

Lois Suhrie is a certified nurse of the operating room (CNOR) who holds a B.S. degree in nursing from Columbia Union College in Takoma Park, Md. She has extensive experience in staff, educational, and management positions within the operating room environment. She is an operating room systems specialist for the American V. Mueller Company, a division of the American Hospital Supply Corporation, McGaw Park, Ill.

Bernard R. Teitz is manager of inventory and logistics of the American V. Mueller division of the American Hospital Supply Corporation, McGaw Park, Ill. He received a B.B.A. in production and operations management from Loyola University in Chicago. He currently is responsible for directing purchasing and inventory control and logistics functions of American V. Mueller and manages its international operations area.

Marty Whitacre is printing services manager of Palm Beach Inc., Cincinnati, a clothing manufacturing firm. He has eight years' management experience in the printing industry and is a member of the In-Plant Printing Management Association.

The editor would like to acknowledge the contribution of **Cynthia Whiting Pendl,** who rendered invaluable assistance in the preparation of this work. Ms. Pendl, who graduated from DePauw University in 1978, is currently in health care sales and works for a large distributing firm in California.